Memoirs
Andrei Gromyko

MEMOIRS

Andrei Gromyko

Foreword by Henry A. Kissinger
Translated by Harold Shukman

DOUBLEDAY
New York London Toronto Sydney Auckland

PUBLISHED BY DOUBLEDAY
a division of Bantam Doubleday Dell Publishing Group, Inc.
666 Fifth Avenue, New York, New York 10103

DOUBLEDAY and the portrayal of an anchor
with a dolphin are trademarks of Doubleday,
a division of Bantam Doubleday Dell Publishing Group, Inc.

Filmset in Linotron Bembo by
Rowland Phototypesetting Ltd, Bury St Edmunds, Suffolk

Library of Congress Cataloging-in-Publication Data applied for
ISBN 0-385-41288-6

Contents

Illustrations

The publishers would like to thank all those listed below for allowing them to reproduce illustrations in this volume.

Between pages 110 and 111
Page 1 – VAAP, The Soviet Copyright Agency (top and bottom right), Andrei Gromyko (bottom left): page 2 – VAAP (top and bottom right), A. Gromyko (bottom left): page 3 – VAAP (top left and bottom): A. Gromyko (top right): page 4 – Popperfoto (top left), VAAP (top right), Camera Press Ltd (bottom). Page 5 – A. Gromyko (top), VAAP (middle), Novosti Press Agency (bottom): pages 6 and 7 – A. Gromyko (top and bottom left), VAAP (all others): page 8 – VAAP (all). Page 9 – VAAP (top), A. Gromyko (bottom left), Popperfoto (bottom right): pages 10 and 11 – A. Gromyko (bottom left), VAAP (all others): page 12 – The Keystone Collection (top left), A. Gromyko (top right), Soviet Weekly (middle), Popperfoto (bottom). Page 13 – The Keystone Collection (top), VAAP (bottom left and right): page 14 – VAAP (all): page 15 – Popperfoto (top left), VAAP (top right and bottom): page 16 – United Nations (left), A. Gromyko (right).

Between pages 286 and 287
Page 1 – United Nations (top), The Keystone Collection (middle), A. Gromyko (bottom): pages 2 and 3 – Novosti Press Agency (top left and right), The Keystone Collection (bottom left), United Nations (bottom right): page 4 – VAAP (all). Page 5 – VAAP (all): page 6 – Novosti Press Agency (top), VAAP (bottom): page 7 – Novosti Press Agency (top), A. Gromyko (bottom): page 8 – Popperfoto (top), VAAP (bottom). Pages 9 to 11 – VAAP (all): page 12 – Popperfoto (top), VAAP (bottom). Pages 13 to 16 – A. Gromyko (all).

Foreword

Andrei Gromyko served his country for fifty years as ambassador, Deputy Foreign Minister, Foreign Minister and President. His tenure of some thirty years as Foreign Minister – from 1957 to 1985 – is without parallel in any major country in this century. He served every head of the Soviet Communist Party since Lenin. Gromyko was relieved of his job by Mikhail Gorbachev, whom he had himself nominated for the office of General Secretary of the Communist Party of the Soviet Union four years before, saying that his candidate had a pleasant smile but teeth of iron.

Gromyko died eighteen months after leaving office. No major Soviet figure attended his funeral.

Soviet politics are brutal. Leaders emerge from an internecine struggle between chieftains of various factions of the Communist Party or from the governing bureaucratic apparatus, the *nomenklatura*. But these chieftains have no other legitimacy than victories garnered in previous internecine struggles. In the absence of elections or other recognized forms of legitimacy, winners are ever bound to feel the precariousness of their position. They can trust only their personal retainers. Every new rule therefore begins with a purge and ends in stagnation. Until now, the Soviet method of government has been more akin to a feudal regime than to a modern bureaucracy – not to speak of a modern democratic state.

It was a tribute to Gromyko's technical mastery that he rendered himself indispensable through five turnovers in the Soviet leadership. But the price he had to pay for his indispensability was the rationalization of ambiguity. To those who were obliged to deal with Gromyko, he appeared unflappable, almost mechanical, well prepared and single-minded. But the concluding chapter of these memoirs dealing with Stalin shows that reality was more complex. Even if one grants that it was written in the Gorbachev period, the chapter contains too much detail to represent simply an opportunistic bow to orthodoxy – all the more so as these memoirs were written after Gromyko had been deprived of all offices.

Gromyko not only recounts a staggering statistical list of atrocities, but gives them concreteness by casting them as human vignettes over a period of thirty years. They are, in fact, the prelude to questions that go to the core of the legitimacy of the Communist system: Was there an objective need for the Soviet Union and its political system to develop along the lines chosen by Stalin? How was it possible to twist the country onto a path of the cult of a single individual whom nobody had ever invested with that power?

Gromyko does not answer these questions; he simply multiplies the tale of mostrosities. But posing them surely constitutes its own commentary. For, in truth, these are unanswerable challenges. The Communist system, lacking legitimacy, rewards the most ruthless, those who, unconstrained by traditions, legal forms or the need for periodic elections, emerge with free reign to consolidate their power essentially arbitrarily. This, in fact, is the primary challenge to Soviet reformers.

Gromyko, undoubtedly a devout believer in Marxist ideology, never resolved the contradiction which he himself raised. Similarly, Gromyko, a dedicated Russian nationalist, always left me with the impression that his dogged persistence was due at least in part to his desire to obscure the weaknesses of the state he represented. Despite the intransigence of his rhetoric, Gromyko's tendency was to stay far away from anything that might provoke physical confrontation. His top priority was relations with the United States. He gave nothing away; but he seemed also careful to avoid showdowns insofar as he had the discretion to do so.

These dichotomies give an intriguing, if ambivalent, aspect to Gromyko's memoirs. He quotes a whole series of statements he made to foreign leaders from Popes to Presidents and in each case reports that they met with the approval of his interlocutor. But what he presents himself as saying is so hackneyed, and the purported agreement is so improbable, that Gromyko – a highly intelligent man – is either striking a pose or – possibly – has his tongue in cheek.

Some events could not have happened as Gromyko describes

them. For example, he quotes me as advocating the division of Cyprus into a Greek and Turkish state during a meeting in Cyprus in May 1974. But the meeting concerned Middle East diplomacy entirely. Cyprus was neither on the agenda nor at that time at a crisis point – this is why Nicosia was chosen as the meeting site in the first place. And one would have to be worse than incompetent to raise the issue of partitioning a host country in a meeting room supplied by the alleged victim.

Similarly, someone seems to have softened the transcript concerning Berlin in my last conversation with Gromyko in January 1989, printed in the Appendix. To begin with, it is interesting that any transcript should exist of a meeting held in the Presidential suite of the Kremlin. In any event, I asked about Stalin's aims in the Berlin blockade of 1948, specifically why he ran such risks so soon after suffering huge casualties in the Second World War. I remember Gromyko saying that Stalin was convinced the United States would not resort to nuclear war over Berlin (despite our atomic monopoly), that an attempt to relieve Berlin would have been resisted, but that Stalin was determined to avoid a general war. The transcript of this conversation weakens these points somewhat and gives the Soviet Union credit for ending the crisis by withdrawing tanks from a confrontation with American armor. But that event occurred in 1961, eight years after Stalin's death and at the time of the building of the Berlin Wall. It had nothing to do with the Berlin blockade.

Still, Gromyko's memoirs convey a very good sense of the ways Soviet leaders wanted their country to be perceived. They exhibit the various strands dominating Soviet thinking before Gorbachev, the main elements of which must still to some extent remain with many of the leaders: the belief in objective factors rather than personal relations; the insistence that Soviet motives are peaceful by definition; and a latent inferiority complex masquerading as truculence.

Recognizing all these tendencies, I rather liked Gromyko. We worked closely together for eight years. Often the butt of heavy-handed joshing by his leaders, he nevertheless dominated the Soviet side of every discussion with his competence. Normally, Gromyko knew every detail of a subject. It was suicidal to negotiate with him without having mastered the record or the issues. He was extraordinarily skillful in accumulating marginal points; he cleverly sought to trade an item which should never have been raised for something really significant. Mirroring the history of his country, which had expanded from a small area around Moscow all the way to the Pacific and the center of Europe not by bold strokes but by relentless pressure, Gromyko relied on the impatience of his interlocutors to extract opportunities. He understood that Western negotiators are uncomfortable with deadlocks and will seek to break every stalemate with new ideas. Against unwary interlocutors this enabled Gromyko to harvest concessions through protracted stalemates. Most likely he needed the stalemates for domestic reasons as well, for he could not have convinced his suspicious superiors that he had in fact squeezed the lemon dry without prolonged deadlock.

Gromyo's dour demeanor made it hard to believe that underneath was a fine, if understated, sense of humor. I met him for the first time during the 1969 session of the UN General Assembly in New York. He walked up to me at a reception and said, "You look just like Henry Kissinger." I replied, "And you look a lot like Richard Nixon." He gave me a wary look and then his face creased with a smile as he nudged me with his elbow. The next year, I was arranging for him to come to the White House to see President Nixon. Gromyko said, "Don't bother to tell me which gate to use. I'll pick the gate and the guard is bound to salute."

In his memoirs, Gromyko states that I gave the impression in my own writings that I had outmaneuvered him. That was not my intention; it is not my view. Statesmen of major countries cannot be outmaneuvered, for one meets them over and over again. Those charged with the responsibility for conducting or designing foreign policy must never leave the territory of analysis for that of mere maneuver. They will be judged in the end not by their cleverness but by their grasp of reality. And this is why – even with one distortion – our mellow last conversation in these memoirs reflects the mutual respect of two men whose duties had made them adversaries.

Gromyko was one of the ablest diplomats whom I have met. He did not embody a great vision or put forward a compelling model of a world order. But neither did the system he represented. As the spokesman of a country that had never prevailed except by raw power, he felt obliged to test his mettle in every encounter. But he protected his country amidst turbulence and confusion;

he masked its weakness by persistence; he achieved important objectives by his skill. Rare is the Foreign Minister to whom one can pay such a tribute.

HENRY A. KISSINGER

September 1989

A note to my foreign readers

August–September 1988 represented a unique watershed in my life. I had become more and more convinced that, like everyone else, I had certain obligations not only to society and the state but also to my family, and indeed to myself.

The Crimea in summer and early autumn is a dazzling spectacle. That year, the heat of the constant sunshine was especially hard to take, and even bathing in the Black Sea didn't help. In the evenings, as is my custom, I took walks along the shore to breathe the cool sea breeze. The sea as usual looked mysterious and vast, and the atmosphere evoked profound personal reflection, and memories of the events of my life, both the good and the bad, the sad and the happy, as in a kaleidoscope. As inevitably as the sea washes back and forth and the sun rises and sets, the question came to mind: 'What does the future hold for me?' In fact, the question was even more precise: 'How much longer can I go on taking part in the complicated business of government?' Such thoughts were bound to lead to the conclusion that it was time to take a rest.

If anyone who has passed seventy years says he hasn't asked himself this question, he is being insincere. In recent years I have thought about it more than once. After all, you don't have to be a philosopher to ask such a question. I confess that I was expecting my family, my colleagues or my friends to express interest in my future plans, however indirectly, yet nobody so much as guessed what I had in mind. Perhaps this is because nature has been kind to me. I have been blessed with good health. Many of my colleagues were not so lucky, and the burden of responsibility seriously undermined their stamina. All my contemporaries, including those with whom I worked closely, have either gone into retirement or died. I tried calling them to mind, but nobody can be resurrected from the past and it was useless to seek their counsel.

I therefore came to the firm conclusion that I would have to take the initiative myself. The time had come for me to drop anchor, so to speak. Naturally I would have to consult those closest to me, above all my family, but I decided to wait until we were back in Moscow, since I did not want to spoil the holiday.

September came. The weather in Moscow was warm and dry and after the heat of the Crimea the evening breeze outside Moscow was refreshing. One morning, before leaving for work, I was enjoying a breakfast cup of tea which Lydia, my wife of fifty-seven years, had made me.

'Lydia,' I said, 'don't you think it's time I retired? I think it's about time myself.'

My question came as a surprise to her. 'Drink your tea, Andrei, everything'll be all right.' She then said something worthy of a lifelong companion: 'Of course, nothing lasts for ever. Our life together is the most precious thing we have, isn't it?'

I agreed, of course. My wife's support has always meant a lot to me.

The last days of my state and party service approached. Before giving official notice of my intended retirement, I took purely personal counsel with Mikhail Gorbachev at the Central Committee on Staraya Square. He told me he would give the matter careful thought. Both the General Secretary and I later expressed ourselves on the matter frankly and in public, as I describe in some detail in this book.

On 1 October 1988 I drove in my black government limousine through the Borovitsky Gate into the Kremlin, where at midday the Supreme Soviet opened in the Great Hall. I took my usual place on the podium alongside Comrades Gorbachev, Ryzhkov and Ligachev, at which point the well-publicised decision was taken. Such moments in one's life are just as memorable as one's high appointments, and as my comrades gave me their warm send-off I felt as moved as I had felt in the past when being given important posts. Above all, I was aware of having fulfilled my obligations to the people, the party and the state. That brief moment is very precious to me.

The next day I left town for Zarechie where I threw myself into writing new material for the foreign edition of my memoirs. Naturally, when one has lived a full working life for decades it felt odd not to be rushing off somewhere or having to make decisions on any number of difficult problems.

My family and I realised that, having been accustomed to the hurly-burly of political life, especially on the international scene, I would not find it easy suddenly to adjust to walking along the garden path of our suburban home or even a city street. But I had to learn to relax, willy-nilly, and I am doing just that: I am taking a course in relaxation. I get advice, some of it quite inventive, from all sorts of people, not just family, about how to spend my free time. And I am grateful to all of them, though I make up my own mind about what advice to accept.

For example, in the past, I used to enjoy hunting, but now I have no taste for it. More and more I have come to believe that even a predatory hawk hovering in the sky has the right to live, and that the momentary satisfaction of man's primeval need to know that he is capable of felling any beast or bringing down a bird is not justified. I know many inveterate hunters do not agree with me and support their 'rightness' with all sorts of arguments; but I am talking about the feeling that visits a man in the evening of his life, when his sense of being at one with nature becomes stronger. It is a time when we change and begin thinking in defiance of current fashion.

My own well tested way of relaxing is not to give up intellectual labour, nor could I even if I wished. I mull over and weigh up the past and my own part in it, and commit much of what I think to writing. I shall continue to do so.

My decision to write this book was not made quickly. Many people suggested that I write it – colleagues at work, relatives, Soviet citizens I had never met, even foreigners. As for myself, although I had the vague intention at some time in the future to begin writing, for a long while I did nothing about it. Only after my seventieth birthday did I decide that perhaps the moment had come.

One reason I delayed was that I was reluctant to have my memoirs published and be measured alongside the work of professional writers. Also, memoirs are only of any worth if interesting to read, and I feared mine might not be. But then I thought: No; I have seen things that few others have seen, and I have known and talked with people professional writers are very unlikely to have met. I decided I would do my best, but in my own way, without a plot, simply writing about my own experiences.

Analysis of the total picture is the business of historians and political scientists. I would stress that I see my own task as narrower: to describe as fully as I can those events in which I myself took part, and those individuals whom fate brought my way.

Clearly much of what has happened over the last fifty years has been of genuinely epic importance, and this is particularly true of the Second World War and the great victory over the fascist aggressor, a victory which has brought lasting glory to our country and its people. Over this period I myself have had dealings with hundreds of people from the widest range of countries – politicians and state officials, military men and scientists, cultural figures and businessmen, and many who could not be fitted into any of these categories. Although I have not set out to give rounded portraits of this impressive gallery of personalities, their inner worlds, their philosophies of life, I have written something about each, using whatever came to hand from my personal experience and selecting mainly those individuals who have stood, or still stand, at the helm of their states, creating and carrying out foreign policy, which is the main axis around which my work has revolved.

When I talk to non-diplomats I often sense that they think of diplomacy as the attempt to outwit one's partners in talks, or to make especially apt remarks, to sparkle with sudden wit or come up with unfamiliar quotations. This is far from the reality. I therefore plan to demonstrate here that the work of an official representative abroad requires many different skills, but first and foremost the ability to analyse problems as they come up and to present them clearly to others in all their essentials.

From 1985 to 1988 I held the post of Chairman of the Presidium of the Supreme Soviet of the USSR, and so I also aim to say something about the vast range of questions with which the Presidium has to deal. Mostly these have to do with the social and economic development of the country, but they are also deeply concerned with its unchanging approach to the consolidation of peace in the world through its foreign policy.

What I have written is in places fragmentary and in some ways incomplete: but recollections cannot of themselves be a total reflection of everything that has happened. That is the way of reminiscences: it is the nature of human memory.

I

At the start of life's path

I am sometimes asked about the origin of my name. In the customary way of old rural Russia, people in my village nearly all took its name as their own family name, and out of the ninety-odd families in Old Gromyki nearly every one was called Gromyko. In the neighbouring village of New Gromyki more than 250 families were also called Gromyko. Less than four miles away there was another village, with more than 200 households, every one of them with the name of Gromyko. You couldn't tell one family from another, and consequently peasants in those villages and hamlets had to invent nicknames for each other. In my family the name of 'Gromyko' was the one registered in the local baptismal and official records, but, following local custom, we used our nickname in everyday life. This nickname was 'Burmakov'. My father, grandfather and great-grandfather had all been known in the village under this name, and I in turn would answer to the name Andrei Burmakov.

The Gromykos are now widely scattered throughout the Soviet Union, but they are all linked in one way or another with the ancient tribes of the Radimichi, and with the area located between the upper reaches of the Dnieper and the Desna, in the Sozha basin, and by the little river Besed.

Gomel, which was the main town of my childhood, is first mentioned in the chronicles in the middle of the twelfth century. It was annexed from medieval Russia in the fourteenth century by the Great Principality of Lithuania and in the sixteenth century by Poland, with which Lithuania was united, returning to the Russian empire in 1772 under the first partition of Poland. In 1924 the Gomel area was designated part of the Belorussian Soviet Repub-

lic. Devastated by the fascists during the war, the town has now
been rebuilt and is a major industrial and cultural centre. I recall
Gomel as a large railway junction with many factories, of which
the most notable was the Vesuvius match factory, where I longed
to work.

The town was located in the so-called Pale of Jewish Settlement,
that is the part of the Russian empire where the overwhelming
majority of the Jewish population were permitted to live. There
were two or three Jewish families in most of the villages of our
district: one of my Jewish friends was David Gurevich, who lived
in the neighbouring village of Khlusy. We remained friends into
our student days. I heard after the war that he had been seized by
the Nazis and shot, simply because he was a Jew. Gomel itself had
a higher proportion of Jews than other parts of the country, but I
don't recall any discrimination against them. But then, with the
abolition of the Pale after the fall of the tsar in February 1917, the
Jews' isolation had ended and they had become fully fledged
citizens.

I was born on 18 July 1909 in the village of Old Gromyki, not
far from Gomel, into the family of a 'semi-peasant-semi-worker'.
This pre-revolutionary designation described a man who did not
have enough land of his own to feed himself and his family, and
who worked away from home in a factory somewhere on a
seasonal basis. In short, ours was a poor peasant household. While
still only a boy of thirteen I used to go with my father to earn
extra money by cutting timber and rafting it downriver to the
factories in Gomel.

I grew up alongside the little district town of Vetka, the majority
of whose inhabitants belonged to a Christian sect calling themselves Old Believers. They were kind, hospitable people and we
liked them. When I was a bit older, I learned that their ancestors
had escaped from the persecution of Patriarch Nikon and the
monarchs of the seventeenth century, and in 1684 had established
the community of Vetka. This community gloried in its artisans:
builders, cabinet-makers, woodcarvers, gilders, icon-painters, en-
gravers. They used to be given churches to build and grand houses
to decorate in Kiev, Petersburg and Moscow. In particular, they
worked with other skilled craftsmen on the magnificent Armoury
Hall in the Kremlin, as well as the Novodevichy and Iversky
monasteries.

Today Vetka is famous for its unique manuscripts and wooden

books. I must confess that all my life I have had a love of old books and pictures. A little while ago the most expensive book ever sold was bought at auction in Paris: it was called *The Apostle* and had been published in 1574 by the early Russian printer Ivan Fedorov. The inhabitants of Vetka must be proud to know that they have a second copy in their local museum!

In putting my early memories down on paper, the question inevitably arises: when did my views of life and the world begin to take shape? I can remember roughly from the age of four. Leaving aside close family bonds, my first strong impressions are of our little house. It stood on the edge of the village and seemed to me at least a hundred years old. It had two rooms, each with one bed and two or three benches, and we lived there with my father's father and mother. Our domestic economy matched the house's simplicity: we had one cow for milk and one horse for labour.

My father, Andrei Matveyevich, was educated, in the basic sense of the word. He had only attended the local four-year parish school but he could read and write. I remember how I envied him his beautiful handwriting: mine has never been up to much. I would try to reproduce the letters as I had been shown, but somehow they always managed to come out disjointed. Still, I didn't do so badly when I used ruled paper.

My father loved telling the family about the battles he'd been in, in Manchuria during the Russo-Japanese War of 1904–5, or in the south-western sector of the Russian–German front during the First World War. I remember him salting his accounts of the latter with sharp words about the Russian generals: 'as for the high command, we troops would always go into battle without enough weapons, especially artillery. There was a constant shortage of ammunition. The German firepower was much greater than ours, which is why the Russian army took such heavy losses.'

According to my father, the soldiers blamed their defeats in Manchuria on their commanders, rather than on the tsar: 'They were afraid to blame the tsar directly. We had a saying: "From Manchuria to Siberia is a short distance – the front is here, and exile's there."'

I hardly ever saw my father with idle hands. Even when he was telling his stories he would be making something or other, planing or repairing or just putting his tools in order. If he was not away on seasonal work, which as a rule would last several months, then he would find some other work to do, maybe preparing firewood for the winter, collecting fallen branches in the forest, and digging up old stumps and bringing it all to the hut by horse.

Usually my father was a man of few words. Working in the fields or the yard, haymaking, or collecting wood in the forest, he could go for hours in total silence. However, there were times when he did allow himself to talk, either with his family around the table or late on a summer evening, when a few of the men – the women did not join in – would gather next to someone's hut on the earthen windbreak, the *zavalinka*.

Once my father and the others were arguing over which country was the richest in the world. Opinion was divided. Some said Germany, because the Germans were robbers: they had even stolen parts of Russia. Others insisted that America was the richest. Nobody thought of mentioning Russia.

Someone said: 'The Americans had a wise President called Theodore Roosevelt. People say he ruled the country well.'

My father said: 'America is probably the richest country – the Americans too have ways of grabbing other people's wealth. Theodore Roosevelt was a cunning President.'

His neighbour agreed. 'Yes, Theodore Roosevelt was a cunning and wise President.'

I have had those words about the 'cunning and wise' American President at the back of my mind ever since.

Such discussions were a common occurrence in the village: the men found them an outlet for their ideas, and from an early age I was allowed to sit in on these sessions.

Everything I have said about my father's capacity for work was equally true of my mother, Olga Evgenyevna. She was born into a poor peasant family from the neighbouring village of Zhelezniki, and had only two or three years of schooling because her father had died early on and she had had to leave school to work in the house and out in the fields. Nevertheless she taught herself to read and write, and she read quite a bit. She had a heart of gold, and spoke only well of people.

She managed to grow a few potatoes, cabbages and cucumbers on the small patch of earth that she looked after, and she dealt with the sowing and planting out of the flax. This occupied an important place in our family budgeting, and without it there would have been no shirts or bedclothes. She had to prepare the feed for the cow, and tended the grain, which was mainly rye. All this work, as well as feeding the family and carefully eking out the food, fell on the women's shoulders in those days, and in our home there was only my mother, my grandmother and my younger sister Evdokia; but she didn't begin helping until I had already gone away to study.

It was from my mother that I inherited my love of books. To both adults and children in the village she was 'Auntie Olya, the professor'. I well recall her telling me: 'You like reading and the teachers think highly of you. Study, and maybe you'll go out into the world.'

In 1933, when I was studying in Minsk, my father went into the forest to fetch kindling and never came back. They found him many hours later inexplicably sick and barely alive. There was no medical help at hand and he died soon after; he was only in his mid-fifties. My mother died fifteen years later, in Moscow. Having spent her whole life in the countryside, she came to the capital a few months before her death for medical attention, but it was too late. I arrived home from the USA two weeks before she died and managed to see her in hospital.

My parents had married just after the Russo-Japanese War, my father then being twenty-seven and my mother nineteen. Their first child was Tatyana, who was born eighteen months before me, but who died when she was about two.

My father's father, Matvei Grigoryevich, had been alive at the time of the emancipation of the serfs in 1861. He too could read. Often, before dinner, I would listen to his precise, slightly drawn-out reading of the Gospels. He finally died in 1927, at the age of seventy-five.

My grandmother, Marfa, is, in my memory, unfailingly kind and gentle. When I was still only very small I remember her using a word I hadn't heard before. I don't recall what I had done wrong, but she wagged her finger at me and said: 'What have you been up to, you little democrat?' That was before the revolution, at a time when 'democrats' were being thrown into gaol and sent into exile – in effect, she was trying to scare me. Indeed, later on I heard the word used many times as a term of abuse. However, as I knew she could never be really angry, since childhood the word 'democrat' has always sounded to my ears like an endearment, not an insult.

My father had two brothers, Nikolai and Ivan, and two sisters, Sofia and Maria. There was already too little of grandfather's arable land to provide food until the next harvest, so that dividing it up into yet smaller allotments at the time of the old man's death caused tempers to rise. Even so, perhaps because such difficulties were suffered by all families in our impoverished region, our family remained close. And we got on well in the village. Visiting or entertaining was always a pleasure, although, as I recall, we didn't care much for alcohol. Nobody in my family drank; but two or three times a year a few young boys in the village would get drunk, most likely hoping for the courage to approach the local girls.

I loved everything about Old Gromyki – the fields and forests, the meadows and rivers. It seemed the best place in the world, even though we often had barely enough potatoes to last us through the winter. The little river Besed was a delight. Small steamboats chugged up it in the springtime – it was too shallow in the summer – and to us children the river bank was like a magnet. We would sit for hours with a fishing rod waiting for a bite, and if anyone actually managed to hook five or six small fish it was considered a real catch: the lucky fisherman felt thoroughly grown-up as he carried his prize home.

When they could, the village children would help the women in the fields, picking flax and hemp, lifting potatoes, reaping and harvesting the grain. It was heavy work, but there were no draught animals – in fact, animals in general were rare, as there was insufficient fodder.

Three kilometres from the village was the large forest of Grafschchina. In the mushroom season, people went fearlessly into the forest. But we thought it had wild animals in it, bandits and even witches; and when our imaginations ran away with us we said there were wood demons too. We really could hear wolves howling there in the winter. You wouldn't go collecting firewood on your own then. Many times, when I went with my father for wood, I imagined how I would defend him from the wolves by letting fly with my axe. Luckily, the wolves stayed away.

Today's city-dwellers will find it hard to understand the magical world of beliefs and legends which country people, especially the children, inhabited seventy years ago. Generally legends were a mixture of superstition and fairy-tale, handed down from generation to generation and meant to demonstrate the importance of keeping one's word, loving one's fellow man, being honest and behaving honourably. But the older children also had magical ways of finding out what the future held. If you wanted to discover your marriage prospects, for instance, you had to go to a deserted hut or old bathhouse outside the village on a dark and preferably foul night, equipped with a flaming torch and a mirror. You placed the mirror so that it reflected the door, which was to be left open. At precisely midnight, the image of your future spouse would appear in the doorway. Only the bravest dared to last out the solitary waiting.

Most seven- or eight-year-olds couldn't have cared less whether the method worked or not, but I and my cousin, Artemka, who was a year older than me, decided to put it to the test. As it happened, my grandfather had a primitive bathhouse away in the woods, so it fell to me to be the hero. Reckoning with the possibility that an evil spirit might turn up instead of my intended, we agreed that Artemka should wait close by, and if he felt things weren't going right he would rush to my help.

He settled down in the bushes armed with an iron bar, while I took up my position in the bathhouse. I lit the torch and sat for a long time. The night was utterly silent and even the village dogs were sound asleep. I felt that I was being watched through the cracks by a thousand demons. Only the thought of Artemka's scorn if I were to desert kept me at my post.

After a while my torch burnt out. Suddenly Artemka decided that we'd been there long enough. He called to me quaveringly: 'Andrei, are you alive?'

I said nothing, just grabbed the mirror, and we both fled, relieved to have escaped with our lives.

Most villagers believed in the supernatural. They had to extract their subsistence from ungenerous soil through unrelenting labour, so it was not surprising that they should find comfort occasionally in the mysterious.

For myself, in the short breaks during work in the fields or woods, if we had not been given any homework at school, I would lie down on the grass and read a book or just daydream. I would ask myself questions like: What are the stars? Why do they twinkle at night? Why do people think God lives in the sky? Who has seen him?

And I would answer: I don't know anyone who has seen him.

I asked my grandmother Marfa this tricky question: 'Who has seen God?'

'Nobody can see God.'

'How can we talk about him, if nobody's ever seen him?'

She replied quite sharply: 'Wait till you get older. Then you'll know all these things.'

There ended the conversation about God.

Other adults said much the same thing. Some claimed that God had so ordered things that man should not know all about him anyway. But we had one close neighbour called Mikhail Shelyutov who was a free-thinker. He declared that the question of the existence of God was under discussion and that there were many scientists who didn't believe in his existence.

From about the age of nine, after the revolution, I began reading for myself the atheistic pamphlets that started to appear. They were easier to find in the district libraries than in our village, but even so my friends and I managed to acquire the principles of atheism, albeit in simplified, popularised form. My family, like many which had hitherto been religious, split on this issue along generational lines. My grandparents remained religious. Their children mostly gave up praying, and, though they would occasionally cross themselves when sitting down to eat, in time they gave that up too, and the beliefs that went with it.

As for my own generation, we practically never crossed ourselves, except at Easter when we would attend the service and listen to the beautiful singing of the choir. We really only went to church because at communion we could have a drop of the quite tasty sweet wine. We thought the priest, Vasily Voltovsky, a greedy man, however, as he only gave us a teaspoonful. Even then it was not always a full one.

I have always loved to read. As a child, whatever I read set my mind working, and in that way I learned to think.

I read whatever came to hand, without any system. Whenever I heard of a book with an interesting title, I would go after it. Once, through friends, I got hold of a book called *Pictorial Astronomy* by Camille Flammarion. The French astronomer would never have believed it had he been told that in a little Russian village a schoolboy was studying his book as intently as if an examination depended on it.

For some reason, all my life I have remembered the first illustration in that book and the caption under it: 'Our earth is hurtling on the wings of Time, we know not whither . . .' Sixty-five years later, when the librarian in the Lenin Library asked which edition of the book I required, I repeated that caption and, when the book was produced, I found that my memory had not deceived me.

As well as books on atheism and nature, I read about Russian history and the exploits of Russian revolutionaries. As my range widened, I became interested in books on travel and geographical discovery, and to this day I remember being entranced by the accounts of the voyages of Captain Cook.

At one time I became obsessed by geometry and trigonometry, and in the summer holidays I went into the woods to measure the distances between trees in order to calculate their height. This gave me a lot of satisfaction, but my interest in maths soon cooled, to be replaced by a love of the human sciences.

Reading through the Russian classics, then Homer and Goethe's *Faust*, led me to wonder whether I shouldn't try writing something of my own, maybe even poetry. So I started to keep a secret notebook and in no time I had composed a dozen poems. But my own critical ability soon won the day and, just as I had written everything in secret, so I burned everything in secret.

I often wondered if I was normal: Why do I want to be alone, usually thinking about some book?

Gradually more energetic, outward-turning activities were added to my solitary musings. Together with friends of my own age and mentality, I found an outlet for my energies in study and community work, and I began to discover something of what I was like. Not a day passed when, along with my friends, I did not 'go to the people', as we dubbed our community work. It sometimes amazed us that adults would listen to us, and apparently even had respect for us, but this gave us still more energy.

As for a general view of the world and human values, until I began reading revolutionary literature, after 1917–18, I had no system of ideas. Nevertheless, some basic opinions were taking shape. For instance, when I observed that the priest, Voltovsky, would ride round the villages on his cart, and the peasants would come out and give him what little grain or oats they could spare, I asked myself: If the priest is spreading the word of God, then why doesn't God feed him? It seemed to me the answer must be that there was no God.

Dialectical materialism had already taken root in the minds of us youngsters. As a Young Communist of thirteen, together with my Komsomol friends, I was already making anti-religious speeches in the village. I can well remember elderly peasant women crossing themselves as they went past the hut where they had been told that Komsomol members were proclaiming that there was no God. And yet, even though my parents and close relatives did not share my anti-religious views, they never quarrelled with me over them.

As teenagers, we wanted to make our mark in the world of art. There were plenty of propaganda playlets included in the pamphlets that came our way, and we chose to perform one that depicted the clash of revolutionary and counter-revolutionary ideas in the stormy years of the civil war. Its two chief characters are Kesha, a 'Red commander', and Vovy, a 'White officer', who have a heated argument.

We gave the part of the White officer to a wild, fiery-tempered boy called Ivan, and when it came to choosing who should play the Red commander the others all called out as one: 'It has to be Andrei. He's always giving lectures – let him take on the White.'

I was flattered by their confidence in me and took the part. We rehearsed in a local school hall. Having neither costumes nor props, we acted in our everyday clothes. We made shoulder-boards of sorts for the White officer, who was to keep peering down at them out of the corner of his eye to see if they were still there. But the best part of his costume was the White officer's new boots, which we polished to a high gloss. My boots, by contrast, were well worn but solid, with metal studs, what we called 'real proletarian' boots. We wore proper gun-holsters, but minus revolvers.

When we got to the political argument between the Red commander and the White officer the White naturally defended the rich. Of the poor he said: 'Someone has to do the work, after all! That's what it's all about. There have to be people to work in the factories and fields and build roads and float rafts down the rivers, and then there have to be other people who manage it.'

The Red commander protested against the idea that the rich, the exploiters, should manage everything. 'Everyone must be equal,' he said. 'Everyone must work. That's why the workers and peasants, led by Lenin, made the revolution.'

The other characters, of whom the Reds were naturally in the majority, were unable to learn their words properly, so we had a prompter tucked away in the corner under strict orders to pay attention. However, since he was awkwardly placed and we couldn't always hear him, we often had to improvise. The prompter also did his utmost, sometimes raising his voice above those of the actors when they weren't following the text. In fact the entire production was rather strange. Still, it all went off well enough, and the leading actors didn't even come to blows, though we got very close to it. When I arrived back home my mother said: 'I thought he was going to tear your new shirt off.'

Anyway, everyone was pleased: not only the actors and the organisers but the audience too. They had sat tolerantly throughout the show, perhaps because they had never seen anything like it in the village before.

That was the last act of my theatrical career.

2

In the aftermath of revolution

In 1914, the news that Germany had declared war on Russia came virtually without warning. The adults reacted sharply. Father said, 'The Germans have attacked Russia. They are strong and dangerous. They always bring suffering.'

That was the first time I sensed what I came to know as love for my country, for its fields and forests and hearths.

The villagers were full of anger at the aggressors, and had an unquestioning faith in their own strength. There was mobilisation, and for the second time my father was conscripted. He served for three years on the south-western front under General A.A. Brusilov. Then, shortly after his return, in October 1917, news of the Bolshevik revolution spread like wildfire around our village.

'The workers have taken power into their own hands,' a peasant told my father. 'We have to march with them. The landowners are kaput.'

There were many words I didn't understand. What was 'power'? What did it mean, 'to march together with the workers'? Surely my grandfather Matvei and the free-thinking Mikhail Shelyutov (whom I regarded as the embodiment of the working man) were not going to set off together somewhere? On the other hand, I knew what 'kaput' meant – the Germans were not far away and German words had come into daily use.

News came from Petrograd that the revolution was being led by 'Lenin and his helpers'. That was the first time I heard Lenin's name, but from the way in which it was spoken I was reminded of the brave knights in fairy-tales who battled with the enemy and always won.

The first change I noticed in the village was that I no longer heard the harness bells warning of the approach of the local police chief whom we all traditionally feared. The village constable disappeared too; he had also been feared, though people used to chat with him and even sometimes answer him back. However, the peasants' most constant and worst fear had always been the thought of the tsar – so much so that even long after the revolution, when life had been completely reordered and the country had gone through major changes, one might still hear a peasant blurt out: 'But what will happen to us if the tsar comes back?'

Our village then suffered a very difficult period. At the beginning of 1918 German forces occupied the western territory, including the Gomel region. In spite of the revolution, unit after unit moved eastwards in a seemingly endless stream. The alarm that the country had felt at the first news of war was completely justified.

The Germans arrived like an enslaving force. The Kaiser's well-drilled troops marched into Russia as if they were on parade. During their occupation they pillaged towns and villages, stole cattle, which they sent by wagon back to Germany, and commandeered horses for their troop transports. In general, they either beat up or killed anyone who stood in their way.

They went from house to house in Old Gromyki, rounding up the cows. I remember as if it were yesterday how three armed soldiers were about to take our cow out of the yard. My father and his two brothers were away in the forest. Only my grandfather was at home. He rushed to get the cow back, struggling desperately. One of the soldiers aimed his rifle at him, but at that moment the cow got its legs tangled in the rope and fell to the ground. This gave the women and children, including myself, aged only nine, and my seven-year-old sister a chance to cling on to grandfather's arms and hold him back.

He took the theft of his cow very hard and seemed lost without her. He grieved: 'What was that damned German thinking of? Did he have to take our last cow, and leave the children without milk?'

For a while the women, including my mother, waited at the outskirts of the village, in case the Germans changed their minds and brought the cows back. But they didn't. The barn, where my little sister and I used to go in the mornings to drink the warm milk, remained empty. Even so in a way I am grateful for the material hardships, of which there were many, for in learning to overcome them I think I strengthened my character.

Even before our area had been overrun, for several weeks we had watched as large numbers of people fled eastwards from the Germans, their carts loaded up with their belongings. They were mostly Poles and Belorussians who didn't speak Russian very well, but the population could understand them and treated them kindly.

The Germans were only stopped when in March 1918 Lenin signed the Treaty of Brest-Litovsk. Although this inflicted great costs in human and material resources on the Soviet republic, it did not affect the fundamental gains of the October revolution which were more important for the country as a whole.

Emerging temporarily from the First World War, the Soviet republic gained a breathing space in which to sort out some of its internal problems, and to set about building the Red Army. Barely eight months later, revolution in Germany overthrew Kaiser Wilhelm II and on 13 November 1918 the Soviet government annulled the Brest-Litovsk Treaty. It was a victory for Lenin's foresight, and by January 1919 the Gomel district was cleared of Germans and the refugees returned to their homes.

The idea took root in my mind that war between states was a great evil and that the invading Germans were our enemies. What did they want our land for? Why did they have to kill Russians? As children we used to play at war, and we always made the Russians win.

Gradually Lenin's New Economic Policy began to work and the Soviet economy became fully established; but it was the shift from compulsory requisitioning to a tax-in-kind that finally persuaded the peasants to get agriculture going and increase output.

I remember an incident in this connection. We had a lecturer who came to the village to explain the policies of the new regime, and to give the people a rough idea of the theory of Marxism-Leninism.

'Marx worked out his teaching on the basis of the latest theories,' he told us, 'using the ideas of other philosophers in a brilliantly selective way, especially those of Hegel. From Hegel he took everything that was good and nothing else. That is to say, he took the rational seeds of Hegel's wisdom.' He asked for questions.

Almost before the words were out of his mouth a quick-witted peasant piped up, referring to the requisitioning of surpluses which often left the peasants without enough grain to feed themselves, let alone to sow: 'You say Marx only took the rational seeds from Hegel, and nothing else. Hegel was lucky. Just the other day, the Marxists came and took *all* our seeds.'

That was before the tax-in-kind that came in with Lenin's new policy. Once the peasants knew how much they had to give to the state and how much they could keep for their own use, they came to see that the new regime understood their problems and this could not but have a good effect on agricultural productivity. For its part, the state then found it easier to feed the towns and the urban working class.

One's psychological and moral world is formed imperceptibly. It is nurtured by the first gulps of air one takes in one's birthplace, by the sound of lullabies and later by the images conjured up by fairy-tales, legends and folk-songs. And of course there is the influence of history, the lives of the great heroes who sacrificed themselves for their country. It is natural to wonder why my childhood experiences should have had such a formative effect on me. I believe this is because they aroused my curiosity, gave me a thirst for knowledge and an urge to save both other people and my country. I felt this so strongly, indeed, that I often imagined myself fighting in the army, defending the country against its enemies, the Tartars, the Swedes, the Japanese and the Germans.

Patriotic feeling used to be engendered virtually at birth. It embraced the sense of being drawn to the house where one was born and uttered one's first words, one's attachment to one's parents and relations, and one's later devotion to the memory of one's home town or village, the hills and rivers of one's childhood. All together, this is what constitutes love for one's country.

Today we generally prefix the sacred word 'patriotism' with 'Soviet'. This reflects an additional devotion to the values of our socialist society and a contempt for the exploitation of man by man.

At the beginning of 1923, I was elected secretary of the village cell of the Young Communist League, the Komsomol. Instructions affecting every aspect of village life were handed down to the local cells by the local Komsomol committee. The Komsomols were supposed to set an example to the peasants and the village intelligentsia, and we took this very seriously.

As I zealously read my instructions, I felt almost as if I was communing with Karl Marx himself. My family put up with my work, but at first did nothing more than that. However, when they saw other villages doing their best to get their own candidates put forward for election they took a more active interest.

In January 1924 Lenin died. It was a fierce winter. I remember struggling through great snowdrifts to get to school, where a funeral meeting had been arranged. Our teachers made speeches, reminding us how much Lenin had done for us and for all the workers and peasants of Russia.

The villagers talked of nothing but the death of Lenin. They asked: 'What will happen now? How are we going to live without Lenin?'

They thought that as Komsomol secretary I ought to be able to tell them. What could I tell them, when I was hoping someone would tell *me*? Then I remembered something I'd heard: 'The revolution was carried out by Lenin and his helpers.' So I replied: 'Lenin has died, but his helpers, the party, still live. And we will live with it.'

After I had completed seven years of primary school and then trade school in Gomel, I went to the technical school in Borisov, not far from Minsk. I lived there in a one-storey wooden house that was famous because Napoleon had slept there at the time he was retreating from Russia with his bedraggled army. It was still called 'Napoleon's', with some irony at the expense of the bankrupt emperor.

I joined the Communist Party in 1931, while I was in Borisov. I had dreamed of doing so ever since I first began to understand the difference between a poor peasant and a landlord, a worker and a capitalist. I received my party card just before the meeting that elected new officials, and at that meeting I was immediately made secretary of my party cell.

I was thrilled by my work in the party. Just as before, as a Komsomol, I was working closely with other people, dealing with the problems of the day, always in the thick of things. Party members in those days – as indeed throughout the history of our state – were in the front line, in the most important and difficult jobs. Not only did we have to explain and agitate in favour of party policy, the main topic at that time being the collectivisation of agriculture, but we were also the first to give up our Saturdays or Sundays to do voluntary work, willingly going wherever we were sent, collecting firewood, unloading wagons, wherever another pair of hands was needed. The party and the Komsomol understood our difficulties and loyally sustained the fire of communist conviction in our young hearts.

We received only a small maintenance grant. Despite the hardships, I remember those days with warmth, maybe because that was also the time when I began my family life with Lydia Dmitrievna Grinevich, a student and the daughter of Belorussian peasants. She was from the village of Kamenki, just west of Minsk.

One day, among a group of female students, I had noticed a beautiful girl. I just couldn't get her out of my mind. Finally I decided: I'm already over twenty; I really must do something about her.

At that age one makes lightning decisions, especially on such matters. We soon got to know each other. I was conquered by her beauty, her modesty and other magical qualities harder to name. It seems to me that these are women's weaponry, against which no man can arm himself. It will be just as well if he never learns to. A thousand Darwins and psychologists can never explain women's particular qualities; it's the secret of nature itself.

The early summer nights were short and, evening after evening, Lydia and I would meet and stroll the whole night through. It was as if we were being carried along in a magic chariot. Only the 'quiet dawns' knew our secret. The film *The Quiet Dawns* was made decades later and was about quite different matters, but its title is so evocative of nature and of my state of mind at that time that I can't help thinking of it now.

One hot summer day I went for a swim in the Berezina. The sun was bright on the fields and a sharp, sweet scent of flowers hung over the meadow on my way. My mind was on nothing but the girl I had just got to know. I happened to be rereading *Eugene Onegin* at the time, and as I walked my thoughts jumped from Tatyana to my new friend and back to Tatyana, although the circumstances were quite different and Pushkin's passionate words figured rarely if at all in our conversations. We simply felt good together. In any case, the most powerful moments in Pushkin's masterpiece occur when the hero and heroine explain why they cannot join their fates one to the other. This was both a warning and an inspiration, implying that you should not miss opportunities in your personal life when they come your way.

As I walked it seemed to me that life was a composition of the sweetest sounds and that people just did not understand this. My thoughts wandered so far away that I almost fell down the steep bank and into the smooth, glittering water below.

I climbed down and spotted two fellow students. Changing rapidly, I joined them and swam to the other side and back. The river was deep but not wide and I accomplished this easily.

The swim woke me up; the chill of the water brought me back to reality from my daydreams. Never again in my life would I feel that sense of spiritual uplift, inner release and purity of thought that I experienced that day as I walked alone in the sunlit meadows.

When I got back to the hostel, I tried to understand what it was I had felt. What was all that about? How could I have been so engrossed in my thoughts that I almost fell down the bank into the river? True, I can swim and nothing much would have happened, but still . . .

The conclusion that I drew from my self-analysis was unexpected and precise: I must tell her everything. We'll have to decide what we should both do . . .

That was how the countryside in the spring and the psychological effect of Pushkin's immortal poem combined to influence my feelings.

Lydia and I got married while we were still students. Life was hard for a time, but after a while we got things organised, including an apartment.

Fifty-seven years have elapsed since those days. Lydia Dmitrievna and I have two children, Anatoly and Emilia. Anatoly is a professor with a doctorate in history and is a corresponding member of the USSR Academy of Sciences, where he is director of the African Institute. Our daughter Emilia is a history graduate and does editing work. We have three grandsons, Igor, Andrei and Alexei, and two granddaughters, Lydia and Anna. One of my grandsons has a son of his own, Oleg. My sister, Evdokia, is still alive and well and lives in Gomel with her daughter Sofia.

The Great Patriotic War did not spare my family. My two younger brothers, Alexei and Fedor, both perished as officers in the Soviet army, one in the early stages of the war, in the Baltic, and the second as the commander of an artillery battery at the crossing of the Berezina near Bobruisk, when the Soviet army was in pursuit of the retreating Hitlerites. My third brother, Dmitri, had a cruel time. During the war he was a member of the resistance against the German occupation, and later was in the army. He returned from the front with his health ruined and died in 1978. Two uncles on my mother's side, Fedor and Matvei Bekarevich, were killed in the war, and my wife's only beloved brother, Arkady, died in the defence of Moscow.

I studied for a further twelve years after leaving primary school: first trade school in Gomel, then technical school in Borisov, then the institute in Minsk and finally postgraduate studies in Minsk and Moscow.

I had decided that I wanted to study the social sciences, and was confirmed in this when, at the age of sixteen, I made up my mind to read Engels's *Anti-Dühring*, whatever the effort. The fact that I was already running political study circles and that I had been elected secretary of the Komsomol collective bolstered my intention. It sounds hard going now, but once I'd started I found I couldn't put the book down, so clear was Engels's exposition of Marx's ideas. I had first heard about Marx's *Kapital* when I joined the Komsomol. I realised it was his major work, and after some months of trying I eventually got hold of a copy. I discovered then what a difficult book it was and noted places that I would study further 'when I was cleverer'.

As I was already a communist, and had been party secretary at the technical school, I found myself being sent on frequent missions by the party authorities, sometimes as often as twice a month. From Borisov, and later from Minsk, I was sent to help in the collectivisation, the consolidation of the collective farms and the strengthening of party work in the villages. Sometimes I had to deal with agricultural procurements also.

After two years of study in Borisov I was appointed head of a secondary school not far from Minsk, in the district of Dzerzhinsk, where my wife was working as a veterinary technician on a state farm. Thereafter I was simultaneously teaching and running the school, and continuing my studies as an external student at the institute.

One day a Central Committee representative of the Belorussian Communist Party came to see me with an unusual offer.

'The suggestion is that you should move on to postgraduate work – if you're interested, of course.'

'But I haven't yet done all my exams at the institute,' I objected.

'Don't worry. Work for the exams, and then, after them, you can go straight into postgraduate work.'

I asked for some time to think it over.

What worried me was the financial aspect. By this time we had our first child, Anatoly, but as a headmaster I was getting a good salary and I was afraid a graduate stipend would lower my family's living standards.

I was sent to talk to the people in Minsk. Professor I.M. Borisevich, who headed the commission at the university there, announced at the end of our interview: 'In view of your educational, labour and social record, the commission proposes that you join the specialist postgraduate course which has just been established here in Minsk.'

I naturally asked, 'What sort of specialists are to be trained here?'

He said, 'We have in mind economists with a broad background, both applied and theoretical. The Institute of Red Professors in Moscow is training social science teachers for our high schools. The idea is to do something similar here, in our graduate school.'

I told the commission frankly that I had had enough of living on a student grant. Borisevich assured me that after a short time graduates were to be paid a stipend in line with the party maximum – in other words, a decent living wage.

'Once you've taken the institute exams, you'll have no hardship,' he went on. 'You're well known here and you'll be taken good care of. The postgraduate course doesn't start for another six months, which gives you plenty of time.' Then he added: 'Whether you accept the offer or not, I happen to know that they intend to transfer you to work in Minsk.'

As I would be leaving Dzerzhinsk in any case, I agreed to the postgraduate course, and in 1933 moved with my family to Minsk. At first we took a private apartment. The professor's prediction about the party maximum had been right, and it was quite adequate for us.

Then the serious work of the postgraduate course began, directed by Professor Borisevich and his assistant, Professor Klimko. I remember that poor Klimko had lost an arm in the civil war. The first six months of the course were devoted to political economy, philosophy and English, and the teaching staff were first class.

We were enrolled in the Belorussian Academy of Sciences and, not long after we had joined, when the Academy put on a reception for some anniversary, we postgraduates were invited together with leading scientists and distinguished academicians. We were amazed to find ourselves treated as equals and placed at their table to enjoy what was for us a sumptuous feast. We realised then that not for nothing did the Soviet state treat its scientists well: evidently science and those who worked in it were highly regarded by the state. I must confess in all honesty that it was after that meeting with the academicians, when I saw how well the state looked after its scholars, that I decided, if I was given the choice, I would enter academic life.

But then, in 1934, an incident occurred which was to affect the entire course of my life. We were told without warning that our group was to transfer to Moscow to a similar institute. We thought about it, and after a while we decided not to protest. As the saying runs: 'If you're a mushroom, into the basket you go.' So in March 1934 my little family, with all our worldly goods packed into three suitcases, moved to Moscow. I well remember my feelings on the journey. An inner voice told me that soon I really would be walking on the famous flagstones of the Kremlin and looking at its walls close up, instead of on a picture postcard.

We were to be housed in Alexeyevsky, a student settlement on the north-east edge of the city. The second Romanov tsar, Alexei Mikhailovich, had had his palace there, though by now all that was left of it was its name. Alexeyevsky was a real student town, with young men and women wherever one looked, and we lived there quite comfortably until we got a really good apartment from the Academy of Sciences in a new block on Chkalov Street, which we shared with a young virologist called Mikhail Petrovich Chumakov. He has since become a world authority on poliomyelitis.

The director of the Moscow institute was M.A. Lurye, an eminent economic theorist. My postgraduate work at the institute was scarcely different from what I had been doing in Minsk, while my party missions in the Moscow region were similar also: dekulakisation, strengthening the collective farms and explaining party policy and the international situation to workers in both town and village. I also had to keep a check on local progress with the party's literacy programme, and lecture on theory – for example, on Lenin's *Development of Capitalism in Russia.*

I recall during one such trip, when it came to fixing up my lodging for the night, the chairman of the local soviet gave me a choice: 'Either you can sleep in a hut where they have a lot of children, which might be noisy, or you can do what other officials have done, and sleep on the hay in a barn.' I remembered sleeping comfortably on hay as a boy, when I had taken the horses to their night pasturing, so I opted for the second choice.

The chairman took me to the barn. When we were in the yard, he casually observed: 'Not so long ago, in another barn nearby, an official who'd been sent here was killed by enemies of the Soviet regime.'

In fact, the night passed without incident. Even so, I did not sleep as soundly as usual.

During my time at the Moscow institute I was lucky enough to attend meetings with some famous revolutionaries in the All-Union Society of Old Bolsheviks. The club had been founded while Lenin was still alive, and had been formally organised in the early 1930s as a place where veteran Bolsheviks could meet to talk over old times, as well as to discuss the current situation.

Only party members of at least eighteen years' standing could join, and by January 1934 the society numbered more than 2000. Its aim, according to its statute of 1931, was to draw on the revolutionary experience of the Old Bolsheviks to help the party educate the young and to collect historical material. Although the members quite often met among themselves, meetings for which we young communists were given tickets were infrequent events which we were very keen to attend.

At one such meeting the speaker was Béla Kun. One of the founders of the Hungarian Communist Party, Kun had been Commissar of Foreign Affairs and of War in the Hungarian Soviet Republic of 1919, and had escaped to Soviet Russia in 1920 when the Hungarian revolution was crushed. He was now a leading figure in the Communist International (Comintern). He was an effective speaker and, discussing the Hungarian Soviet Republic, he identified the bourgeoisie and landlords as the sworn enemies of the workers, and said they would only be defeated if the workers were well organised and led by their own party. He mentioned Stalin, but tactfully, only in passing. Kun was clearly a militant revolutionary with a sound knowledge of the situation in his home country. He handled facts easily and spoke without notes.

At the same meeting we heard a speech from V.G. Knorin, a

Latvian revolutionary who had taken part in the 1905 revolution in Russia, and was now on the Executive Committee of the Comintern. Knorin spoke about the international situation, stressing the task facing the communist parties. Pointing out that the rise to power of fascism in Germany had complicated the position, he resisted the temptation to make predictions. We particularly noticed how carefully he avoided lightweight, unsubstantiated theories about the future of Europe and the world. This was wise of him. Hitler's ravings about expansion had appeared in books and pamphlets, but they had yet to become Nazi Germany's state policy, and the plans of fascist aggression were still far from clear.

Practically everyone who spoke at these meetings said how important it was for the party to crush the Trotskyist opposition. This was accepted as an appropriate thing to say. Even so, in 1935 the society was closed down as a result of Stalin's policy, and the names of some of its more outspoken members ceased to appear in the press.

In 1936, after three years of postgraduate study, which included further English-language classes and writing and defending my dissertation, I was given a job as a research assistant at the Academy of Sciences Institute of Economics, which was then headed by the academician M.A. Savelyev, an Old Bolshevik and comrade of Lenin.

I assumed that my position as a research worker was stable and permanent. I had a secondary job as a teacher of political economy at the Moscow Institute of Civil Engineering, where my students included several who became famous later. At that time teachers were frequently as young as their students, which was true in my own case, and I often felt awkward; I would have liked to look older than I was.

At the same time, I had a party job running a circle for the political and economic education of scientific workers at a large factory in Moscow. It consisted of about thirty people, and topics included foreign as well as domestic affairs. I was to learn later that the commission of the Central Committee which selected candidates for the diplomatic service took these classes into account when planning my career.

One day at the end of 1938, having been made scientific secretary of the Institute of Economics, I was summoned by the then president of the USSR Academy of Sciences, the botanist Vladimir Leontyevich Komarov. I was puzzled at being called by so eminent a scholar.

He announced: 'We want to make you scientific secretary of the Academy's branch in Vladivostok.'

I cannot say I found this an appealing offer, so I said, 'I'm still only a young research assistant. The job requires at least a doctor of science.' What I was actually thinking was: If the president of the Academy were a psychologist rather than a botanist he'd no doubt see through me and I'd be on my way to Vladivostok.

Luckily he agreed to leave things as they were, but urged me to reconsider.

As events turned out, I was not destined to continue as a research worker. At the beginning of 1939 I was invited to a Central Committee commission that was selecting new personnel for diplomatic work. When I was called in I immediately recognised V.M. Molotov and G.M. Malenkov.

I was told: 'You are being considered for transfer to work of a foreign policy nature, probably diplomatic.'

I am not sure even now why the commission picked me. No doubt the frequent trips I made to explain the party line on domestic and foreign policy played a part, and the fact that I was at the top of my postgraduate group in learning English may also have helped. When I was asked what I had read in English, I mentioned a few books and then added one that had interested me: *Rich Land, Poor Land*, by the American economist Stuart Chase. Nothing more was said, though I felt I had the commission's approval.

A few days later I was summoned once more to the Central Committee, where they told me: 'You are to be transferred from the Academy of Sciences to the diplomatic service – if you agree.'

A short conversation ensued and I told them I accepted. Later, when I was ambassador in Washington and then in London, I completed and in 1957 (under the pseudonym G. Andreyev) published a book called *The Export of American Capital*, for which Moscow State University conferred a doctorate of economics on me. In 1961 under the same pseudonym I published a monograph, *The Expansion of the Dollar*, continuing the same theme in 1982 with another monograph called *The External Expansion of Capital: Past and Present*. My research work in this important area of economics to a great extent helped me in my main work.

3

On the eve of war

During the 1930s, while the Soviet Union was getting stronger and the people were building socialism, the international atmosphere had steadily worsened. One could feel the leaden clouds of war approaching.

One after another, countries were falling victim to the aggression of Germany, Italy and Japan, as these powers set out on the road to the Second World War. Britain, France and the USA meanwhile adopted a policy of appeasement, and desperately sought means of deflecting the spearhead of the attack from themselves on to the USSR. This is well known now. The disquieting pages cannot be torn from the history books.

This policy had been crowned in September 1938 by the Munich agreement made between the ruling circles of Britain and France and Nazi Germany. Yet in less than a year the fire of the war had spread, and in the eyes of the whole world the belief that fascist aggression would leave the West alone had collapsed.

As for the Soviet Union, throughout the 1930s she struggled consistently to create a system of collective security in Europe, using her weight and influence to curb the aggressors and avert the catastrophe. This inevitably placed heavy demands on Soviet diplomacy. Her lone efforts were not, however, sufficient, and Britain and France rejected Soviet proposals and were unwilling to join our effort to stop the aggression. It was becoming clear that the European nations were standing on the threshold of a world tragedy. In this situation, the USSR tried in every way at least to delay the onset of war, and to gain time to prepare for the onslaught.

★

By age and conditioning, like the rest of my generation, I did the work I was assigned, and whenever I took stock of my position it seemed to me that I was doing things right. When I thought I'd like to be a 'Voroshilov marksman', I entered the shooting competition and won the award. Similarly, I earned myself the 'Prepared for Labour and Defence' badge.

I had felt drawn to reading Lenin while I was still a youth, and the profundity of his views consistently impressed me. But there were words and ideas I still did not always understand, so I made a vow: if I didn't understand something, I would read and reread it, and think it over, and ask people who knew, and keep on at it until I *did* understand. I have kept this vow in relation to Lenin all my life.

It would be immodest of me to suggest that the theoretical knowledge I gained from my reading was adequate and that everything was absolutely clear to me. I was always aware that I needed constantly to improve myself. The only thing I can say for sure is that all the reading I did in my youth formed a sound basis for what was later of use to society.

In the spring of 1939 I began to work in the Commissariat of Foreign Affairs in Moscow. I must admit I began my new job as director of the American section with some trepidation.

I had my first meetings at the US embassy, and from the outset I studied their diplomats closely. The US ambassador to the USSR at the time was Laurence Steinhardt. The man did so little to advance the cause of Soviet–American relations that I wondered why President Roosevelt, who seemed to have such a broad world view, had chosen him for the job. To the satisfaction of both sides, however, Steinhardt did not remain long in Moscow.

There had been two US ambassadors in Moscow between the establishment of relations in 1933 and Steinhardt's term. The first, from 1933 to 1936, was William Bullitt. This was the same Bullitt who had arrived in Moscow in 1919, as the Red Army was in full advance, charged by President Wilson with the task of negotiating an end to military operations in Russia. Lenin then had talks with him and was obliged to reject every one of his proposals, since they were all aimed at the restoration of capitalism. No doubt Roosevelt sent Bullitt as his first ambassador because he had experience of the Soviet government. As ambassador, however,

Bullitt conducted a consistently unfriendly line towards the USSR, trying in every way to give Washington the view that the Soviet Union was weak, and putting a tendentious interpretation on everything he saw and heard in Moscow. He maintained this attitude after he had been transferred from Moscow to Paris, and even later still, in 1944, during the Second World War, when Roosevelt was trying to encourage Americans to think well of their Soviet ally, Bullitt wrote an article in *Life* entitled 'Peace, the view from Rome', which was so anti-Soviet that it aroused the indignation of progressive forces in the USA.

His successor in Moscow, Joseph Davies, was a colourful, positive figure who served as ambassador from January 1937 to June 1938. Utterly different from Bullitt, Davies urged the US administration to develop good relations with the USSR, especially trade relations. He was a prominent and respected figure in the Democratic Party – his wife was famous as Marjorie Post – but there were some good-natured jokes about the two of them while they were in Moscow. One must remember that at that time there was a lot of anti-Soviet propaganda being put out in the USA. The press and the politicians were not only attacking the Soviet system, they were also spreading a mass of myths – for example, that the Soviet people were starving and living in a state close to collapse.

Anyway, the new ambassador decided he must somehow organise the cellars and store-cupboards of the American residence, so he had all manner of food supplies sent to Moscow: if there was no sugar, better take half a ton of it; if there was no porridge or butter, better take a ton of each. He wanted the Bolsheviks to know that the American ambassador drank his American tea with American sugar and ate his porridge made with American oats and flavoured with American butter. Though clearly exaggerated, these stories did the rounds in both capitals, briefly lightening the atmosphere in that often dismal time.

Seeing things quite differently from Bullitt, Davies was convinced that Britain and France were making a mistake in trying to appease Hitler and isolate the USSR, and quite a few in the US administration agreed with him.

Davies at once established a normal businesslike relationship with Stalin – of whom he would later speak to Soviet officials, including myself with warmth and respect. He generally took the constructive point of view: 'When we are examining practical

issues in our mutual relations, we must start off by setting aside
the ideological and social differences in our two systems.' Roosevelt was impressed by this approach, and it gained support among
influential American circles as Nazi German aggression grew.

I got to know Davies several years later, when I was working
in the USA. We met frequently, visited each other's homes and
generally had a good working relationship. He lived on the outskirts of Washington in what looked like the typical house of a rich
American. The architecture was designed to look 'democratic': it
had no statues of lions or dragons or madonnas, and no fountains;
but its exterior was deceptive. On entering, one was astounded
by the luxury. At once, one recognised American architectural
efficiency – the finish was luxurious and comfortable but, most
of all, it was well concealed from the outside.

There were European paintings and furniture, and the Davieses
had bought unique treasures from the storehouses of Russian empresses, objects of fabulous value. I remember during one dinner
my wife reached for a salt-cellar and found she couldn't move it.
I noticed her embarrassment and asked what was the matter.

'I can't pick up this salt-cellar,' she whispered. 'It must be fixed
to the table.'

It was a massive object, evidently made of solid gold, and we
discovered that it had once belonged to Catherine the Great. But
at least, now that she knew that its secret lay simply in its weight,
Lydia soon won her struggle with it.

My wife and I often attended big receptions which the Davieses
laid on. The name and wealth of the former ambassador to
Moscow attracted American 'high society', most of them in the
administration or the business world. On these occasions I had
frequent conversations with Senator Thomas Connally and Con-
gressman Sol Bloom, the Senate and House of Representatives
chairmen of the Congress commission on foreign relations, respectively. Both pursued Roosevelt's line on the USSR.

Senator Connally was an interesting man in many respects.
Once, when we were both guests of the Davieses, he bravely
spoke up in favour of opening a second front in western Europe
– and this at a time when one only whispered such things in
Washington. Davies was more discreet, but Connally defended
his idea. 'It's quite wrong,' he said, 'for the US not to help the
Red Army to a victory. From the point of view of our own
national interest, the US should come out as a war power. And

we can do that best by direct involvement in the fighting, not simply through Lend-Lease. It's already plain that the Red Army is carrying the day and that Hitler is all but finished.'

It is customary in America for rich men to show themselves to the world in a certain way. The Davieses had a luxury yacht, for example, and my wife and I were once invited out on it. Among all its other facilities, there were even special tablets you could take so as not to feel sick. True, we didn't go far from New York harbour, but I remember the wonderful view of the great city. I also recall, however, the dirt and the heaps of garbage on the shore, the oil slicks and the piles of cardboard boxes and broken glass on the wharves.

Davies was always smartly turned out and courteous. Not for him the eccentric clowning one sometimes met in rich American businessmen and middle-rank officials – the sort of people who would put their feet on the desk and give you the soles of their shoes to look at.

Davies had another, less fortunate habit. In the manner of exalted twentieth-century Anglo-Saxons, he liked to prance about on a horse. Now you hardly ever saw someone riding a horse in an American city, but Davies's estate was outside town, so he could indulge himself. Unfortunately, during one such ride in the late 1950s he had a bad fall. He clung on to life for a while, but did not recover. His wife, Marjorie, outlived him by a few years.

There is scarcely a book in the USA about foreign policy during the war or after in which you will not find the name of Joseph Davies. In 1941 he headed the President's committee for co-ordinating the work of all organisations dealing with aid to the Allies.

Two days after Germany invaded the USSR, Davies declared: 'The world will be amazed by the scale and determination of Russia's resistance.' He spoke out in the press, on the radio and at countless meetings, calling on the Americans to shed their prejudices about the USSR and its people. He called persistently for the opening of a second front. His book, *Mission to Moscow* (1941), and the film of the same name, helped to strengthen American sympathy for the USSR. He was also the organiser of the National Council for Soviet–American Friendship and its honorary president.

In May 1946 he stated: 'Peace can be secured only by universal recognition of Roosevelt's legacy – the unity of England, the USA and the USSR.'

For his successful activity in helping to cement friendly Soviet
–American relations and fostering the growth of understanding
and trust between the two countries, in May 1945 Davies was
awarded the highest Soviet decoration, the Order of Lenin. He
earned the right to lasting respect in the USA and the USSR.

Let me return to 1939, however. I had been in charge of the
American section in the Foreign Commissariat for no more than
half a year when one day one of my bosses called me in and said:
'You're wanted at the Kremlin, to see Stalin.'

I hadn't been expecting this. Up till then I had only seen Stalin
at a distance in Red Square, when he was taking a parade, and
once at a large meeting in the Great Kremlin Palace.

I arrived at the Kremlin at the appointed hour and found a short,
upright man in the anteroom to Stalin's office. I introduced myself
and he replied: 'Poskrebyshev.' He was Stalin's assistant and
secretary. He went in and announced my arrival.

And so I found myself in Stalin's office. It was simply furnished,
and entirely functional. There was a small writing table, at which
he worked when alone, and a larger table for consultations, where
I was to sit many times in the future. This was where his meetings
usually took place, including those of the Politburo.

On this first occasion Stalin was at the larger table. Standing
beside him was Molotov, the Commissar for Foreign Affairs,
whom I had already met. They greeted me, first Stalin and then
Molotov. Stalin opened the conversation.

'Comrade Gromyko, we're thinking of sending you to the
Soviet embassy in the USA, as second in command.'

Diplomats, like soldiers, are supposed to be ready for sudden
moves. Even so, frankly I was somewhat surprised by this proposal. I made no comment, however, and with his customary
brevity Stalin went on to list the areas in US–Soviet relations to
which I should have to pay special attention.

'The Soviet Union,' he emphasised, 'ought to maintain reasonable relations with such a powerful country as the United States,
especially in view of the rise of the fascist threat.'

He added some concrete advice on various issues, which Molotov supported with some remarks of his own.

'We're not sending you to the USA for just a month, maybe
not for just a year,' Stalin said, watching me attentively. Suddenly

he enquired: 'And how do you get on with the English language?'

I replied, 'It's a struggle which I think I'm gradually winning, though it's a difficult business without conversational practice.'

At this, Stalin offered me some advice which I found perplexing: 'From time to time, Comrade Gromyko, you ought to go into American churches and listen to the sermons. The ministers speak clearly and in good English, and what's more they have good diction. You know, when Russian revolutionaries were abroad, they always used to follow this practice to improve their knowledge of foreign languages.'

This flummoxed me. How could Stalin, an atheist, I thought, advise me, another atheist, to visit American churches? Was he maybe testing my soundness? But I bit my tongue and said nothing, and perhaps it was just as well.

Of course, I didn't attend any churches in America – perhaps the only time when a Soviet diplomat failed to carry out an order of Stalin's. But one could imagine the effect on the nimble American newspapermen if the Soviet envoy were seen to attend church: 'Maybe the professional atheist isn't an atheist after all?'

That was my first visit to Stalin.

After leaving the Kremlin, as always, I thought over what had happened. I knew that ambassador K.A. Umansky had recently been recalled from Washington, evidently because he was not to the centre's liking. That meant I was trusted and was being given an important mission. I learned later that both Stalin and Molotov had grievances against Umansky, and though he returned to the USA as ambassador it was plain that his days there were numbered. After Hitler's attack on the USSR the opinion arose that perhaps Roosevelt would be impressed if the ambassador to the USA was a diplomat with a broad international reputation gained through association with the League of Nations. Therefore M.M. Litvinov was appointed ambassador, though only for a short time. From later events it became clear that Stalin had seen this as a temporary measure, simply for improving US–Soviet relations.

Immediately after the meeting with Stalin, my family and I prepared to leave for the USA. I had never been abroad before and the journey, through Romania, Bulgaria and Yugoslavia, to Genoa, where we were to embark, was full of interest.

Italy was the first capitalist country where I was able to observe life closely. At every step, I was struck by sharp social contrast, especially in people's clothes. I also noticed that whenever two Italians gathered together it seemed that one of them was making a speech to the other, while the second one, without waiting, would chime in with a speech of his own; and all around them it would appear that other, equally argumentative, assemblies were going on. In Genoa I remember typical Italian narrow streets, with the washing hanging out on lines stretched across from window to window. I wondered how anyone could tell their own laundry from their neighbour's, but evidently they could. I thought Russians would get it mixed up. You needed experience.

Now, with Umansky, who was returning with us to the USA, we boarded the Italian liner *Rex* (later sunk by the British at Bari) and set sail for Naples. I had been under the impression that everyone sang in Naples, but not a soul was singing while we were there, as if to spite me. We made the trip to Vesuvius – Umansky, my son Anatoly and I – and visited the ruins excavated from under the volcanic ash. And what ruins! The guide gave us a lurid account of the Pompeian way of life and morals, so full of juicy details that I doubted if the Pompeians themselves had known so much about their own goings-on. At one point, the guide lowered his voice to a well-practised murmur and said: 'And now you are going to see a very touching sight.' Slowly he led us to a particular spot, plainly counting on a special financial recognition for his services, and, as he revealed two entwined human skeletons, he said: 'You can guess what *they* were doing.' He then added: 'Throughout the centuries, buried under ash and lava, they have shown in their own way that love is stronger than death.' It did not sound banal when he said it.

Both in Genoa and Naples, and also on the Italian roads, we noticed great numbers of soldiers. Wherever one looked, one saw uniforms. I had the impression that they were constantly raising their hands in salute to each other, and that, although the Italians had the reputation of being somewhat undisciplined, they even tried to stay in step when walking along the street. I remarked to Umansky: 'Doesn't it seem to you that the Italian soldiers would like to look like Germans?' He agreed with me. But it still seemed to us that if one asked any of these groups of soldiers to give us a lyrical rendition of 'Ave Maria' both soldiers and officers would have burst into song, forgetting the uniforms in which Mussolini's regime had decked them out.

Then we were off to sea again. I recall a notable incident while we were crossing the Atlantic.

The captain of the *Rex* invited Umansky and myself to his cabin on 7 November, the twenty-second anniversary of the October revolution. Toasting us in fine Italian wine, he announced quietly: 'To the great October revolution. To Lenin!'

Naturally we were moved by this and warmly joined in. But, recalling the toast later, we said that if the Duce had known about it things would not have gone too well for our captain.

A few days later, having experienced our first Atlantic storm, with my wife and children – seven-year-old Anatoly and two-year-old Emilia – I reached the USA. We left the liner and were met by a car on the quayside. Immediately we found ourselves in the embrace of the vast city of New York – though 'embrace' is not perhaps the best word to describe the sensation, for the streets seemed too narrow and we felt hemmed in by the huge buildings. Not surprisingly, Anatoly asked me if the Americans lived in the city all the time or only during the day.

I explained: 'They live here all the time. But they're not all Americans – on 61st Street there is the Soviet consulate, which sent this car for us, so there are Soviet people who live here too.'

My first impressions of this modern Babylon were not so different from what I had read in Theodore Dreiser, Jack London or Ernest Hemingway. However, being as it were inside the belly of the monster, I realised much more clearly that, with the aid of wealth and technology, mankind is capable of creating something completely alien to his nature.

We spent less than a day at the consulate, where we were received by the consul-general, V.A. Fedyushin, and then set off by Pullman train to Washington.

The US capital was and still is a much quieter place than New York. Its industry consists mostly of small-scale artisanry. Even at that time, half its population was black.

Washington provides the élite with the huge governing mechanism it needs to administer the vast state. An important part of this mechanism, and the part with which the Soviet embassy has its main dealings, is the foreign and diplomatic service. I began at once to arrange essential visits, above all at the State Department.

Although I was struck by the ease with which these meetings were arranged for me as second in command at our embassy, the administration was clearly cautious in its attitude to the ambassador, Umansky. I thought someone in the State Department must have taken a dislike to him and was out to injure him. It could have been no accident that the press was always spreading rumours of a personal nature about him. I had to take this into account, as a new man on the stormy sea of political life. This was happening moreover at a time when the threat of Nazi aggression against the USSR was becoming plainer.

I first met President Franklin Roosevelt at the opening of the National Gallery. Despite his physical disability, he made his speech standing up, using carefully concealed support. As I looked at him, I thought of his bravery and willpower. Though he was in a constant battle with his illness, he seemed calm and assured.

Studying the country where one is posted is an important part of any diplomat's brief. And so, in the middle of 1940, using my responsibility to inspect the conditions under which Soviet specialists were working in various American factories, I was able to explore some of the country's industrial cities.

Accompanied by my colleague, V.I. Bazykin, I visited factories in Chicago, Detroit, Cleveland, Buffalo, Cincinnati, Milwaukee, Worcester and Camden, and talked with the Soviet specialists working there. Living cut off from home, they were obviously pleased to see us, and were hungry for news of what was happening in the USSR and in US–Soviet relations, which were then strained. American ruling circles were interpreting the Soviet–Finnish war, which had just ended, in their usual anti-Soviet way, and were condemning the unification of the Baltic republics with the USSR.

The trip gave me solid factual material about the American hinterland, more than one could ever find in the press. We visited the Ford Motor plant in Detroit, where they gave us detailed explanations of the technology, and we watched as finished engines came off the conveyor belt after dozens of operations.

In Chicago we attended the Democratic Party Congress, at which President Roosevelt's candidacy for his third term was to be decided. Several thousand people were present. One presumed that all the shouting was for the Democrats, but it was impossible to tell in the great roar, which sounded as if an earthquake was approaching. The chairman, Senator Alben Barkley, constantly hammered his gavel in a vain attempt to restore peaceful conditions.

Out on to the platform stepped the senator from Alabama. Bald and middle-aged, he thrust his arms in the air, stood there for one minute, then two minutes, and eventually began to speak. Naturally, not a word could be heard. So he stopped, raised his arms again and stared upwards, waiting for the audience to take pity on him. But he waited in vain: no one was listening.

Beyond the yelling and the chaos, however, it was easy to hear the cries of ecstasy every time the name of Roosevelt was mentioned. The meeting wanted to show that his third term was assured. Roosevelt's success in the election was guaranteed. The majority of Americans wanted it, and the Soviet people felt the same way.

And so we returned to Washington. I was thirty years old. At Harvard, John Kennedy, aged twenty-two, was studying law and the institutions of the bourgeois state. At the other side of America, in Hollywood, Ronald Reagan was a rising star, having just made *Hell's Kitchen*.

4

As ambassador in war's dark days

Among those responsible for US foreign policy before, during and since the Second World War, nobody has ever tried to give a precise answer to the question: what measures did the USA take to prevent the outbreak of war?

Historians and politicians who have analysed the events of those years have given various replies. They have claimed that the USA did its duty before the war by condemning the expansionist aims of Hitler and his allies. But none of them has asked what would have happened if the USA had come out on the side of the countries calling for peace, above all the USSR, and declared its determination to create a mighty, united force to oppose aggression. They do not ask this because the USA in fact had no plans and undertook no steps to deter the aggressors. Mere condemnation, at best erratic and consisting of a few tired speeches by administration officials, was hardly a sign of any very firm intent to take a stand against Hitler.

Washington's attitude only changed when the USA felt the heat of war itself. And, hard though it may be to believe, even the treacherous attack by Germany's ally, Japan, on the American fleet at Pearl Harbor in December 1941 still did not open the eyes of all Americans to the danger to peace and freedom posed by Germany and her eastern ally. There were still American politicians who wanted the Soviet Union and Germany to bleed each other white, clearly hoping that the USA would be able to have the last word in settling the terms of the eventual peace.

This must not be forgotten. While the Soviet people pay full tribute – voiced many times by our leaders – to the American contribution to the victory over Germany and Japan, the fact is that the USA did not do what it could and should have done to avert the war itself.

From my own experience as a diplomat, I can say that this situation made life difficult. The attitudes that gave rise to it, moreover, would often have an effect on the actual conduct of the war.

In the summer of 1941, with still six months to go until Pearl Harbor, Washington was going about its normal, peaceful life. Congress was in recess and the administration dozed, as civil servants cheerfully set off for the weekend with their families. But in the Soviet embassy, with more and more information coming from Moscow and the US administration, the tension mounted.

It was 4 am on 22 June in Moscow when Hitler's bombs began to fall on Minsk, Kiev, Kaunas and other Soviet cities, and shells were bursting inside the Brest fortress, but in Washington it was still the evening of the 21st. Late that day, American radio, citing European sources, announced: 'German forces have crossed the Soviet frontier.' On Moscow Radio, early next morning, we heard the announcement that Germany had broken the non-aggression treaty, signed with the USSR in August 1939, and attacked the Soviet Union. The war had begun.

Figuratively speaking, history's verdict on Hitler and his henchmen was to crucify them for the appalling crimes carried out on their orders. Not on a cross, for they violated every religion, but on the bloodstained swastika that surmounted the bunker where the chief war criminal of them all gave his last gasp. The efforts of those who like rummaging in the dustbin of the past to come up with dubious offerings for the public seem therefore all the more strange.

From time to time we are even told that the Soviet–German pact of 1939 was the means used by the Nazis to start the war. For its part, the Soviet Union has shown with the utmost clarity that the pact was the result of the policy of a number of Western powers which did not wish to join the USSR in blocking Hitler's path to aggression and the unleashing of war. In attacking the Soviet Union, Germany not only demonstrated the criminal nature of the Nazi clique but also accentuated the guilt of those Western politicians who had declined to combine the efforts of the states seeking to preserve the peace.

The fact that Hitler's Germany was a lying and criminal regime is plain for everyone to see, but it is important to note that Stalin was convinced that Hitler would honour the treaty and that therefore the USSR would not be drawn into the war by a German attack. And once Stalin settled on an idea he would cling to it. No amount of warning messages – whether from London or Tokyo – could shift his *idée fixe*. Nevertheless, this does not mean we should seek excuses to whitewash pre-war Western policy and blacken the Soviet Union. Objective analysis of the causes and consequences of the events of that period refute any such notions.

Usually, when Western sources discuss the non-aggression pact they raise the question of an alleged secret protocol, supposedly signed by Molotov and Ribbentrop. This protocol is said to have registered an understanding between the two sides on the need for certain territorial changes to be made in the countries lying between Germany and the USSR.

This story is not new. It was being peddled before the Nazi war criminals were brought to book. The Soviet chief prosecutor at Nuremberg labelled it a forgery, and correctly so, since no such 'protocol' has ever been found, either in the USSR or in any other country – nor could it be. The Soviet prosecutor's declaration was a challenge to all those who wished to believe the forgery. After all, he made his statement right in front of Hitler's Foreign Minister, Ribbentrop himself, sitting there in the dock.

It is well known that lies spread quickly, regardless of whether they are fabricated decades ago or now.

Henceforth, Soviet foreign policy sought every means of international co-operation to secure the most favourable conditions for the total defeat of the fascist aggressor and the liberation of the European nations. The USSR and its diplomats strove to strengthen the anti-Hitler coalition and to open the second front, but the path was long and hard.

The Washington embassy on 16th Street became the channel for systematic contacts and the transmission of messages between top Soviet and US leaders. This was a new phenomenon, and the documents which have been published show what vital questions were raised and settled in this correspondence.

As a rule, when the Soviet embassy received a letter from Stalin addressed to Roosevelt, the President's military aide, General

Edwin Watson, would be asked to come to the embassy, a procedure agreed with Roosevelt. Everything was done with extreme
urgency. Having received Stalin's letter from me – I was by then
privy to such matters – the general would at once deliver it to the
President, a matter of fifteen minutes or less.

The President once said to me jokingly, 'I don't suppose Watson
gives you much peace these days, with all his visits?'

'Mr President, we welcome his visits,' I replied. 'Anyway, they
follow the same procedure in Moscow with your messages to
Stalin.'

Discussions with Roosevelt were always about key issues of the
day, and my meetings with him remain deeply etched in my mind.
I still firmly believe that he was one of the most outstanding US
statesmen. He was a clever politician, a man of broad vision and
special personal qualities.

When I replaced M.M. Litvinov as ambassador in 1943, I
remember presenting my credentials and saying: 'As Soviet ambassador to the USA, I will work for co-operation between our
countries and for strengthening our relations as allies.'

Roosevelt replied, 'I regard the development of friendly Soviet
– American relations as a matter of absolute necessity, and in the
interests of both countries.'

These remarks were not made as part of the customary formal
speeches at a presentation of credentials. Instead, in the course of
normal conversation, the President had suggested to me in his
typically direct way: 'You give me your speech and I'll give you
mine and they'll be printed in the press tomorrow. Let us talk
rather about setting up arrangements for the meeting of US, Soviet
and British leaders.'

He had in mind the forthcoming Tehran conference, and his
businesslike, direct style made a big impression on me. He was
saying, in effect: Let's put protocol aside, there's a war on. It was
as if he could read my thoughts, and it seemed to me then that
the man in the White House was not just an aristocrat concerned
with dressing up his thoughts so as to impress, but a powerful
man of action.

Roosevelt never made one feel under pressure to react at once
to any of his ideas. He liked to use original turns of phrase which
came to him easily, but he obviously wanted to explain his
thoughts, and he liked going back to them, repeating them in
another way and in a new perspective. He was fond of a joke, and

he appreciated the same in others. At the same time, if one was attentive – and I had plenty of opportunity during the five years I knew him – one could catch a glimpse of sadness in his eyes. He smiled sometimes to disguise the anguish caused by his disease.

In 1921, while holidaying with his family on Campobello Island, Maine, he had lost the use of both legs through polio, of which there was then an epidemic in the USA, and the doctors could do nothing. But, although Roosevelt realised that his disability would be with him for the rest of his life, he did not give in to it, and managed by sheer willpower – especially when making public speeches – to appear bold, determined and above all healthy.

He was called upon frequently to address all kinds of audiences. His half-hour 'Fireside Chats' on the radio from the Oval Office became a tradition, and he appeared on television for the first time in 1938, before it came into regular use in the USA in 1941. Whether at meetings, or on the radio or TV, Roosevelt always spoke slowly. He pronounced his words clearly and expounded his ideas simply. He did not resort to gestures: the expression on his face was sufficient, inspiring and determined. His speeches made Americans feel good and fired their determination, and during his lifetime he earned the accolade of the National Association of Teachers of Oratory as 'the greatest of all modern American orators'. No other President of the USA that I ever met could compare with Roosevelt in this regard.

Another of Roosevelt's unusual traits was that he never used harsh words in conversation, even against his political opponents, excepting, of course, America's enemies in war. Whenever a harsh word seemed in order Roosevelt would resort instead to humour and, although his witty barbs could be pretty painful, from personal observation, at Yalta for example, I can say that he consistently showed great self-control, trying even at moments of great tension to introduce into the atmosphere a helpful note of compromise.

In this respect he differed sharply from Churchill. Indeed, they were altogether different in both character and physique. It is well known that Churchill often became irritated during discussions, though he did make an effort at both Tehran and Yalta to keep his temper within the accepted norms.

During talks before the Yalta conference I noticed Roosevelt smile ironically when he mentioned Churchill's name to me. This was almost certainly because from the lively correspondence between the three leaders, concerning the Polish question and German reparations, Roosevelt knew just how different Stalin's attitudes were from Churchill's. In fact, Roosevelt's style was much more like that of Stalin, who never allowed his words to outstrip his thoughts. Churchill, on the other hand, at times became emotional and let his feelings show, at which point Roosevelt would do his best to defuse the situation. This is not of course to suggest that the President was compliant. He firmly defended America's interests, and tried to gain every advantage he could, but he did it more subtly than Churchill, and with greater tact.

It should also be emphasised that, although as a representative of the bourgeois class Roosevelt naturally expressed its interests, he belonged to that group of the American ruling circles who took a realistic view of the international situation and of the need to develop Soviet–American relations. It was after all not until he came to power in 1933 that the USA established diplomatic relations with the USSR.

Roosevelt's meetings with Soviet officials were of a special nature. Despite the limitations due to differences between the two social systems, there was always a wide area in which mutual understanding could be achieved; and this fact is something of which Washington officials today would do well to take note.

The many articles and books on Roosevelt concentrate understandably on his political achievements as President. Furthermore, as there are now very few contemporaries of Roosevelt left who knew that remarkable American personally, much of the literature on him is inevitably a paraphrase of what was written years or even decades ago, with the number of inaccuracies steadily increasing. Practically no objective works depict Roosevelt as a man; therefore, since photographs or newsreels do not tell us much, I thought I would add a few more brushstrokes of my own to his portrait.

Franklin D. Roosevelt was welcoming and always had a kind word for a foreign representative and his country. If the meeting was in his office, he behaved informally. For example, because of his affliction, he would sit throughout the interview, but in such a way that one was not made aware of his physical disability. Despite his medication, Roosevelt probably suffered pain during meetings, but he never showed it – although he could not always hide his fatigue, especially towards the end of his life.

He had an open face. I have met people who swear that it was possible to tell from his face how Roosevelt felt about any particular issue, and I fully agree with them.

He always referred respectfully to Stalin. Admittedly he pronounced the name wrongly, with the stress on the *-in*, but I never corrected him, for I had seen how he simply ignored others who tried.

It has often been said that President Roosevelt decided practically all questions on his own and seldom felt the need to discuss policy with others. This was not so. In fact, he had a circle of advisers whom he regularly consulted on both domestic and foreign policy matters. It is true that once his mind was made up he did not waver in making a decision, but first he would always elicit the views of friends and others whose competence he trusted. He liked competent people.

He once said to me, 'There are so many problems, it makes my head swim. I need clever people to help me resolve them properly.' He would advise me, when I was Soviet ambassador, to 'see Harry Hopkins about this tricky question. He may not have the answer to every question, but he'll do his best, and he'll give me an accurate account of it afterwards.'

Hopkins was regarded as a clever man, albeit complicated. Apart from a brief spell (1938–40) as Secretary of Trade, he held no important posts, but he was always at hand for Roosevelt, whose views on war and peace he shared. Known unofficially as the 'President's deputy', 'White House chief of staff', 'chief national security adviser', Hopkins was in fact all three. This was the secret of his success in Washington. Hopkins was not only Roosevelt's eyes and ears; he was also his feet. At the most critical moments in American history, it was Hopkins the President sent abroad on important missions. In January 1941 it was Hopkins who flew to London to see Churchill. In July 1941, only a month after the German attack on the USSR, Hopkins was in Moscow talking to Stalin. Roosevelt so trusted Hopkins, moreover, that he never gave him his instructions in writing.

I had several confidential talks with Harry Hopkins, some of them in our embassy, where he occasionally brought his wife, much to the pleasure of my wife and myself. I especially remember one conversation with Hopkins in which he raised the subject of the future.

'So, what will relations between the USA and the USSR be like after the war?' he asked. 'It's more than plain that Germany is going to be on her knees. The President hasn't the slightest doubt about it.'

This chat took place long before the Yalta conference, but at a time when the Red Army was already advancing west.

Hopkins continued: 'Roosevelt often raises this question when he tries to look ahead. A lot of people have asked him about his hopes for US–Soviet relations. But he hasn't made up his mind yet. It depends on many factors – the main one being the stance the USSR adopts as a great world power. Still, from the little the President has said, he obviously believes that the USA ought to do everything possible to lay the foundations of good future relations with the USSR.'

I replied: 'All the messages from Stalin that I have delivered to the President, as well as through you, Mr Hopkins, have been full of respect both for the President and for your country. If both leaders have similar views, that surely says a lot already. I have to say, though, that Stalin has not always had favourable responses, even to his most urgent requests.'

I explained one particular case that I was thinking of: 'A few days after Hitler's attack on the USSR, the Soviet embassy in Washington received a cable, signed by Stalin, requesting the US government to supply the USSR with armour plating for tanks, of which we were in acutely short supply. We did not, however, receive a helpful reply and in fact the USA delivered nothing to us. This left both Moscow and the Soviet embassy with a sense of bitterness.'

'Yes, I know,' Hopkins said. 'Inevitably not everything the Roosevelt administration has done has pleased Moscow. But we've got things straightened out now, surely? We've supplied you with warplanes and trucks and ships, and quite a bit of food, too.'

It would have been tactless to argue with him; but the truth was that during the first year after Hitler's attack, at the worst time for the Soviet Union, the USA sent us practically nothing. Only later, when it was clear that the USSR could stand its ground, and on its own, did the deliveries gradually begin to flow.

'It used to be,' Hopkins went on, 'that the President devoted most of his time to the country's domestic situation. But since the Japanese attack on Pearl Harbor and America's entry into the war against Germany he has spent far more time thinking about the future and relations between you and us.'

Of course, Hopkins was devoted to the capitalist order and American democracy, and on ideological questions he remained a representative of his class. Nevertheless, as Roosevelt's confidant and a patriot, and in the name of victory over fascism, he achieved great things in the cause of US–Soviet relations.

Hopkins's views were shared to a great extent by the Secretary of the Treasury, Henry Morgenthau, Jr, with whom I developed excellent relations. Morgenthau was forceful on the post-war world order: 'Germany must not be allowed to resume an aggressive policy; she has committed enough crimes under Hitler. Neither we nor you must let it happen again.'

He did not think that the line would meet resistance among influential politicians in America.

'The military are quite determined,' he said. 'And American business even more so. After all, they don't want to have to face a powerful competitor on world markets.'

It is curious that Morgenthau should have made such categorical assertions. One might have thought that it was part of his job to know that, throughout the war, American monopolies used their capital to help German industry produce weapons for Hitler's army. The evidence supporting this fact was splashed all over the US press soon after the end of hostilities and it is hard to believe that Morgenthau knew nothing about it during the war. On the other hand, the recesses of US policy were at times so impenetrable that possibly even senior figures in the administration had no idea of the scale of American and German wartime collaboration. But it's not surprising that the investigation into this collaboration begun by Congress at the end of the war was rapidly wound up.

On the future of Germany, Morgenthau's were perhaps the most radical solutions being proposed. 'The best way to avert aggression in Europe,' he told me once, 'will be to dismember Germany and even to resettle part of her population in other parts of the world, say, North Africa.' True, he would qualify this by saying: 'The President hasn't been over this plan yet, though he does know such ideas exist.'

Among the many contacts I had with high officials in the Roosevelt administration, Vice-President Wallace deserves special mention. Descended from Scottish and Irish landowners who had emigrated to the USA in the first half of the nineteenth century, Wallace, like the rest of his clan, held the views of the petty bourgeoisie, which feared the omnipotence of big monopoly capital and sought a 'middle' path of social development. Of broad educational background, Wallace was at home with economics and statistics, biology and genetics, and he was interested in history and philosophy. He was regarded as an authority on agricultural science and had published several important studies. For seven years before becoming Vice-President in Roosevelt's third term, Wallace had occupied the post of Secretary for Agriculture and was the theoretician of agrarian policy in Roosevelt's New Deal.

Most of the highly placed people in the American political arena thought of foreign policy only in terms of instant results, but Wallace was not one of these. At the epicentre of the political struggle, he worked for active co-operation with the USSR against fascism and for a stable peace after the war. He was convinced that no major question of world politics could be solved without the USSR, whether during or after the war, and he was bold enough to say openly that the Soviet contribution to the victory was decisive. He said: 'The Russians will cause enemy losses . . . at least twenty times more effectively than the rest of the Allies put together.'

As a supporter of Soviet–US co-operation, Wallace wrote in his diary, as early as January 1943, that problem number one after the war was going to be the maintenance of good relations with the USSR. In 1942 he was contemplating visiting the Soviet Union and he learned to speak Russian quite tolerably. A visit to Russia in May 1944 gave his knowledge more solid foundation, and after his return he told me more than once that his tour of the Soviet Union had made an enormous impression on him.

While acknowledging that the USA and USSR had different social systems, he would invariably revert to the idea that both countries could co-operate fruitfully: 'I believe,' he said, 'that Soviet–American co-operation should above all mean averting military confrontation between us.'

Someone else with whom I also had good relations, and who was extremely close to Roosevelt, was Harold Ickes, the Secretary of the Interior. Hopkins, Morgenthau, Ickes and Wallace, like Roosevelt, all shared the view that the differences between our two social systems should not stand in the way of co-operation to defeat our common enemy and build peace after victory. Clearly these views expressed the interests of the American people. Yet, tragically, a totally different political strategy emerged in the early years of the 'cold war', when the American administration began to preach the doctrine of naked force and to set in motion the arms race.

Wallace could see the course America's foreign policy was taking. Those in charge were steering it further away from the wartime co-operation with the USSR. This much was plain in the earliest years of the Truman administration.

Roosevelt had made Wallace Secretary of Agriculture in 1945, but in the next year, with Truman as President, he was replaced and thereafter held no official post. As presidential candidate of his own newly formed Progressive Party, Wallace failed in the 1948 election. Most politicians at that time were competing to whip up public hostility to the USSR and the other socialist states. Washington's policy became increasingly aimed at serving imperial pride, and this found open expression in the cobbling together of aggressive military blocs, the spread of a dense network of American bases on foreign territory and the broadening of America's overseas economic influence. In consequence, for people with Wallace's attitudes the outlook was bleak.

Wallace had the ability always to set one at one's ease. My first impression of him was that he looked like a Russian: medium build, brown hair, an open, pleasant face and a reserved smile. Although he always appeared slightly embarrassed and constrained in his movements, this did not prevent him from talking freely, or mixing and being attentive, especially when he was the host, and his ability to get to know people was remarkable.

His relations with the Soviet representatives were invariably good. I remember one incident with special warmth. The phone rang at seven o'clock one morning, an unusual event in the ambassador's apartment at that time of day.

'Hello?' I said.

'Andrei Andreevich, this is the duty officer at the embassy. A man has just called here. He apologised for the hour and said he was Vice-President Wallace.'

'The Vice-President? What did he want?'

'He asked me to pass on some tablets for your wife and left. I have the tablets here.'

It turned out that Wallace's wife had been telling my wife the day before about some wonderful slimming tablets that were hard to find. Now Wallace had got hold of some and brought them personally to the embassy. A trivial incident, but it reveals something of his thoughtfulness.

Our meetings usually took place in Washington, but one day he said: 'Why don't we take a trip out of town with our wives and have lunch somewhere? It'll give us a chance to talk on our own.'

I had no objection. He then added: 'You wouldn't mind if the Swiss ambassador and his wife came along too?'

That was also fine by me.

'As it happens,' Wallace said, 'the ambassador and I are married to close relatives.'

At the appointed hour – it was a Sunday – Lydia Dmitrievna and I set off for the meeting-place, some forty miles out of town. It turned out to be a wooden bungalow, modest-looking but extremely comfortable inside.

The lunch was well organised, and in the course of it the Swiss ambassador gave me the important piece of information that his government would be interested in restoring diplomatic relations with the USSR. Naturally I showed proper interest. Our diplomatic relations with Switzerland had been broken off in 1923, at the time of the assassination in Lausanne of the Soviet plenipotentiary, Vatslav Vorovsky.

'I will report what you have said to Moscow at once,' I promised him. 'Speaking for myself, I would very much like this idea to be taken further.'

And so it was: Soviet–Swiss diplomatic relations were soon restored.

Towards the end of the lunch at the bungalow, Wallace indicated that he wanted to talk to me alone. We got up from the table, leaving the ladies with the Swiss ambassador, and sat down at a small table in a far corner of the large room.

The Vice-President said: 'Now that it looks pretty certain that the Allies are going to win the war, we have to take the opportunity to make a big improvement in US–Soviet relations. Present Allied ties must not be weakened. I'm very concerned about this, because certain guys here, particularly in big business, are undermining the friendly feelings that the exploits of the Red Army have aroused in the American people.'

I told him he was absolutely right. 'After all, we became allies because the fundamental long-term interests of our two countries demanded it. As for the attitudes of American business, we think the administration could use its influence more to alter them. Business, after all, is not monolithic. In our view, business circles worldwide could benefit greatly from the development of contacts with the USSR. The opportunities are going to be colossal after the war – especially when you consider how much plant and equipment the Soviet Union is going to need for rebuilding the industry Hitler's barbarians have destroyed.'

I met Wallace twice later, when he was no longer Vice-President. He came to see me in New York in 1946 and on that occasion was interested in only one thing: 'What do you think of my chances in the 1948 presidential election?'

Of course, I gave him an encouraging response, although I was frankly perplexed by the question, for it showed that he did not have a very accurate knowledge of the mood of the electorate. America's ruling class was now preparing to use the 'big stick' in world affairs – the policy President Theodore Roosevelt had fought for at the beginning of the century – and the American public had already been subjected to a mighty wave of propaganda in favour of it. After this talk, therefore, I must admit I had the impression not only that Wallace had lost contact with the pulse of political life but that he also lacked experienced advisers.

At around the same time, Wallace invited my wife and myself out to his country house, about a hundred miles from New York. When we arrived, it turned out to be a substantial, well-managed farm, producing young horned livestock and chickens.

Wallace explained: 'The chickens are my main business; the rest is not up to much. Come and see the chicken-houses.'

We saw thousands and thousands of chickens. It was obvious that every task connected with this business, right down to cleaning out the chicken-houses, was done properly; and it seemed that the former Vice-President was not above doing much of the work himself if necessary.

One of the pillars of the Roosevelt administration before and during the war was undoubtedly Cordell Hull, Secretary of State from 1933 to 1944. It was under Hull that diplomatic relations were established between the USA and the USSR. Respected and trusted by the President, he was regarded in the Soviet embassy as an authoritative political figure. Even so, while Hull followed Roosevelt's line on Soviet–US relations, we quickly realised that he was not entirely wholehearted in this. During the war, how-ever, the military situation demanded that Hull keep his private feelings very much in the background.

Tall and grey-haired, Cordell Hull had great charm and tact, and I cannot recall an occasion when the conversation turned sharp. If difficulties arose on a question, he preferred to leave it temporarily unresolved, or hand it over to his subordinates. When he himself was obliged to take an opposite position, he would try to present it with flexibility, and in velvet tones. This of course changed nothing, but it did help to relieve the strain as one took one's leave.

Hull was not one of those statesmen – common today – who like to say they are servants of the people. He was rarely seen at a public forum. Lacking oratorical skill, he spoke quietly and slowly, so much so that one sometimes thought he might be unwell. He did not like speaking before large audiences, especially if they were unofficial, and much preferred an intimate group of two or three. Our contact continued for fully five years, right up to his retirement as Secretary of State in November 1944 on health grounds, at the age of seventy-three.

The first Under-Secretary of State was Sumner Welles, who, although subordinate and not a member of the cabinet, played an important part in wartime US diplomacy. By personality and education, Welles had the mark of an Englishman, and he tended to exploit this quality. When a foreign diplomat called, he would immediately rise regardless of his visitor's rank, unhurriedly ap-proach precisely the number of steps he thought appropriate, and languidly murmur: 'Do sit down.' Everything in Welles's behaviour was carefully thought out. His manner was always correct, but he was strict about what questions were to be dis-cussed, and he had two favourite phrases for opening a conver-sation: 'I am listening' and, if the visitor had come at Welles's invitation, 'Please hear our statement out.'

Welles was a frequent visitor at the White House, and Roosevelt personally listened to his opinions. Interestingly, in a book (*The Time for Decision*, 1944) which came out after the turning-point of the war, he made his views on Western big business quite clear: '[they] were firmly convinced that war between the Soviet Union and Hitler's Germany could only be in their interests. They as-serted that Russia would definitely be defeated and hence Commu-nism would be liquidated.'

Even so, in Soviet–American relations Welles was generally given the unpleasant jobs, such as making representations or declarations. Our embassy staff knew this, and when someone had to make a visit to the State Department he tried if possible to see other assistants. Still, it proved some consolation to us to learn from conversations with other foreign embassies that his contacts with them were in the same spirit.

Not a sociable man, Welles died while out walking alone in the countryside.

Among the other state officials of Roosevelt's administration whom our embassy had frequent occasion to meet were James Forrestal, Secretary of the Navy, and Henry Stimson, Secretary of War.

I remember Forrestal as a relatively young man, sociable, lively and energetic. In all our talks, he would declare we must fight the war to a total victory and he was not above cursing the Führer in the sharpest terms. Forrestal preferred intimate meetings, visiting us in the embassy and inviting us back to his house, where the atmosphere was always friendly. He once regaled us with the story of how his wife was robbed of her precious jewels during a reception. The story, which had incidentally appeared in the press, was intriguing and as complicated as any Agatha Christie mystery. Forrestal's witty remarks in telling it, however, were somewhat overdone. A lively man, bustling with energy, Forrestal found it hard to sit still for any length of time, and preferred to pace the room, waving his arms, as he cursed Hitler and his minions. If a wall map was at hand, he couldn't resist giving a summary of the military position and with the aid of a pencil making a few 'strategic' moves, usually of a naval character. He knew his subject well.

His death in 1949 was entirely unexpected and deeply tragic: he threw himself out of the window at the hospital where he was undergoing treatment, and just before making his fatal leap he gave a frenzied cry: 'Russian tanks!' How sad that his mental recesses could have harboured such delirious fears about the danger supposedly coming from the Soviet Union, which he had so admired during the war.

The Secretary of War, Henry Stimson, was hardly less complex a personality than Forrestal. As Stimson had been Secretary of State during Calvin Coolidge's Republican presidency (1923–9), his inclusion in the Democratic administration was unusual but clearly a calculated tactical move by Roosevelt. But the fact is, of course, that since both parties represent the interests of the same class, the bourgeoisie, any differences between them are insubstantial.

I recall Stimson as an old man, Anglo-Saxon in appearance and demeanour. His voice and manner of speech were unexpressive, but what he said was always concise and thoughtful; however sparingly he might say so, he was in favour of US–Soviet co-operation, and for its continuation after the war.

If one adds the army chief of staff George Marshall to the list of those senior officials who frequently called for good US–Soviet relations, it becomes clear that during the war the top level of the US military viewed the Soviet Union in quite a positive light. The subsequent change in Washington's approach derived from decisions taken at a high political level, and behind it stood all-powerful capital, the monopolies, the arms business.

George Marshall was a significant military and state figure during the war. Chief of staff in 1939, he was in charge of US land forces in 1939–45, and I would meet him in Washington during his short trips from Europe. Marshall's importance can be gauged from the fact that he was included in the work of the Tehran, Yalta and Potsdam conferences, and the administration counted on his authority after the war as well. As Secretary of State in 1947–9, however, Marshall gave his name to the plan to carry out the Truman Doctrine in West Germany and other countries of western Europe, its aim being to consolidate capitalism and prevent progressive social change from taking place. Later Marshall became a supporter of the creation of NATO and he ended his political career as US Secretary of Defence. On George Marshall the diplomat's morning-coat and army uniform seemed to fit equally well.

After Pearl Harbor, the Americans were dogged by the thought that the USSR might not hold out and that the anti-Hitler coalition might not be strong enough to beat the fascists. In consequence, one of the Soviet embassy's tasks – and it was one to which we gave great importance – was to inform the American public about the course of the Soviet struggle against the Nazi aggressors and reinforce America's faith in the inevitability of victory.

It is an interesting fact, and worth mentioning here, that the widow of Woodrow Wilson never attended a reception at any embassy except that of the Soviet Union. When she was asked why, she replied: 'I go in order to salute the Soviet people for their resilience and bravery in the fight against the common enemy.'

Big business and the millionaires and billionaires were equally concerned, if possibly less admiring. One of them was Nelson Rockefeller, whom I was to meet quite often. Roosevelt wanted to use the name of Rockefeller, the symbol of rich America, to disarm criticism of his economic experiments, so he gave this prominent representative of the family a job as co-ordinator of Latin American affairs. My meetings with Rockefeller had nothing to do with Latin America, of course, but concerned US–Soviet relations and international politics, about which he was rather well informed.

Many times he said to me, 'I'm among those who want normal, even good relations between our two states.' True, I had the impression that he was not sure quite how these relations were to develop after the war, but this did not prevent him from expressing some bold thoughts.

'I don't care what the professional politicians in the administration say about my ideas,' he bravely proclaimed on one occasion. 'I want to say frankly what I dare say no one has said to any Soviet representative. Of course, the USA and the USSR are different countries. In your terms, your country is socialist, ours is capitalist. I would put it this way: America is a land of private initiative, whereas the Soviet Union is a land of social initiative. So what then? You stay as you are and we'll stay as we are. The way we do things is just fine for us Americans.'

After a short pause, he remarked: 'The President himself recently expressed the same idea to me that neither side must try to foist its own system on the other. Any attempt to do so can lead only to trouble. This is precisely the philosophy that lets the USA ally itself with the Soviet Union.'

He went on: 'When I was deciding whether to join Roosevelt's administration, and took stock of his view, I came to the conclusion that the USA could only gain from co-operation between the two strong allies. Not only will the broad cross-section of American business not suffer, on the contrary it will gain a vast market in the Soviet Union for its goods. Of course, a certain part of the American business community will always look on you with suspicion. But as soon as we're sure you're not trying to start a revolution here we'll feel better about doing business with you, and when that happens the entire Rockefeller dynasty will be in favour of good relations with the USSR.'

He then asked, as if in passing, 'How will Germany come out of the war?' And he gave the reply himself: 'No doubt she'll be in a state of ruin. But what then? The Allies will have to face up to this question.' Qualifying it as his own opinion, he added: 'If Germany resurrects her economic potential, the USA will have a serious competitor. The past has shown that she is capable of rebuilding her industry rapidly. But the Allies can keep her wings clipped – especially if they act in accord.'

To give him his due, even when he was Vice-President in 1974–7, Rockefeller's attitude to the Soviet Union was always correct. Though he was at the opposite political pole, he never showed open hostility, but always proceeded on the basis that both countries must coexist peacefully.

At the end of one meeting he said to me frankly: 'I see a turn to the right in American public opinion about the Soviet Union. New winds are blowing, and it's hard to say where they will carry our relations.'

I replied: 'Soviet policy towards the USA will continue as before. Did you know, Mr Rockefeller, that the USSR voted, with its European friends, to have the United Nations head-quarters based in the USA, and that New York was chosen because of this? And do you know why?'

'Not for sure,' he replied.

'Moscow,' I told him, 'wanted to make sure the Americans did not lose their interest in international affairs. We were afraid the USA would revert to isolationism, in which case there could be no knowing which way some European states would go.'

Later on, while not betraying open hostility to the USSR, Rockefeller did show some duplicity. On the one hand, he expressed the need for peaceful relations, and, on the other hand, he called for a strong America, an armed America, an America in which big business would run the country and decide its policies in domestic and foreign affairs.

I often met Rockefeller, both officially and unofficially, and I remember one occasion particularly well. My wife and I had received an invitation from Rockefeller and his wife to a dinner in our honour. We arrived at the plush restaurant and found a large company of big businessmen and their wives waiting for us. The table was set in the Rockefeller manner, that is to say, in understated luxury, in which the main feature that night was a sea of flowers. Our hostess declared that she couldn't eat unless there were flowers on the table, and they had to be to her taste.

I asked her, 'Are flowers your hobby?'

She replied, 'No, I have a different hobby.' After a pause she explained: 'I'll let you into a secret. My hobby is moving from one apartment to another. Moving, buying furniture and arranging it. I adore arranging furniture.'

I confess I thought then of those Americans I saw on the streets in Brooklyn, who spent the night in unheated houses with broken windows, because the owners thought it not worth their while to keep them up. However, one would not say such things to the hostess on such an occasion.

As usual, the topics of conversation were extremely varied: a little politics, a little business, a bit about literature and the theatre, children, relatives, who lives where, how one spends one's free time. On the subject of children, people in that circle were clearly amazed if someone had their children living with them in town: children should be kept somewhere away from the family, preferably out of town.

Whenever the élite of the business community gathered together, it always struck me that they spoke quietly and unhurriedly. It was as if each participant wanted it known that he had no need to raise his voice to make others listen. And this was the atmosphere at the Rockefellers', even when the talk was far from the world of business.

In this respect, Americans are very different from the English. Both in the business community and among those involved in British political life, there is much more argument, noise and bustle, so that superficially everything seems more democratic. In Britain, questions and answers and would-be witty remarks about one's opponent are a common feature. Perhaps this derives in part from the ways of the ancient British Parliament. It is not done to read from a text in Westminster. Debates must be conducted spontaneously, and everyone must be able to hear them, since this appears more democratic – a belief that somehow radiates from Parliament to society at large, and to the business community as well.

★

America's permanent representative to the United Nations in the late 1950s and early 1960s was Henry Cabot Lodge. A distinguished figure in the upper reaches of American politics, Lodge was famous because of his father, a senator who in 1918 had opposed President Wilson over the Treaty of Versailles. The opposition in Washington led by Lodge senior disrupted the US ratification of the treaty, was a major cause of Wilson's defeat in the election and was widely regarded as having shortened his life. The senator's son was scarcely less stubborn in his loyalty to the most reactionary tendencies in American politics. Until the end of his term at the United Nations, Lodge junior remained a firm adherent of John Foster Dulles, who would not even hear of peaceful coexistence.

Lodge once asked me: 'What exactly do you mean by peaceful coexistence? Here in the USA, and perhaps in other countries too, people don't have a very clear idea of what you really have in mind.'

Yet again I gave my explanation, underlining the main point: 'Whatever differences there may be between states, they must be resolved by peaceful means, that is, by talks. Peaceful co-operation and peaceful competition – that is what I mean by coexistence.'

Lodge had listened very carefully to what I said. 'That's an interesting idea,' he replied. 'But it's one thing to have it as a dream and quite another to apply it as a basis of practical policy.' It was not a very reassuring reply.

Lodge's successor at the UN was Senator Warren Austin. Unlike some other US statesmen, Austin knew how to have a serious discussion on foreign matters with his Soviet counterparts. Even so, although we had frequent talks which usually resulted in clarifying each side's point of view, they rarely brought us any closer together.

Austin once asked me: 'How is it possible to reconcile the interests of the socialist states with those of the Western democratic states?'

Dulles himself might have envied this formulation of the issue.

In answering him, I drew his attention to the facts of history: 'Germany, the USA and Britain, despite their similar social structures, were on different sides during the war. Then the USA and Britain became allies of the USSR, despite the differences in their social systems. The experience of the war shows social differences are no barrier to co-operation and coexistence.'

Austin thought for a moment and then said: 'I have to admit

your reference to states during the war is persuasive, but I cannot see any likelihood that the USA will accept the principle that you are defending. Today's questions of practical policy such as disarmament and arms control are quite another matter.'

During my time in the USA, I had dealings with people who were so utterly detached from the country of their birth and education that I would call them political dinosaurs. One of these was Eduard Beneš, President of bourgeois Czechoslovakia. In May 1943 he had come to the USA from London, where he was President of the Czechoslovak government in exile, to sound out Roosevelt on the future of Europe and of his own country in particular. The Czech people at that moment were hungrily absorbing the news of the Red Army's westward advance. The peoples of Europe were becoming aware that their liberation from the fascists was coming from the east. While Beneš and his government were far away, the Czechoslovak people were fighting fascism, widening the partisan struggle against the Czech and Moravian protectorates and the pro-fascist regime in Slovakia.

One day the State Department called and said President Beneš would like to see me. I agreed.

I arrived at Blair House, a three-storey house in the early American style, next door to the White House, and the official government residence for senior foreign visitors, where I met Beneš in the spacious drawing-room.

Beneš opened the discussion deferentially: 'The eyes of the world are on the Soviet Union. Everyone expects that the brilliant Soviet armed forces are going to liberate the people from the fascist yoke.'

At his request, I gave him the latest news from the front.

'In the name of the Czechoslovak government and on my own behalf,' he said, 'I want to affirm our friendly feeling for the USSR, and I am sure the whole Czechoslovak people feel the same. The time is coming when the closest friendship, growing out of the natural sympathies of our two peoples, will bind Czechoslovakia and the USSR with strong ties.'

He then discussed British and US policies, wartime and post-war. As I listened to him, I thought of the pre-war squabbles in the League of Nations, where Beneš – a nimble and wily politician – and the British, French and other Western delegates had lulled the people by minimising the danger of aggression. As President of Czechoslovakia, Beneš stands judged by history for having toyed with fascism, and for having accepted the conditions agreed in Munich in September 1938 by the British, French, Germans and Italians on the division of Czechoslovakia, thus setting his country on a course of capitulation in the face of fascist aggression. And now here he was sitting in front of me and assuring me of his friendship for the Soviet Union. But I made no mention of his past; it was hardly the place for me to rebuke him. Nor did he deserve any compliments. We therefore stuck to topics in which it was easiest to avoid personal remarks.

I thought he looked hale and hearty, showing no signs of physical and psychological stress, and I was struck by the way in which he frequently drew imaginary lines and arrows on the table, representing the movement of armies or state policies. There was barely enough room for his gestures. In both appearance and manner, in his measured and carefully modulated tone of voice, Beneš acted very much like a professor, perhaps of law. And it all seemed to be done to show off his great oratory, even though he had an audience of only one.

To the end of his life, Beneš remained a bourgeois politician with no conception of the real thoughts and hopes of the working people. Supported by Czechoslovak reactionary forces and relying on them in the immediate post-war years, he did his best to obstruct the revolutionary changes that were occurring in his country. In February 1948 the flow of events carried Beneš far from the people, and he took part in a reactionary conspiracy, supported by imperialism and aimed at overthrowing the people's regime, restoring capitalism and taking Czechoslovakia into NATO. He went into retirement when the plot failed. His political career was at an end.

Another Czechoslovak politician whom I met many times, and whose destiny was extraordinary, was Jan Masaryk. The son of Tomáš Masaryk, President of Czechoslovakia from 1918 to 1935, he was brought up in a bourgeois republic and was basically Western in his orientation. He spent the war years in England, in 1940 as Foreign Minister of the Czech government in exile, and from 1941 as its Deputy Prime Minister. After the liberation of the Czechs by Soviet forces, as soon as the last of the occupiers had been got rid of, Masaryk faced the choice of either serving the people or finding himself on the other side of the barricades.

At first he chose the former course and in April 1945 was made
Foreign Minister.

During the first three years after the war, I met him frequently.
Our first meeting was in 1945 at the founding conference of the
United Nations in San Francisco. The Czech delegation was
cordial towards us and we responded in kind.

Masaryk was tall, and gave the impression of being well
muscled. He moved slowly, and never hurried, even when rising
to speak at the sessions. He spoke in a measured way and with
long pauses, during which he no doubt studied his own thoughts.
Anyone who took this slowness as a reflection of his mental
capacity would have been mistaken, however. In San Francisco
he plunged enthusiastically into the busy, tense atmosphere. This
situation demanded that people express their positions clearly on
the main questions on the agenda.

At that time, Czechoslovakia was represented by a National
Council in London, recognised as the government of that country
by the anti-Nazi coalition powers, including the Soviet Union.
While Beneš, as head of that government, was wary in his attitude
to the USSR, Prague had just been liberated by Soviet troops and
Masaryk as Foreign Minister tried to maintain close contact with
the Soviet delegation. We met almost daily, not only at the sessions
or in committee, but also informally, and although the Czech delegates avoided any criticism of the USA, Britain and other Western
powers – no doubt acting on orders from Prague – the Soviet delegation was pleased with the Czech position as a whole, since even
on issues where we had differences with the Western Allies our
position usually coincided with that of Czechoslovakia, as of the
other East European countries. Throughout the conference, in fact,
the Czech and Soviet delegations maintained the closest co-operation. All this was, of course, a reflection of what was happening
in Czechoslovakia, the growth of the Czech Communist Party's
influence and the bankruptcy of its bourgeois politicians.

As Czech Foreign Minister, Masaryk later headed his country's
delegation at the sessions of the UN General Assembly and would
visit our delegation's country house at Glencoe, while we were in
turn frequently invited to be his guests. He was an interesting man
to talk to, but found it difficult ever to say a hard word. If one
observed him closely, he seemed always to be contemplating, not
something he had said, but rather what he had left unsaid –
especially when a difficult issue came up, such as the attitude of

the Western states to the Soviet Union or the people's democracies.

Sadly Masaryk ended his career not on the side of his people. Evidently unable to free himself from the weight of the past, he could not devote his outstanding abilities to the service of socialist Czechoslovakia, and his physical death followed soon after his political demise: in 1948 he killed himself.

During the Roosevelt era one simply could not count the number of cables and letters of sympathy and friendship we Russians received at our embassy and consulates, both from individual Americans and from all sorts of organisations. This was primarily thanks to the policy the Roosevelt administration had adopted towards the USSR as a victim of aggression. It was this feeling on the part of ordinary Americans that Truman tried to stifle, by distorting history and by mocking the mutual sympathy of the two nations. Admittedly Churchill made a speech on 5 March 1946 at Fulton, Missouri, which was the signal for the formation of a broad anti-Soviet bloc, including the USA, but one speech would not have been enough to turn American public opinion against Soviet Russia. Reactionary forces still had to stir up a wave of mass propaganda to create the desired effect.

Interestingly, in the autumn of 1945 Eleanor Roosevelt came to a reception at our embassy, having just returned from London.

'I'm just back from Great Britain,' she said, smiling broadly. 'I was accompanied by John Foster Dulles. You know, I'm convinced he just doesn't trust the Russians one bit.'

'Why? Why shouldn't he trust us?' I asked.

The President's widow replied: 'I think Churchill has a lot of influence over him.'

Evidently she was not well informed about the Dulles family. During the war, John's brother, Allen, had even had secret talks in Switzerland with representatives of the Nazi leadership about a separate agreement, and at that time one brother was as reactionary as the other. John, moreover, was soon to inspire the US anti-Soviet policy of 'a position of strength'. On the visit with Eleanor Roosevelt, therefore, it could well have been Dulles who had put Churchill in an anti-Soviet mood. It was the time when faint stirrings could be felt of the distrust that would gain full force in the cold war.

There is something I would like to say now which many

Western readers may think far-fetched. None the less I would like it to be taken seriously.

The time has come when people have to look at their neighbours in a new way. To save the world from catastrophe we have to unite and abandon the previous course of confrontation. But if someone advocates pluralism in politics he must understand that not only the Americans and British, the Swedes and Australians, the Swiss and Italians have the right to choose their own social path of development: the Soviet people and the Cubans, the Nicaraguans and Ethiopians, the Angolans and Namibians, the Chinese and Vietnamese have the same right.

In their hearts, the Americans know that their hostility to socialism arises mainly from the fact that the socialist countries reject private ownership, as distinct from personal property which one earns by the sweat of one's brow.

Having gone through a complex period of development, Soviet socialism is now spreading its wings, developing democracy and openness, restructuring its house on its Leninist foundations. Far from being feared, it invites collaboration.

In a world where nations recognised the right of social choice, there would be no grounds for dangerous confrontations, and disarmament would release vast resources for peaceful construction and the resolution of many global problems.

The Soviet people do not hanker after what is not theirs, but neither will they give up their heritage. What are most precious to us are our socialist ideals which, combined with the technical expertise of other countries, will raise our people's standard of living. That is what *perestroika* is all about, and since the 27th Party Congress we have rolled up our sleeves and got to work on it.

Mankind's main enemy today is not one ideology or another – it is not ideologies that fight – but the weapons of mass destruction. Humanity's shame and misfortune is war, and war must be thrown on the scrapheap. That is the only sensible approach to the realities of the modern world, where everyone must have a place. Otherwise mankind will not survive.

People of reason must not allow themselves to be trampled on by militaristic thinking: this can only bring tragedy, the destruction of the gift of life and the undeserved end of mankind in the manner of the biblical Armageddon.

People must speak up against this now, and passionately, while there is still time to create a stable peace on earth.

5

American culture

During the war there was an explosion of interest in the Soviet Union among American cultural figures. As a rule they would have been remote from politics, but, with so much of the world ablaze and so much blood being spilt in Europe and elsewhere, many leading personalities of stage, screen, literature and music made contact with the Soviet embassy and came to our receptions.

Lillian Hellman, the famous playwright, had in fact formed her progressive views earlier, in Republican Spain, and anti-fascism remained a theme throughout most of her work. Then, during the war, President Roosevelt sent her on an unofficial trip to the Soviet Union lasting several months in order to cement cultural links between the two countries; there she was received by Stalin.

On her return we were dining in a small restaurant when she told me: 'I'll never forget this trip and my meetings with the Soviet people. I also went to the front, where I met General Chernov. He reckoned he would be liberating Warsaw some nine or ten days after my arrival and he invited me to accompany the army to the city. He even asked me to come all the way to Berlin with him. I wrote him a letter later, but then I heard he'd been killed two days after liberating Warsaw.' She spoke with sadness.

Of middle height with large eyes, she was an unremarkable woman to look at, but she possessed clear judgement, plenty of human feeling and also great civic courage. Uncompromising in her views, she remained true to her ideals of humanism, duty and truth. Vilified and ostracised for several years, during the McCarthy period she was subjected to insulting interrogation and investigation by Congressional committees. Although she afterwards admitted to having come close to a breakdown several times, none of their threats ever silenced her and she maintained her dignity throughout, scorning those who wanted to destroy her. 'I cannot and do not wish to fake my conscience to suit this year's fashions,' she wrote in a letter to Joseph McCarthy, Chairman of the House Committee on Un-American Activities. The moral strength she showed in those dark days, when the FBI and the McCarthy committee made a mockery of America's conscience, could not but be admired by decent people in the USA and abroad.

After the war Hellman again visited the USSR – of which she later wrote a vivid account – where she was always warmly received as a friend and where her plays are well known. Her three powerful socio-psychological dramas, *The Children's Hour*, *Watch on the Rhine* and *The Little Foxes*, have been put on in all the best Soviet theatres, and the playwright herself participated in the staging and rehearsal of *The Little Foxes* in Moscow.

The outstanding black singer and actor Paul Robeson earned an enormous reputation in the thirties, forties and fifties among Americans at large, but above all among the black population. His mighty voice attracted big crowds and he always performed to packed houses. His fame spread abroad and he was invited to tour many European countries.

Robeson never lost an opportunity to meet Soviet people. He was relaxed with us, like a friend. I particularly remember his meeting with the Soviet delegation in San Francisco in 1945 during the founding conference of the UN. Many times he visited the USSR, and he was invariably greeted with warmth. His son, Paul – we called him Pavlik – learned to speak Russian and with his father and mother was a frequent visitor at the embassy.

We used to have impassioned conversations. A supporter of Roosevelt's policy towards the USSR, Paul never sought to avoid political topics, and was especially impressed by the fact that there was no national or racial prejudice in Soviet society. 'Whereas in America,' he would say, 'first it's the pro-fascists, then the Ku Klux Klan.' Robeson felt it personally when friends were humiliated because of their race, and he would denounce the authorities in strong language for doing nothing to stop the racists.

He learned a bit of Russian himself. I once read him some verses of Pushkin and he asked me to write them out for him; in a short time he was able to read them himself. He read English literature too, and he joked that he and Shakespeare were old friends.

'A marvellous playwright,' he said. 'He gave great force to his Othello. The character took me over, and I would prowl around the house at night. My wife used to laugh and say she was scared of me when I was preparing to play the part. I would reassure her by pointing out that I hadn't once tried to strangle her.'

Reactionary America could not forgive Robeson his progressive views, above all for his good relations with the Soviet Union. Eventually the government took its revenge on him for speaking out against racial intolerance, and for being a talented singer and actor and for being famous in other countries. They took their revenge on him for being Paul Robeson.

He was persecuted by various means. Either his successes would be ignored or he would be attacked for his behaviour off-stage. He understood what was going on, but he stuck to the path he had set himself.

One day he said to me: 'You know, it looks like the American authorities are thinking of depriving me of the right to go abroad, even to perform. I think that's the way things are going.'

And he was right. In the last years of his life, Robeson was forbidden to leave the USA. He was simply refused permission to travel abroad, and his family were subjected to the same hostile restraint.

Americans, especially the blacks, will long remember this talented, wise, honest singer, great actor and patriot. And we Soviet people will remember a friend and supporter of good relations between our two states. He loved both countries, if in different ways.

I had always wanted to know what sort of person Charlie Chaplin was. I'd seen his films even when I hadn't any money to buy a cinema ticket – they used to be shown in Gomel in the park, and my friends and I used to watch them through the cracks in the fence. It was not the best way to see a film, but the miracle of cinematography – and it was still a miracle then – worked its magic even through the park fence.

Our first meeting was at an official charity reception in New York during the war in aid of Allied wounded. I was ambassador by then and was eager to find out whether Charlie was just a brilliant comic, without much brain, or whether he was something more.

I was standing and talking to some diplomat or other when the man I knew so well from the cinema came up to me with a charming smile: 'How do you do, Mr Ambassador. I'm Charlie Chaplin.'

The smile suited him and as a matter of fact rarely left his face. We only knew the happy Chaplin at that time; the sad one was yet to appear.

Having greeted him, I said: 'You know, everyone who goes to the cinema in my country knows you well. And, now that the Soviet people have heard about your speeches against fascism and in support of the Soviet Union, they feel still more sympathy for you.'

We got on to the Soviet cinema and Chaplin remarked: 'I'm not terribly familiar with Soviet films, but from what I have seen I have a great impression of positiveness. There's nothing degenerate or vulgar about them.'

I made up my mind to ask him a question that had often puzzled me: 'Why don't you make films from books by the great European writers, like Byron, Goethe, Balzac?'

Chaplin answered completely without embarrassment: 'American filmgoers want to see stories that give them a feeling of optimism about everyday life, stories that create a happy mood. Most people go to the movies to leave their troubles behind, to have a good time. It doesn't matter if the film's a fantasy or a farce. After all, life itself is pretty farcical. A film can only show a tiny fragment of all this, but the fact that my films are popular shows that mine is the fragment people want to see.' He spoke without posing or bragging.

I next asked him, 'Are you familiar with the works of any Russian writers?'

'Yes, I know *War and Peace*, of course, and some of Turgenev and Dostoevsky.' He then added: 'I've heard of Pushkin and Lermontov, but I haven't read them, I'm afraid.'

As we parted warmly, Chaplin said, 'I wish you victory.'

The next time I saw him was at a diplomatic reception in London, and we greeted each other like old friends. He had left the USA for good, but had not yet settled in Switzerland. His departure from the USA had been preceded by a campaign of vilification against him, both as a man and as an actor. Many people in the West wondered how such a great artist could suddenly be so unacceptable to the authorities. Why was he being slandered in America?

I asked him a tricky question: 'What are you at the moment – American or British?'

He replied with a wry smile: 'I guess I'm not really an American.' Then he added, suddenly serious again: 'I'm fed up with having mud slung at me – especially as I don't know what for.'

We moved away from the group and he went on: 'Judge for yourself. I've been slanged for having married more than once, but if that's a crime then millions of Americans are guilty of it. I've just been unlucky in that area. Nobody can accuse me of behaving unfairly to any of the wives I divorced. I'd have thought I'd been punished enough by life as it is, but there seem to be people who want to punish me more.'

He looked at me almost pleadingly, as if for my sympathy.

Getting agitated, he went on: 'They're persecuting me because I have views which show in my films and which they don't agree with. First they attack my morals, then they find legal grounds: they're trying to prove I haven't paid all the tax I owe on my US earnings. It's all part of a campaign against me, and American law is so fashioned that if the government is against you you're sunk, even if you're completely innocent. That's why I've said goodbye to the USA.'

He broke off. Suddenly he said, as if to himself, 'Now, why am I telling you all this?' And immediately he gave the answer: 'First, because even though I'm not a communist I admire your country's honesty. Secondly, because I know you would never use my words to harm me.'

I knew of course that for years Chaplin had been regarded in certain circles as a leftist radical, if not actually a communist. So I said: 'I confess I'm touched by your trust, and I'd like you to know that your confidence is safe with me – we Soviets are guided by our moral principles, which are clearly different from those of the men who are intriguing against you.'

We were photographed together by a British journalist and I still have that photo: it reminds me of a wonderfully wise and attractive man.

There are film actors and film actors. In my experience the majority of actors either consciously serve those with a particular artistic and ideological viewpoint or are simply consumed by materialism. But there are also actors with genuine star quality who also manage to retain their own moral convictions, actors who believe that they have a duty to inspire a sense of nobility in others.

I was much impressed by a talk I had with one such actor, Edward G. Robinson. The conversation, in a restaurant near our embassy, was intimate and frank, and during it Robinson gave us a striking picture of the film industry in America.

'The American film industry is run by a bunch of ruthless millionaires. The only thing that matters in the business is profit. As far as the screen bosses are concerned, how the millions are made is secondary. For them, anything goes, as long as the cost of a film is earned several times over, once it's been released. These people know nothing about morality or social justice.' He added: 'I may be no expert in economics or finance, but I've certainly seen a fall in the moral standards shown on the screen.'

He was somewhat agitated and one could see that it was a painful subject.

'More than once,' he went on, 'I've had to ask myself in moral terms if I should take on a role. And I can't say I've always made the right decision. Several times I haven't been pleased with my performances – I mean in the sense of the way of life I present on the screen and the image I create. Still, most of the time I've managed to resist the conditions laid down by the Hollywood bosses.'

He complained: 'American films are overdoing vulgarity and debauchery. It's called naturalism, and the saddest thing is, film audiences are being brought up on this stuff and they like it. So the producers make more to satisfy the demand they themselves have created. It's hard to fight against them. And who's going to fight, anyway? The battle is so unequal.'

I asked him, 'Isn't there any group of other well-known actors like yourself, and maybe producers, who are trying to influence the cinema in more positive directions?'

'There are no organised groups like that,' he replied. 'And in the USA they wouldn't last long, either. Any actor who tried it would soon find himself starving.'

It was obvious our guest was full of resentment for the people who held the fate of the film industry in their hands.

'So that's how it goes for a great number of film actors,' he concluded. 'Every day they have to dish up behaviour that insults everything good and decent in mankind.'

After that conversation I could well understand why Edward G. Robinson had joined the National Council for American–Soviet Friendship, then headed by Corliss Lamont.

Marilyn Monroe – she had a reputation of always being late, but she came early to meet the Soviet delegation, perhaps to get a good seat. She was about fifteen feet away from us.

After the official part of the reception was over and the guests were leaving, I was passing her table when she suddenly turned to me: 'Mr Gromyko, how are you?' Although we'd never met before, she spoke as if we were old friends.

Mostly out of courtesy, I replied: 'Hello, I'm just fine. And how about you? I've seen a lot of your films.'

She held out her hand and said something, but I missed her words, and the crush of people was already pushing me into the next room. But at least I could tell my children I had actually talked with Marilyn Monroe.

Monroe was then at the peak of her career, a screen idol in many countries, always smiling and happy. But then, three years after I met her, we got news in Moscow that she had committed suicide. How could that happen? Always the happy, radiant Marilyn, and now suicide – and only thirty-six years old. Drugs were mentioned, but the stories made no sense.

The years came and went. Then in the early 1980s articles began appearing in the Western press to the effect that Marilyn had not killed herself but had been the victim of a conspiracy. The roles she played in films may have made her look simple-minded, but in fact she must have known a lot. She had been acquainted with some of the highest state officials, and would have talked to them on many important matters, including politics. Not long before her death she had been seeing both John and Robert Kennedy. And that was in a period – the spring of 1962 – of important military and political events: the USA exploded a megaton bomb and Polaris missiles were put into commission. Many people meanwhile had come to regard Marilyn as a Red on account of her good relations with the Soviet Union and Soviet culture, and her friendships with people of left-wing views, in particular her future husband Arthur Miller and his friends. Some officials even accused her openly of becoming a communist. This was of course rubbish, but her good relations with the USSR did not escape notice – after all, she had spoken up for human rights in the USA – and she was under constant surveillance in Hollywood.

It emerged in the 1980s that back in 1955, before she was even thirty years old, a secret dossier had been opened on her. The American authorities have admitted that they have an 'extensive' file on her, and according to the *Sunday Times* in London this dossier contains material on foreign policy, as well as questions of defence. The paper says that in the eyes of the special services Marilyn Monroe had become a 'security risk'. So they simply got rid of her. Whether this is so or not, maybe the future will tell.

Obviously many foreign writers have already written about America. Even so, everyone sees his surroundings in his own way, so perhaps my own impressions of America and the Americans are also relevant. I worked in the USA for eight years, with only one short break, and I often came up against Americans in their ordinary lives, as well as in politics. At first we rented a small house in a quiet Washington street and then, when I was made ambassador, we moved to the embassy on 16th Street, a five-minute walk from the White House.

America in the late 1930s and early 1940s made a big impression on me. At first glance, American cities seemed utterly unlike not only Russian cities but also the European ones my wife and I had seen, which were much calmer and where one could feel the breath of history. If you compared New York with, say, London or Florence or Venice, you would think they were on different planets.

Here it was the breath of technology one felt, and innovation, and everywhere the buildings seemed to shout after you: 'We're not like you Europeans. We make noise, we hum, we roar, and we like it. The dollar, the dollar, that's all we want.'

Yet, strange though it may seem, American towns eventually came to remind me of Russian towns. For a long time I couldn't work out why, and then I got it. At first I'd been distracted by the striking external differences between, say, New York and Moscow, but then, as I became immersed in the everyday life, I realised that they both absorbed the new and cast off the old in the same way.

In any big American city everything is in motion. When we first arrived, New York was already inundated by cars, and the metallic clang of the overhead railway was augmented by the rumble of trucks and the frequent howl of the police and fire-engine sirens, day and night. The cacophony excited the population and clearly affected their psyche, and without it New York would not be New York.

Unfortunately, in recent decades, Moscow has been going the same way. Under the pressure of urbanisation, many of its old streets and squares have been defaced with bland, indefinable architecture. Dozens of interesting buildings have been destroyed. Straight streets and straight lines now dominate, and the national character of the city has been lost. The environment has been spoiled, the city has become noisier.

The noisy streets of New York were as straight as if they'd been drawn with a ruler. The buildings looked gigantic. On the other hand, Washington was quieter. As the capital, populated mostly by government officials, it was as it were a counterpoint to New York, and no building was (or is) allowed to be higher than the cupola of the Capitol.

One odd feature of the Washington of those days was the extraordinary number of dogs that were allowed to roam free, and I recall an incident in this connection.

Out of sheer curiosity our young son, Anatoly, went into the local church during the sermon. He told us about it: 'I'm sitting and listening. The preacher drones on for a while and then, at the end of his sermon, he starts to get excited and ends up practically screaming. The people aren't exactly bored, but they aren't very joyful either. Then they start passing a huge cup around and everyone's throwing money into it, sometimes even paper money. But I had practically nothing on me. What could I do? It would be shaming not to give something, so when the cup was about to reach our row I got up and left. People gave me disapproving looks and one old man even hissed at me. But I felt better once I went outside. I wanted to get home. I saw the bus approaching the stop and started to run like mad to catch it, when all of a sudden I was being chased by a lot of dogs. One dog howled just like the Hound of the Baskervilles and it bit me just as I was jumping on the bus. If I was superstitious, I'd say I was being punished for ducking out of the church like that.'

We were worried about the bite, but the American doctor we

consulted reassured us: 'Nothing to worry about. We haven't had rabies in Washington for many years now.'

Anatoly's remark reminds me of the many American super-stitions I encountered. Despite all their technological achieve-ments, most Americans still seem to believe in miracles, raising the dead, astrology, magic, witchcraft, all kinds of messiahs, vampires and fortune-tellers.

However, Americans have one quality which we Soviet people can admire unreservedly – their business efficiency. Its roots presumably go back to the time when pioneers came to settle and survived the harsh conditions only through the sweat of their brow and sheer guts. American efficiency struck me right away. Americans don't work at half-speed. Whether they are selling hot-dogs or popcorn on the street, or building an apartment house or a shopping mall, growing wheat at home or drilling for oil in foreign parts, they don't just work well, they work with total dedication. They never hold meetings to discuss what would seem to us to be important questions about methods. They simply know they have to work better than anyone else, and if they don't they know they'll soon be unemployed. The world of American business makes full use of the fear of losing one's job, and idlers, layabouts and drunks get no wages.

With the exception of communists, all the people I spoke to in America liked to talk about American democracy, yet none of them seemed to have a clear perception of what real democracy, real rule by the people, actually is. They used words learned in school, like their fathers and grandfathers before them.

Even George Washington's contemporaries in slave-owning America talked about freedom and thought they were living in a democratic country. Under Abraham Lincoln they talked about the power of the people, and in Theodore Roosevelt's day the press glorified the American democracy which the administration was imposing by force on the peoples of other countries, especially in Latin America, while at home the working masses were being squeezed harder and harder by big business.

So what is the situation like today? Soviet visitors to the USA are struck by the strange (to them) sight of people standing in line for a job, or for unemployment benefit, or just for a bowl of soup. If you ask someone how he got into this situation, he'll tell you:

'I haven't got a job, my family's got nothing. I've tried looking for work, but I haven't found any.' And if you ask him who's responsible he'll say: 'That's how it is. This is a democratic country – one guy finds a job, another doesn't.'

It's obvious that since childhood this man has believed that unemployment, with all its consequences, is a feature of democracy. Even the most oppressed minorities, the blacks, the Puerto Ricans and Hispanics, sing the same refrain: 'The United States is a democratic country.'

As for the American trade unions, they are concerned entirely with the workers' material interests, not with questions about the social order, or domestic and foreign policy. They may participate in presidential elections, but even then they only have the chance to vote for a representative of the ruling class. If you ask a trade-union member whether he regards the USA as a democratic country, he'll say he does, and he will say this regardless of the glaring fact that eight or nine million Americans are daily denied subsistence. His conviction is not shaken even by legislation which has taken away from workers many of the social gains they struggled for, only to transfer the resources to the military budget. After all, American democracy is also a democracy of the military-industrial complex, and the Pentagon's arms race is big business.

As for the views of those at the top of US society, in business or the arts, they overwhelmingly proclaim that in America democracy is at its most perfect.

The economist John Maynard Keynes, for example, although he was an Englishman, fits excellently into my comments on American democracy, since many of his ideas about state interference in the economy were practised in the United States. Admired by Western theoretical economists and American millionaires alike, Keynes's ideas were embodied in the policies Franklin Roosevelt applied in order to overcome the economic crisis that had brought him to power. The main principle he stressed was that the ills of capitalism could be overcome by means of state-monopoly regulation.

I first met Keynes in 1943 in Atlantic City at the United Nations Relief and Rehabilitation Administration (UNRRA) Council, one of the first wartime conferences held to discuss the economies of the countries occupied by Hitler. Keynes was there on behalf of the British government and, although he remained in the background, he was an influential figure among those who set the tone for the conference.

For instance, he told me on one occasion: 'The Western Allies, above all the USA and England, have common interests, not only in the war against fascism, which we're going to win. They will have just as much interest in co-operating after the war.'

Although he was careful not to make predictions, he seemed to suggest that Britain's colonial empire would be in a parlous state after the war, in which case Britain would be in need of economic help from her powerful American ally.

I asked him, 'Isn't it threatening for Britain to be in a situation where she can no longer be independent of America?'

Instead of replying directly, Keynes said, 'Take note of Britain's great potential, which I'm sure she will still have after the war.'

I then asked him, 'How would you apply your theoretical views to the difficult period that is going to come for the anti-Hitler powers?'

Weighing his words, Keynes replied: 'I don't believe in social-ism. The capitalist countries will continue to develop along the same path they have followed for hundreds of years. That doesn't mean the world is going to be divided into black and white. Elements of convergence will occur, and the governments of the capitalist countries are going to need much more flexibility in dealing with economic problems. It is therefore logical to antici-pate more state interference than ever before – but in harmony with the interest of the entrepreneurs, rather than against them. It is important that both sectors assist in overcoming the state's economic difficulties.'

By 'difficulties' Keynes no doubt meant 'crisis', so I asked: 'What, then, is your view of Marx's arguments about the inevita-bility of economic crisis in capitalist society?'

His answer was curious for the time: 'I recognise that Marx's argument had good grounds. But capitalist society has now de-veloped and the possessing class has learned from experience how to cope with upheavals in the economy.'

I said, 'One of the main points in Marx's political economy was his theory of the law of surplus value and his analysis of the inner workings of capitalism. What is the main thing in what is now called Keynesianism?'

He thought for a while and then said: 'To be brief, the main point in my theory of state regulation is the need to maintain both effective demand and full employment.'

The capitalist countries achieved neither of these basic aims after the war. Neo-Keynesian schools were formed, some leaning to the left, some to the right, but none of them helped to save capitalism from its constant ills. Since the Second World War, the capitalist economies have been characterised not by effective demand but by almost permanent inflation and vain attempts to avert economic crisis, which have manifested themselves as falls in production, under-use of capacity, and fluctuations in the investment and currency markets. As for full employment, just ask the millions who are out of a job.

My personal impression of Keynes was of a man who knew his own worth. His imposing appearance set him apart. Elegant in a dark suit of superb English cloth, he preferred to talk of big things and did not indulge in the social chit-chat so beloved of his fellow countrymen. An interesting man, a subtle conversationalist, a scholar of prodigious talent, he intelligently served his class and the system in which he and his forebears had grown up.

When the subject of America is being discussed, I am often asked, 'What are Americans really like?' This is not a naïve question. There are research institutes in the Soviet Union entirely devoted to the study of the United States. Their books are widely read, their articles appear in the press and their members appear on television. Their observations of America and the Americans are very impressive. And yet even they have probably missed much. I myself have wondered if I really know the Americans. I spent in all more than eight years in the USA on party and government work, not counting all the trips of one or two weeks, but I still can give no clear answer. I can, however, identify some common features, some characteristic traits.

I am, for example, firmly of the view that public opinion in America is less well informed than it is in Europe, and one of the main reasons for this is that the people at the top, who control the news media, hand out biased information, especially on foreign policy matters as they relate to the USSR and the life of the Soviet people. Another typical feature of average Americans is that they will say, 'You look like a million dollars', meaning, 'You are looking well'. I have known so many Americans who, when talking about their friends or family, refer to their success in life, when that success has consisted simply of building up capital. No one earns more praise in the USA than a good businessman. People don't usually ask: 'How did he make his capital, where did it come from?'

Americans cannot see that capital yields a profit to its owners only because other people are exploited. Ordinary Americans see people out of work or suffering racial discrimination, and millions homeless and illiterate, but there are countless distractions to cloud their view, to distort their normal human responses. There are of course people in the USA who openly and courageously carry on the struggle for equality, who do not bow down to the dollar, but they are very few. Once upon a time, before the name of Abraham Lincoln had dimmed, fighters for freedom sought refuge in America from foreign oppression. But today it is seldom fighters for freedom who seek refuge there any more; it is those who want to get closer to Mr Dollar.

What, then, is the attitude of ordinary city folk to Soviet people on the human level? In this, I have to say that the Americans are no different from people in other countries. They are courteous and civil and they want to know more about the USSR. Throughout my time in America, apart from occasional anti-Soviet demonstrations organised by various minority groups, neither I, nor any of my family, nor any of my embassy staff, was ever insulted or shown disrespect. On the contrary, we noticed that Americans showed special courtesy when they were dealing with Soviet citizens. There were unfortunate incidents, of course, but these were with either junkies or thieves, and such people don't usually stop to ask for your passport. Ordinary Americans have always received Soviets with great interest and still do. This applies not just to officials but to others, such as representatives of public bodies, artists, scholars and tourists.

For example, in 1943 two major figures of Soviet Jewish culture, the famous actor and chairman of the Jewish Anti-Fascist Committee Solomon Mikhoels, and the Yiddish poet Itzik Fefer, came to appeal to the American Jewish community for support for the Soviet war effort, and they made a big impression on the American public at large. They addressed audiences mostly in the large cities, such as New York and Washington, and were everywhere received rapturously. As soon as they arrived in Washington, they asked us to arrange contacts for them with a wide American public, and we did whatever we could to assist the venture.

In the course of their brief stay in the USA, Mikhoels and Fefer acquired hundreds of new friends who in turn began to participate in various kinds of public activity aimed at developing friendship between our two countries. Mikhoels in particular left a deep impression with his bitter attacks against the Nazis. Many of the most varied social groups wanted to meet him, since he was well known in America as a great theatrical figure.

Certainly, American culture is rich and varied, and, as I have had frequent occasion to observe, not devoid of sharp contradictions either.

The great Czech composer Antonín Dvořák, who for three years in the last century was director of the National Conservatory in New York, where he composed his *New World Symphony*, declared that the American composer who incorporated Negro melodies in his music would become the founder of the American school. That composer was to be George Gershwin, who took the blues and the spirituals and the chants of the slaves on the plantations of the old South and made them his own. He became famous and the world became aware of the existence of an authentic American musical culture.

I arrived in Washington two years after Gershwin's death, but I well remember the yard-high lettering on the billboards advertising his opera *Porgy and Bess*.

But it is the exception that proves the rule, and a strict rule it is. Profit is the pitiless filter through which everything to do with culture and art and the country's spiritual life has to pass. Only that which promises a return on capital can survive. There is nothing obvious to suggest which cultural figures are to merit praise, but there are countless means which determine who shall be raised up and who cast down. One is the press and the mass media, and for the most part and in the last analysis they serve the interests of the ruling élite.

There are occasions when a talent appears that in other circumstances would do credit to the USA and enrich the cultural life of other countries as well; but society's tentacles and the ultimate subordination of everything to the laws of capitalism distort such talents, in both the literal and metaphorical senses of the word.

Such a case was surely that of the short-lived singer Elvis Presley. Performing in a style that was just short of indecent, he was the idol of American youth for twenty years. His managers did everything to squeeze the last drop out of this gifted performer and America was amazed by the prolonged resistance Presley put up against his exploiters. The people who were pushing him further along the path of vulgarity succeeded only in breaking the health of this goose that laid the golden egg. He became seriously ill, and the media was full of it. Instead of treatment, however, he was given more contracts for countless performances that would bring huge profits to his backers. It was well known long before his death that he was addicted to narcotics and stimulants, but the octopus would not loosen its grip. Presley's talent collapsed and he died at the age of forty-three.

There are of course Americans who understand what is going on and who condemn it. But they are helpless against the almighty dollar and the spiritual devastation it wreaks.

6

Tehran and Yalta

To travel from the Soviet Union to the United States during the war, when the direct transatlantic route was out of the question, was no simple matter. The only reliable way was to fly right across Siberia and the Soviet Far East to Alaska, then south through Canada and the western United States and across to Washington. I made the trip three times.

The route across Siberia and Alaska was arduous, and our pilots nicknamed it 'the Mazuruk line', after Hero of the Soviet Union Major-General Ilya Mazuruk, a famous pilot and chief of polar aviation.

The flight from Washington took five days, one way. Siberia seemed endless. The plane flew on for hours, but always below was the taiga. That was when I first realised just how vast our country is. Somewhere above Yakutia we observed a huge fire, its broken front extending for tens of kilometres into the taiga. The glow made me think of what it must be like on the front, where at that time our soldiers were dying.

I flew that route for the last time in 1944, and on that occasion the weather produced some surprises for us. I had been appointed head of the delegation to the Dumbarton Oaks conference which was to produce the UN Charter, and the delegation included leading experts on international law. We flew without incident to Chukotka, but then we were stranded for more than twenty-four hours in the tiny settlement of Uelkal, on the shore of the Krest gulf. The plane could not take off because of the weather. The wind was hurricane force and though it was August one could feel the cold breath of the north.

Uelkal consisted of a few huts. After we had been settled in one we were told: 'If you want the evening to pass more quickly, you'd better try the mobile cinema next door. They're going to show the war news.'

As we got outside we had to grab hold of each other to stay upright. 'Next door' was 200 metres away and we could cover the ground against the wind only by helping each other. After much time and no little effort, we reached the small building where the film was being shown. It was packed. The whole population was there, consisting of women, children and old men, all the young men having been mobilised, as everywhere else in Russia.

They started with the news. The turning-point in the war had long passed and the Red Army was advancing steadily. Every scene showed another victory, and the audience became very excited. Then a war adventure film was shown. Many such films were being churned out at the Alma Ata studios during the war. Most had little artistic merit, with the enemy shown in caricature, but they gave harmless entertainment to people who were longing to see just about any film, as long as it was about the war. The same thing was going on all over the country and, to tell the truth, in our embassies too. There in the Far North the audience was enthralled, and, although the little hall was stifling, nobody left before the very end.

Getting back to our hut was even harder. The wind literally blew one off one's feet.

The hurricane had ceased by morning but we were still unable to take off because the weather ahead was too bad. So we stayed a few hours and got to know something about the life of the local Chukchi, an ethnic group whose living conditions had recently begun to improve under the Soviet regime.

We visited the local kolkhoz (collective farm) and found that the manager, a Chukchi, had studied in the Leningrad Peoples of the North Institute. Shortly before the war he had contracted tuberculosis and been advised to go straight back to Chukotka, where the climate and food would soon get him back to health.

'I wasn't taken for the front because of the TB,' he said, 'but now the disease is getting better. I feel fine here at home.'

He told us how worried he was for the children of the men at the front, and how the women had replaced the men doing typical jobs of the Far North, such as fishing, hunting and reindeer-herding in the tundra. It touched us that even this tiny settlement in far-off Chukotka was sharing the hardships of the entire country, anxiously waiting for news from the front of victory over Nazi Germany.

The turning-point of the war had come in the winter of 1942–3. As the Red Army began its victorious advance, this turn of events gave rise to a host of problems requiring urgent attention and it was plain the Allies must meet to discuss not only how to fight the war and secure victory but also how to lay the foundations for the post-war organisations of peace.

Three such conferences took place between 1943 and 1945 – Tehran (28 November to 1 December 1943), Yalta (4–11 February 1945) and Potsdam (17 July to 2 August 1945) – and the decisions taken at all three are published and freely available. Even so, there is still lively public interest in them, as people want to know the true course of events during and after the war – especially since these decisions have been deliberately falsified by some politicians in the West who claim that they were not well founded and even call for them to be repudiated.

Certainly American officials are reluctant to recall certain facts about Tehran, and in London they are even less enthusiastic. And yet this conference was very important, representing as it did a significant stage in the development of Allied relations.

The proposal that the Big Three meet in Tehran was contained in a message of 5 November 1943 from Stalin that I personally delivered to Roosevelt. In his reply the President wrote: 'The whole world is waiting for us three to meet, and the fact that you, Churchill and I will get to know each other personally will have far-reaching consequences . . . and contribute to the further worsening of Nazi morale.'

My post involved me in all the painstaking work of the three countries in organising the conference, as well as taking part in it and then carrying out its decisions. I shall dwell on the three most important issues discussed.

Firstly, the idea of opening a second front. Britain's position, which Churchill defended with zeal, was that the enemy could be defeated through attrition by carrying out a series of operations on his southern flank: in northern Italy, the Balkans, Romania and other German satellites. The real point of this policy was plain: to stand in the way of the Soviet armies' advance on Berlin and, by occupying south-eastern Europe, to obtain for the Western Allies an opening to the Soviet Union's western borders.

At Tehran, Stalin actively urged the Allies to open a second front in western Europe as soon as possible. He tried repeatedly to make Churchill commit himself to a date for landing Allied troops in Europe, but could get nothing out of him. On one occasion, barely able to contain himself, he rose from his chair and said to Voroshilov and Molotov: 'We've got too much to do at home to waste our time here. We're not getting anywhere.'

In confusion, and obviously afraid that the conference might break up, Churchill hastily announced: 'The marshal has misunderstood me. I can give an exact date – May 1944.'

The atmosphere relaxed immediately and the participants continued working. The Western Allies adopted a more constructive approach and, although they did not quite keep to the May 1944 date for the invasion of France, 'Overlord' – the code-word for the operation – took place on 6 June of that year.

Secondly, the Tehran conference was an important milestone in another respect. By the time it took place there was no doubt about the defeat of Germany and her allies. But what then? Those who took part in the conference knew this question was knocking at their door.

The Soviet Union, the USA and Britain all regarded it as essential that any possibility of further aggression from Germany should be excluded. The US and British governments had not yet officially revealed their plans for dealing with Germany when she had been defeated, but rumours had percolated from one capital or the other that plans were being hatched to split Germany up into small states. At Tehran, both nations brought this idea out into the open. Although it was clear that neither Roosevelt nor Churchill had any plan worked out, they shared the belief that special attention be paid to Prussia as the most aggressive part of the German Reich, that its wings should be clipped by reducing its territory.

Having listened to the American President and the British Prime Minister, Stalin made the following comment:

'On the field of battle, Prussians, Bavarians, Saxons and the troops from other parts of Germany all fight with the same determination. In my opinion, the German question cannot be solved by breaking up the unified German state. You cannot eliminate Germany like that any more than you could eliminate Russia. A solution should be sought through the demilitarisation and democratisation of Germany as a whole. Nazism and the

Wehrmacht must be liquidated and the criminal leaders of the Third Reich must be put on trial by the people.'

He then made a simple but wise suggestion: 'As this question needs some thought and further work, representatives of the three powers should get busy on it.' The others agreed. The matter was complex and indeed would not be settled until 1945, at Potsdam.

The fate of Poland was the third vitally important issue discussed at Tehran. Our allies were plainly aware that the Soviet–German front was approaching Polish territory and bringing closer Poland's liberation, and they were afraid therefore that the Polish democratic forces, which had mounted a mighty anti-fascist resistance, might form government organs that would be loyal to socialism and friendly to the Soviet Union.

The governments of the USA and Britain wanted post-war Poland to follow the old bourgeois–landowner path. They were trying to bring about the return of the country's reactionary government in exile, and to this end were urging the Soviet Union to re-establish diplomatic relations which had been broken off on 25 April 1943 because of that government's openly anti-Soviet stance.

The policy pursued by Washington and London was manifested by the fact that, having broken an earlier agreement with the Soviet Union, the exile government effected the removal from Soviet territory of locally formed Polish army units. The Polish exile government also put forward absurd demands concerning the Polish–Soviet border. Roosevelt was the first to speak of this at the official sessions on the Polish question, but Churchill quickly gave him his most active support. How could he not? The Polish exile government was entrenched in London and enjoyed open British protection.

On the Polish question, Roosevelt clearly had one eye on the forthcoming presidential election, in which he wanted to gain the support of the seven million Polish Americans, many of whom had been influenced by widespread anti-Soviet propaganda in the USA. At the same time, Roosevelt was wary of Churchill's wish to impose a government on Poland that was blatantly hostile to the USSR. With good reason he believed that such an attempt could lead to a split in the Allied ranks. In an interview in the *New York Times* of 19 January 1944, the US ambassador to the USSR, Averell Harriman, dissociating himself from the Polish exile government's line, frankly observed: 'This government is deciding the future of Poland on the basis of a British and American struggle with Russia. I don't see that we have any interest in such a situation.' It was a statement that did him honour.

Were there good reasons for the Soviet Union to restore relations with the Polish exile government? On balance, no. Not only was that government carrying on hostile intrigues against us, but its policies were also increasingly diverging from the interests of Polish people, and in consequence it was steadily losing their support. Churchill and Roosevelt saw the recklessness of this and even tried to talk reason to the Polish government, but in vain. The reactionary Polish exiles were determinedly heading for the scrapheap.

The parties to Tehran also expressed their views on Poland's future borders. To demonstrate his ideas on where the borders between the USSR, Poland and Germany ought to be, Churchill used three matches, one for each.

'These matches,' he said, 'must be moved west in order to settle one of the main questions standing before us – the guarantee of the Soviet Union's western borders.'

It is worth noting that our legal right to such a guarantee was here recognised by Britain and the USA.

Seeking to clarify exactly how Churchill's matches could be applied to the issue, Stalin stated: 'The Soviet Union recognises the Soviet–Polish border of 1939 and regards this as just.'

The border he had in mind was the one which had been created by the reunification of western Belorussia and western Ukraine with the Belorussian and Ukrainian Soviet Republics, respectively.

The Tehran conference finally adopted the formula: 'the core of the Polish state and people must be located between the so-called Curzon Line and the River Oder.' These words incorporated the Soviet point of view, and it was also agreed in principle that Königsberg and its hinterland would be transferred to the Soviet Union.

Thus the Soviet Union at Tehran set the solution of the Polish question and its borders on a path that would satisfy both the interests of the Polish people and the needs of European and international security. We could not permit post-war Poland to be turned into a convenient bridgehead for anti-Soviet adventures. Stalin made this perfectly clear to Roosevelt and Churchill and they fully appreciated the logic of his position.

In order to strengthen the alliance and speed the end of the war,

Stalin then announced that the USSR would enter the war against Japan. In precise terms, he said: 'After Hitler's Germany has been destroyed, the Soviet Union will give the necessary help to the Allies in the war against Japan.'

Briefly but significantly, the Allies also discussed the outline of their post-war collaboration in securing a stable peace, and expressed in general terms their views on the creation of an international security organisation. No firm decisions were taken on this issue, but the idea of three-power collaboration for international peace found expression in the Tehran declaration: 'We are sure that the agreement between us guarantees a stable peace. We fully recognise the high responsibility that lies on us and on all the United Nations to bring about a peace that will meet the approval of the mass of the nations of the earth and that will eliminate the calamity and horrors of war for many generations to come.'

All the participants considered Tehran to have been necessary and useful. Most importantly, it fixed the date for opening the second front in France, thus shortening the war and reducing the loss of life. 'The mutual understanding we have reached here', as the declaration, signed by Roosevelt, Stalin and Churchill, stated, 'guarantees us victory.'

Churchill made an effective symbolic gesture at the conference by handing Stalin a sword of honour for the people of Stalingrad, sent by George VI as a token of the British people's respect.

On returning from Tehran, Roosevelt gathered his cabinet and told them with great warmth about the co-operation which had characterised the conference and about the contribution made by the Soviet delegation. The majority of Congress recognised the importance of the conference, and the newspapers prominently carried such headlines as 'Allies vow to make three-pronged attack' or 'Big Three reach full agreement in Tehran'.

Such discontented voices as there were were drowned in the general approval. It was in these circumstances that in December 1943 I first visited Cuba to present my credentials as envoy. We had established diplomatic relations with Cuba and I had to double up as envoy. Bad weather on the way back meant we had to stay overnight in Jacksonville, Florida. I remember it well, since it was New Year's Eve and the hotel owner, on learning that the Soviet ambassador and his wife were staying at his hotel, wanted to express his admiration of the Soviet army's victories, and, to

please us, he said, 'I've made a surprise for you: a Russian supper.'
You could call what we were served only relatively 'Russian', but
it was a sincere expression of American friendship for the Russian
people and we were touched.

After Tehran, Roosevelt was ill for a while, and so it was not
until early February 1944 that I had the chance to discuss with him
the results of the meeting of the Big Three.

He began by emphasising the good terms he was on with Stalin.
He then summarised how the conference had gone, and finally he
told me: 'To achieve agreement, it was often necessary to put
pressure on Churchill. He turns towards compromise rather
slowly, I'm afraid. But turn he did, and we reached some pretty
useful understandings.' As he talked about Churchill, the President
bestowed on me one of his charming 'Roosevelt' smiles and made
it plain that the British Prime Minister was a partner who gave
him plenty of trouble.

A little over a year after Tehran, the Big Three met again, this
time in February 1945, at the Livadiya Palace in Yalta, in the
Crimea, where the last of the Romanovs had once enjoyed sumptuous holidays.

Everything looked triumphant and majestic. Stalin entered the
conference hall with the Soviet delegation following behind.
Silence reigned. Roosevelt and Churchill were already in their
places. Stalin approached the table and greeted Churchill, who
had risen and come forward towards him, and then Roosevelt,
who could not rise quickly without help and remained sitting.

The first session dealt with military questions. Our delegation
included a group of military experts headed by deputy chief of
Red Army staff General Alexei Antonov. He had sessions with
his US and British counterparts on a daily basis to exchange
information and agree joint military actions, and at the first session
he reported on the Soviet–German front.

By this time the Allies had landed in Normandy, and a worrying
situation had arisen in January owing to a German breakthrough
in the Ardennes. Churchill had requested help from Stalin, as a
result of which the Soviet High Command had decided to speed
up their plans. Although Soviet troops were not yet fully prepared
to go over to the attack – a plan is a plan – the offensive was begun
on 12 January. Antonov reported that Soviet troops had fought
for eighteen days over a distance of 500 kilometres, that forty-five
German divisions had been destroyed, that the roads linking the

enemy's grouping in East Prussia with central Germany had been cut, and that the Germans had had to move troops from the western to the eastern front.

The news was impressive. The Soviet troops had provided considerable help to the Allies, and both Churchill and Roosevelt listened attentively. The Soviet general then proposed that the Allied advance in the west be speeded up, that they bomb the German columns and transports as they moved eastwards and that they prevent the enemy moving his troops out of Italy.

Roosevelt was listening intently, while Churchill puffed away on his cigar and never took his eyes off the speaker. Although the translation was not simultaneous, Churchill watched the speaker, not the translator.

When Stalin spoke, which as a rule he did briefly, his opinions often grated on the ears of the Western leaders. Although his phrases in themselves were not harsh, still less crude, and he was tactful, what he said made a powerful impression.

It was striking that, while Roosevelt reacted to Stalin's remarks calmly, even with understanding, Churchill did so with barely concealed irritation. The British Prime Minister tried not to show his feelings, but his cigars gave him away. He smoked far more of them when he was tense or excited. The number of his cigar stubs was in direct proportion to the stresses of the meeting. Everyone noticed it, and mocking remarks were made about it behind his back.

It should be said in fairness that Stalin had a liking for Roosevelt – which could not be said about his attitude towards the British Prime Minister. To some extent he may have been showing sympathy for the President's infirmity, but I and other Soviet officials were convinced that a more important reason for this difference of attitude had to do with the politics of the two Western leaders.

I cannot remember a single occasion at the conference when Stalin misheard or misunderstood a major statement from either of his two partners. His memory worked liked a computer and missed nothing. As never before, during the sessions in the Livadiya Palace, I came to realise just what extraordinary qualities this man possessed.

Stalin made sure that every member of the Soviet delegation was fully informed about what he regarded as the most important tasks facing the conference. He ran the work of the delegation with an assurance which conveyed itself to all of us, especially those sitting at the conference table.

Despite the lack of time, Stalin still found opportunities to talk with those within the delegation who were able, because of their position, to express a judgement or maintain contact with the Americans and British. These internal meetings varied in size, depending on the circumstances. On one occasion Stalin arranged a sort of cocktail party, during which he exchanged a few words with each member of the Soviet delegation, moving about slowly and with a pensive look on his face. From time to time he came to life and even made a joke. He knew everyone by sight; in fact, it was a matter of pride to him that he knew a great many people and could remember their names and often where he had met them. It would always impress.

Stalin moved on from group to group, stopping to ask questions. It was noticeable that he himself said very little, but listened attentively to what the others were saying. I had the feeling he was working all the time, preparing himself for the next meeting of the Big Three.

Approaching me, Stalin asked, 'What are the main social elements that Roosevelt can count on for support inside his country?'

I replied: 'The American President above all defends the interests of his own class, of course – the bourgeoisie. His domestic policies may encroach to some extent on the interests of the large monopolies, and right-wing extremists sometimes make the absurd accusation that he is sympathetic to socialism, but it's only a propaganda ploy by people who don't want the USA to have good relations with the USSR.' After a short pause, I summed up my answer: 'At the moment, Roosevelt as President has no rival. He feels secure.'

As far as I could judge, it was to these words that Stalin attended most of all.

Stalin also organised an official dinner for Churchill and Roosevelt to which the core personnel of the three delegations were also invited. There were not too many people present and one could hear everything anyone said. Naturally, everyone was keen to hear whatever the three leaders would say. Stalin was lively and made jokes, provoking friendly laughter which helped to produce a relaxed atmosphere. Major questions were not discussed during the dinner, and mostly the three leaders threw short, pithy comments back and forth. In essence, they were agreeing that they must secure a rapid end to the destruction being wrought by Hitler's army and do their best to see that Germany never rose again as an aggressor.

I do recall one of Stalin's less formal remarks during the dinner, however: 'History has recorded many meetings of statesmen following a war. When the guns fall silent, the war seems to have made these leaders wise, and they tell each other they want to live in peace. But then, after a little while, despite all their mutual assurances, another war breaks out. Why is this? It is because some of them change their attitudes after they have achieved peace. We must try to see that doesn't happen to us in the future.'

Roosevelt said, 'I agree with you entirely. The nations can only be grateful for your words. All they want is peace.'

At that moment, Churchill was in conversation with Molotov and so did not join in.

Everyone at the Yalta conference knew that the decisions taken in the Livadiya Palace had immense significance for the peaceful future of Europe. We felt we were at the focus of history and that Justice was standing by, scales in hand.

The three historic personalities, Stalin, Roosevelt and Churchill, together possessed immense power and influence. How much more they could have done, had there been sufficient agreement. Sadly, however, there were many questions on which they did not agree. The issue of German reparations to the USSR, in particular, was never resolved. Stalin and the rest of the Soviet delegation wondered what Roosevelt and Churchill were thinking when they dismissed this question. Didn't they realise that, if the Germans were made to pay even twenty or thirty billion dollars, it would represent no more than a drop in the ocean? The damage they had done to our country was later assessed at 2600 billion roubles, so were our allies perhaps thinking that the Soviet economy should not be allowed to recover too quickly?

Each of the three leaders spoke several times on this issue, the President less than the others. Although he was ready to admit the possibility of some nominal compensation, he could not name a sum. He also avoided direct confrontation with Churchill, who was not willing to concede even a symbolic gesture of reparations for the USSR.

When all three men had made their positions clear, Stalin leaned towards me and asked in a low voice: 'What should I make of

Roosevelt? Does he really disagree with Churchill, or is it just a ploy?'

A tricky question. Still, I gave him my opinion: 'There are differences between them, but one must be aware that he is correct in his behaviour towards the British Prime Minister. Even so, that same correctness would never stop him bringing unofficial pressure on Churchill. If he hasn't done this, I hardly think it's accidental.'

Stalin seemed to share my assessment. When the session was over and we were getting up, he said quietly, as if to himself, 'It's possible the USA and Britain have already agreed on this with each other.'

This suspicion was to be confirmed later, at the Potsdam conference, when the Americans joined the British in refusing to discuss Soviet reparations seriously and the USSR faced opposition from both powers. True, Roosevelt was not at Potsdam, his place having been filled by Truman. I doubt if Roosevelt's carefully vague remarks at Yalta caused his successor at Potsdam much difficulty.

Similarly, Churchill's position was endorsed by the Labour government which came to power in Britain during the Potsdam conference. Although the Labour leaders, Attlee and Bevin, had often spoken in the Soviet Union's favour about her terrible war losses, at Potsdam – now Prime Minister and Foreign Minister respectively – their vocabulary had altered and they were far more sparing in their generosity.

During the Yalta conference, Stalin was living in the old Yusupov Palace, in the village of Koreiz, a short distance from the Livadiya Palace. There he had his study where he received delegation members and held meetings. The ambassador to Britain, F.T. Gusev, and I had rooms in an adjoining wing and were often in Stalin's study.

In the early evening, and sometimes the morning too, General Antonov arrived to discuss the situation on the front. As a delegate I was present at one such meeting, and for the first time I was able to watch Stalin following the war news. It was obvious from his demeanour that he was pleased with the situation. He questioned Antonov about particular military formations and it became plain the plan of attack by our forces had already been drawn up and approved. Neither Antonov nor Stalin mentioned our losses, but clearly the enemy was retreating, and fast.

Stalin asked, 'How well equipped are our forces for the operations in Poland?'

Antonov had evidently foreseen this question: 'They have what they need. But it won't be easy – the enemy will put up desperate resistance, as he knows the loss of Poland will have disastrous consequences for the Nazi leadership.'

The military surveys gave us all a much needed boost. Serious political clashes had begun to take place in our meetings at the Livadiya Palace. One morning, before leaving Koreiz for Livadia, I was in my room and got a call to report to Stalin at once.

He was alone when I arrived in his study. I greeted him and asked, 'The beginning of the conference seems very tense – how are you feeling?'

Stalin replied, 'I feel perfectly normal.'

I realised he was worrying about other things than the state of his health. A special messenger had just delivered an urgent letter in English for him, and he handed it to me.

'This is from Roosevelt,' he said. 'I want to know what he says before the session begins.'

I gave him an impromptu translation and he occasionally asked me to repeat a phrase. The letter was about the Kurile Islands and Sakhalin. Roosevelt reported that the US government recognised the USSR's right to the half of the islands of Sakhalin and the Kuriles under Japanese occupation.

Stalin was very pleased. He paced the room, repeating, 'Good, very good!'

I observed: 'In the 1905 peace talks after the Russo-Japanese war the USA helped the Japanese to annex considerable Russian territory. But presumably this new US position rehabilitates them in our eyes, as it were, after the support they gave Japan then?'

He seemed to agree that America had 'rehabilitated' itself. After a few seconds, as he pondered the contents of the letter, he spoke his thoughts: 'This is an important letter. The Americans recognise the justice of our position on Sakhalin and the Kuriles. Now in return they will try to insist on our participation in the war against Japan. But that's another question altogether.'

I noticed that something else seemed to be bothering him. 'May I go now, Comrade Stalin?' I asked.

But he suddenly shot a question at me: 'Tell me, what do you think of Roosevelt? Is he clever?'

The question did not surprise me, as I knew I was not the first man he had asked. Also I knew from the many letters from Stalin I had passed to Roosevelt that even when Stalin did not take the same position as the President, he held him in high regard.

I replied: 'Comrade Stalin, Roosevelt is a highly intelligent, very capable man. Just the fact that he got himself elected President for a third and then a fourth term speaks for itself. Of course, he was helped by the international situation. And a lot of it was also due to the capable job the Democrats did in popularising his name. But his talks on the radio, his "Fireside Chats", also made a big impact on millions of Americans.'

Stalin remarked laconically: 'That was smart of him. Yes, he got everything right.'

He had what I would call a smile of solid satisfaction on his face. It was an expression I had noticed when he was feeling good, when the discussion was about someone to whom he was well disposed. As I left him, I had the feeling that his positive response to Roosevelt's letter would have an influence on the session that was to start in about an hour's time.

Certain significant events had led up to the letter. Already, back in Tehran, Roosevelt had asked Stalin about Soviet help in the war against Japan. It became apparent then that the opening of a second front by the Allies was being linked to the USSR's willing-ness to help the USA in the East. The USA and USSR reached an understanding in principle on that occasion, but it was not regarded as a firm agreement, and the final word on the question was not given until after Roosevelt's letter about Sakhalin and the Kuriles. That was why, in my opinion, Stalin was so pleased by Roosevelt's letter. Several times he walked across the room with it, as if he didn't want to let go of it, and he was still holding it when I left him.

That day I watched Stalin and Roosevelt with special attention. I thought they must both be thinking that they had bridged an important divide, and it may be that the position taken by the US President and his administration on Sakhalin and the Kuriles, as well as on the second front, to some extent explains Stalin's favourable attitude to Roosevelt as a person.

The conference also spent a lot of time on Poland's future frontiers and the composition of her government. It was decided that the frontier should follow the old Curzon Line, with some adjustment in Poland's favour. There was no serious disagreement over the need for Poland to acquire some territorial additions in the north and west, although there was disagreement over their extent.

The Soviet side proposed that Poland's western border be the Oder–Neisse line. However, the Americans and British opposed this on the dubious grounds that the Polish population would not be able to master the resources of the new territories, and the Yalta conference was thus unable to fix Poland's western frontier. This would be done plainly and decisively at Potsdam, thanks to the consistent position taken by the USSR.

Understandably, a sharp confrontation took place at Yalta over the composition of the Polish government, since the question concerned the political nature of a reborn Polish state in a strategically important part of Europe.

The Soviet Union took the view that a future Poland must not be governed by the people who had led her to a national catastrophe, but by the democratic forces that had fought against Hitler to free their country and restore Polish statehood. It was perfectly logical, therefore, that the USSR should recognise a provisional government in Poland that would represent the interests of the democratic forces. (On 21 April 1945 the Soviet Union concluded a treaty of friendship, mutual aid and post-war co-operation with that government.)

While not acknowledging the provisional government, the Western powers did at least see the impracticability of returning the exile government from London to Poland. Therefore at Yalta Roosevelt and Churchill proposed the dissolution of both the exile and the provisional governments and the formation of a new provisional government which would include the chief members of the reactionary government in exile. Both Western leaders defended this position stubbornly, aware that, though it represented for the West a rearguard action, it was an important one.

In seeking an understanding on this, the USSR was prepared to compromise: the USSR and the democratic forces of Poland agreed that the provisional government be supplemented with uncompromised politicians both from within Poland and from Polish exile circles. This became the basis of the resolution adopted at Yalta. The USA and Britain recognised the new government and withdrew recognition from the exile government, which then ceased to exist.

At the conference, Stalin made an announcement about the USSR's approach to Poland: 'Our concern is not simply that

Poland borders on our country, though that is important. The essence of the problem lies much deeper. Throughout history, Poland has served as a corridor for unfriendly armies to attack Russia. . . . Why have our enemies been able to pass through Poland so easily up to now? Above all, because Poland was weak. The Polish corridor cannot be physically closed by Russian forces from the outside . . . only . . . from the inside by Poland's own forces. And for that Poland must be strong. That is why the Soviet Union is interested in the creation of a strong, free and independent Poland.'

Then there came rumblings at the conference of difficulties over the creation of the United Nations. The conference at Dumbarton Oaks had decided many issues, but there was still the question of the veto and special rights for the permanent members of the Security Council. After discussion, the three leaders agreed that a conference be held in San Francisco on 25 April 1945 to settle the final text of the UN Charter.

As soon as the conference was over, the world learned that a central problem discussed at Yalta was the future of Germany. The three leaders had reached understanding on Germany's unconditional surrender and on laying the foundations for the democratisation and demilitarisation of the country. Prompted by the Soviet Union, the parties solemnly declared that it was not their aim to destroy the German people, but that only when German militarism and Nazism had been uprooted would the Germans be able to enjoy a peaceful, dignified life and take a respected place among the other nations.

The final conference document, 'Unity in the Organisation of Peace as in the Conduct of War', represented an agreement between the three leaders to preserve and strengthen in peacetime the collaboration that had existed during the war. The outcome of the conference meant the final collapse of Hitler's hopes for an Allied split. Instead it was the Third Reich that broke apart and was consumed in the flames of war.

There have been attempts now and then to present the decisions of the Yalta conference as if they were intended to carve Europe up into spheres of influence for the great powers. This is pure fantasy.

As if foreseeing the possibility of future slanders against the conference, President Roosevelt told the US Congress: 'This conference means the end of the system of unilateral action, closed alliances, spheres of influence and all the political intrigue that was indulged in for centuries.'

It was well said.

If they are objective about the conference, politicians today cannot but admit its historical importance for Europe and the world as a whole. The three powers agreed: to bring to an end Nazi Germany's violence; to convene a United Nations conference to create an international organisation for the preservation of peace; to establish in this new organisation the principle of unanimity of the powers through their permanent membership of the Security Council; to adopt a declaration to co-ordinate their actions in solving the problems of a liberated Europe. The three powers also agreed on the treatment of Germany after her unconditional surrender and on the just and immediate punishment of war criminals; on the creation in Germany of three special zones for the three powers, plus France; and on Far-Eastern questions.

German reparations to the USSR, the Polish question and Poland's borders were not finally agreed at Yalta, but the discussions there played their part, especially on the Polish question, which would be settled at Potsdam.

One can feel the anger in the statements of some Western politicians who claim that the USA and Britain made unjustified concessions to the USSR. They should read what their fathers and grandfathers said and wrote during the war in praise of the Soviet people's sacrifices for the sake of victory over the common enemy. The Soviet Union honestly carried out its duty as an ally, both on the battlefield and at the conference table.

7

Potsdam

It was a clear day. I was in San Francisco at work on the UN Charter. Foreign Commissar Molotov had already departed for Moscow, leaving me as head of delegation. I was suddenly called to the phone. The day was 9 May 1945.

'Mr Gromyko?'

'Yes, who is it?'

'Leopold Stokowski. I must congratulate you. Your great country has won victory over the Germans.'

We had all been waiting impatiently for this moment, yet it came unexpectedly. Leopold Stokowski was the first to call me.

And so it began. I remember Victory Day as a stream of congratulations from every side. All sorts of people rang up: Eugene Ormandy, Charlie Chaplin, diplomats, government officials, various public organisations and of course Russian emigrants who still had patriotic feelings.

A little later, Lydia Dmitrievna called me from Washington, her voice breaking with emotion: 'People haven't stopped coming. There's a long queue at the gate. Everyone's ecstatic. Thousands of people are congratulating us and hoping you'll go out and say something. We've told them you're in San Francisco, but they still say, "Let the Russians come out, we want to congratulate them."'

Clearly the whole world was aware of the colossal sacrifices the victory had cost us. And not only had the Soviet armed forces done their duty – Soviet diplomats had made their small contribution, too. Later, at a Kremlin reception in honour of army leaders, Stalin told them: 'Good foreign policy is worth two or three armies at the front.'

In the USA at that time, the great majority of Americans greeted Soviet citizens with great warmth. It is known now, however, that the US secret service, in the person of Allen Dulles, had been conducting separate peace talks in Switzerland with certain leaders of the Third Reich whose interests were represented by General Wolff. Hearing about these talks, Stalin sent the President a message expressing his indignation at the activities of the US special services, and on 12 April 1945 Roosevelt signed a message to Stalin in which he spoke of his firm intention to strengthen co-operation between the USSR and the USA. That was the last letter he wrote to Stalin, and the last he wrote in his life. He died later that evening, and so did not live to see the victory for which he had done so much.

A yawning gap, with enormous consequences for international affairs, appeared in American political life. Roosevelt's place was taken by Vice-President Truman and almost at once serious strains developed in Soviet–US relations.

On Victory Day President Truman appeared on American television. He spoke about the victory, but in an official, cold manner. The nation was rejoicing, the whole of America was triumphant, yet the face of the President was stony. It came as no surprise later when he and Churchill did their best to disrupt the good relations that had been built up during the war between the USA and USSR. After all, this was the self-same Harry Truman who, when Germany attacked the Soviet Union, had made a statement which became famous beyond his country's shores: 'If we see that Germany is winning the war, we should help Russia, but if Russia is winning we should help Germany, and let her kill as many Reds as possible.'

A sign of Roosevelt's goodwill towards the USSR had been to invite Molotov to attend the San Francisco conference in the spring of 1945. Molotov had accepted, but by the time he and I arrived Roosevelt was dead and it was Truman who received the Soviet guests. As ambassador I accompanied Molotov to the White House.

I had seen Truman only a few weeks before. Then he had been reasonably friendly, but now, as he talked to Molotov, he was harsh and his demeanour was cold. Before Roosevelt's death, Truman had wanted to create a good impression of himself in Moscow, but at the meeting with Molotov it was as if someone else had been put in his place. Whatever was suggested, whatever the topic of conversation, his attitude was negative and sometimes he seemed not even to be listening to us.

It was plain that he was not pleased with the results of Yalta as regards the UN and some of the principles of its operations. He was stridently pugnacious and found fault with practically everything said by us about the international organisation and the need to prevent aggression from Germany. Molotov had been instructed to raise with Truman the question of the forthcoming first session of the United Nations General Assembly, at which the USSR was prepared to speak in unison with the USA on some issues. The discussions never took place.

Quite unexpectedly – still in the middle of our talk – Truman suddenly half rose and gave a sign to indicate that the conversation was over, in effect breaking off the meeting. We left.

In analysing that meeting, one might conclude that Truman had behaved in this way because, as he now bore the highest office, he had been informed that America had just become the only country in the world to possess a new weapon of terrifying destructive power, the atom bomb. With this weapon in America's hands, Truman evidently felt he could dictate terms to the Soviet Union.

Stalin was of course informed of the meeting, but he never referred to it in my presence. I am, however, convinced that he took a very unfavourable view of Roosevelt's successor, a man who felt and did nothing to hide his hostility to the power which had borne the heaviest sacrifices in the war against the common enemy.

As soon as Nazi Germany had been defeated, there arose the practical need to take stock of the situation by convening another conference of the three Allied leaders. A progressive mood was growing in Europe and throughout the world. The conference took place at Potsdam, in the still-smoking ruins of the Third Reich, and as ambassador to the USA I was a delegate. It was an especially important event in my political life.

A great amount of preparatory work was necessary before the conference, and I went to Moscow to do my share. Stalin and the Soviet leadership mapped out our country's main aims, paying particular attention to the more obvious controversies which would arise. Thus the Soviet delegation was well prepared and we set off for Potsdam determined to seek agreement.

Truman represented the USA. For Stalin personally he was a

totally unknown figure. Naturally Churchill knew Truman better, and from the opening days of the conference, for as long as Churchill was still taking part, it was noticeable that he and Truman understood each other almost intuitively. During the conference Churchill was replaced by Attlee; but the new Labour government fully adopted the line taken by Churchill, and Truman and Attlee easily found a common language.

It is worth recalling some aspects of the conference. Although some of its foreign participants have already written about it, there are inaccuracies in their accounts.

As Potsdam was located in the Soviet zone of occupation, all the logistics and security for the delegates were our concern. The Soviet delegation was housed in Babelsberg, a small town a few minutes' drive from Potsdam and a former residence of the German kings. The conference itself took place in the Cecilienhof Palace. When all the Soviet delegates had assembled, Stalin looked the place over, the staircases and corridors, and commented: 'Hmm, nothing much. A modest palace. Russian tsars built themselves something much more solid!'

The entire route from Babelsberg to Cecilienhof was lined with security guards, soldiers placed at six-yard intervals. In addition, fifty yards beyond these men was a further line of guards, spaced further apart.

Stalin frequently invited Molotov to travel in his car. He also invited me, usually because he had questions for me about Truman, the mood of American political circles and so on. At first, when Stalin sat in the folding-seat of his ZIS, while Molotov and I were given the main back seat, I felt somewhat awkward; but I later discovered that Stalin actually preferred that seat, since it was in the middle of the vehicle and he found it less bumpy.

At every crossing and in all the squares there were Soviet women traffic police with flags. They were immaculately dressed in new army uniforms of a very fine cut, and in all their movements they were so graceful that they could almost have passed for ballet dancers. We were told that the American and British delegates found them as delightful as we did.

Both at Yalta and at Potsdam I worked close to Stalin and I would like to describe some aspects of his dealings with people through the prism of the conferences. My impressions of Stalin at meetings, my general observations of him, the episodes that have stuck in my mind, either from the conferences or during conversations with foreign officials visiting the Soviet Union – all these come together to form my image of the man as I then saw him. On the other hand, I do not set out to define what Stalin was. I just observed him while I was doing my job, and my impressions of him were secondary to the work in hand. I therefore do not want to present my view of him as a complete or incontrovertible truth.

At Yalta Roosevelt became ill and the session was deferred for the day. Stalin wanted to visit him and he asked Molotov and me to accompany him. We went to the President's rooms on the first floor of the Livadiya Palace where the empress had once slept. The window opened on to a beautiful view of the sea.

The President was delighted to see us, as he was confined to his bed and had hardly any visitors. He was clearly tired and drained, though he tried not to show it. We sat with him for maybe twenty minutes, while he and Stalin exchanged polite remarks about health, the weather and the beauties of the Crimea. We left him when it seemed that Roosevelt had become detached, strangely remote, as if he could see us, yet was gazing somewhere into the distance.

We were descending the narrow staircase when Stalin suddenly stopped, took his pipe out of his pocket, filled it unhurriedly and, as if to himself, said quietly, but so that we could hear: 'Why did nature have to punish him so? Is he any worse than other people?'

Despite his basic harshness of character, Stalin did just occasionally give way to positive human emotions.

Next day Roosevelt was back to normal and the sessions restarted, though the fatigue did not leave his face throughout the conference. He had only two months to live.

I repeat: Stalin sympathised with Roosevelt the man and he made this clear to us. He rarely bestowed his sympathy on anybody from another social system, and spoke of it more rarely still.

Naturally, everyone in Stalin's entourage or who worked closely with him took pains to observe him closely, catching his every word and gesture. After all, the more imposing the thundercloud, the more warily one watches it. For his contemporaries, to be in Stalin's company, still more to talk to him or to be present during a conversation, was something special. One was aware how much depended on the will of this man.

This in one way contradicts the Marxist view of the role of personality in history. Outstanding personalities are the product of conditions in a particular time. On the other hand, these people can and do influence the course of events and the development of society. Marx, Engels and later Lenin all based their philosophical works on a recognition of this.

What was the most striking thing about Stalin at first sight? In whatever situation, the first thing that one was aware of was that he was a thinking man. I never heard him say anything that was not precisely relevant to the matter in hand. He did not like preambles, long sentences or verbose speeches. On the other hand, he was patient with people who, because of a lack of education, found it hard to order their thoughts neatly.

I was always aware, watching Stalin speaking, of how expressive his face was, especially his eyes. When rebuking or arguing with someone, Stalin had a way of staring him mercilessly in the eyes and not taking his gaze off him. The object of this relentless stare, one has to admit, felt profoundly uncomfortable.

If he was seated when speaking, he was apt to shift his weight from one side to the other, sometimes emphasising a thought with a movement of the hand, though in general he used gestures sparingly. He spoke quietly, evenly, almost as if muffled, and raised his voice rarely. Even so, whenever he spoke there was total silence, however many people were there. His speeches had an original style. His thinking consisted of precisely formulated, non-standard ideas.

As for foreign officials, he did not exactly pamper them with his attention. If only for that reason, seeing and hearing Stalin was regarded by them as a major event.

Stalin was always unhurried in his movements. I never saw him increase his pace, and it seemed to me that time itself slowed down when he was at work.

Very often at small meetings, while someone was giving a report, Stalin would simply pace the room, listening and making comments as he did so. He would walk a few paces, stop, look at the speaker and the others in the room, maybe go closer to gauge their reactions, and then recommence pacing. Then he would go and sit at the head of the table, and remain there, quite still, for several minutes, which meant he was waiting to see what impression the speech was making on the others. Or he would ask: 'What do you think?' Those present would try to answer briefly, avoiding superfluous words.

It was noticeable that Stalin never carried a file of papers with

him, whatever kind of meeting he was attending, including the
international conferences. I never saw him with a pencil or pen in
his hand. He was never seen to make notes. Whatever materials
he needed he kept in his study. He worked at night, and was
generally more friendly at night than during the day.

He always turned up for a session of the international conferences prepared. When the delegation went with him, they knew
what he would speak about. He did almost all the talking for the
Soviet Union. His chief support on foreign affairs was Molotov.
When necessary, Stalin would lean over and consult with a member of the delegation before speaking.

I recall an occasion when the discussion was about the stubborn-
ness of the German resistance towards the end of the war, when
even a blind man could see it was all over for the fascists. Several
people had something to say on this. Stalin listened to each one
and then, as though summing up a debate, he said: 'That's all
true, I agree. But still, one must recognise one characteristic that
Germans have, and that they have shown in more than one war,
and that is the doggedness and determination of the German
soldier.'

Then he added: 'History shows that the most dogged soldier of
all is the Russian; then comes the German, and in third place . . .'
He paused before he said: '. . . the Pole, the Polish soldier, yes,
the Pole.'

Stalin's assessment made a big impression on me. The German
army was by then virtually destroyed. One would have expected
him to describe this army of aggressors, rapists, pillagers and
hangmen in the harshest terms. Yet Stalin had set the German
soldier in an unemotional historical context.

Stalin was one of those few leaders who would never allow bad
news from the front to obscure his assessment of the facts, or his
faith in the party, the people and his armed forces. It later transpired, however, that the stress and the colossal difficulties of the
war had taken their toll on Stalin's health, and one can only be
amazed that, despite it all, he lived to see the victory.

Did Stalin take care of his health? It struck me that he always
looked tired, but I never saw a doctor with him throughout all
the Allied conferences. I don't think it was bravado on his part.
He simply didn't like the long walks which the doctors invariably
prescribed. As for his appearance, he was of medium height. His
perfectly tailored marshal's uniform suited him, and he seemed to

like wearing it. If he wasn't wearing uniform, then it would be something in between uniform and civilian dress. Sloppiness in dress was not in his nature.

Stalin's face was rather podgy. I often heard it said that he bore the scars of smallpox, but I don't recall ever seeing any, and I was close to him many times. It was not true that he was prone to put on weight easily. Of course, as a man who did no physical labour, he had a tendency that way, but he was careful to curb it. At table, I never saw Stalin over-active with the knife and fork; one could say he ate rather slowly and sparingly. He did not drink spirits, but he liked dry wine and always opened the bottle himself, first studying the label carefully, as if judging its artistic quality.

People often asked about his attitude to art and literature, and my own impression is that he loved music. He enjoyed the concerts arranged in the Kremlin, especially singers with strong voices, male or female, whom he would applaud vigorously. I personally saw how during the Potsdam conference, in full view of everyone, he kissed the violinist Barinov and the pianist Gilels, who played beautifully after the official dinner, and he was moved also by certain singers at the Bolshoi, men like Ivan Kozlovsky.

I recall that once, when Kozlovsky was performing, some Politburo members loudly requested a folk-song. Calmly, Stalin intervened: 'Why put pressure on Comrade Kozlovsky? Let him sing what he wants. And I think he wants to sing Lensky's aria from *Eugene Onegin*.'

Everyone laughed, including Kozlovsky, who immediately sang Lensky's aria.

As for his taste in literature, I can state that he read a great deal. This came out in his speeches: he had a good knowledge of the Russian classics, especially Gogol and Saltykov-Shchedrin. Also, to my own knowledge, he had read Shakespeare, Heine, Balzac, Hugo, Guy de Maupassant – whom he particularly liked – and many other western European writers. It was also apparent that he had read a lot of history, as he often quoted examples that could only have come from historical sources.

It has been justly remarked that in his behaviour Stalin was always correct. There was never any familiarity or slapping on the back, which sometimes passes for geniality. Even when he was angry – which I have seen – he never exceeded the permitted limits, and he rarely swore.

I do remember, however, an episode that took place in 1950,

when the puppet government of South Korea was being egged on by the USA to start war on North Korea. The outbreak of war in Korea created serious international tension, since everyone realised it could lead to a wider conflict.

One day before the Security Council was convened, Moscow was deciding what position the Soviet representative should take, and, further, whether the Soviet delegation should even take part in the session, when the USA had written a letter to the Security Council that was both insulting and an open provocation.

Having read a cable from Ya. A. Malik, the Soviet UN representative in New York, Stalin phoned me in the evening: 'Comrade Gromyko, what instruction do you think we should send on this?'

I said: 'Comrade Stalin, the Foreign Ministry has already prepared an instruction for your approval. The main points are a decisive rejection of the rebukes directed at North Korea and the Soviet Union, and an equally decisive condemnation of the USA for its part in unleashing aggression. Secondly, if the Security Council introduces a motion against North Korea or the Soviet Union, or both, Malik must use the right of veto and prevent the vote.'

I waited for Stalin's reaction. He said, 'In my view, the Soviet delegation should not attend the Security Council session.'

He added some sharp comments about Washington's hostile letter to the UN. Even so, I felt obliged to draw his attention to an important consideration: 'In the absence of our representative, the Security Council will be able to do what it likes, including sending troops to South Korea from other countries under the guise of being UN forces.'

But my argument made no impression on him. He was not going to change his mind, and he actually dictated the instruction himself – something he did very rarely. Forty minutes later the text was transmitted to Malik.

As is well known, my warning to Stalin was justified. The Council passed a resolution cobbled together by Washington, and military units from various countries were sent to South Korea under the label of 'UN forces'. On this occasion, Stalin, guided for once by emotion, had not made the best decision.

Stalin liked people with wit. He himself used this weapon economically. I never heard from anyone, during his lifetime or after, that he abused it. But he also liked people who thought logically, and was impatient if he gave an order and got an immediate, unthinking response.

For example, while on holiday in the south of the country, he once gave one of his security officers the order: 'Get me Ras Kasa on the phone at once.'

The officer immediately responded, 'Very good!', and rushed off to carry out the order.

Ras Kasa was one of the Ethiopian chiefs who at that time was putting up tough resistance in the war against the Italians, but there was simply no telephone line to his mountain fastness in Ethiopia. So after a while the young security man, half dead with worry, returned.

Hopping from one foot to another, he reported: 'Comrade Stalin, there's no way we can get through to Ras Kasa, as he's somewhere in the mountains of Ethiopia.'

Stalin had a good laugh and said: 'And you're still working in security?'

Another, sadder example. A little while after Stalin's death, I was in Molotov's study and he told me about Stalin's last moments.

'The members of the Politburo went to see Stalin, having heard he was not well. In fact, he was very ill. One day during his illness, we were standing by his bedside: Malenkov, Khrushchev, myself and other members of the Politburo. Stalin kept falling into semi-consciousness, then coming round again, but he was unable to say anything.

'At one moment,' Molotov went on, 'he suddenly came to himself, and half opened his eyes. Seeing familiar faces, he then pointed slowly at the wall. We all looked where he was pointing. On the wall there was a photograph with a simple subject: a little girl feeding a lamb with milk through a horn. With the same slow movement of his finger, Stalin then pointed to himself. It was his last act. He closed his eyes never to open them again. Those present took it as a typical example of Stalin's wit – the dying man was comparing himself with a lamb.'

Khrushchev described Stalin's last moments in virtually the same words.

I have decided to express my thoughts on Stalin, firstly, because I was his contemporary, and have seen him in many different situations during and after the war, and, secondly, because people rightly ask what attitude to take to him, since he had so many confusing qualities.

Stalin will provoke controversy for decades, if not centuries. A man of large calibre, he successfully held the Communist Party together after Lenin's death, and for a further thirty years played a determining role as the leader of a great power facing momentous tasks. Red Army men and partisans died with his name on their lips.

However, it is wrong to see only his positive side, since he was a tragically contradictory figure. On the one hand, he was a man of powerful intellect, a leader with the unshakeable determination of the revolutionary, and also the ability to find common understanding with our wartime allies. On the other hand, he was a harsh man who did not count the human cost of achieving his aims, and who created a monstrously arbitrary state machine that sent multitudes of innocent Soviet people to their deaths.

The names of his victims must never be forgotten. General Secretary Gorbachev spoke with great force about Stalin at the ceremonial session celebrating the seventieth anniversary of the October revolution, and his words expressed the thoughts and feelings of the Soviet people. The Soviet nation feels justified anger against Stalin for the tyranny he exercised over utterly innocent people. Beside his mass of crimes, the worst evils of Russia's past autocrats and their henchmen pale into insignificance. The snake of Stalinism slowly stifled its victims, using the most cunning ploys and attacking with equal lack of mercy the worthy representatives of the Bolshevik Old Guard and ordinary Soviet citizens, workers, peasants, intellectuals, communists and non-party people. No wonder those who survived are still angry.

But this should not be allowed to overshadow our nation's achievements, in both war and peace. These achievements are great, and they were accomplished despite Stalin's monstrous crimes. Justice demands that we see the dark pages, but also the heroic pages of our history.

The day before the Potsdam conference opened, our military suggested to Gusev and myself that we take a tour of Berlin, which was something we had already decided we very much wanted to do.

Now, on the ground, we observed the ruined capital of Hitler's Reich, and there were precious few undamaged or even half-destroyed buildings to be seen. Only some of the smaller houses in the outlying districts remained unscathed. I remember the difficulty our jeep had in negotiating the Unter den Linden, littered as it was along its entire length by collapsed walls. There were bricks, mountains of bricks everywhere.

Our officer escorts suggested we take a look first of all at the Führer's former Chancellery. We reached it with some difficulty, as the route was obstructed by fallen buildings, tangled masses of girders and concrete blocks. Our jeep could not drive right up to the Chancellery building, so we had to walk the last lap.

Every step of the way was guarded by Soviet sentries who courteously passed us along the line to each other right up to the grand entrance, though there was nothing very grand about it now, as the building had been practically destroyed by the bombardment. There were still some walls standing, albeit riddled with countless bullet-holes and yawning shell-holes. Only fragments of the ceilings remained, and the windows gaped black.

The Chancellery made a strange first impression. The architects seem to have incorporated an air of diabolical severity, intended to inspire a feeling of reverence and fear. One could have no positive reaction to the building. We were told by many Germans that it had been a gloomy place even before it was destroyed. If one drastically reduced it in scale in one's mind's eye, keeping the proportions as they were, this Hitlerite citadel would resemble an ancient tomb.

We passed through halls which Hitler and his henchmen had used for gatherings and ceremonies. For some reason, apart from its floor and ceiling, the main hall had been less damaged. The doors, windows and chandeliers, as in most of the other rooms, bore signs of the battle and most of them had been broken.

We descended into the underground part of the building, which went down several floors, on one of which we found an auxiliary electric generator. Our escort commented: 'The whole of Berlin could have been plunged in darkness, but here the lights would still be burning.'

The lower floors presented a scene of chaos. Evidently the Chancellery garrison had put up a desperate fight, and many shells, bombs and grenades had found their target here. The place was littered with fallen iron and wooden girders and ceiling supports and huge lumps of concrete.

Along both sides of the narrow corridor were compartments of some sort that had been distorted by explosions. The corridor itself seemed to stretch the entire length of the building, and as one made one's way through it, on duck-boards, one had to be careful not to fall into the water, which was quite deep. No doubt a shell had hit the water main.

The whole thing induced a gloomy and depressing feeling. Photographs of this underground chaos, if they exist, would make a fitting illustration for Dante's *Inferno*.

It was with a feeling of great relief that we emerged from that building, reminiscent of a gun-emplacement and so recently the lair of the chief fascist criminal himself, and filled our lungs with fresh air.

We were then taken to see another sight – Hitler's bunker. If one were looking for a monument to symbolise a curse on everything criminal and anti-human that was associated with the Nazis then the ruins of that bunker would do perfectly.

Cylindrical in form, some nine metres high and five metres or so in diameter, it appeared to have been carved out of solid rock. The entrance led down into a cellar full of water. Shapeless lumps of reinforced concrete blocked the path from one part of the bunker to another. I had the feeling our troops had done a good job in destroying the madman's last hiding-place. Powerful explosions had dug deep craters all around the bunker.

The scene of the ruined Chancellery and the bunker, embodying as it were the collapse of Nazi Germany and its criminal regime, made an indelible impression on us.

We were also taken to a place alleged to be Goebbels's house, though practically nothing was left of it. The Soviet officers told us that when the corpses of Goebbels's six children were found in the cellar of the Chancellery, they were brought out on to the street. Soon after, they found the bodies of Goebbels and his wife not far from the bunker. All the corpses were laid in a row and covered up. Only a restricted number of people were allowed to view and identify them.

It is hard to convey the depressing, eerie feeling all this created in me. Before committing suicide, the fascist big-mouth had given orders for his wife and children to be exterminated. The murderer-mother tells her children: 'Don't be afraid, the doctor's going to give you an injection that they give to all children and soldiers.' On Magda Goebbels's orders, the Nazi doctors give the children an injection of morphine, the children become semi-conscious, and Frau Goebbels slips a capsule of potassium cyanide into each of their mouths, breaking it first. Then she kills herself.

There are few crimes in history that compare in sheer moral decay and harshness with what that pair of murderers did. Like scorpions in a tight corner, they stung themselves to death.

After my tour of the ruins of Berlin, I came to the Potsdam conference table with impressions of destruction still fresh in my mind.

Now that the enemy had laid down his arms, one would have expected the atmosphere at Potsdam to be triumphant; but instead protocol reigned. The heads of delegation greeted each other and expressed their proper pleasure at meeting, but at the round table there was not the warmth that the world wanted to see and that the sacrifice of the fallen demanded.

The conference sessions were chaired by each head of delegation in turn. From the outset, the US President and the British Prime Minister showed caution and coldness, and the further we progressed, the plainer this became. On almost every main question there was disagreement: for most of the time, the talks were tense, and although nobody actually banged the table, it was clear to all that the path to understanding would be a stony one, and that some questions might not be agreed at all. Throughout the talks Stalin and the Soviet delegation showed respect to their partners, and tried to introduce a feeling of trust. To some extent this softened the harsh atmosphere created by the other two delegations.

We in the Soviet delegation watched Truman intently. After all, although he had exchanged messages with Stalin, he had not yet had to discuss questions of principle at this high level. We wanted to see what made him tick, what were Washington's aims in Europe, especially in Germany, and what was their foreign policy in general.

Our common opinion finally was that Truman had come with the aim of conceding as little as possible to the USSR and of maximising the possibilities for tying Germany in to the Western economy. In his opinion, for example, Roosevelt had given too much to Stalin at Yalta on the German reparations question: he viewed potential agreement only within that framework, and it goes without saying that in this respect Churchill was his trusted ally.

Long before the conference, the USA had been making intense efforts to develop the atom bomb, and later, when many facts pertaining to its invention were made public, the behaviour of Truman and Churchill at Potsdam became clear. The US Secretary for War, Stimson, wrote in his memoirs that Washington had thought it essential to delay deciding post-war European and other problems until the USA had the trump of the nuclear weapon in its hand.

Certainly, until the timetable for making the bomb had been met, the American President tried to delay the Potsdam meeting, and it was in fact postponed at his request from June to July. He waited impatiently for the results of the test and when he finally got them – on 16 July 1945, secretly, just one day before the opening of the conference – he obviously felt he would be able to take a tough line in the talks.

This was immediately apparent in the initial discussions on eastern Europe. Truman loudly made the unsubstantiated claim that the Soviet side had not fulfilled the obligations agreed by the three powers in the Crimea. We firmly rejected this assertion, as well as Washington's attempts to interfere in eastern Europe which reflected its expansionist ambitions there and in other areas of the world.

The US side was therefore compelled to recognise that, without the bomb as an open political factor, in effect as blackmail, nothing would come of their tough stand. Accordingly, a few days later, on 24 July, as Stalin was making his exit after the session, the President held him back and said: 'I have something to tell you in confidence.'

Stalin stopped and waited. Truman said, 'The United States has built a new weapon of great destructive power which we intend to use against Japan.'

Stalin took the news calmly, showing no emotion – a reaction which apparently disappointed Truman.

Very soon afterwards, however, a meeting took place in Stalin's residence at Potsdam which has etched itself in my mind. Only Stalin, Molotov, Gusev (the Soviet ambassador to Britain) and I were present. When we entered, Stalin and Molotov were waiting, and it was evident they had already been discussing the questions to be raised with us two ambassadors.

Stalin's first question was: 'Well, what about German reparations to the Soviet Union?'

Molotov immediately jumped in and reminded him in broad outline of what the Allies had said on this topic at the end of the Yalta conference. He spoke harshly about Churchill's position: 'Churchill has obviously made up his mind not to allow any agreement on this. I still think we have to raise the question again at Potsdam, and insist categorically on a realistic level of compensation for the appalling damage done to our economy.'

Stalin agreed: 'Britain's position, and America's, for that matter, is unjust. It's not the way allies should behave. The USSR is being cheated, cheated because the Americans have already shipped out the best equipment, complete with all its documentation, for the various technical laboratories in the sector occupied by Anglo-American forces. I don't know what Roosevelt's attitude would have been had he been alive, but Truman doesn't even know the meaning of justice. So the question of reparations must be discussed at Potsdam. It is of fundamental importance.'

Molotov asked me for my opinion and I told him I considered the Soviet position well founded and convincing, and in my view it should be defended at Potsdam. Stalin then raised the matter which turned out to be the main point of our meeting.

'Our allies have told us that the USA has a new weapon, the atom bomb. I spoke with our own physicist, Kurchatov, as soon as Truman told me they had tested it successfully. We will no doubt have our own bomb before long. But its possession places a huge responsibility on any state. The real question is, should the countries which have the bomb simply compete with each other in its production, or should they, and any other countries that acquire it later, seek a solution that would mean the prohibition of its production and use? It's hard at this moment to see what sort of agreement there could be, but one thing is clear: nuclear energy should only be allowed to be used for peaceful purposes.'

Molotov agreed and added: 'And the Americans have been doing all this work on the atom bomb without telling us.'

Stalin said tersely: 'Roosevelt clearly felt no need to put us in the picture. He could have done it at Yalta. He could simply have told me the atom bomb was going through its experimental stages. We were supposed to be allies.'

It was noticeable that, even though Stalin was annoyed, he spoke calmly. He continued: 'No doubt Washington and London are hoping we won't be able to develop the bomb ourselves for some time. And meanwhile, using America's monopoly, in fact America's and Britain's, they want to force us to accept their plans on questions affecting Europe and the world. Well, that's not going to happen!' And now, for once, he cursed in ripe language. A broad grin appeared on the face of my good friend Gusev.

Of course, Stalin did not touch on the scientific or technical aspects of the problem. But it is widely known that, while in Potsdam, he contacted Moscow several times to give instructions to the experts on this matter.

When later I weighed up what Stalin had said, I came to the inescapable conclusion that, even though he had seemed to speak lightly, his words must be regarded as the backbone of Soviet nuclear policy for many years to come.

Gusev and I were about to leave when Stalin put another question, which had no direct relation to politics: 'What do our ambassadors think about the organisation of the conference? Are our allies satisfied with the arrangements?' Of course, it was the second part of the question he was most interested in.

I replied: 'The Americans, of whom I've seen more than the British, for obvious reasons, have said more than once that the entire conference has been well organised. There have been no incidents, although the British have given a hint worth mentioning. Churchill was so riveted by our women traffic police, in their marvellous uniforms, that he dropped his cigar-ash all over his suit, but he suffered no further injury.'

Stalin smiled, possibly for the first time during the meeting.

I should now like to touch on some other aspects of the Potsdam conference which have been dealt with inaccurately in Western sources.

The Polish question aroused heated discussion, as it had at Yalta. All three leaders knew it would come up, and so it did, almost every day.

Shortly before the conference opened, a Provisional Polish Government of National Unity, headed by Edward Osobka-Morawski, had been formed in accordance with the decisions at

My birthplace in Old Gromyki

My parents

My parents in 1914 with myself and my sister Evdokia

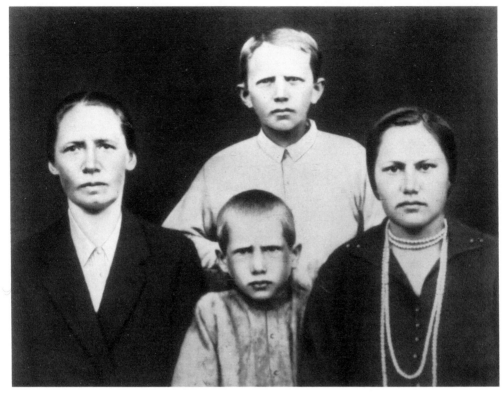

My mother in 1931 with Fedor (born 1922, died on the Front in 1943), Dmitri (born 1917, wounded in the war, and died in 1978) and Evdokia, now living in Gomel

Aged 20, in 1930, with Lydia, then aged 17

As a student in Minsk in 1931

With Lydia in 1942 in Washington

Anatoly and Emilia in 1943 during our time in Washington

Washington 1944, with A.A. Sobolev (left) and Golunsky (Soviet diplomats in Washington)

LEFT Edward G. Robinson

RIGHT With Paul Robeson
in Washington in 1945

BELOW RIGHT I met Charlie
Chaplin in London in 1954.
Here he accepts the
European Cultural
Foundation's Erasmus
Prize in Amsterdam, 1965

The Yalta conference.
V.M. Molotov, Winston S.
Churchill (I am to
Churchill's right) and
Franklin D. Roosevelt
salute on their arrival at
Simferopol in 1945

The Conference begins. I
am seated two along from
Stalin's left

Stalin and Roosevelt
during the discussions.

The negotiating table at Potsdam

The Potsdam Conference. On the left is Postoev, the interpreter. Golunsky is standing, in uniform

BELOW Chairman of
Supreme Soviet (i.e., Head
of State) Mikhail Kalinin
conferring on me the
Order of Lenin

TOP I stand behind Harry S. Truman and James Byrnes

ABOVE With Stalin and Truman at Potsdam

With Dmitri Manuilsky, permanent UN representative of the Ukraine government (*left*), and Earl Warren, governor of California

The Big Five at the San Francisco conference later in the year. I am on the top right

With Ernest Bevin in 1946 when he was Foreign Secretary (I was then Deputy Foreign Minister)

LEFT August 1952. With equerry (probably) on my way to present my credentials to the Queen, after my appointment as Soviet ambassador to London

ABOVE Travelling by coach to Buckingham Palace. In all it took three coaches for full protocol to be observed

With Ho Chi Minh in 1957. Kliment Voroshilov sits betwe

With Zhou Enlai in China in 1957. The man in glasses i
Topolev, the aircraft designer

In China with Khrushchev in 1959. Liu Xiaoqi sits to Mao's left, while on my ri
is Mikhail Suslov, on my left Alexei Antonov

With Dwight D. Eisenhower in the White House at the time of Suez in 1956

I met Gamal Abdel Nasser on several occasions. This meeting was in 1969, at his presidential palace in Cairo

Dean Rusk sees the joke, New York 1965

With Maurice Couve de Murville in 1965

With General Charles de Gaulle in 1966

Chancellor Konrad Adenauer, aged 86, in 1962

With Jawaharlal Nehru in India, 1960

After the tea ceremony, Kyoto 1966

After addressing the UN General Assembly on the strengthening of international security and on the prohibition of chemical weapons, September 1969

Alone for once

Yalta, and, while the USA and Britain had been compelled to establish diplomatic relations with it, they were dragging their feet over dissolving the Polish government in exile.

Detailed discussions concerning the formation of the provisional government took place, and the conference noted the views of an invited Polish delegation, headed by Boleslaw Bierut. The three powers then accepted a resolution expressing their satisfaction at the creation of the provisional government. The resolution also stated that the establishment of diplomatic relations between the USA and Britain and the Polish provisional government terminated their recognition of the former Polish government in London, which in fact no longer existed.

This was clearly in Poland's interest, since it facilitated the consolidation of the provisional government's position. Among the members of that government, however, were some, like S. Mikolajczyk, who did not merit the nation's confidence. Ignoring Poland's national interests, they would take a path which led to total political bankruptcy.

Realising that consolidation of the provisional government in Poland had dashed their hopes of turning that country into a 'cordon sanitaire' against the Soviet Union, the USA and Britain then tried to evade a Potsdam decision on the location of Poland's western border. They did not succeed. Thanks to Stalin's arguments for a border along the Oder–Neisse line, and the weighty reasoning of the Polish delegation which manifestly demonstrated the justice of their case in terms of history, economics and security, and also taking into account the situation on the ground in the territories which had been ceded to Poland, Churchill and Truman finally agreed that the Oder–Neisse line should be accepted as Poland's western border.

Even so, their agreement was conditional upon the Soviet delegation's acceptance of their positions on German reparations, and these became one of the most contentious issues at the conference. The Soviet case for compensation was more than well founded. From the northern Caucasus, the Volga, Moscow and Leningrad to the western frontier lay a zone of virtually scorched earth, ruined cities and villages, piles of bricks and twisted metal where factories and office buildings and apartment blocks had stood. More than that, Hitler's Luftwaffe had also bombed towns that lay between Moscow and the Urals, and it all had to be rebuilt, in many cases from the ground up. Yet neither Churchill nor Attlee nor Truman was prepared to acknowledge the Soviet position; they insisted that Germany should not have to pay reparations.

During a break, Stalin said privately to his own delegation: 'The English and the Americans want to throttle us. But never mind, we got through the civil war – we'll get through this too.'

As a result of the talks, however, the USSR did make definite concessions on reparations and thus made possible agreement on Poland's new western border, as it had been proposed by the Polish delegation. Thus, for the first time in her history, the problem of Poland's state frontiers was finally and justly settled. The inviolability of this frontier later received ratification in international law in the treaties between Poland and East Germany (1950) and West Germany (1970), the Soviet–West German treaty (1970) and the Final Act of the Meeting on European Security and Co-operation (1975).

Our side was less successful, however, in achieving agreements on the democratisation, demilitarisation and de-Nazification of a united Germany. In promoting the idea of Bizonia, then Trizonia, and then a separate West German state, Washington, London and, in due course, Paris all showed that they did not want a united, genuinely democratic, demilitarised Germany. Later Soviet proposals along these lines were unfailingly rejected. As a result, after a number of intermediate stages, two independent German states emerged, the GDR and the FRG.

Today, in the countries which were our allies during the war, there are people who argue for the reunification of the two Germanys, and they attack the USSR for opposing such unification. They are being dishonest. What they really want is for West Germany to swallow up East Germany. They know perfectly well that it was the Western powers who crudely broke the spirit and the letter of the Potsdam agreement on the future of Germany by drawing West Germany into NATO.

All Germans, wherever they live, should remember that the Soviet Union never wanted the dismemberment of Germany. It was the USA and Britain who at the three-power Allied conferences proposed tearing Germany apart.

The Potsdam conference did not consist only of talks. The heads of delegation arranged various events to show their mutual respect, such as luncheons and dinners, souvenir photographs, and at all of them Stalin, Truman, Churchill and then Attlee gave the newsmen plenty of photo-opportunities.

There is a photograph of the Big Three at the conference table at Potsdam that has stuck in my mind. It has a special quality that derives, I think, from the electricity in the air. Everyone at the round table clearly feels the nervous tension. It can be seen in their faces, especially the faces of those in the front row, where the special staffs are seated. We are all in a state of extreme concentration, and this shows: nobody is smiling.

I remember another, happier occasion, when Truman had arranged a dinner. After we all got up from the table he sat down at the piano and played something he had evidently practised very carefully – he was of course well known as an able amateur pianist. When he'd finished, Stalin praised him and said laughingly: 'Ah yes, music's an excellent thing – it drives out the beast in man.'

To be truthful, it wasn't quite clear whom Stalin had in mind as the one whose beast had been driven out. Even so, Truman chose to be very pleased at his words.

Only my heightened awareness of the historic occasion can explain why I still have so many images in my mind from that conference. I particularly remember the first day.

There is Truman. He is nervous but he mobilises all his self-control so as not to show it. It looks at times as if he is about to smile, but this is a false impression. I have the feeling that the President is somehow huddled into himself. No doubt the fact that he has no experience of meetings at such a high level, and never met Stalin before, plays a part. But to give him his due he is never rude or discourteous. He is helped by the fact that all his major statements are prepared in advance, so he only has to read them. In discussion his extempore comments are usually brief, but his advisers and experts are in constant consultation with each other and from time to time pass him notes.

And Churchill. That veteran politician makes only short statements, as a rule, but he loves to stretch out individual words. The words he wants to underline are pronounced harshly. He almost never uses a prepared text. It is said that he likes to learn his speeches by heart, and my impression of him is certainly of an experienced orator who knows how to present his rhetorical stock-in-trade.

Attlee. Our delegation is right in its prediction: if Labour gets in, they'll follow essentially the same policy as the wartime Coalition. At the conference Attlee scarcely speaks. Maybe when the delegation discusses domestic policy he speaks up, but mostly he's quiet as a mouse. Maybe the experienced Labour leader is afraid of saying something that the press would pick up, and of losing Labour some support.

Stalin. He looks calm and steady. So does the Soviet delegation as a whole.

Also interesting were the dinners at which the three leaders met either to work or to relax.

One did not have to be a psychiatrist to see that each of the Big Three knew his part. Certainly two contrasting worlds – capitalist and socialist – were represented, but all three men still had to find some understanding.

Everyone listened carefully when Roosevelt spoke. We studied the twists and turns of his thinking and his sharp judgements and jokes. What he said was important for the future of the world, and we knew it.

When Churchill spoke he knew how to sparkle and make a joke, and he expressed his ideas well. One felt he was on familiar terms not only with politics but also with history: he had after all fought in the Boer War at the beginning of the century.

Then, quietly, almost casually, Stalin would begin to speak. He spoke as if only the other two were in the room. He showed neither restraint nor any desire to make an effect, yet every word sounded as if it had been specially prepared for just this occasion and just this moment.

It was noticeable that, when Stalin was speaking, even when the subject was not high policy, Roosevelt would often try to convey his attitude to what was being said, either with nods of his head or by the expression on his face.

Even at that time, it would have been hard for even the most unobservant person not to notice the authority and respect that was accorded to Stalin by the other leaders. First and foremost, this was clearly due to the unexampled feats of the Soviet people in the war. The monolithic unity of the Soviet people had made an enormous impression: the working class, the peasantry and the intelligentsia in a single upsurge had risen to defend the country against a powerful enemy.

8

Creating the United Nations

Even during the war, the Allies had already recognised the need for some sort of united nations assembly, an organisation whose main task would be to preserve peace more effectively than the League of Nations had been able to. From a preliminary exchange of ideas on the creation of such a body, the Allied powers soon went on to detailed talks about its nature, its structure, its rules and obligations. The basic work on the United Nations Charter was done at the Dumbarton Oaks conference of 21 August to 7 October 1944. I represented the Soviet Union and our approach was clear: we were determined to create such an organisation and we were determined that it should be effective. The three delegations met in a cosy house in Dumbarton Oaks, which is a suburb of Washington: Britain and the USSR were represented by their ambassadors in Washington, and Assistant Secretary of State Stettinius represented the USA.

The work was exceptionally intense. Plenary sessions, working groups, meetings of heads of delegation and many other kinds of meetings took place. The participants all knew they must reach agreement and one by one all but the most difficult questions were settled.

The Dumbarton Oaks conference agreed 90 per cent of the issues concerning the creation of the UN, the main question left unsettled being that of the division of powers between the Security Council and the General Assembly. This controversy reflected the participants' different positions on the question of the need for unanimity among the five permanent members of the Security Council, the body which would bear the main peace-keeping responsibility. The US position was that, should one member of the Security Council fail to agree with the other four, then that member's vote should not count in the Council's decision-making. Britain took the same position.

The American position created a serious risk that the great powers might be put into confrontation with each other, and thus it undermined the co-operation without which the UN could not function. The US position in fact allowed the UN to be turned into an instrument for imposing the will of one group of states upon another, above all upon the Soviet Union, as the sole socialist member of the Council. The states which had a majority in the Security Council might therefore be tempted to use force, rather than seek mutually acceptable solutions.

In opposing the American proposal, the Soviet Union argued that all decisions should be agreed unanimously by the three victorious powers as well as France and China who, by common consent, should enjoy the same rights. In other words, the basis of effective action should be the principle of unanimity among the five permanent members of the Security Council, with the right of veto to be available should that unanimity not be achieved.

Roosevelt realised the importance of the unsettled issue, and invited me to the White House to talk it over with him. He opened by underlining the importance of the Security Council, and then went on to lay out the position which his people had defended at Dumbarton Oaks. I did not feel he was particularly emphasising the issue, however; rather he was looking for a way of removing the difficulties.

I explained the Soviet position: we did not have room to retreat from our position, just as our troops at Stalingrad knew that they could not retreat further east than the Volga.

There was no outcome from this meeting, but, as the President was clearly concerned to find a means of reconciliation, I felt hopeful that the search for agreement would succeed. And, although agreement on the veto was never reached at Dumbarton Oaks, we still felt confident that the USA and Britain would alter their positions, since they obviously knew that without this there would simply be no United Nations.

And so it happened. The question of the veto was settled at Yalta, by means of a proposal by Roosevelt basically corresponding to the position the USSR had been arguing from the start: Security Council decisions, apart from matters of procedure, must be agreed unanimously by all the permanent members.

Many in the West have wondered why Roosevelt gave in to the USSR, and he has been criticised for it. But in fact he performed a great service to the world and the step he took can be explained very simply: more realistic than others in Washington and London, he recognised that the Soviet Union simply could not give up the principle of unanimity.

Once agreement in principle had been reached at Yalta on the right of veto, there still remained the question of how any issue to be put before the Security Council was to be designated as important or merely procedural. Although Yalta had not dealt specifically with this, the fact that a general understanding had been reached made it possible at San Francisco (25 April to 26 June 1945) to agree a joint declaration by the USSR, USA, Britain, France and China, which stated that a question would be considered procedural if all the powers agreed that it was.

At San Francisco, for the first time ever, representatives of a wide range of states gathered under one roof to build a reliable barrier against future wars. What was this barrier to be, how would one measure its reliability, what should we build into its foundations?

The envoys of those European countries which had borne the main brunt of the war now shouldered a heavy responsibility. Of course, we in the Soviet delegation noticed that there were markedly different reactions to our proposals at the conference. Countries like Poland, Czechoslovakia and Yugoslavia were close to us on most important questions, although the complex situation still existing in those countries did sometimes make itself felt. On the other hand, the representatives of Australia, New Zealand, the Union of South Africa and a number of Latin American countries – all countries that had not been touched directly by the flames of war – viewed the Soviet position with little understanding. There was also a certain reserve among some countries of Asia and North Africa.

As for our wartime allies, their policies seemed to have two faces, one which recognised the Soviet position, and another which served their own narrow interests. Even so, the manner in which discussion took place at San Francisco compares very favourably with the vituperative discussions at today's international meetings. The vocabulary of the capitalist world in those days was not embellished by such gems as 'acting from a position of strength', 'the crusade against communism', 'the Soviet Union is an evil empire' and so on.

Agreement on a preliminary review of all important issues was achieved in restricted meetings of the Big Five before the San Francisco conference opened. This proved easily done, since all five knew that without it nothing at all would be achieved, and they knew, moreover, that agreement between the USA and USSR would have decisive importance for all the other countries.

The American representative in San Francisco was again Edward Stettinius, who was by then Secretary of State. With the departure of Molotov after a short time, I became head of the Soviet delegation. The heads of the British, French and Chinese delegations were, respectively, Anthony Eden, Georges Bidault and S.V. Sung; then later the British ambassador to Washington, Lord Halifax (accompanied, it seemed at the same level, by a senior Foreign Office official, Alexander Cadogan), Joseph Paul-Boncour and the leading Chinese nationalist diplomat of the period, Vi-Kyuin, known as Wellington Ku.

As it turned out, during the conference's plenary sessions the chief impulse in putting questions, in overcoming disagreement and finding acceptable solutions came from the US and Soviet delegations. The shaky situation of Chiang Kai-shek put its mark on the Chinese delegation. Even the veteran Wellington Ku looked distraught. He was mostly silent, and not even the US representatives, who showed most concern and respect for him, could dispel his evident gloom.

Meetings of the steering committee, which had been created at San Francisco, and included the Big Five heads of delegation, were hardly different from plenary sessions. The presence of the heads, however, clarified one's view of their political line on the questions under discussion. It was also easier to ask for explanations at these restricted meetings, since one was talking directly to the people invested with the most power.

The Soviet representatives felt throughout the conference that the Western delegates were people from another world, thinking in another language. Moreover, our rudest opponents were often not the great powers, but rather their dependents. This was most noticeable of the British dominions, which had not yet acquired their own political identities. Herbert Evatt of Australia, Peter Fraser of New Zealand and Mackenzie King of Canada all made themselves look silly as they tried to drown the right of veto in a torrent of words. Obviously the British were using their loyal partners to front for them when they themselves found it awkward to come out against the principle of Security Council unanimity.

Apart from these sessions, there were meetings of the three, the USA, USSR and Britain, and more frequently meetings between only the USA and USSR, when a greater degree of understanding was usually reached.

One such meeting between myself and Stettinius took place when debates on the right of veto for the five, the powers of the General Assembly and the fate of the colonial territories were in full swing. Everyone knew that the wording of all decisions for inclusion in the UN Charter had to be got exactly right, since a shaky charter would be ineffective and virtually impossible to amend.

Stettinius and I met alone. Our old friend, the right of veto, came up straight away. One might have thought that it had been settled at the Yalta conference, but now there was a new boss in the White House – Truman – who did not like much of what Roosevelt had accepted at Yalta. Admittedly the administration had not decided it was going to bury the principle of unanimity whatever the cost, but Truman was determined whenever possible to shake the understanding we had reached.

I drew Stettinius's attention to the following: 'There can be no backing away from the Yalta agreements. The USSR believes that, without a decision on the right of veto within the spirit of Yalta, it will frankly be impossible to create the proposed international organisation. We hope therefore that the US delegation will, not merely formally but rather actively, defend the principle of unanimity of the permanent members of the Security Council.'

Stettinius listened carefully and replied: 'I concede that to endanger the Yalta understanding would mean an enormous risk, and I promise to see that all US representatives do not permit any confusion on this issue.'

I had the feeling Stettinius himself needed to sort out his own thinking. In his mind, the Secretary of State still supported Roosevelt's line, but that did not mean he had the authority to override those in the Truman administration who disagreed with him.

I should add, however, that in the latter part of the conference Stettinius made no small effort to see the forum did not collapse.

A decision had to be taken as to which questions should be given to the Security Council and which to the General Assembly, that is, what issues should be subject to veto.

The USSR argued that all important issues of war and peace should go to the Security Council. Washington and London – supported by the representatives of many, mostly smaller, countries – argued for a division that would give the General Assembly more rights and the Security Council fewer. This attempt to hand over many of the Security Council's powers to the General Assembly was based on America's confidence that it could easily obtain a majority there and so put through any resolutions it liked. The clear result of this tendency would be to shift the balance of responsibility for the preservation of peace from the Security Council to the General Assembly, and the line separating the functions of each body hence became a major issue.

Tension grew steadily at the five-power meetings as it became clear that President Truman had issued directives which cut straight across the Yalta agreements, and the US–British position on the division of powers was not going to be reconciled with the Soviet position unless one side gave way.

A host of resolutions now poured forth giving the General Assembly the right to review virtually any question that was not concerned with sanctions against a state. But Stettinius was basically sympathetic to the Soviet Union's position that there should be a proper division of powers, and, after some tough talking, a possible agreement emerged: the Assembly would be able to discuss any question put by any state or group of states, but it could only issue a consultative opinion, and it would be for the Council to take binding decisions.

The Soviet delegation further declared: 'Our country will not agree to any UN Charter that might sow the seeds of a new military conflict.'

The opponents of the veto then gave in.

Everyone relaxed; jokes became more frequent. In just a few days the climate had changed. Clause 10 of chapter IV of the Charter appeared, limiting the powers of the General Assembly in the spirit of Yalta, and including the veto.

★

The discussion at San Francisco took another sharp turn when the subject arose of former League of Nations mandated territories. In the light of the wartime rise of national liberation movements in colonial and dependent countries, a solution to this problem was urgently needed.

The USSR was in favour of giving these countries their independence, while many of the Western powers, especially Britain, were naturally for retaining colonial rule. America's position was peculiar. Washington tended to view colonial empires as an anachronism and made no secret that it would shed no tears were they to be dismantled. Therefore, with one eye on the USSR, US representatives made the point that the colonial powers had done well out of their possessions economically, and that enough was enough. In any case, it was time the old masters moved aside. Stettinius sarcastically remarked that the colonial powers should recognise that times had changed and that they should now say goodbye to their colonies.

At the same time, however, the USA was already hatching plans to take over the protectorates of the Mariana, Caroline and Marshall Islands in Micronesia – which in due course they did, thus breaking the UN Charter with an act of flagrant imperialistic robbery.

The USSR meanwhile argued that international trusteeship should facilitate the achievement of independence by these peoples, and tried to include in the Charter not merely self-rule, as the US draft proposed, but independence.

A sharp discussion also took place on an issue that had not been raised at either Yalta or Dumbarton Oaks, namely whether states would have the right to leave the UN if for any reason they did not wish to remain. It would seem to be a simple issue, but it was in fact complicated, since any loss of this right affected the question of the sovereignty of states. On the one hand, no state should leave an organisation devoted to the preservation of peace. However, a state might believe that the organisation was not doing its job. Alternatively a state might wish to leave the UN and simply occupy a position of neutrality. Should it be deprived of that right?

The USA, Britain and France made a great show of concern that the UN should not be weakened by allowing the exit of any member state. But any such attack upon the principle of national sovereignty, a principle sacred to international relations, would have made possible interference by one state in the domestic affairs of another, and would, moreover, have enabled the UN itself to meddle in the internal affairs of member states.

I introduced a resolution opposing this and the majority of delegations adopted our position.

During the conference, I met Stettinius often. After Roosevelt's death, the great majority of his immediate aides left office, either from choice or because they were replaced. Stettinius, however, managed to hang on for a while. This was explained to some extent by the fact that he represented big business: before the war, he had been chairman of the board of the United Steel Corporation, a company any President and any administration must take into account. Nevertheless, three months after Roosevelt's death, Stettinius was replaced by James Byrnes, who was more to Truman's taste.

I have a very clear image of Stettinius – his hair the colour of fresh-fallen snow – sitting at the conference table. He spoke evenly, always finding a word for each head of delegation, never raising his voice, and what he said always sounded the same: this is black and that is white. He tried not to go too deeply into problems; I think he regarded discussion of difficult political issues as no more than a painful duty. Holding his high position in the steel industry must have left its mark on him. Nevertheless, despite his coming from another social order, I must say I found Stettinius was the sort of diplomat with whom I could talk and come to an understanding.

I should mention that in his meetings with us Stettinius never argued for the advantages of private enterprise, American democracy or the American way of life, and he had plenty of opportunities.

One such was the occasion when he invited me with my wife and son, Anatoly, to join him and his wife, Virginia, for an outing on his yacht around Manhattan Island. It was fine weather and we were going to be shown the bridges and monuments and so on.

As the yacht sailed along, he suddenly said: 'Look! There's Wall Street.'

No explanations were necessary, but I was struck for the first time by the modest appearance of this, the headquarters of capitalism. One end of the street terminates at the ocean – which is why it is best viewed from a boat – and the other end winds up in a cemetery.

For about a year after leaving office as Secretary of State, Stettinius was the US ambassador to the UN, and held no further posts. In 1950 he published his book *Roosevelt and the Russians: The Yalta Conference*, in which he gives his view on Soviet–US relations.

Senator Arthur Vandenberg, an influential figure as head of the Republican opposition in the Senate, enjoyed considerable influence in the US delegation, although he tended to function best in its internal deliberations, rather than at the restricted or general meetings, where he preferred to sit silent.

Before the war he had been against diplomatic recognition of the USSR and shared the view that Hitler was not a threat to the Western powers. Soon after the war broke out he stated that 'it has no relation to America', and in February 1941 he opposed Lend-Lease. Throughout the war he had opposed Roosevelt's policies, openly attacked the idea of a second front in Europe and called for US troops to be concentrated in the Pacific. Nevertheless, bearing in mind his influence in the Republican Party, Roosevelt had invited him to join the US delegation to San Francisco. At the end of the conference, heeding American public opinion, Vandenberg made a speech in favour of ratifying the Charter.

Vandenberg's influence on foreign policy grew after Stettinius was replaced following Roosevelt's death. He virtually became Byrnes's right-hand man and revealed himself as an opponent of all post-war co-operation between East and West.

After Anthony Eden left San Francisco, Lord Halifax became the head of the British delegation. Jokingly nicknamed the Watchtower by the other delegates, Lord Halifax is as sharp in my mind today as if I had only just met him.

Having been an MP since 1910, he had held a number of ministerial posts as well as being appointed Viceroy of India in 1926. Before the war his influence on British foreign policy was considerable and he had been among those who sought an agreement with Germany against the Soviet Union. Foreign Secretary in Chamberlain's government, which negotiated the Munich agreement, he continued in this post in Churchill's coalition government which came to power after the beginning of the war.

In his post-war memoirs of 1957, Halifax tries to shrug off his responsibility for the policy of appeasement and shifts the blame on to other British and European politicians who allegedly let events in Germany get out of control. The Munich agreement he calls a 'terrible and sad affair, but the lesser of two evils'. Even after everything Europe had gone through at the hands of fascism, Halifax thought the greater evil would have been the organisation of determined resistance to Hitler. Right up to his death, he never recognised the efforts made by the Soviet Union to avert war.

I met Halifax in Washington. He had become British ambassador in 1940. A refined aristocrat, he tended to seek the company of men he considered the powerful of this world, among whom he firmly numbered himself. He would talk to me readily about the situation at the front, and enjoyed passing on the tittle-tattle he had picked up in the corridors of power. The Americans earlier had assessed him unflatteringly as Foreign Secretary, and he liked to pay them back. Once, in the presence of US representatives, he let drop some of the opinions he'd heard about them in London high society.

What Halifax could not stand was to be reminded of his position on Germany before the war, and as a rule this would not be mentioned in his presence. I, too, did my best not to make him feel uncomfortable.

I do not recall him as easy to get on with. Nevertheless he was interesting to talk to. He collected gossip about the war, presidents, governments, international meetings, Nazi intrigues with the neutrals, the whisperings of foreign diplomats. When he was especially interested in hearing something, he stretched his already unusually long neck still further. It was not worth trying to talk to him, however, on such things as economics, unemployment, monopoly profits or trade unions. He was an arch-conservative in his views.

We never discussed the political system, world outlook or ideology of the Soviet Union. More than once he let it be known that he did not regard himself as sufficiently well versed on these subjects. Only one thing he was sure of and that was that things were done differently in the USSR.

He was determined that Britain should survive – he repeatedly made this clear – and she would only survive if Hitler's military machine were smashed. He understood the Soviet role in this perfectly.

At the meetings of the Big Five in San Francisco, one felt strongly that Halifax had no real knowledge of the matters under discussion, and didn't have much interest in them. He often seemed to be observing the proceedings with a vacant, almost absent-minded stare. And when he did feel like saying something – first checked with Cadogan – he would express his thoughts in so ornate a way that few could understand him.

On a number of questions I had to remind him of commitments he had made in earlier conversations, but which he was evidently now prepared to jettison. Not that he was openly unfriendly to us, but Halifax and the rest of the British delegation at San Francisco never made us feel confident that they would keep their promises.

In the middle of 1946 he retired as ambassador to Washington and returned to England, ending his political career. The San Francisco conference was his final appearance in the field of foreign policy. There followed a period of loneliness and tending his lawns until, in 1959 at the age of seventy-eight, he died.

My memories of the personalities I met at San Francisco would not be complete without brief mention of the French head of delegation, Joseph Paul-Boncour, as French a Frenchman as you could find. Short of stature, dressed in exquisite taste, with totally white hair which tended to stand up on end and which he kept vigorously brushed, he seemed to have walked straight out of the pages of a Balzac novel.

By the time we met, he had already had considerable political experience and had made a brilliant career. At twenty-five he had been head of the Prime Minister's office, then a member of the Chamber of Deputies, and at thirty-eight Prime Minister and Foreign Minister. He took part in many international meetings and lived until 1972, just short of his hundredth birthday.

Although he often expressed the point at issue in any matter dividing the Soviet Union and the Western powers with more subtlety than either the US or the British delegates, he always supported them. He was on the whole a modest man, however, and it must be said that his moderation was occasionally helpful in finding solutions.

Once during a dinner, I asked him, 'How do you envisage France's future in the difficult situation that exists?'

His reply was unusually bold: 'France must stand on her own two feet as an independent state. De Gaulle understands the soul of the country, and the country will follow him.'

This was at a time when relations between de Gaulle and Roosevelt had been strained and Truman had not yet made up his mind about the obstinate general who was not afraid to say no to Washington when he thought France's interests were not being served.

Among the statesmen attending the San Francisco conference, Field Marshal Smuts, who headed the delegation of the Union of South Africa, was a rather original figure. It was the first time the Soviet delegates had ever met such a man: he was like a fragment of the past, receding ever further into history.

The son of an Afrikaner farmer, Jan Christiaan Smuts received a brilliant education at Cambridge and returned to South Africa at the age of twenty-five to become state attorney of the Transvaal. A leader of the Boer struggle for independence from British colonial rule in 1899–1902, he had no sympathy for the interests of the black majority population. In 1905 he was sent to England for talks on self-government for the Boers and returned home advocating co-operation with the British. He held many ministerial posts and was Prime Minister of the Union of South Africa several times. He was responsible, at the Paris peace conference after the First World War, for putting forward the idea of mandates, which the imperialists were to use to mask their dominion over the 'non-self-governing territories'. In 1939 he replaced the pro-German government in power at that time, and became Prime Minister, Foreign Minister, Minister of Defence and chief of the armed forces all at once. He was awarded the honorary rank of field marshal by the British Crown in 1941.

At San Francisco we called him 'the last of the Mohicans', as he was possibly the only leader of the Boer rising still living.

He spoke rarely at the conference. This form of activity, he must have felt, was not for him: he could make more sense with a rifle than with speeches and declarations.

Smuts liked driving around the streets of San Francisco in an open car. He was very impressed when the public recognised him, and he would wave his hand in acknowledgement and evident pleasure.

'You should be aware, Mr Gromyko,' he confided, 'that during the Boer War I took Churchill himself prisoner.'

'That did not prevent you from becoming a prisoner of his politics later,' I retorted.

The field marshal made no objection: I don't believe he understood the point of my remark.

I had met Smuts in the St Francis Hotel, where the Soviet delegation was housed. What had brought him to the meeting?

He explained: 'This sort of big conference is new for me. Of course, much of what goes on at the plenary sessions and in the committees is clear enough, but there are some things I don't understand.' He added: 'As for the right of veto, our delegation is content to leave everything to the five powers.'

He did not mention that his delegation was supporting those who wanted to undermine the unanimity rule.

'But my delegation, and I myself,' he went on, 'view with dismay the fact that the draft Charter makes no mention of God.'

I questioned the grey-haired field marshal: 'What has God got to do with it?'

He calmly explained: 'Look what is happening. Whatever clause in the Charter is being discussed, nowhere does it say that God is standing behind it all. States, like people, must fear God and be guided by his will, and this should be seen in the Charter.' He made it clear that in his opinion the League of Nations had failed because the states had not heeded the will of God.

I looked at him and tried to see if he really believed what he was saying. Judging by the exalted look on his face and the zealous way in which he delivered his lengthy monologue, he clearly believed every word. What he had said brought into sharp focus the mysterious wall which exists between the minds and feelings of religious people and those who see only the physical world of nature and science.

Having said his piece, Smuts waited for my response.

I started by saying: 'The United Nations is going to consist of different states which have different religions and ideologies, including dialectical materialism.' I paused. He was listening closely, so I went on: 'You know, of course, that the Soviet people and its guiding force, the Party of Communists, is governed by the scientific teaching of Marxism-Leninism. Our philosophy excludes any belief in a supernatural force. Although we have freedom of religion, we are an atheistic state. How can we talk about God in the Charter of an organisation whose purposes are strictly of this world? The Charter must direct all the member states towards guaranteeing peace between the nations. This is what all countries must start from, regardless of their social structure or ideology.'

I could not tell what he was thinking. Eventually he said: 'While I do not share your basic approach, I do see the consistency of your argument as the representative of your country. Apparently my wishes in this matter will not be met.'

He had come to sound us out, no doubt having already spoken to some of the Western delegations, but he did not raise the question of God in the conference. Neither did the Western powers make the question a serious issue; there were already enough important earthly questions that needed settling.

We said a respectful goodbye to the field marshal.

At San Francisco, and later at the first four sessions of the General Assembly and a number of other international meetings up to 1953, the Soviet Ukrainian delegation was invariably headed by Dmitri Zakharyevich Manuilsky, for whom I had the deepest regard.

A senior party figure of pre-revolutionary vintage, he had worked in the Comintern before becoming Foreign Minister of the Ukrainian Republic. He was a modest man who stood out among Soviet diplomats for his wide knowledge of the social and political sciences, having completed his education at the Sorbonne in 1911 and maintained a lively intellectual interest all his life.

We first met at San Francisco, where we worked together in the nucleus of our three delegations (USSR, Belorussia and Ukraine). He was not fond of figures and detailed work: his strength lay in analysing problems with a broad perspective, where his long experience came into play. He also had a very lively sense of humour. He could give excellent verbal character sketches, and in the middle of a political discussion would suddenly remember something amusing and relevant that had happened to him in one of the many countries he had lived in.

Once he told me about a visit he made to the famous Grévin Waxworks Museum in Paris, which had been the model for the equally famous Madame Tussaud's in London. There were not many people at the Grévin on that occasion and Manuilsky decided to play a joke on two women visitors. He went on ahead of them, took up a pose among a line of waxworks and froze as the women approached.

They went right up to him. One of them said, 'He really does look real!'

At which Manuilsky twitched his moustache and solemnly told her: 'Madame, I want to come alive.'

The women shrieked and ran. They only realised the truth when they had already covered some ten yards.

'Yes, Andrei Andreyevich, it really did happen,' he assured me.

The American authorities provided working conditions for the visiting delegations that were tolerable, but hardly more than that. They helped personnel to find hotels, but as for rented accommodation it was a case of cash on the nail, and quite a lot of it too.

As the receiving country, the USA ought to have set up official arrangements to create a welcoming atmosphere for the first major post-war international conference. Instead, President Truman did not honour the opening ceremony with his presence, and the US government limited itself to token representation at the level of Governor Warren and the mayor of the city. Admittedly the message of welcome sent by the President said: 'Never in history has there been a more important conference or a more needed meeting than the one we are opening today in San Francisco.' But an enormous chasm clearly yawned between what he said and what his administration really believed.

The lack of consideration shown by the administration was made up for to some extent by the city of San Francisco itself, with its steep, handsome streets, its romantic, low-rolling mist, the beauty and engineering genius of the Golden Gate Bridge and the magnificent redwoods nearby.

The decision where to locate the United Nations was taken at San Francisco by agreement, in effect, between the two great powers. In view of our joint war effort with America's allies, and bearing in mind Washington's repeated assurances that the USA would collaborate to prevent the outbreak of a new war, the USSR accepted, as a friendly gesture to Washington, that the United Nations should be housed in the United States.

However, the proper procedures had to be gone through first and an executive committee was created, with fourteen states represented, including the five permanent members of the Security Council. The committee met in London to begin its work six weeks later, on 15 August 1945, in Church House, a historic building in the centre of the city near the Houses of Parliament. It had been agreed at San Francisco that, following this executive committee's work, a preparatory commission, comprising all the member states, would meet and that these two bodies would deal not only with the location question but also with a large number of other UN organisational matters.

In the preparatory commission every member state was allowed to vote and also to submit its own proposals on the location of the UN headquarters. Not everyone was in favour of having it in the USA. Various European capitals were mentioned, the three most commonly cited being Copenhagen, Paris and Geneva, with Monaco also named on one occasion. Debates were often heated. Copenhagen did not acquire a majority, for, although no one had anything convincing against it, neither did anyone come up with anything particularly in its favour.

Paris, or some other French city, was popular with many delegates, but some of the larger European states looked askance at this idea, as it would give the French an advantage over London or Washington. Rome did not figure, since Italy, as one of the aggressors, was not one of the founding members of the UN.

Geneva was hotly defended by some, who emphasised Swiss neutrality and the city's amenities, but its opponents argued that the new organisation should not be housed where the impotent League of Nations had been.

Everyone understood that the place that was chosen would receive a big influx of hard currency, deriving from the services needed for a large number of overseas visitors, and also would acquire long-term jobs for many of its citizens. However, no one admitted this. Instead, the chief reasons mentioned included:

Europe is closer to Asia and Africa.
Europe already has a Palace of Nations.
Europe is where two world wars were started, and so security is especially important for Europe.
Europe is the centre of modern civilisation.

The argument against Europe was: placing the UN headquarters in the USA would be an expression of recognition by the anti-Hitler coalition states of America's part in the war.

Characteristically, this argument was not put by the USA itself.

But the US delegates were carrying out intense behind-the-scenes activity, and eventually the US representative at the preparatory commission, Adlai Stevenson, read a resolution approved by Congress, inviting the United Nations to the USA. A stormy debate was followed by an open vote which went as we had expected: in favour of Europe twenty-three, against twenty-five, with two abstentions; for the USA thirty, with fourteen against and six abstentions.

It would, however, be many months before the final location was settled, with municipal authorities in San Francisco particularly keen to be chosen.

In fact the first session of the General Assembly took place in Central Hall, London, at the beginning of 1946, with fifty-one delegates. Today there are one hundred and fifty-nine.

At the first session the US delegate announced that his government had found a place in New York and nobody raised any objection. For the first three or four years, the Security Council was located about twenty-five miles from New York at Lake Success on Long Island, while the General Assembly met in Flushing Meadow, a suburb of New York City. But neither site was suitable for the organisation's work, and everyone knew that the United Nations would eventually settle in Manhattan. It was a gift of Nelson Rockefeller's that made this possible. With characteristic acumen, Rockefeller realised that the considerable costs he was incurring in giving away a piece of real estate would yield vast profits in the future as a result of the increase in value of other land and property he owned in the vicinity of the UN building.

It was fundamental to the thinking of the UN's creators that its work must be in the hands of an authoritative figure. However, as soon as they started to define that figure's powers for inclusion in the Charter, disagreements arose. The US and British delegates wanted to accord this figure wide powers – wider than those possessed by even the most powerful state. We asked where one would find someone whom both the West and the East could trust so completely, but there was no reply.

In the end a compromise was reached and went into the Charter: the Secretary-General, as the chief administrative official, would be personally responsible only for the working of the UN secretariat; but he could also draw the attention of the organisation, even that of the Security Council itself, to any situation which in his opinion needed it. His functions, however, should not include investigating these situations himself by means of commissions or groups. This formula was not intended to reduce the Secretary-General's status, only to give a sober and realistic definition of his functions. Had he been empowered to take political decisions, conflicts would inevitably have arisen.

It was not easy to select a Secretary-General, but after considerable effort Trygve Lie, the Norwegian politician, diplomat and lawyer, was chosen.

After the liberation of Norway in the spring of 1945, Trygve Lie had returned from London to Oslo and became Foreign Minister in Einar Gerhardsen's government. He took part in the San Francisco conference and later headed the Norwegian delegation to the General Assembly in London in 1946.

The Soviet Union supported Trygve Lie, counting on his impartiality, which, however, lasted only a short time. It was not only his personal political outlook that played a part here, but the fact that most of his apparatus was staffed by Americans or personnel from other Western countries. Thus all the documents, information and proposals that settled on his desk first went through an American sieve, and no secret was made of this.

The first Secretary-General was not a man of strong character. He could create a fuss and when he did his athletic physique could be quite impressive, but those who knew him also knew that his fund of disapproval or anger would quickly run out and be replaced by a conciliatory mood – which itself would probably not last very long either.

In most of the many meetings I had with him in London and New York, he would assure me of his good feelings for the USSR and he would praise the feats of the Red Army in liberating the north of Norway. But in the sharp clashes that took place on the floor of the General Assembly or in the Security Council he nearly always favoured the western shore of the Atlantic, and as the years passed he gave way to the pressure of American ruling circles more and more.

In the UN annual report of 1948, he virtually exonerated the USA and Britain from their frequent failures to carry out the UN's resolutions, and he praised the expansionist Marshall Plan. He also actively used his position to support America's aggression against the Korean people by masking US troops under the flag of the UN.

If I was asked to judge whether or not Trygve Lie was a good Secretary-General, I would have to say that he was not.

It took a long time to find his successor. There were many candidates, but the circle steadily narrowed down to one on whom in 1953 the five permanent members of the Security Council could agree – Dag Hammarskjöld, who until then had held various posts in the Swedish government.

Everyone was watching him. We had believed we could develop good working relationships with him, but, despite his initial, visible efforts to preserve objectivity, his line of conduct strayed further and further from that ideal. Our efforts to keep him within the framework of the acceptable failed, and when the winds of the cold war began to blow more fiercely they seized hold of Hammarskjöld and carried him away. Even London and Washington sometimes felt uneasy at the over-obvious zeal with which he oiled the wheels of NATO, but he continued to drift in an openly anti-Soviet direction.

He was perfectly aware of what he was doing. Clearly, since he must have known that when the election for a new Secretary-General came round he could not count on Moscow's support, he was so intoxicated with the praise he received from Washington and other NATO countries that he had decided: I shan't be here that long, anyway, so to hell with objectivity.

I remember a conversation I had with Hammarskjöld during the General Assembly, not long before his fateful trip to Africa in 1961, when he was killed in an air crash. Our permanent representative, A. A. Sobolev, was with me at this meeting. Hammarskjöld seemed unusually talkative, delighted with his own rhetoric as he tried to justify his actions, and the two of us needed to do quite a bit of manoeuvring to get him to remain silent for a moment.

We of course said what we had come to say, putting our position on the need to give realistic aid to the newly independent African countries. We said: 'They must be protected from the intrigues and pressures of the imperialist countries. This is especially so of the former Belgian colonies.'

Afterwards, half joking, half serious, Sobolev summed up his impression of the meeting: 'I wonder what pills he'd taken to get into such a state before seeing us?'

The lesson of Trygve Lie, and still more that of Dag Hammarskjöld, was that the Secretary-General must be someone who was known for his objectivity, and who understood that he could do his job properly only if he acted impartially.

Finding another Secretary-General took a lot of time and effort. But the choice finally came to rest on U Thant, then Burma's Deputy Foreign Minister and a close associate of the Prime Minister, U Nu, who had done much to develop Soviet–Burmese relations. U Thant was European in his manner and, as a diplomat, lived in the English style.

Even so, five years after his election, he confessed to me: 'It looks like my honeymoon with this organisation is over.'

This surprised me, as such a belief had not shown in his demeanour.

He said, 'There's a positive army of Americans working in the secretariat, many of them from the special services, and they say I'm not being fair to the USA.' He was very distressed about it. 'This is not the case. The fact is, they don't like me being objective towards the USSR and the other socialist countries.'

He made similar remarks to me on subsequent occasions; but as a cautious man, of genuinely neutral outlook, he managed to hang on in the job until 1971. Then he retired through ill health and went to Burma, where he died soon after.

9

The arms race

In April 1946 I was made permanent Soviet representative to the United Nations, and not long afterwards I became Deputy Foreign Minister. Since then there has hardly been a day when the problem of disarmament has not been on my mind. I have taken part in countless meetings at every level and engaged in bilateral talks with representatives of many other states.

Arms control and reduction are fundamental for a security system. One cannot repeat this too often to anyone who wants to understand these matters.

At the Genoa conference of 1922, under direct instructions from Lenin, Soviet Foreign Commissar Chicherin said: 'Our state proposes universal arms reduction, and then the threat of war will be removed.' This has been the Soviet approach ever since.

From 1946 onwards, in the UN alone, the USSR has introduced more than a hundred initiatives towards ending the arms race and achieving disarmament. The USSR made the first proposal on universal and total disarmament combined with universal supervision, and there have been countless Soviet proposals to limit or stop the arms race.

Back in 1946, when the memory of war was still fresh, the UN established a special commission which met in London with the participation of the USSR, the USA, Britain, France and Canada. It soon emerged that only the USSR was in favour of disarmament, while all the others blocked every proposal aimed at disarmament and ending the arms race.

The American representative was Adlai Stevenson, a leading figure in American political life in the post-war years. At the commission Stevenson stubbornly repeated that it was impossible for the US administration to accept any resolution on disarmament.

Stevenson once invited me to dinner at his residence, where he confessed to me frankly that even discussing disarmament was not acceptable to the USA. There in London, he admitted for the first time: 'Big business in America cannot conceive of existing without arms manufacture. Nobody in Washington takes the idea of disarmament seriously. But I can't say that openly at the commission.'

I could not have asked any representative of the administration to be more frank than that.

'But in that case,' I replied, 'what do you think is the proper course for countries to take on this issue?'

'Controlled rearmament,' came the reply.

So it was to be rearmament.

Stevenson was by no means the worst American politician in the field of international relations. But when he became the Democratic presidential candidate he obviously had nothing attractive to offer the American voter on foreign policy, particularly in relation to disarmament, so it is not surprising that he was defeated.

After the war, there were many talks on disarmament, and they took place on every level, including the highest. The USSR put its questions pointedly.

'Why does the US need to install bases in other countries?'

'Against what enemy are these bases being built, or those previously built being preserved?'

Stalin asked these questions, Molotov asked them, and Soviet conference delegates asked them. These questions are just as pertinent forty years later.

I remember how stubbornly Western leaders resisted discussing the question of their foreign bases. For instance, I recall President Eisenhower, sitting in his country retreat at Camp David, listening to Khrushchev. The President's face was stony, his gaze fixed somewhere just above his guests' heads, if not higher. This was not the Eisenhower who had been widely advertised as the man who just couldn't help smiling. Here, when disarmament was mentioned, he said nothing. And Truman before him had behaved in the same way, at best saying: 'American bases overseas are serving peace.'

At our Vienna meeting in June 1961, President Kennedy was

hard put to it to find arguments in defence of US foreign bases when we asked him: 'Why does the US have so many bases and troops in Europe? Surely they have no enemies there?' At least Kennedy denied that the US intended increasing their troop numbers in Europe. He also agreed to give the matter further thought. In this connection, I think the following conversation should be revealed.

During my visit to New York in September 1963 to attend the General Assembly, Secretary of State Dean Rusk came to see me. He said, 'The President wants to find ways of improving relations with the Soviet Union and reducing tension.' He went on: 'Could we go for a ride out of town and carry on our conversation?'

I realised something serious was afoot, and of course accepted.

We drove beyond the city limits, where Rusk reported the President's message: 'Kennedy is thinking of reducing the number of US forces in Europe.'

We discussed this walking along the side of the road.

It seemed to me that common sense about this issue had at last gained the upper hand in Washington. The question had been present, visibly or invisibly, at almost every Soviet–US meeting since the war, whenever NATO policy and the remilitarisation of West Germany were discussed. The Soviet view was that US forces and bases in western Europe represented an obstacle to peace. Kennedy's idea therefore seized our attention.

I reported what Rusk had told me to Khrushchev, and said: 'If the President has the political strength to carry out his idea, he'll be doing a great thing for Europe, for the world and for the USA. Well, we'll just have to wait and see.'

Sadly, however, the President's days were numbered.

Thinking of Kennedy, I am reminded of what Roosevelt had said at Yalta: 'The United States will take all reasonable measures to preserve peace, but not at the cost of maintaining a big army in Europe three thousand miles from the USA. Therefore American occupation will last only a relatively short time.'

And yet not one of the post-war administrations has wanted to talk about reducing US forces in Europe – or anywhere else, for that matter.

During my work with the UN Atomic Energy Commission, I had frequent dealings with Bernard Baruch, the US representative.

He had been appointed as a well-known figure from the world of big business, who also knew how the Washington machine worked.

I had first met Bernard Baruch in Washington in 1941. On that occasion he spoke in a friendly way about the USSR, not of course out of sympathy for socialism, but out of antipathy for fascism. Even so, he said: 'The USA and Britain must do their duty as Allies and open the second front. I have spoken about this to the President.' That was at a time when many Americans, especially those occupying high posts in the state machine, were reluctant even to mention the second front.

He had been nicknamed the 'economic dictator' in the First World War, and, though this was an exaggeration, he did have enormous influence. During the Second World War he was the President's adviser on the war economy, and one conversation with him was enough to show that he understood both the surface phenomena and the deeper processes of the economy. For him the interests of monopoly capital were sacred, and presumably his advice helped the Roosevelt administration to strike a balance between those interests and the needs of the war effort.

After the war, with the formation of the Atomic Energy Commission, Baruch and I had an official reason for meeting. Since he was already seventy-five years old, it is not easy to understand why Baruch accepted the post as US representative on the commission, which certainly brought him no glory. The 'Baruch Plan' (as the press dubbed it), which he presented but which was really the Pentagon's plan, boiled down to making sure that the USA retained the monopoly on nuclear weapons. The intention was that the USSR and the rest of the world should to a significant extent place their security in Washington's hands. The USSR found this unacceptable.

The actual intention was to be camouflaged by the creation of an international body to monitor the use of nuclear energy. However, Washington did not even try to hide the fact that it intended to take the leading part in this body, to keep in its own hands everything to do with the production and storage of fissionable material and, under the guise of the need for international inspection, to interfere in the internal affairs of sovereign countries.

One day I received a very graciously worded invitation to visit

Bernard Baruch at his Long Island estate; the occasion was either his birthday or some other celebration. As a colleague on the commission, I accepted.

We arrived at a well-appointed, comfortable house. The other guests included leading lights in the business and academic communities, and, after we had all raised our glasses several times to our host's remarkably good health, Baruch came up to me and said in a low voice: 'I'd like to have a brief chat, just you and me. Let's talk about atomic weapons.'

I replied: 'Fine, I'd like that. I also want to say that we should meet more often for this purpose.' We moved away from the other guests and I went on: 'Although we discuss this issue at least twice a week, the main thing, of course, is not the number of meetings we have but their result.'

'Are you thinking of just US–Soviet meetings, or four-sided ones, with the French and British too?' Baruch asked.

I explained our position: 'Both forms of contact are acceptable to us, but if your administration thinks bilateral contacts are preferable that's fine.'

He seemed to be expecting this reply and said: 'I think bilateral talks would be especially useful,' adding, 'Washington will anyway consult with London and Paris on issues that interest the four powers.'

And that was what we agreed.

He then went on: 'The US government cannot understand why you will not accept the American position. This briefly comes down to the need to create some sort of international authority able to monitor state atomic industries. It would receive reliable information about the manufacture of nuclear weapons, and all governments would therefore be sure that the international agreement which they will have signed was being strictly observed.'

I asked him, 'Can you say what sort of authority this would be and what powers it would have?'

Until now, neither Baruch nor his advisers, such as Oppenheimer, had ever been precise about this new authority or its exact functions, and it was evident Baruch found my question hard to answer – clearly because he and his advisers had been ordered not to be specific.

Nevertheless Baruch gave me a broad hint: 'This international inspecting body must guarantee to provide complete monitoring of all the world's industries dealing with fissionable material. In other words, it must be competent, and it must have sufficiently wide powers to exclude any possibility of deception.'

He was thus confirming that under the US plan all the inspectors would be experts in the field. Inevitably, therefore, at that time they would all be Americans.

I replied: 'You and your government should not forget that an even more fundamental nuclear issue still divides us: namely, how are nuclear weapons to be controlled and how should future decisions on them be taken? These are decisions for the five powers in the Security Council. This principle was recently endorsed in the UN Charter and hence applies also to the Atomic Commission, which is a body created by the Security Council. The USSR is not prepared to give way on this.'

Baruch gave a blunt refusal: 'The USA cannot agree with that position.'

These were the main differences, then, within the commission. America had established a monopoly on the manufacture of nuclear weapons and wanted to retain that monopoly. Any references by the USA to some sort of international government which would settle all problems were purely propaganda. No serious politician in Washington believed in this supranational government – it was simply Truman's policy of avoiding any agreement with the USSR until the Potsdam resolutions could be 'reinterpreted' in America's favour.

Washington's propaganda machine worked without stopping, pumping out claims that the Soviet Union was barring progress towards any effective agreement, and avoiding any mention of America's efforts to maintain her monopoly on the manufacture of fissionable material. Even a number of major scientists were distracted by the idea of an international authority.

This campaign was remarked on in a letter from a number of eminent Soviet scientists, including the president of the Academy of Sciences S.I. Vavilov, the director of the Physics and Chemistry Institute A.F. Ioffe and the director of the Electro-Chemical Institute A.N. Frumkin. Their letter emphasised that the American position was unacceptable.

Whether Baruch himself thought the USA was making unjustified claims I do not know. But, if he were alive today, I wonder what he would say about the US claim to have the right of first strike against the USSR The Baruch Plan, so energetically trumpeted by the American side, was stillborn, and it could not have been otherwise, given its content and aims.

Years later I met Baruch – in his house facing Central Park in New York – with A. A. Sobolev, our permanent UN representative, and Baruch's son, who was also a businessman.

Baruch wanted to reminisce about his plan, and he made some ironic remarks about it. I had the definite feeling that he now doubted the Truman government's irreproachability, so finally I asked: 'Mr Baruch, a long time has passed since our squabbles in 1946. What do you think of the position you were defending then?'

He replied, 'I no longer defend everything in the plan they gave my name to.'

Sobolev and I did not rub salt in his wounds.

Later in the conversation Baruch complained: 'Americans today are being strangled by the high cost of living. The prices of everyday things have leapt to God knows what heights, even by comparison with wartime.' The idea of a millionaire grumbling about the cost of living was bizarre, but he continued bitterly: 'Even I am affected by the high prices. It's not so easy any more, for instance, to get domestic help. I've been look-ing for a new butler for months. I want to get rid of the son of a bitch I've got now, as he's started stealing from my wine cellar.'

Sobolev and I had a good laugh afterwards over the miseries of being a multi-millionaire.

I saw Baruch a few times at our UN mission. On the last occasion he came through the door and took up a boxer's stance, to remind me of the great fights – including Joe Louis's – he had taken me to see in 1946. He was friendly and categorically condemned hostile US statements about the USSR. As he was leaving, he said: 'Mr Gromyko, have you read my book, *How I Became a Millionaire*? I sent it to you in Moscow not long ago, at the UN mission.'

I replied, 'I did get the book and have nearly finished reading it.'

'Well, what do you think of it?'

Joking, I answered, 'I've tried following your advice, but noth-ing has come of it.'

We both laughed and said goodbye until the next time. But there was no next time. He died aged ninety-five.

All decent people, including those who do not agree with socialism, have urged that the monster of the nuclear weapon should not be uncaged and allowed to cause a world catastrophe. Some were closely involved in its production. And after Hiroshima it is well known that such eminent scientists as Albert Einstein, Robert Oppenheimer and Frédéric Joliot-Curie supported the call to prevent its continued production.

In early 1939, Joliot-Curie in France, the Hungarian Leo Szilard and the Italian Enrico Fermi, both working in the USA, had come separately to the conclusion that, under certain conditions, one could produce a chain reaction in a uranium nucleus which would be accompanied by an explosion of monstrous force. They also calculated that Nazi Germany had the resources with which to make a nuclear weapon. Their guess was confirmed: the Nazis had occupied Czechoslovakia and had already banned all exports of the uranium ore being mined in Jáchymov.

By this time Albert Einstein was living in the USA. In the 1920s the creator of the theory of relativity had been heading the Physics Institute of the Kaiser Wilhelm Society in Berlin (as the German academy of sciences was called), but with Hitler's rise to power and Nazi persecution of Jews he left for America. On 2 August 1939 Szilard persuaded Einstein to sign a letter to Roosevelt which described the work of Joliot-Curie, Fermi and Szilard, and called on the administration to take note of their research, since it could lead to the production of a new type of bomb of unimaginable force. The object was to beat Hitler to it. The President's note, 'This demands action!', was dated 11 October 1939.

It was not until 6 December 1941, however, that the White House actually decided to go ahead with the development of nuclear weapons, and it was not until 13 August 1942 that the Manhattan Project was launched, co-ordinating all the work connected with the new weapon and headed by Robert Oppenheimer. The USA put two billion dollars into making three bombs; 150,000 people were employed; and two new towns had to be built in secret. Then, as the project was nearing completion, on 25 March 1945, Einstein and Szilard sent another letter to Roosevelt. Five years before, they had urged him to make the bomb; now they tried to prevent its being used.

I well remember my meeting with Einstein. It took place in the Waldorf-Astoria in New York. Naturally, we talked about the atom bomb, as it was then called. Everyone was talking about its use, the ash having hardly yet dispersed above Hiroshima and Nagasaki.

'The papers have been printing more and more reports about the atom bombs dropped on Japan,' I said. 'What will happen next? Everyone wants to know.'

I was greatly impressed by his answer. As always, he expressed himself quietly. 'I have told President Roosevelt that, in connection with the atom bomb, misfortune awaits us all. My opinion is now widely known. The boys here do not fully realise the fate that awaits the round ship we are all in, including the Americans.'

By 'boys' he meant the American politicians, and by 'round ship' he meant the earth.

He went on: 'If it depended on the scientists, I think the overwhelming majority of American scientists would call for the ban of this appalling weapon.'

He mentioned several names, including that of Ernest Orlando Lawrence, an eminent physicist whom I knew well. He had been awarded the Nobel Prize for his work on atomic physics in 1939, and during the war the Soviet Academy of Sciences had asked me to confer on him the status of honorary academician.

I recall one particularly remarkable statement Einstein made during our talk: 'If I had known that Hitler was not going to be able to develop the atom bomb, I would never have supported the American atomic research programme.'

I met Oppenheimer and Joliot-Curie several times, the former when he was working as scientific consultant to Bernard Baruch in the UN Atomic Energy Commission, and the latter when he was head of the French Atomic Energy Commission and adviser to the French representative on the UN commission, Alexandre Parodi. By now Oppenheimer had recognised the threat posed by nuclear weapons, and he and Joliot-Curie opposed their continued production and spoke repeatedly of the need to ban them. Oppenheimer was careful to avoid phrases which could be interpreted as direct disagreement with the US government's official position, even though it was plain enough what he meant. Joliot-Curie on the other hand, while tactful about the official line of the Western

powers, was openly negative towards the US position being taken
in the talks. We were impressed by his nerve.

Official circles in the West began to look at them both with
suspicion, and then to condemn them openly, especially Oppenheimer. We found him very obviously strained in our conversations – evidently being constantly tailed had left its mark.
Needless to say, he did not talk about this. The US authorities punished him even so, accusing him in 1953 of 'disloyalty'
and denying him access to secret information. It was his political
death.

Similarly, after Joliot-Curie's had been the first signature on the
Stockholm Appeal in March 1950, calling for an irreversible ban
on atomic weapons – an appeal which within six months had been
signed by half a billion people – Bidault removed him as France's
supreme commissioner on atomic energy, and he was not permitted to work at Fort Châtillon, France's main centre of research,
where he himself had started up France's first nuclear reactor.
After this, Joliot-Curie devoted himself to the struggle against
nuclear weapons and became the head of the Universal Peace
Committee.

More and more scientists now support this view, and as a result
certain responsible political figures in the West have been willing
on occasion to discuss disarmament, but as a rule their words are
mere rhetoric and they rarely do more than shuffle the issue off
into some committee or other, where it dies a death at the hands
of the pettifoggers.

I had a characteristic conversation with Dulles once on this
subject. It took place during the San Francisco conference. Dulles,
an unofficial adviser to the US delegation, expressed an interest
in the Soviet armed forces and asked me: 'Tell me, please, Mr
Gromyko, is the Soviet Union going to keep its multi-million-man
army for a long time after the war?'

I replied, 'We will decide that question when the time comes.
For the moment it is too soon to say.' I then asked Dulles, 'And
what do you think the USA will do with its forces in Europe and
Asia after victory over Japan?'

He answered: 'I do not hold an official post in the Truman
administration, so what I say is my own opinion, but in my view
the bridgeheads we have taken on the Pacific islands, and will take
in Japan itself, should be maintained by the United States.'

When Dulles became Secretary of State some time later, he

translated what he had said to me into the language of official foreign policy. Under him, the question of disarmament was hermetically sealed, and his obstructionist spirit lived on for ten to fifteen years. In Washington there was no sense of alarm about the arms race, and efforts were made to reverse even those agreements partially limiting arms production that had been negotiated under Presidents Nixon and Carter.

It has long been axiomatic that the militaristic course in world affairs is the policy of those for whom the arms race is big business. Writing that capitalism will eschew no means to acquire excess profit, Marx quotes the English publicist, T.J. Dunning: 'Guarantee ten per cent and capital will do anything, guarantee twenty per cent and it really comes to life, at fifty per cent it is ready to cut off its own head, at one hundred per cent it will trample every human law, and at three hundred per cent there is no crime it will not risk, even if it means the hangman's noose.'

Human reason revolts against the idea that scientific genius, the highest skills of workers and colossal resources should continue to be wasted on weapons of destruction. The people are right to demand an end to this madness.

The railroad millionaire Averell Harriman was a most distinguished figure in American life, coming to prominence as the representative of those in big business who were able to think realistically about the Soviet Union. I knew him for more than forty years.

Harriman went into politics in the thirties, under Roosevelt, holding a number of administrative posts, in particular as adviser to the President on industrial and financial questions.

Then came the war. The Soviet leadership, as Roosevelt knew, did not have a very high opinion of US ambassador Steinhardt, then in Moscow. His panic reports that the Soviet capital would fall to the Germans and that the front would collapse were widely known. His successor, William Standley, was in Moscow little more than a year (April 1942 to September 1943) and left no trace of having been there.

Roosevelt's next choice fell on Harriman, who had already accomplished a number of political missions for the government. For instance, he had been the President's special representative in England to implement the Lend-Lease agreement, and at the end of September 1941 had been the US delegate to the three-power Moscow talks dealing with war deliveries.

When his new job came up he visited me at the Soviet embassy in Washington, where he praised the Soviet people in their struggle against the Nazis and also expressed the view that the USSR and USA must find a common language.

He arrived in Moscow as ambassador in October 1943, bringing his daughter with him, and was often received by the Soviet leadership. His experience in business, where there are always problems between workers' representatives and the entrepreneur, helped him on the diplomatic front. We saw how astutely he had learned to develop his argument in the course of the discussion, listening carefully to what was said before giving a firm opinion. At his own request, early in 1946 he was transferred as ambassador to London and his place was taken by Walter Bedell Smith.

Harriman's influence was no longer what it had been under Roosevelt. On the other hand, post-war Democratic presidents frequently used his services for important political missions. He spent some time as Secretary of Trade, and later he was the President's special aide on international affairs and Assistant Secretary of State.

I particularly remember his invaluable contribution to negotiations for the 1963 treaty banning nuclear tests in the atmosphere, in space and underwater, which was signed eventually by myself, as Soviet Foreign Minister, Dean Rusk and the British Foreign Secretary Alec Douglas-Home.

The signing had been preceded by talks in Moscow in July of that year with Harriman and the British Minister for Science, Lord Hailsham. As work on the treaty came to an end, one barrier still remained: we needed to know under what conditions any party to the agreement would have the legal right to withdraw. The USSR proposed that a state could exercise its sovereign right to withdraw if exceptional circumstances threatened the higher interests of that state. The British representative soon got the go-ahead from London to accept our proposal, but the US representative would not agree, since he said it would conflict with the President's instructions.

During a break in the talks, I suggested to Harriman that he pick up the phone in the next room and call President Kennedy. I told him: 'As the signing is being held up by this one obstacle, I think the President ought to know.'

Harriman took my advice and phoned the White House. Kennedy at once gave him permission to accept our proposal; when we sat down again, all three delegations approved the Soviet text and within an hour the full draft had been initialled. What Harriman did seems simple enough, but someone with less influence and experience might have acted differently and started a lengthy correspondence with Washington – and God knows what that would have produced.

To the end of his life Harriman spoke up for peaceful coexistence, condemning anti-Soviet positions taken by Washington and insulting remarks about the socialist system in the Soviet Union. He took part in the talks which led to the end of the war in Vietnam, and he frequently spoke up against the arms race.

As I was writing my thoughts about Harriman, I heard the sad news of his death. It is hard to accept that he is no more, that we shall never again hear his voice, soberly calling on the USA and USSR to live in peace.

Following the test-ban treaty of 1963, a whole system of agreements came into being: on research in space (1967), non-proliferation of nuclear weapons (1968), the ban on nuclear and other weapons of mass destruction being deployed on the sea-bottom (1971), the convention on banning the development, manufacture and use of biological and toxic weapons and on the destruction of such weapons (1972) and the convention banning military and other substances harmful to the environment (1977). The bilateral Soviet–US anti-ballistic missile treaty (1972) and its codicil (1974), and the temporary agreement limiting strategic offensive weapons – SALT-1 (1972) – were especially important.

People who are familiar with the USA often express sadness at the contradictions in the political life of that country. This particularly applies to Washington's behaviour in the field of disarmament. The Strategic Arms Limitation Treaty of 1979 (SALT-2), for instance, is an excellent case in point. The last stage of the treaty came during the presidency of Jimmy Carter and, in the course of agreeing the terms, I visited the President several times. On one occasion in the White House, he said to me: 'The United States accords enormous importance to this treaty. It must be concluded. The United States stands firmly behind this.' Yet only a short time later the same Jimmy Carter was ensuring that the treaty would not be ratified by Congress. His pretext was that Soviet policy in Afghanistan at the end of 1979 made ratification impossible. The fact is, however, that all the really important American decisions concerning arms limitation in the broadest sense had been taken before, not after, Soviet involvement in Afghanistan.

NATO's decision to increase its annual budget for fifteen years had been taken in May 1978; in December 1979 the US President had decided on a five-year growth of America's military strength to the highest level ever; and in December 1979 NATO took the extremely dangerous decision to redeploy new American medium-range nuclear missiles in Europe. Thus it had already become plain by December 1979 that the ratification of SALT-2 was off, and events in Afghanistan were quite irrelevant. All in all, Washington seems to have used them as a figleaf to cover up the nakedness of its arms race policy.

The situation grew worse when Reagan came to power. American and NATO arsenals must already have been full to the rafters, and yet frenzied multi-million-dollar arms programmes were voted in one after the other. And now a new and extremely dangerous development has been thought up: weapons in space.

If one were to use the latest technology to take a photograph showing the global scale of military preparations by the USA and her allies, one would see a panorama that would appal any objectively minded person: multi-warhead missiles, strategic bombers, an armada of warships, hundreds of bases around the world and a vast stockpile of all kinds of arms.

It will be said: 'What about the USSR and all the weapons it has on the ground, in the air and on and under the sea?'

We answer: 'Yes, they are there, but through no choice of ours.'

In practical terms, only Nixon and Ford gave any attention to the issue of disarmament, and Carter partially, since it was during his presidency that the understanding, reached by President Ford in his talks with Brezhnev at Vladivostok in October 1974, was put into force.

Why should this be so?

Only one answer seems possible: those who set the policies of many Western powers and support the build-up of nuclear arms and the militarisation of space must at that time have decided that, since it is not possible to secure a world with only one social system (their own), then they will let anything happen. Either the capitalist world triumphs, or the whole world must fall into the abyss. Since then, however, much has changed for the better.

In January 1986, Gorbachev announced a bold and ambitious new programme for the complete destruction of nuclear weapons by the end of the century. This was ratified by the 27th Party Congress and approved by the political consultative committee of the Warsaw Pact. Even if we accept that a great deal of time will be needed to carry out this radical solution to the problem, reason still demands that everything be done to stop the arms race now, and eventually to destroy nuclear weapons.

There is cause today to believe that not only leading scientists but also the majority of ordinary people understand the truth about nuclear weapons and recognise man's profound responsibility in the matter. Even so, some states are still far from pursuing the logic dictated by the nuclear age. Strange as it may seem, there are still influential people who try to prove that the existence of such weapons actually helps to keep the peace. They claim that nuclear weapons are 'the chief support for peace and peaceful development'. And fear of nuclear weapons is proclaimed as 'the greatest blessing for mankind'. This is the most blatant hypocrisy.

Whenever I have met leading world figures, as soon as the discussion touches on basic issues they will muse about where things will end if the arms race is not stopped and if it is extended into space. Such people are not isolated individuals. Their contemplation and hesitation reflect a definite sense of alarm that is now universally felt.

At times today, even entire Western political parties waver when they are faced with making a definite decision concerning the arms race. The British Labour Party is a case in point. When it was in power it agreed to the deployment of new US missiles in western Europe, including Britain. Then, when the Conservatives under Margaret Thatcher won the parliamentary elections and adopted a strong policy of nuclear rearmament, the Labourites began to recognise the importance of arms limitation and the complete elimination of nuclear weapons.

Let us take another example. As we know, Washington asked West German Chancellor Schmidt for permission to deploy further US nuclear missiles in West Germany, and no arm-twisting was needed to get him to agree to this step. Once they were in opposition, however, Schmidt and the other leaders of the German Social Democrats adopted a more responsible stance, and called for an end to further deployments and for an effort to seek ways of reducing the armed confrontation in Europe.

These things tell us that there is a pendulum effect at work in the political and public life of the NATO countries. This alone justifies our doing everything possible to explain our policies. Of course, nobody can determine when doubt becomes hesitancy, hesitancy becomes conviction, and conviction becomes practical action, but one thing is certain: out of the clash of different tendencies in the whirlpool of international life, in the last analysis the wish for peace will triumph.

10

England and the English

People make their first visit to England with enormous interest. What's London like? What about the famous Tower, Westminster Abbey, Buckingham Palace? Where's Shakespeare buried? What are the English like? These were the questions in my mind when I arrived there for the first session of the UN General Assembly at the beginning of 1946.

The worst war in human history had just ended. Europe was in mourning but also rejoicing, grieving for her dead but triumphant in victory. The Soviet leadership, and Stalin personally, were determined to continue to co-operate with the Western Allies, including Britain. During the Potsdam conference, however, changes had occurred on the British political scene. The Labour government of Clement Attlee had replaced the wartime government of Winston Churchill, and even the British themselves were not sure at first what the new government's policies would mean.

In the event, there were some minor social changes, but they did not alter the essence: the class face of power remained the same. Internally, the social foundations which had taken centuries to form were not even subjected to serious erosion. As for the impression made abroad in the months following the election, it was essentially the same: nothing had changed or was likely to.

The Soviet side did hope, however, that the Attlee government would have a more objective view of the Soviet position, at least on international issues such as the fate of the colonial territories. A wave of national liberation movements was rising in certain regions and the question of their future urgently needed to be addressed.

A council of Foreign Ministers met in London in September–October 1945 to deal with many questions raised at Potsdam, but in particular with Italy's colonial possessions in Africa. The USSR was firmly in favour of giving these colonies their independence, and the Soviet delegation made the concrete proposal that the USSR be given the United Nations trusteeship for Tripolitania, with the aim of facilitating the sovereignty of Libya.

This proposal met fierce resistance from both London and Washington. Ernest Bevin was especially zealous; any Conservative Foreign Secretary would have envied his colonialist fervour. As a result of this, serious divisions arose, and at one point Bevin made an inexcusably rude remark to Molotov.

Molotov at once demanded, 'Mr Minister, I ask you to withdraw that.' When this challenge produced no result the Soviet minister got up and made for the door. 'In that case, I cannot participate in the council's work.'

To Bevin's discomfort, protests broke out all round the table. Quickly realising what he'd done, he called out: 'All right, I take back what I said.'

But Molotov either did not hear him or, more likely, did not catch his meaning and continued rapidly towards the door. Had it closed on his back, it would probably have been the end of the meeting.

Without hesitation, I called after him in Russian: 'Bevin has taken back what he said.'

Molotov was at the door, but when he heard me he returned to the table and after several minutes the meeting resumed. As for Bevin and Molotov, they hardly looked at each other.

Bevin was a colourful character, of course – he simply did not observe the commonly accepted norms of behaviour. A major trade-union figure in the Labour Party, and a genuine original, he evidently thought that, coming as he did from the lower orders, he had the right to behave as he liked.

He once said to me: 'I'm on good terms with your ambassador, Gusev. We have good contacts and things are going fine.'

In fact, the main feature of Gusev's conversations with Bevin consisted in Bevin trying to steamroller him. The ambassador would present a question to the British Foreign Secretary, request a reply and then sit patiently, while Bevin boomed on in his thick, bass voice about everything but the matter at hand.

From my own conversations with Bevin, I gained the impression that his knowledge of history, like his knowledge of science, was very vague. He once admitted: 'Though I have to do a lot of diplomatic work, I've hardly read a book on it, and there's not much chance that I ever will, either.'

There was something appealing in such frankness. Another side of Bevin I did not like at all. When he was talking with other delegates or ambassadors – no distinctions were made – he would use quite unacceptable expressions. His vocabulary seemed to rest uneasily between the refined speech of an Oxford don and sheer gutter language.

We used to joke among ourselves in the Soviet delegation that, if you joined Bevin's qualities to those of Attlee, then you'd get what you wanted. Attlee lacked Bevin's abrasiveness but also his forthright nature. He represented the English school of manners at its best. It was torture for him, however, if he had to speak first at a meeting, so it was perhaps fortunate that his time in the corridors of power was brief.

I was appointed ambassador to London in June 1952. Stalin called me to the Kremlin for a talk. Pacing the room, as always, he underlined the importance of my new post: 'England has the opportunity now to play a major role in international affairs. But it's not clear which way the English, with all their sophisticated diplomatic experience, will direct their efforts.' He broke off, and came up close to me: 'That's why we need people there who can help us to understand their thinking.' He was brief and to the point. That was my main instruction.

I handed my credentials to Queen Elizabeth II, though she had not yet been crowned. Before this, I had met her father, George VI, at the beginning of 1946 when he was giving a dinner in honour of the delegates to the first session of the General Assembly. At the end of the meal all the guests rose from the table, which was laid with massive gold cutlery, and, as we moved into a spacious drawing-room, I found myself alongside the King, evidently not by accident. Suddenly I heard him say: 'Let us go into the middle of the room for a little chat.'

On his own initiative, the British sovereign started urging me earnestly that it was essential that the wartime contact between the USSR and Britain not be lost. Naturally, I supported this view. Our conversation attracted the attention of the other guests but aroused no surprise. Both countries were, after all, wartime allies. I will not hide the fact that the conversation with the King made a good impression on me.

My second meeting with the King and his charming and highly cultivated wife, Queen Elizabeth, took place at a reception for delegates at the same UN Assembly. I remember their courtesy to the Soviet representatives, and to the Ukrainian and Belorussian diplomats as well. A little way off, also receiving the guests, were the present Queen Elizabeth II and her sister, Princess Margaret. I had a brief, polite but extremely friendly conversation with the two princesses. Princess Elizabeth impressed the Soviet delegation with her seriousness and courtesy. I remember her interesting, if brief, comments on Russian literature and art, and on the people whose bravery the English admired.

As Queen Elizabeth, she made the same impression on me when I handed her my credentials in 1952. I was struck by her mature judgement on questions connected with relations between the USSR and Britain.

The ceremony took place in the reception room at Buckingham Palace. We Soviet diplomats, noting the quality of the finish, thought that, with a few more metres in the width and a much higher ceiling, it would run a close second to St George's Hall in the Kremlin. As for the range of colour and the furnishings, however, Buckingham Palace was on the whole gloomy, in keeping with Anglo-Saxon taste.

I saw Churchill again, also in 1952, when I was ambassador and he was Prime Minister. I found that all he really wanted to do was to reminisce about Stalin and Roosevelt during the war and to talk about the meeting of the Big Three at Potsdam. He liked making the trip into the past, and if I hadn't interrupted him he would have gone on for ever.

That's how it was again in 1953 when I paid him my last visit before returning home to Moscow, where I had been summoned to become First Deputy Minister of Foreign Affairs. Stalin had just died.

Churchill spoke about Roosevelt at Yalta. 'I was afraid the President would not be well enough to go through with it. He was ill almost every day. It was his old affliction coming back. He was also under enormous stress.'

I nodded. 'Stalin was also rather worried about the President's health. He even visited him, first sending word that he should not try to get up, or go to any trouble. And that's how it was. Stalin did not burden him, he only wished him a speedy recovery. I was there myself – it was a touching scene.'

Our meeting ended on a positive note. Churchill accompanied me to the door of Number 10, where the photographers were waiting. He's there in the photograph of our last meeting, with his inevitable cigar and his inimitable Churchillian smile. Two days after our meeting he sent me more than two dozen of his small water-colours, bound in an album.

During my various visits to Britain I met many British political figures, but from them all I would like to single out Anthony Eden, who was Foreign Secretary three times – in 1935–8, 1940–5 and 1951–5 – and in 1955–7 was Prime Minister.

Some time in my youth, while reading and rereading the classics of English literature, I created an image in my mind of what I thought was the typical Englishman: tall, gaunt, slightly phlegmatic and almost always smartly dressed in black. Sadly, my first live Englishman, who was teaching my group when I was a graduate student in Minsk in 1933, was distinctly below average height and not in the least smart.

When I was sent abroad on my diplomatic work, I soon realized that, physically, many of the English are not very different from people of Slavic origin. But, if one is thinking of the intellectual type, who likes to talk politics over one of the famous whiskies with his visitor from abroad, then I would say Anthony Eden was exactly my typical Englishman. I would go so far as to say he was a living model of what a subject of the British empire should be.

He had the enviable quality, in a politician, of being able to start up a conversation on the smallest pretext. It seemed to me that everyone in the room was ready to respond in kind to Eden's enchanting smile. It all looked so natural. He was, of course, helped by the ample stock of appropriately gracious phrases that graduates from Oxford and other privileged institutions have at their disposal. I cannot remember any time, either as Foreign Secretary or as Prime Minister, when he even raised his voice. It was just not his style.

I single out Eden, not because he occupied a position in any way different from that of other leading Conservatives of his time, but because he possessed an innate ability to seek compromise. Participants in talks sometimes felt that the path ahead was blocked, that a wall stood between them. Then all of a sudden, the next day, or even in a few hours, Eden would appear with his readily adjustable smile and an ingeniously new approach that eased the situation – even if what he had to say did not eventually bring agreement any closer. So, on the one hand, he was a politician who created crises, such as the tripartite aggression against Egypt in 1956, and on the other hand, his methods acted like life-belts at talks.

I met Eden most often at post-war Allied conferences, and in London after the Conservatives had beaten Labour in the 1951 election. As always, he was polite and ready to talk about anything. The topic that interested him most was the relations between the victorious powers, as they were affected by the position in Europe. He often worried about European issues, especially in relation to Germany. Unfortunately, at the time we met, I felt that he was representing a country that was already tied by joint obligations to the USA and the other NATO countries. Though he said we should not allow a worsening of Soviet–British relations, the feeling remained that he spoke without conviction. Truman and Dulles were already at work, relations between the Allies were going downhill, and ruling circles in Britain were not keen to stop the rot.

I remember something else from my meeting with Eden. He was seriously ill. He told me he had jaundice and was not feeling well. He said he would feel better for a while and then it would get worse again. Usually lively, quick in his movements and loving a joke, now he looked limp and motionless, though intellectually he was as lucid as ever. He was still the interesting man I had enjoyed talking to in Berlin, Geneva and San Francisco.

His political career came to an abrupt end in the Anglo-French –Israeli aggression against Egypt, and in January 1957 he resigned, to be replaced by Harold Macmillan.

Macmillan had played an important part in the Conservative Party since the beginning of the Second World War and held various ministerial posts in Conservative governments. When he was Prime Minister, his view of foreign policy was based on strengthening Britain's ties with the USA within the framework of NATO. He was in favour of West Germany's rearmament and the political and economic integration of western Europe.

Macmillan's term as Prime Minister was characteristic of the cold war. During his visit to the Soviet Union in February–March 1959 he had talks with the head of the Soviet government, N.S. Khrushchev, and as Foreign Minister I took part. The chief questions on the agenda were, of course, the situation in Europe, relations between East and West Germany, the remilitarisation of West Germany and East–West relations. The arms race and disarmament were touched on in almost every talk, and the British position presented by Macmillan excluded the least possibility of any understanding or the slightest movement.

Khrushchev did not exactly help matters by inviting Macmillan to have the talks in 'Stalin's remote cottage', a beautifully decorated house outside Moscow, so called because it had been built for Stalin.

The atmosphere was none the less businesslike: nobody banged the table and a calm tone was maintained; but nothing was achieved. In all, the results of that visit amounted to the fact that a senior guest had actually come and a meeting had actually taken place. That was all.

A second episode took place during the fifteenth session of the General Assembly in the autumn of 1960. The Soviet delegation was headed by Khrushchev, and Macmillan headed the British delegation. The debate became heated at times. In all the General Assembly debates, as well as in its many committees and sub-committees, the Soviet Union and leading NATO countries were in constant confrontation.

I remember, on 28 September, one particularly sharp speech by Macmillan on fundamental questions of East–West relations. The delegates were listening to him intently. Suddenly, at the point where Macmillan started using especially strong language against the Soviet Union and her friends, Khrushchev bent down, took off his shoe and started hammering it on the desk in front of him, the sound of the shoe on the bare wood resonating around the hall, while he shouted out: 'The Soviet Union is for universal disarmament with universal monitoring, and it's the Western powers that are doing the undermining!'

It was a unique moment in the history of the UN. To give Macmillan credit, he went on with his speech as if nothing was happening. Soviet and American security men immediately formed a circle around the Soviet delegation. I was on Khrushchev's right, and the permanent Soviet representative, V.A. Zorin, was on his left, and sitting immediately in front of us was the Spanish delegation, who ducked out of the way, just in case the owner of the shoe decided to give an encore.

The atmosphere was strained. One of the Spaniards of ambassadorial rank got up, stepped out of range of the shoe, turned and yelled at Khrushchev: 'Ve do not like you! Ve do not like you!'

Nobody was surprised at that, as our relations with Spain at that time were terrible, and our diplomatic relations with them non-existent, since the country was still under Franco.

It seems funny now, but at the time no one, either among the delegates or in the public gallery, was laughing. They were all too amazed. One of the chief actors that day had lost his temper. A pity, but it does happen.

Leading figures in Britain at that time often said that Macmillan was haughty and vain. I personally observed this to be the case, but no more than in other pillars of the Conservative Party. In October 1963 Macmillan retired from politics and returned to his publishing firm. Prime Minister and publisher – an interesting combination.

Macmillan was succeeded by Alec Douglas-Home, but he was not Prime Minister for long. The Conservatives were defeated in the 1964 election and Labour came to power. When the Conservatives came back in 1970, Douglas-Home was made Foreign Secretary in Edward Heath's cabinet.

I met both of them many times. They both acknowledged the importance of developing co-operation between the USSR and Britain but, alas, in practice the Conservative government hardened its attitude to the USSR. In the autumn of 1971 the government even instituted a gross provocation against the USSR, accusing a number of Soviet personnel in England of 'impermissible activities', and ordering them to leave the country. The accusations were false, and the Soviet government issued a strong protest.

Soviet–British relations stagnated for a while, but then in 1973 conditions were ripe for a visit by Foreign Secretary Douglas-Home, and it took place in December.

I have very lively memories of Douglas-Home. He was a mild-mannered man: it was not in his nature to speak harshly, especially to a foreigner. One must, however, qualify this. After talking to him for a while, one realised that something did not quite match his moderate manner. Resting now on one leg, now on the other, he would insist – quietly, of course – on expounding his ideas, without stopping, through to the bitter end. If he was obliged to give his partner in conversation a break, he would just be waiting for his side of the tournament to begin again. There were no sudden, still less brilliant, breakthroughs in my meetings with Douglas-Home, but at least each one left a civilised impression that made the next meeting easier.

It is hard to say what judgement history will pass on Lord Home's role. He added sharpness to the outline of British foreign policy. He also liked to run ahead slightly. His government would hardly have made up its mind on an issue before Alec Douglas-Home would blurt their decision out. It used to be possible to tell exactly which way British domestic policy was going from Douglas-Home's statements at international meetings. However, his elaborate arguments and rationalisations carefully never contradicted American policy. For this reason, he was always respected in Washington, and little real progress in Soviet –British relations was made until Labour came back into power in 1974.

Harold Wilson's predecessor as leader of the Labour Party in opposition was Hugh Gaitskell. We had established contact when I was ambassador in 1952–3, and I remember a conversation with him when he was a guest of the Soviet embassy. At his request we were alone. His comments on general questions of policy were not particularly original: they contained a measured dose of criticism of the USA and a similarly measured emphasis on the need to improve Soviet–British relations.

He was clearly not keen to go deeper into his views on East–West co-operation and, while arguing for peaceful coexistence with countries having different social systems, he stuck to a pretty firm line of supporting NATO and allied relations with Washington. For appearance's sake, Gaitskell was not above criticising Washington, but by the time it came down to real policy his anger had cooled.

Indeed, the Labour Party shares much of the responsibility for the way in which, after the Second World War, Britain's foreign policy became increasingly dependent on the American line. History will judge the Labour Party harshly for its solidarity with Washington, and for its lack of any independent line in foreign affairs when it was in power.

At one point during our conversation, Gaitskell stretched out his hand to me and I reached out mine to him. Then we both burst out laughing at this spontaneous gesture. We realised, however, that although it was a joke it was a significant one.

Gaitskell said, 'When all is said and done, Labour is a socialist party, isn't it?'

'You would know better than I,' I declared.

And we both laughed again.

Picking up what he had just said, I asked him: 'As leader of the Labour Party, could you explain to me the direction in which your party wants to take the country? Up to now, Labour has not done much to reshape either the economy or the social structure. Nobody takes mere nationalisation seriously as a means of undermining private ownership.'

Gaitskell declared: 'The Labour Party does not, of course, adhere to the teachings of Marx. We regard them as entirely inappropriate for England.' He went on: 'Certainly Labour stands for social transformation – but not the radical changes that Marxism dictates.'

I asked, 'If Marxism doesn't suit the Labour Party, then what is your guiding philosophy? No serious party can be without some fundamental principles. What are yours?'

He replied, 'The Labour Party follows the teaching of the Fabians. They are the people British socialists most respect.'

In saying this, Gaitskell tried to give the impression that there were no different opinions within his party. But in fact, of course, he belonged to its right wing, whose theoretical credo was some brand of 'democratic socialism'. When he went on to explain this credo, he naturally wanted very much to prove that it was different from that of the Conservatives, but he failed utterly. He did not accept the concept of class ideology, for example, but when he went into detail, apart from some propaganda debating points from electoral campaigns, it turned out that the ideological foundation of Labour's political activity was the ideology of the ruling class, the bourgeoisie, plus some petty-bourgeois admixtures.

Yes, the English middle class have arranged the whole educational system so as to make the social sciences work in their favour. That is true of philosophy, political economy and all branches of history. And it is worth adding that, in my experience, Britain's statesmen, both Labour and Conservative, her social figures, diplomats and clergymen, all have a very scrappy knowledge of the human sciences. In essence, what they have is selective, pragmatic, a hard-headedness of the crudest kind. Bishop Berkeley himself would give them high marks for mastering his ideas on subjective idealism. Needless to say, there are people in Britain who stand head and shoulders above those I have mentioned here; but they are mostly people (including communists) who have acquired their knowledge outside the walls of the recognised universities.

Gaitskell's successor as leader of the Labour Party was Harold Wilson, a man who left a significant mark on his country's history. President of the Board of Trade in the first Labour government, Wilson and the leader of the left wing, Aneurin Bevan, resigned from Attlee's cabinet as a protest against cuts in the social services.

When Labour returned to power in 1964, after a thirteen-year absence, Wilson became Prime Minister. The government's domestic policies led to genuine reforms in economic and social life and to gains for the trade unions. In foreign policy, however, the government was in favour of Britain's active participation in NATO and co-operation with the USA on several important issues, for instance, Vietnam, the Middle East, European security and disarmament. Growing discontent with Labour's policies led to their electoral defeat in 1970 and they went back into opposition for a further four years.

Wilson became Prime Minister again in 1974. Both inside his own country and abroad, Wilson had the reputation of being a master of political manoeuvre, an experienced and skilful politician who knew how to use a situation. I can personally attest that his reputation was well earned, for, in February of the following year, he visited the Soviet Union. The talks which took place at the highest level were important in bringing about mutually beneficial co-operation between the USSR and Britain. They concluded with the signing of a protocol which envisaged the deepening of political consultations on international problems, as well as questions of bilateral relations. Also signed was a joint declaration on the non-proliferation of nuclear weapons and two long-term programmes, one on the development of economic and industrial co-operation and the other on scientific and technical co-operation. In the joint declaration, both sides asserted their intention to work together to extend détente to all regions of the world.

In March 1976 I arrived in London for talks with Prime Minister Wilson and Foreign Secretary James Callaghan. This was my last meeting with Wilson, who had already decided to resign, as both Prime Minister and leader of the Labour Party. The reins were taken up by Callaghan. It was plain to me during our meeting that Wilson was retiring from active political life with regret, and he did everything to make the meeting as unconstrained and friendly as possible.

I want to emphasise that Wilson was well disposed towards the Soviet Union, not in terms of our fundamental socialist philosophy, but in terms of realising more deeply than many others that the USSR and Britain must learn to live in peace and to co-operate to prevent war. His frequent visits to Moscow bear witness to this, and it was characteristic of him that, after retiring, he became the honorory president of the GB–USSR Association.

James Callaghan, the new Labour leader, tended to the right wing of the party. As Prime Minister, he wanted Britain to maintain close ties with the USA. He believed that, standing firmly on the ground of NATO and the EEC, Britain should fill the role of bridge-builder or connecting link between the Commonwealth countries and the USA and also between the USA and the countries of the Common Market. Even so, during the first period of Callaghan's government, the positive trend in Anglo-Soviet relations continued. Trade grew, as did scientific, technical and cultural co-operation.

I have known Callaghan for a few dozen years and his manner has never changed. Seeing him for the first time, you might think he was a Russian. The open, amenable look and the measured smile suggest readiness to start a conversation. He is never forced or tense, and always looks as if he's about to slap you on the back.

Wilson and Callaghan were an interesting pair. They seemed to have been born to work with each other, and they did quite a bit of good for Britain.

Callaghan was less abrupt than Wilson. Rather than saying outright, 'I don't agree with you', he preferred the more cautious 'Maybe one could put it this way . . .' before giving his version. I must say I felt quite a lot of sympathy for Callaghan. Though a man of few words, what he said was always weighty. He would soften his position by saying, 'I will listen to what you have to say with pleasure', and add, 'Let's not rush. The Soviet Union and Britain will still be here tomorrow.'

I enjoyed talking to Callaghan and people like him and Wilson. A particular stratum of the Labour Party was raised in precisely this spirit.

★

What is Britain's political picture today? The Conservative govern-ment has adopted a position of unconditional support for America. The old British lion is becoming senile. Countries which were once part of the great British empire – now modestly known simply as the Commonwealth – are with good reason becoming more refrac-tory in their attitude to London. They often vote against Britain in the United Nations, particularly as a sign of protest against Lon-don's collaboration with the racist regime in South Africa.

Even in these circumstances, the Soviet Union has tried to maintain the positive gains in our relations of previous years. We point out the dangers for Europe and the world inherent in Tory policies. Gorbachev spoke about this personally to Margaret Thatcher during his visit to Britain in December 1984 and again when they met in the Kremlin in 1985.

Contemporary England is a product of the England of yester-day. Parliament's decisions are a complex fabric woven of a thousand threads through which influence is brought to bear on the legislators by the bourgeoisie who really rule the country. One way or the other, they inevitably get their wishes through. The most varied subjects can be discussed in Parliament for days and weeks, being rejected, amended, changed from one point of view to another. But in the end they emerge rounded off, in the form of finished decisions, elegant, smoothed out and presenting no hindrance to the ruling class in using its power.

Sometimes a snap election takes place, and you think something unusual is about to happen; but, after any election, the bourgeoisie is still in power. And that's the only thing that matters.

The two main political parties, Conservative and Labour, follow each other in and out of government. They each know that whatever majority they gain at one election they are going to have a minority at some future election. This ties them together with one string, visibly and invisibly.

If one looks at Parliament, the armed forces and the civil service, one sees that they regenerate themselves. England, in fact, is a living example of Marxist-Leninist teaching on the base and the superstructure.

Moreover, if one notes that British capital is closely meshed with American capital and that the multinational companies have become a malign influence in the international arena, then the essence of the British system of power, with its open and secret corridors of that power, becomes even clearer.

At the front in the cold war

With the same sense of excitement that I had felt in August 1948 on returning home after eight years in the USA, I left London for Moscow in April 1953, to take up my new post as First Deputy Minister of Foreign Affairs. But the years had passed and unfortunately the cold war had become a reality. The creation in April 1949 of the North Atlantic Treaty Organisation (NATO) had been preceded by a loud propaganda campaign, involving politicians, historians, economists and journalists, whose single message was the 'communist threat' and the 'purely defensive character' of the future military bloc. One of the chief activists in this campaign was Walter Lippmann, whose articles on the need for military alliance came out in all the main mass-circulation organs. Every article would include a dose of hostile references to the USSR.

Among the major generators of the idea of NATO and the ideology of the cold war was Dean Acheson, Secretary of State from 1949 to 1953. His handwriting was also visible in the Truman Doctrine and the Marshall Plan. Methodically and persistently, Acheson did all he could to bring NATO into being. He had no difficulty finding assistants. It was just a matter of providing government dollars for anyone willing to say what the reactionaries wanted to hear. It is accepted practice in the USA to invite academic establishments to advise on foreign policy.

One of the worst examples of US aggressiveness in international affairs was the Korean war. But Soviet moral and material aid helped to support the Korean Democratic People's Republic (North Korea), and the USSR played an important part in opening the armistice talks which were successfully concluded in 1953.

The situation in the Korean peninsula has not yet been resolved and the position in the Far East remains unstable. The USSR supports North Korea's proposal that American troops be with-drawn from South Korea, thus providing a sound basis for the peaceful reunification of the country without outside interference.

It should be noted also that the USSR greatly facilitated the signing of the Geneva accords on Indo-China, bringing to an end the bloody war launched by the French against the people of that region.

In 1953 Truman, Churchill's partner in launching the cold war, was replaced as President by Dwight D. Eisenhower.

History is full of examples of hitherto unknown figures coming to the fore during great events, usually connected with wars. Eisenhower was just such a man. In only ten years he made the leap from being a virtually unknown staff officer in 1941, to supreme commander of Allied forces in Europe in 1943, to Presi-dent of the USA in 1953.

He possessed no special qualities. It was circumstances which were mainly responsible. When America entered the war, Roose-velt had to find top military personnel in a hurry, and this helped Eisenhower up the ladder. When a commander-in-chief for Allied forces was needed, they looked for an American general who was good at staff work and handling people – Eisenhower again. Then, when he entered the presidential election in 1952, it was with the support of big corporations and companies involved in arms production that his victory was secured. For financial-industrial monopolies like those of Rockefeller, Morgan, Du Pont, Mellon and other billionaires, Eisenhower's policies were their policies, and they consequently used every means and spared no expense to get him back into office when he stood again as Republican candidate in 1956.

Eisenhower's eight-year term in the White House was character-ised by an increase in reactionary domestic political feeling. Arms production speeded up steadily. The slogans of the arms race and the cold war embraced all aspects of US domestic and foreign policy.

The Korean war ended in the first years of Eisenhower's presidency. Then both sides signed the Indo-Chinese agreement in Geneva, and it looked as if the heat was going out of the ten-sion between East and West. Washington, however, had other ideas.

In 1955 a meeting of the heads of government of the USSR, USA, Britain and France took place in Geneva. Sharp exchanges occurred revealing serious differences between the former allies. Eisenhower, Eden and Edgar Faure fiercely argued that NATO was a force for peace, especially in Europe, while in fact their plan was aimed at swallowing up East Germany into West Germany, and whitewashing the remilitarisation of West Germany in peace-loving propaganda.

In an effort to deprive the three Western powers of their notion that the Soviet Union was not doing its part in consolidating peace, the Soviet delegation, consisting of Khrushchev, Bulganin, Molotov, Marshal Zhukov and myself, announced that the Soviet Union was willing to join NATO. We argued that, since NATO was dedicated to the cause of peace, it could not but agree to include the USSR.

It is hard to describe the effect this announcement had on the Western delegations when it was made by Bulganin, as President of the Council of Ministers. They were so stunned that for several minutes none of them said a word. Eisenhower's usual vote-winning smile had vanished from his face. He leaned over for a private consultation with Dulles; but we were not given a reply to our proposal.

After the meeting, Dulles caught up with me in the corridor and asked, 'Was the Soviet Union really being serious?'

I replied, 'The Soviet Union does not make unserious proposals, especially at such an important forum as this.'

Dulles was about to add something, when Eisenhower came up. Now a smile did appear on his face, as he said: 'We must tell you, Mr Gromyko, that the Soviet proposal will be carefully examined by us, as it is a very serious matter.'

At later meetings of the four powers, however, it was evident the Western delegations did not wish to discuss our proposal further and they simply steered clear of it, giving mysterious, oracular smiles whenever it was mentioned. The fact is, NATO simply did not know how to deal with it and so they simply hushed it up. Often I have mentioned our proposal to US officials of later generations and very few of them have ever heard of it.

At our suggestion, Zhukov paid a visit to Eisenhower. According to Zhukov's account, Eisenhower withdrew into himself and merely mouthed a few platitudes. I could see that Zhukov was upset and, on our way back home, he made the comment that the

Soviet Union must 'keep its powder dry', a view shared by the other members of the delegation.

I met Marshal Zhukov many times, especially after I became Foreign Minister. He was then Defence Minister. Two meetings stand out in my memory. The first occurred when we went to Bucharest together in April 1957 to sign the Soviet–Romanian treaty on the legal status of Soviet forces temporarily based in Romania. Since we sat next to each other we soon got talking, and I noticed he was always more relaxed when he was not in Khrushchev's company.

Speaking of the war, on the flight to Romania, Zhukov said: 'Winning depended to a large extent on the determination of the troops and the officers. The certainty that we were going to win kept up everyone's spirits, from privates to generals.' The marshal's words referred to the stern measures employed towards the end of the war to reinforce discipline among the troops – harsh actions with which he personally had been associated.

With undisguised pleasure, Zhukov talked about the new missiles that were being supplied to the army. There were as yet no intercontinental ballistic missiles, but the great powers had major new ballistic weapons and Zhukov was pleased with the range over which ours had been successfully tested.

He also made a number of comments about Stalin which may seem significant. Though Stalin was dead and Khrushchev had made his famous speech about him at the 20th Party Congress in 1956, Zhukov nevertheless said: 'I acknowledge the enormous service Stalin rendered as supreme commander.'

On the subject of Khrushchev's part in any military operations during the Second World War or their preparation, however, he said absolutely nothing. On the other hand, Khrushchev himself often liked to recall his trips to the front and his contacts with various military people.

There have been recent reports in Soviet sources to the effect that Zhukov recognised that the Soviet military leadership was to blame for the fact that our forces were unprepared to meet the fully armed Nazi aggressor. I never got that impression from him myself, but I do remember his saying: 'Before the war, the political decision to arm fully was taken very late, and that was the main problem.'

Although he never expressed such thoughts in the presence of former members of the Politburo, he also spoke bitterly of the enormous damage Stalin had inflicted on the country by his massacre of the top echelons of the army command. 'Of course, I regard them as innocent victims,' he said. 'Tukhachevsky was an especially damaging loss for the army and the state.'

Many people, especially journalists, have pointed out Zhukov's harshness as a war leader and have suggested that he lacked self-control. Maybe at the front, especially during the fighting, he was severe, but in my experience he never lost control of himself. I know him as a man of principle. It is absolute nonsense to suggest that he exaggerated his own role in the war. In any case, how could he overemphasise his own part? His service to the Motherland is the jewel in the crown of the Soviet people's greatest victory.

Another leading Soviet military figure of whom I have always had the highest opinion is the Defence Ministry chief during the sixties and seventies, Marshal Andrei Antonovich Grechko. A country's foreign policy has to stand on the solid foundations of an efficient economy and a reliable defence force. Equally, the armed forces of any state cannot but feel the influence of its foreign policy. My working contacts with Grechko therefore were systematic, and hardly a day passed when we did not discuss some problem where defence and foreign policy overlapped. As a result, our proposals were commonly submitted to the Politburo over both our signatures, and Brezhnev gave his support to our work.

I first got to know Grechko properly in 1955, when he was commander-in-chief of the Soviet Army Group in Germany, and I quickly realised he was more than a military expert. He could discuss US foreign policy, NATO as a whole and the policies of other states. He had the ability to listen and was always willing to change his mind if he found his own judgement unconvincing. Although he could not be counted among the great orators, in a small company of friends he was transformed: he could analyse information, marshal his arguments and draw brilliant conclusions. I think our military historians will always recognise the debt we owe him as an army chief, patriot and communist.

Fairly soon after the four-power meeting in Geneva, Washington took a course officially announced in 1957 as the 'Eisenhower doctrine', according to which the USA claimed the right to use armed force to impose its authority in the Middle East. The doctrine (which, overtly and covertly, was widely followed) envisaged opposing national liberation movements and intervening in the internal affairs of other countries in the region under the guise of resisting the 'communist threat'. It blatantly contravened both international law and the UN Charter.

The Soviet Union repeatedly pointed out the dangers for peace in the Eisenhower doctrine. They were demonstrated in the plots which were hatched against the independence of Syria, and the aggressive US action in Lebanon in 1958, which developed into the US Middle East policy we see today; yet our protests were ignored.

In September 1959, however, Eisenhower sought political contact with the USSR, and invited Khrushchev on an official visit to the USA. The talks covered a wide range of topics, in particular the circumstances surrounding Berlin. The Soviet side stressed the importance of settling these on the basis of a German peace treaty and normalisation of the situation in West Berlin and its environs. The US position made such an approach impossible. Understanding was, however, reached that talks on West Berlin should be continued, and that the four powers should meet again in May 1960.

Eisenhower was courteous to the Soviet delegation throughout the visit. He tried to create a pleasant atmosphere and in general behaved as though he wanted constructive relations. As a further sign of this, he invited Khrushchev and others in the Soviet delegation to the official presidential retreat at Camp David, located in wooded hills some forty-five miles from Washington. The residence consists of a number of green-painted wooden cottages, and the main building is a simple one-storey house containing a moderately sized living-room with a massive fireplace, and a number of bedrooms in the wings.

The place was first used by Roosevelt in the early days of the war. He called it Shangri-La, after the land of eternal youth in James Hilton's *Lost Horizon*, and made frequent use of it as a country retreat. Truman used it less often. Eisenhower revived the practice, however, renaming the place Camp David, after his grandson. The Americans have a tendency to give names to places. What we might call a peasant hut they would give the name Golden Rock, just because there was a brown stone nearby, maybe no more than six feet high.

American presidents often invite senior foreign guests to Camp David: it is ideal for such meetings, as I found on a number of occasions.

Khrushchev's arrival was preceded by an odd little conversation. Just before he came in, Eisenhower joined in a chat I was having with Dulles.

The President looked distinctly tired. He complained, 'My health is playing up', and added: 'It's my heart. It's giving me trouble and I've got to be careful.'

Dulles and I listened sympathetically. Eisenhower continued: 'It turns out that the best thing for it is to have a brandy before going to bed. If I'd done that, I could have avoided the heart attack I just had.' He was smiling, but to show he was being serious he said: 'That's not just my opinion, it's what my doctor says – the famous cardiologist, Professor White.'

Professor White did indeed help Eisenhower for a time, but his heart trouble eventually caused his death.

Before leaving Washington, Khrushchev invited Eisenhower and some of his cabinet colleagues to an official farewell dinner at the Soviet embassy. My neighbour at the table was the President's wife, Mamie, as she was affectionately known. She spoke sympathetically about the Soviet people:

'You've been through so much. We know how hard things were in the war. We know what you lost.' Even so, she felt obliged to conform to the current fashion: 'But it now looks like the Soviet Union wants to impose its system on other countries. There's a lot being written about that. It's what a lot of people here think. Is it true?'

I told her, 'Don't believe everything you hear,' and added that we strictly observed the principle of non-interference in the affairs of other countries.

Mamie's response was typical of her. With disarming spontaneity, she said, 'They don't say anything about that over here, for some reason. I've never seen it in the Bible either. And the Bible is my handbook.'

Keeping a straight face, I had no choice but to agree with her. 'That's right, the Bible doesn't say anything about it.'

Khrushchev's visit in fact amounted to little more than a routine occasion, with no real change in attitudes, and the joint communiqué reflected this.

Soon, however, an incident occurred which made Soviet–US

relations even more difficult: the invasion of Soviet airspace on 1 May 1960 by the US U2 spyplane, shot down by Soviet missiles in the region of Sverdlovsk. The fact that it had been planned was plain to see, as the pilot, Gary Powers, himself confirmed. But Washington behaved defiantly and tried to deny the obvious. So the Soviet Union demanded an apology from the US government, and went on to table a question on the subject at the preliminary four-power meeting, which took place in Paris on 16 May, prior to the summit arranged the previous year for later that month.

The general tension was obvious from the circumstances of that meeting. The heads of delegation assembled in the hall, and Khrushchev entered first, followed by Defence Minister Malinovsky and myself. We went at once to our places and stood at the table waiting for the others. Two or three minutes later President Eisenhower and his aides entered. He was about to move forward to greet Khrushchev, but met his icy stare, understood the situation and remained where he was. No greeting took place: the two leaders did not even shake hands. President de Gaulle and Prime Minister Macmillan, observing normal practice, shook hands with the other delegates.

This somewhat unusual overture boded no good. After a few words from de Gaulle, Khrushchev took the floor: 'This meeting can begin its work if President Eisenhower will apologise to the Soviet Union for Gary Powers's provocation.'

In a barely audible voice, Eisenhower replied, 'I have no intention of making any such apology, as I have nothing to apologise for.'

Everyone realised that to carry on sitting would be to start a competition over who could outsit the other. Therefore, without uttering a word, everyone got up and left the hall. The USA did not give the USSR the apology it deserved and the meeting, which might otherwise have done much to reduce world tension, was broken off.

The French President tried to save the situation by telling Khrushchev that although Eisenhower was wrong in principle he should be forgiven, but nothing came of this approach.

Even so, Eisenhower deserves credit at least for a statement he made in his farewell address in January 1961, in which he warned against the influence which was being felt from 'the conjunction of an immense military establishment and a large arms industry'.

He said: 'We must guard against the acquisition of unwarranted influence, whether sought or unsought, by the military-industrial complex.'

Americans who knew the political situation would often say, 'If Dulles didn't exist, we'd have to invent him.' There was something in this. The faithful servant, convinced and steadfast and, in his own way, capably defending the interests of the military-industrial complex – such was Dulles.

Born in Washington in 1888, the son of a theology teacher, the grandson of one Secretary of State and the nephew of another, as early as 1907 John Foster Dulles was in the US delegation to the Hague Peace Convention, was an adviser to the US delegation at the Versailles Peace Conference in 1919 and in subsequent years carried out many diplomatic missions.

Closely involved in big business, Dulles was on the board of a number of corporations and banks, and headed the powerful law firm of Sullivan and Cromwell, whose services were used by sixty companies, representing a large slice of American industry. Sullivan and Cromwell were members of the pro-fascist America First Committee, and Dulles and his wife personally made large contributions to this body. Appointed president of the foreign commission of the National Council of the Church of America in 1941, Dulles was on its extreme reactionary right wing. In 1944 he became vice-president of the Association of New York Lawyers and chairman of its international law section. The cults of the cross and the sword seemed to fit well together in him. Having become a millionaire himself, he zealously defended the interests of big business and the increasing expansionism of US foreign policy.

I first met Dulles in 1945 in San Francisco, at the conference steering committee, and I observed him for about fifteen years thereafter. Throughout that time he was consistent. He never adapted himself to the man in the White House, whoever it was. Neither Roosevelt nor Truman regarded him as an errand boy. Bible in hand, he would always defend right-wing positions.

Although his style was angular and sharp, he was not a born orator. He spoke slowly, calmly and quietly, but his words made an impact. Everyone knew he was the voice of monopoly capital, which ran America, and as a participant in the Foreign Ministers' conferences in London (1945), New York (1946) and Moscow (1947) he exerted a strong influence on the US government's positions.

In the early 1950s he held a number of posts, becoming virtually a permanent adviser, but he could get no higher. He was active in the electoral campaign of 1952, giving Eisenhower his support and drafting the Republicans' foreign policy. He ascended the last rung of the ladder in January 1953 when he became Secretary of State, and his stamp was thereafter plainly visible on every aspect of US foreign policy and diplomatic activity, above all on Soviet –US relations.

Dulles invented the idea of 'brinkmanship', which he regarded as an advanced way of conducting external affairs and which he embraced until the end of his life. His name is closely associated with the militant course of US policy and hostility to the USSR, in which few other US politicians could outdo him.

What can be said of him as a man? That is not so easy, since it is hard to imagine him outside the politics he represented. My impression of him, talking to him alone, is that, while he was not exactly confused, he would often begin hesitantly, as if trying to find the right wavelength. Also, he was constantly fidgeting: he would shift from one foot to the other, and very rarely look you in the eye.

Was he well educated? Undoubtedly, if one took the standards of the West, where the humanities are taught in strict conformity with the needs of the ruling élite. During one of my visits to Washington he invited me to his home, with the Soviet ambassador Menshikov. He received us in a living-room-cum-library and proudly showed off his large collection of books, some of them antiques.

Apparently to impress us, he led us to a bookcase containing the works of Lenin and Stalin, published in the USA.

'Here is Lenin, here is Stalin,' he said. 'Their selected works. I'm working on the dictatorship of the proletariat right now, looking into what has been written about it and what it really means.'

He showed us some of the pages he had marked with comments and underlinings and exclamation marks; obviously he took his reading seriously. I had the chance to see some of his marginal notes which, although banal, showed he was sharply critical of everything he'd read. The ambassador and I thanked him for his hospitality and wished him luck with his studies of Marxism-Leninism. Dulles laughed out loud, and so did we. We understood one another very well.

In the summer of 1959, when the Foreign Ministers of the four powers were meeting in Geneva to discuss Germany, an adjournment was suddenly announced: John Foster Dulles had died. Only a few months earlier he had left his post as Secretary of State through illness and become a special consultant to the President. Now we all had to go to Washington for his funeral.

We all flew together. A little way in front of me was the new Secretary of State, Christian Herter. He was lame and used crutches, so we always let him go ahead.

Somewhere over the Atlantic, the US Secretary of Defense Neil McElroy came over to me and asked: 'May I join you, Mr Gromyko? There are one or two things I'd like to talk over with you.'

'Be my guest,' I replied.

I knew perfectly well that no Secretary of Defense was going to say anything on his own initiative to the Soviet Foreign Minister, especially with the Secretary of State sitting in the same plane.

McElroy began talking about what he called the 'yellow peril', that is, China. 'The yellow peril,' he said, 'is now so great that it just cannot be dismissed. And it's not just a matter of taking it into consideration – it has to be dealt with.'

Although I could guess where he was going, I said nothing and let him carry on.

'We ought to combine against China.' He stopped to see what effect this had on me.

Soviet–Chinese relations at that time were difficult, to say the least, with armed clashes taking place on our borders.

In reply I said: 'You and I – that is to say, the USA and the USSR – have the much more important job of finding a solution to the difficulties in Europe and trying to improve Soviet–US relations.'

'But, still,' he insisted, 'there's a big problem here. We both have to think about it.'

That was the end of the conversation.

I understood, as I was no doubt meant to, that it was really the Secretary of State, not the Secretary of Defense, who had spoken to me.

I told Khrushchev about McElroy's overture when I got back

to Moscow. He said my reply had been the right one. The issue was not raised again, either by us or by the USA.

In February 1957 I was appointed Foreign Minister. The aggressive intrigues of imperialism continued to provoke serious crises in various parts of the world, and in April 1961 American mercenaries mounted an invasion at the Bay of Pigs in Cuba. The action, which ended in ignominious failure, led to the postponement of an agreed Soviet–US summit meeting.

The purpose, therefore, of the Vienna meeting (3–4 June) between Khrushchev and John F. Kennedy, the new President, was to establish contact between the two leaders and to discuss the basic issues of Soviet–US relations. Disappointingly, although the conversation was conducted in frank terms, and went on longer than planned, it did not result in success.

Meanwhile US foreign policy had led to a new upsurge of tension, with Cuba as the epicentre. Even after the defeat of American mercenaries at the Bay of Pigs, Washington had not changed its course on Cuba. Instead, on the pretext that Cuba was being turned into a 'base for communist penetration into America', a loud propaganda campaign about the 'Soviet threat' in the region was launched. On 4 September 1962 President Kennedy made a statement in which he cast doubt on the legitimacy of measures being taken by the Cuban government to secure the defence of its own country. The statement contained direct threats to Cuba if she did not back down. On 11 September the Soviet government called on the USA 'not to lose its self-control and soberly to assess where its actions could lead', and suggested a path to the normalisation of the situation in the Caribbean.

The preparations for imperialist intervention continued, however, and therefore the Soviet and Cuban governments reached agreement on the further reinforcement of Cuba's defences. The appropriate arms were installed, including rockets. This was a purely defensive measure. At the same time, Cuba pointed out that, if the USA would give effective guarantees that it would not carry out an armed invasion of Cuba and not help other countries to invade either, Cuba would have no cause to reinforce her defences.

In the face of the mounting international crisis, the USSR undertook active diplomatic efforts to find a peaceful settlement.

On 18 October 1962, on the instructions of the Soviet leadership, I met President Kennedy in the White House. Understandably, most of my talk with Kennedy was devoted to the Cuban problem, while other international issues, in particular Germany and West Berlin, took a back seat.

I put the Soviet position to the President. 'I should like to draw your attention,' I said, 'to the dangerous development of events in connection with the US government's attitude to Cuba. For some considerable time, the American side has conducted an unrestrained anti-Cuban campaign and made attempts to block Cuban trade with other states. Calls for aggression against that country are being issued in the USA. This course can lead to serious consequences for the whole of mankind.'

Kennedy replied, 'The point is, the present regime in Cuba does not suit the USA. It would be better if there was a different one there.'

I asked him: 'But what basis does the American leadership have for supposing that the Cubans ought to decide their domestic affairs according to Washington's judgement? Cuba belongs to the Cuban people, and neither the USA nor any other state has the right to interfere in her internal affairs. All the statements we hear from the President and other officials, to the effect that Cuba is a threat to US security, are groundless. It is enough to compare the size and resources of the two countries, one gigantic, the other tiny, to see that the accusations against Cuba are obviously false.'

I then emphasised my point: 'The Cuban leadership, and Fidel Castro personally, have stated to the world more than once that Cuba has no intention of imposing its system on anyone, that she stands firmly for non-interference between states in domestic affairs, and tries by means of talks to settle all outstanding questions with the US government. And yet, although these statements are supported by actions, those who call for aggression against Cuba say they are inadequate.' I added, 'The only way to solve the overwhelming majority of international problems is through talks between states, and declarations in which governments explain their positions.'

This gave the President clearly to understand that, if the USA had any claims against Cuba or the USSR, then she should settle them by peaceful means. Threats and blackmail were out of place.

I then told President Kennedy in the name of the Soviet leadership: 'Should the USA undertake hostile actions against Cuba, or against states which have good relations with her and which respect her independence and give her aid at a difficult time, the Soviet Union cannot play the part of bystander. The sixties of the twentieth century are not the middle of the nineteenth century, not the time when the world was divided up into colonies, and not the time when the victims of aggression could only be heard weeks after any attack. The USSR is a great power and will not be a mere spectator when there is a threat of unleashing a big war in connection with the question of Cuba, or in connection with any other part of the world.'

Kennedy asserted, 'My administration has no plans to attack Cuba, and the Soviet Union can take it that no threat to Cuba exists.'

He then made an important admission: 'The action in the area of the Bay of Pigs was a mistake. I don't deny that the Cuban problem is a serious one, but I am restraining those who are in favour of actions which could lead to war, as long as such actions are not provoked by the other side.'

Kennedy's interpretation of the situation was that it had been made worse by the Soviet Union's installation of weapons in Cuba. He then read a formal statement, vindicating the US plan to place a blockade around Cuba: 'We are only talking about banning ships from calling in at US ports for cargoes, after they have made deliveries to Cuba.'

Again I was compelled on behalf of the Soviet leadership to state: 'The Soviet Union urgently calls on the US government and the President personally not to permit any steps to be taken that are incompatible with the interests of peace and order and in accordance with the UN Charter.'

Contrary to later assertions made in the West, at no time in our conversation did Kennedy raise the question of the presence of Soviet rockets in Cuba; consequently there was no need for me to say whether there were any there or not.

Furthermore, I told the President: 'Soviet aid to Cuba is aimed exclusively at strengthening her defensive capability and developing her peaceful economy. Using Soviet instructors to teach the Cubans how to handle defensive weapons cannot be seen as a threat to anyone. The USSR answered Cuba's call for help because the call was simply a response to an impending danger.' I concluded by saying: 'Mr President, allow me to express the hope that the USA now has a clear understanding of the Soviet position on the Cuban question and of our assessment of US actions in relation to that country.'

At the end of the meeting I carried out one further instruction from Moscow: 'I have been asked to convey a proposal from the Soviet leadership for a Soviet–American meeting at the highest level to settle vexed international questions and to review questions of difference between the Soviet Union and the United States.'

Although Kennedy responded favourably to this proposal during our talk, later the same day I was informed that the American side felt that such a meeting, were it to take place in 1962, would lack preparation and hardly be fruitful. Washington, therefore, while not rejecting the possibility of a summit meeting, postponed it indefinitely.

I should add that my conversation with Kennedy had been full of sharp turns and sudden breaks. He was nervous, though he tried not to show it, and kept contradicting himself. After making threats to Cuba, he would say Washington had no aggressive intentions against that country. In fact, as it later emerged, at that very moment the President, in the strictest secrecy, with a group of his closest colleagues – Vice-President Johnson, Secretary of State Rusk, Defense Secretary McNamara, Attorney-General Robert Kennedy, General Taylor and a number of other presidential aides and advisers – had been considering different ways of landing an invasion force of American troops on Cuba.

The day I spoke with Kennedy I also met Dean Rusk. In the course of our conversation the Secretary of State affirmed: 'The USA has no intention of carrying out an armed invasion of Cuba, even though the island is being turned into a bridgehead for an attack on the USA. The Cuban regime does not conform with the interests of the security of the Western hemisphere.'

Rusk expressed his particular dissatisfaction about the appearance of Soviet weapons in Cuba, although, like Kennedy, he did not ask specifically about our rockets.

In reply we said: 'Cuba is compelled to draw conclusions from the attempted invasion in 1961. This was prepared by Americans on American territory and armed at American expense. If Washington has claims against Cuba, for example of a material kind, then the USA has every right to enter talks with the Cubans to settle them.'

Rusk gave no reply to this.

Then followed a significant discussion on the question of American bases outside US territory in close proximity to the Soviet border.

I said: 'You obviously will not deny the presence of American military bases and numerous military advisers in Turkey and Japan, let alone Britain, Italy and other West European countries, as well as Asia and Africa. Thus the USA may have bases in those countries and conclude military treaties with them, yet you do not believe the USSR has the right to help Cuba to develop its economy and strengthen its defensive capability – precisely that, its defensive capability.'

Demonstrably avoiding a reply on the main question, he said, 'The Soviet Union is exaggerating the role of US bases abroad.'

My talks with Kennedy and Rusk made it plain that the US administration did not wish to make an objective analysis of the situation, nor to use peaceful diplomacy as a means to settle the problem. All this came out of the confused and excited mood which then dominated leading US circles. President Kennedy was under pressure from the hawks who were insisting on a test of strength, and the fact that common sense eventually gained the upper hand shows that Kennedy, who had been visibly thrown off balance, was in fact a statesman of outstanding intelligence and integrity. My conversation with him was perhaps the most difficult I have had with any of the nine presidents with whom I had dealings in my forty-nine years of service.

A few days later, on 22 October, in an address to the American people, the US President declared the naval blockade against Cuba that he had mentioned to me earlier. He also sent a personal message to the leaders of the Soviet government. On 23 October the Soviet government replied that the US blockade must be seen as 'an unprecedented act of aggression', and drew the attention of other countries to the fact that Washington was prepared 'to push the world towards the abyss of an armed catastrophe'. The Soviet declaration underlined that, if the aggressors unleashed war, the Soviet Union would make the proper response.

During the Cuban crisis, an intense correspondence was being conducted through diplomatic channels. The Soviet side, seeking a peaceful solution, officially submitted compromise proposals on 27 October and these became the basis for a settlement. The USSR agreed to remove the rockets, regarded by the USA as offensive, on condition that the USA would respect the inviolability of Cuba's borders and undertake not to carry out aggression against her. The USSR also required that in return the USA would remove its rockets from Turkey.

In reply, the President gave his assurances that no invasion would take place and also promised to lift the naval blockade. Driven by the acute struggle going on in US political circles, however, the White House made a statement on 27 October 1962 attempting to prove that there was no connection between the problems of security in the Western hemisphere and those of Europe, and that the Cuban crisis must be settled before there could be any undertaking to deal with other problems.

Despite this public stance, the question was discussed in confidence, and the President did take a decision in principle to remove US missiles from Turkey – and that in the end is what happened. As a result of the diplomatic struggle, the main problems of the Cuban crisis were settled, and at a press conference on 20 November President Kennedy announced the lifting of the naval blockade.

On 7 January 1963 First Deputy Foreign Minister V.V. Kuznetsov and the permanent American representative to the United Nations, Adlai Stevenson, sent a joint letter to UN Secretary-General U Thant, in which they stated that 'although the two governments have not solved all their problems' they believed that the level of agreement achieved made it unnecessary to place the Cuban crisis on the Security Council agenda.

The letter went on: 'The governments of the United States and the Soviet Union express the hope that the measures taken to avert the threat of war in connection with this crisis will lead to the settlement of other differences between them and to a general lessening of tension.'

Common sense as well as a sense of responsibility had prevailed.

I had first met John F. Kennedy in 1945 at the San Francisco conference, where he was a special correspondent. He asked me for an interview and we met in the St Francis Hotel, where the Soviet delegation was staying. I remember to this day the detailed questions he put, mostly about the Charter of the new organisation; it was clear that he knew his way around foreign policy issues, and he spoke with assurance about Roosevelt's opinions. On almost no single question of substance concerning the UN Charter did he take a different position from ours. Even where the US and Soviet positions were opposed, Kennedy listened to what I had to say, and even expressed understanding of our motives. Only someone with access to the White House or to people close to the President could speak as he did.

Half jokingly, I said, 'Did you have a hand in preparing President Roosevelt's proposals on the UN for the Yalta conference?'

He replied, 'No, I didn't, but I've got good contacts with people around the President and my father is a friend of his.'

That explained a lot.

When we met for the first time in the White House, after he had been elected, he remembered our meeting in San Francisco.

I remarked, 'You know, Mr President, I formed the opinion then that you were no ordinary newspaperman.'

He laughed.

During my visit he introduced me to his family, his wife and his two children. The gathering took place on the well-kept lawn in front of the White House before our talk, at which we were joined by A.F. Dobrynin and G. M. Korniyenko.

Both in the USA and abroad, public opinion saw it as a bold step when in his speech at the American University in Washington, on 10 June 1963, Kennedy called on the American people directly to drop some of their cold war stereotypes and support him in restraining the military-industrial complex. This speech showed that Kennedy was looking ahead further than the captains of the arms industry and the Pentagon; it could be regarded as the outstanding act of his presidential life.

My last meeting with him left a deep impression in my mind. It took place two months before he was assassinated.

As I entered his study, I found him smiling and as usual in a good mood. He said, 'Why don't we go out on to the terrace and talk one to one without interpreters?'

Naturally I agreed, and we left the room.

He immediately began to talk about the internal situation in the USA: 'The fact is, there are two groups of the American population which are not always pleased when relations between our two countries are eased. One group consists of people who are always opposed to improvement for ideological reasons. They are quite a stable contingent. The other group are people "of a particular nationality"' – he meant the Jewish lobby – 'who think that, always and under all circumstances, the Kremlin will support the Arabs and be an enemy of Israel. This group has effective means for making improvement between our countries very difficult.' He ended briefly: 'That is the reality. But I think it is still possible to improve relations, and I want Moscow to know that.' He stopped, obviously wanting to hear what I had to say.

I replied: 'I want to underline first of all that we understand very well that the two groups you mention do not represent the opinion of your country as a whole. Surely the ordinary people are not in favour of tension between the USSR and the USA? They want good relations, and many facts show this. Not only the Soviet people but the American people too approved the agreement over the Cuban crisis. And the President's contribution to obtaining agreement is well known.'

I stopped and looked at him. But he was clearly waiting for me to continue.

I went on: 'As for affairs in the Middle East, has not the Soviet Union in the past called for the establishment of two independent states on the former territory of Palestine, one Arab and one Jewish? Both our countries have made similar proposals. Everyone needs to be reminded of this. Therefore there is no need for the part of the population you have mentioned to feel aggrieved at us.'

At the end of our conversation, Kennedy said, 'I just wanted you to know some of the difficulties the President of the United States has to face when dealing with questions of Soviet–US relations.'

The conversation then continued in the President's study with others present.

I don't know why, but when I first heard the Tass report of Kennedy's murder it was that talk on the White House terrace that came into my mind – what he had said about there being opponents to his policy.

It is now over a quarter of a century since Fidel Castro took the Cuban helm. It is not given to many people to become a legend in their own lifetime, but my meetings with Castro, in Moscow and frequently in Havana, have convinced me that he is a giant in mind and heart and in his services to his people.

He once told me that, while still a student, he read the *Communist Party Manifesto*: 'I realised that it contained the true path to national and social liberation for my country.'

People who knew Fidel in his childhood and youth say that his qualities of leadership within a collective group were clear from an early period – in school, university and then in his revolutionary, party and state activity. This is above all explained by his intellect, his dynamic personality and enviable physique.

From the earliest days of the revolution, Castro zealously developed physical culture and sport on a national scale. To this day, he hardly misses a major international baseball, boxing or volleyball match that takes place in Cuba. He often invites senior overseas visitors to join him on such occasions, Scuba-diving remains one of his great pleasures. 'The colourful underwater world always delights me. It brings me a sort of spiritual peace.'

One of Castro's closest comrades-in-arms was Che Guevara. If there were a world pantheon for people who have made the deepest impression on the struggle for freedom in the name of social justice, then the ashes of Che Guevara would be buried there.

Che Guevara once told me how he had become head of the National Bank of Cuba in 1959. 'After Batista had been overthrown and power was transferred to the people,' he said, 'we leading activists were meeting with Fidel so he could distribute responsibilities among us. When we got to who should handle the economy, Fidel asked, "Tell me, friends, which of you is an economist?"'

Che paused. 'I thought he had said, "Which of you is a *communist*?", so straightaway I said, "I am," at which he said, "OK, you handle the economy."'

I laughed out loud and Che continued: 'By the time the misunderstanding was cleared up it was too late – no other jobs were left.'

He was later made Minister of National Industry, a post he held from 1961 to 1965.

Che used to come to Moscow for talks on economic co-operation, in which I took part, and it was plain that he had a sound understanding of Cuba's needs; in general he was a competent partner in the talks, both firm in defending his views and also tactful.

Che Guevara also took part in the United Nations General Assembly. As head of his country's delegation, he spoke on 11 December 1964 on Cuba's position in the international situation, condemning imperialism and US interference in Cuba's internal affairs and the US blockade – which incidentally is still virtually in being. The Assembly was full to capacity and the delegates applauded Che's speech.

So great was the Cuban counter-revolutionaries' hatred of Che Guevara that they fired off a bazooka at the UN building while he was speaking. Luckily they were bad shots and the shell fell into the river. UN security guards arrested a woman called Pérez, a Cuban counter-revolutionary who was carrying a knife with which she intended, in her own words, 'to kill Che Guevara'.

Before Che left New York, the Soviet delegation hosted a dinner in his honour to which we invited heads of delegation of other socialist states. The Soviet side was represented by the three delegations of the USSR, Ukrainian and Belorussian republics. The occasion was memorable for its warmth and cordiality, and everyone toasted our Cuban comrade on his speech to the UN.

After dinner, Che and I had a tête-à-tête. He told me: 'I'm going straight from New York to a distant land, to help the people there in their struggle for a dignified life and freedom.'

In 1967 the news flashed around the world that Che Guevara had been brutally murdered in the jungles of Bolivia by enemies of her people and of freedom.

The essence of US policy in international affairs had been fully revealed at the beginning of 1965 by Washington's armed intervention in Vietnam.

The US President at the time was Lyndon Johnson. As Vice-President he had taken over in 1963, on the assassination of John Kennedy, being sworn in on the plane back from Dallas to Washington, and in the election of 1964 he managed to retain the presidency, helped partly by the popularity of the dead President whose legacy he had promised to uphold. The results of Johnson's policies are well known. They led to a worsening of social and racial conflict within the country and gross errors abroad, the worst being the war in Vietnam. It was therefore no surprise, when speaking in 1968 shortly before the next election, that Johnson shed a tear as he announced that he would not be standing – but it was far too late for tears.

Despite the many meetings I and other Soviet officials had with our US counterparts over the question of Vietnam, we faced an impenetrable, unhearing wall. By the end of the sixties, everyone, including the White House, realised that the US army of intervention numbering over half a million men was hopelessly bogged down in the Vietnam jungle. Neither the bombing of North Vietnam nor bombing missions over Laos and Cambodia had brought the results the US strategists were looking for in the 'dirty war', as the Americans themselves call it. Instead the war caused serious dislocation in the US economy, emptied the state treasury and hit the taxpayer hard.

The Johnson administration made attempts to ask the Soviet Union to assist the USA in finding a way out of the Vietnamese impasse, but nothing came of these, since Washington obviously wanted to achieve the impossible – to get out of Vietnam and remain there at the same time.

In 1966 the 23rd Congress of the CPSU had declared that the USSR and the other socialist countries would provide the necessary support to Vietnam, and this declaration ought to have been taken seriously.

The collapse of Washington's adventure became a fact. The USA was compelled to end the war and conclude the Paris agreement on Vietnam. In all, the USA lost 60,000 men dead and more than 300,000 wounded, and the government spent the colossal sum of more than a hundred billion dollars.

As a result of the Vietnam people's victory, the Socialist Republic of Vietnam arose, the People's Democratic Republic of Laos entered the family of socialist states, and Kampuchea (Cambodia), which had been through the bitter torture of war and then the horror of the bloody regime of Pol Pot, also gained its freedom.

12

Europe: old and forever young

Europe is often called 'an old woman', but maybe she is old yet forever young. Have not almost all the most advanced ideas come into the world from Europe – freedom, equality, fraternity? The more than half-century through which I range in my book is a period of enormous interest, but any slice of Europe's history provides a treasure-house for the historian.

Since the end of the Second World War, European governments have been consistently preoccupied with the question of how a new war can be averted and conditions created for peaceful co-operation. How can Europe, with its rich culture and great political experience, guard against armed confrontation? Surely common sense dictates that a secure peace can only be based on respect for the political-territorial realities that came into being on the continent as a result of the war? That has always been the Soviet Union's starting-point.

As we know, with the end of the war several European states acquired new frontiers, and these are just. The stability of those frontiers recognised in the Yalta and Potsdam agreements is central to Europe's security. The position a state takes on this issue is an important indicator of its policy on European affairs and of how much its statements in favour of peace represent its real intentions. The Soviet Union and its Warsaw Pact allies hold to the view that Europe's frontiers – north, south, east or west – are inviolable.

Security can be guaranteed only by the joint efforts of the socialist and capitalist countries, and the idea of pooling efforts to this end was realised in the Soviet and other socialist countries' proposal to hold an All-European Conference on Security and Co-operation. Despite difficulties, the idea met with success in

Helsinki on 1 August 1975, when thirty-three European countries and the United States and Canada signed the Final Act.

The conference drew a line below the Second World War, confirmed Europe's frontiers and fixed the fundamental principles of peaceful relations between states. Furthermore, the follow-up meetings in Belgrade and Madrid represented a great achievement for the approach to reducing tension by means of dialogue.

Facing each other in Europe are two mighty groups of states, the Warsaw Pact and NATO. The European policy of the USSR and its allies has therefore been expressed in initiatives intended to restrict the participants in these groups, and to bring about the eventual dissolution of these organisations. Special mention should be made of the joint proposal by the socialist countries to conclude a non-aggression treaty which would help to remove much fear and distrust.

Relations with France have always occupied a prominent place in the USSR's European and international policies. In the 1920s and 1930s France had as it were set the tempo and conducted the orchestra of states which pursued anti-Soviet policies. The lessons of the war, however, demanded that Franco-Soviet relations be put on a sensible footing and called on both countries to co-operate.

One particularly frustrating meeting I had as ambassador in Washington was in 1945 with Léon Blum, who had headed the Popular Front government between 1936 and 1938, during which time he had emerged as a true right-wing socialist. His inconsistency, political opportunism and cowardice towards Nazi Germany undoubtedly made Hitler's task of conquering France in 1940 much easier. Blum had been interned by the Nazis and shipped out of Germany, and now he was here before me in our embassy in Washington.

He said, 'First of all, I would like to express my respect for the great country of Lenin which resisted and gained victory over Hitler's Germany.' After I had thanked him he then asked, 'Are you aware of the enormity of the tasks which face Europe, and which face our two countries?'

Answering his own question, he mentioned the role of the USA only in passing. Rather, he repeated several times: 'We must establish friendly Franco-Soviet relations. That is the main issue for Europe.'

For my part, I said, 'The Soviet Union has always sought to have good relations with France, even though at times we were repaid with black ingratitude. You remember those times?'

Blum said nothing. He obviously did not like to recall the pre-war period.

However, we parted on a friendly note and expressed the hope we might meet again.

After he left I concluded that it was not so much what he had actually said that was important, but rather what he had hinted at indirectly.

A year or so later Blum was again heading the French government, though only for a few weeks. If this government is to be remembered for anything, it should be for unleashing a bloody war in Indo-China in a vain attempt to preserve France's colonies there. It was as if an evil fate hung over Blum that he could not escape.

Those responsible for France's foreign policy quickly realised that it was important to create and maintain good relations with the Soviet Union. Such was the position adopted by that outstanding Frenchman, Charles de Gaulle. During the war years, in exile abroad, de Gaulle had headed the French Resistance forces, and it was under his leadership that in December 1944 France entered a treaty of alliance and mutual aid with the Soviet Union – a treaty sadly to be virtually annulled by subsequent French policy.

During his visit to Moscow in December 1944, de Gaulle met Stalin, and later he had talks with other Soviet leaders, including Brezhnev, both in Moscow and in Paris. An outstanding statesman, de Gaulle was also one of the most perspicacious politicians in the West, playing a major part in the creation and development of the process of détente.

'The breeze of détente' was how I happened to describe relations between the USSR and France in 1965 during a visit to Paris as Foreign Minister. This 'breeze' gathered strength in subsequent years and became a benign wind blowing over Europe, given powerful impulse by contacts at the highest level; during this time bilateral issues were settled and key questions of world politics reviewed. Such bilateral documents as the Franco-Soviet Protocol of 1970 and the Principles of Collaboration between the Soviet Union and France of 1971, as well as others, formed a sound basis for relations.

Over the last two decades I made frequent trips to France, took part in virtually all talks at the highest level, and received French foreign ministers in Moscow.

I met de Gaulle on several occasions and he was so dominant in his country's political life for nearly twenty years that I would often think of what the French sometimes said: there are two towers in France – one is the Eiffel Tower, the other is de Gaulle. His social policies were not, of course, progressive, and in foreign policy he held to a course in the post-war years which brought France into NATO. However, even within NATO he preserved his own identity and he asserted it more than once in his own inimitable way.

During my visits to Paris as Foreign Minister, de Gaulle would invariably receive me in the Elysée Palace, and as a rule our meetings were of a frank and well-intentioned nature. He was good at avoiding sharp corners in conversation, since he had the enviable ability not to react to a question that seemed at all tricky. On the other hand, he had a way of so constructing the discussion that, while actually sticking to his own position, he gave the impression that he was inclined to agree with his companion. Even on those frequent occasions when no agreement at all seemed possible, de Gaulle had a reassuring formula: 'Anything is possible.'

He was a fine orator. At official dinners and luncheons he would speak smoothly and almost never from a text. He had a phenomenal memory and used it to good effect.

The name of de Gaulle belongs among the great names of France, and yet his grave is to be found in a modest cemetery 150 miles from the capital in the village of Colombey-les-Deux-Eglises, in the department of Champagne. It was to this place that the general finally retired. He lived there with his family in a small two-storey house to which he added a six-sided tower topped by a small cone. In the tower was his study, where he spent many hours in contemplation writing his memoirs. Unlike Churchill, who hired a whole team of researchers and writers and produced his 'memoirs' volume after volume in rapid succession, de Gaulle painstakingly wrote and rewrote his memoirs himself by hand. He tried to make them as much a work of art as a work of politics, and he succeeded. People asked him how, not being a writer, he had managed this, and he would reply:

'It was torture. It would take three agonising pages of draft to get one finished page. My daughter, Elisabeth, would type them up and I would then go over the text again three more times. Believe me, it was appalling work.'

Worthy of mention also is de Gaulle's comrade-in-arms, André Malraux. As a member of de Gaulle's first government (1944–6) he was in charge of the Gaullist party's propaganda services and in 1959–69 was Minister of Culture. It is not often that a leading intellectual can also be called a politician, but Malraux was without doubt one such exception. A famous writer, an active fighter against fascism, the commander of a squadron of foreign volunteer pilots who fought on the side of Republican Spain, and during the Second World War a brigade commander in the French Resistance, he accepted the ministerial post because he believed profoundly that he could do more for his country as a politician than solely as a writer.

I recall a conversation I had with Malraux during my official visit to France. The first thing that struck me was his modesty: though he was a famous writer and one of the most highly cultivated people in France, he talked always about other people, about politics and the world situation, cultural matters and Franco-Soviet cultural relations. He was the very embodiment of high intelligence, and he was voluble but thoughtful on any question I cared to ask. Naturally the so-called German question was impossible to avoid, and he seemed to expect it.

I asked him, 'Do you believe that those who decide policy in the North Atlantic bloc will prevent the rebirth of militarism in West Germany, where there are still many Nazis?'

Malraux replied, 'France will do her duty. You can believe in General de Gaulle.'

'Is General de Gaulle going to determine NATO policy on his own?'

'No, of course, not alone,' Malraux answered. 'But de Gaulle has his own special opinion of the Germans which no one is going to shift.'

I then asked him: 'How do you combine your ministerial responsibilities with your creative work?'

He smiled. 'I thought you'd ask me that. Well, I can sum it up by saying that I have practically no time for my own writing. My public work absorbs all my attention.'

We were standing in a spacious hall, holding the obligatory cup of coffee of every diplomatic reception.

Malraux said, 'I believe that artistic people, whatever field they are in, can do their country a good service if they will offer their talent and their spiritual force in the cause of peace.'

After de Gaulle's retirement, the policy of developing good relations between France and the USSR was on the whole continued by Georges Pompidou. I do not propose to assess Pompidou's domestic policies, but rather to set him in the context of foreign policy. He inherited the political capital accumulated by France under de Gaulle, and attempted to build on it through summit meetings with Brezhnev in the 1970s. Two issues were dominant at these meetings: first, that the USSR and France should do everything possible to prevent a new war; and, second, that it was essential to establish practical relations in keeping with the interests of détente.

At each meeting the German question would invariably arise, and on the level of general principle the French agreed with us that West Germany must adopt a peace-oriented policy. However, when we drew their attention to the fact that West Germany's obligations to NATO were hardly compatible with such a policy, the French response was often couched in such a convoluted, elaborate, rococo style that one completely lost the thread of their argument.

Such meetings inevitably left us with an unpleasant aftertaste. We would wonder: Have the French really forgotten so soon? Why do they place strictly tactical considerations above the more fundamental need never to permit a new war?

During one of my meetings with Pompidou he observed, justifiably: 'It is essential that we develop Franco-Soviet economic relations.'

I agreed with him, but pointed out that successful Franco-Soviet economic ties really depended on the French government giving its practical support.

Pompidou took my point, but the record shows that the French government's support was never more than half-hearted. We repeated our argument when Giscard d'Estaing became President, and it still applies today.

My impressions of Pompidou's last meeting with Brezhnev, in which I took part, in March 1974 at Pitsunda in the Caucasus, are sad. Pompidou was seriously ill at the time. At Adler airport, near Sochi, Pompidou and Brezhnev, and Foreign Minister Michel

Jobert and I, greeted each other warmly. Smiling and gesturing in the most welcoming way, Pompidou behaved like a real Frenchman, but we were all appalled by the waxy hue of his face. He had medical staff with him, but there was no hiding the fact that the President's last weeks, if not days, were ticking away.

We went from Adler to Pitsunda by helicopter. It was clear the President was tired. In view of his illness, a very light regime was adopted during the talks, but even so at times one noticed an unnatural concentration in him as if, although he was listening attentively, his inner gaze was directed elsewhere. Pompidou's intellect, however, was as sharp as ever. He expressed his thoughts concisely and clearly and the talks were conducted in the usual friendly, businesslike atmosphere.

We all accompanied Pompidou and his entourage from Pitsunda back to Adler airport. It was distressing to watch the President getting in and out of the car; despite his efforts not to show the pain, his face betrayed his suffering.

That is how I remember him. Three weeks later he was dead. He was an outstanding French statesman and it was entirely fitting that the new cultural centre in the capital should bear his name.

I have happier memories of my meetings with Valéry Giscard d'Estaing, both as a member of the French cabinet and then as President, though I shall again restrict myself to foreign policy and my impressions of him as a person.

Giscard's political centrism inevitably coloured his views on foreign policy, including the sphere for which he had been responsible as Economics and Finance Minister, namely economic relations with other countries. Even so, when he became President on the death of Pompidou, Giscard did as all his predecessors had done and tried to demonstrate his loyalty to the Western allies – even though already in 1966 France was no longer part of NATO's military organisation and was striving to preserve her own national image.

So, after coming to power, Giscard declared that he intended to continue the policy of de Gaulle and Pompidou, which could be summarised thus: in the interests of détente and peace the USSR and France not only should but *must* collaborate. As for preserving France's image as an independent state, this was of course contradicted by France's loyalty to NATO on issues of a military nature, a fact we repeatedly drew to the attention of the French government and its President.

Both sides, however, tried to build on what was common to our foreign policy, namely an interest in establishing peaceful co-operation between states. At the beginning of December 1974 Brezhnev made a working visit to France. The Soviet leader was meeting Giscard for the first time as President, although we already knew him as a partner in talks on another level.

I quickly realised that Giscard d'Estaing had a pretty sound understanding of the basic problems, although he mostly held a diametrically opposed view from mine – as was the case when we discussed nuclear weapons, the NATO bloc and events in Afghanistan. Giscard was always well prepared for talks. As a rule he produced factual arguments, and I never once saw him show impulsiveness or haste. He did not pay much attention to protocol, either. I was much impressed by this: the formalities are there simply to ease discourse, not to make it more difficult.

There are a number of amusing stories about Giscard the man. I myself was particularly surprised by one event which took place during Brezhnev's visit. The Soviet delegation was housed at the ancient château of Rambouillet, outside Paris, where the talks also took place. The French delegation came by car from the capital and we all waited in the little vestibule for the head of their delegation to arrive.

Suddenly we heard the clatter of a motor above the château and a small helicopter landed on the lawn. Out stepped Giscard. One of the Frenchmen remarked, 'The President was flying it himself.'

The Soviet delegates took this to be a joke, but after the talks, when we went outside on to the lawn to say goodbye to our host, we were amazed to see him take the controls, gently lift the helicopter into the air, circle above the château, wave his hand to us and fly off towards Paris.

We were told, 'Despite his official position, the President also never misses the chance to drive his car himself. The Elysée security staff go crazy.'

We heard some time later that, after a minor road accident involving the President's car, common sense prevailed.

Another amusing episode comes to mind. During our visit, the world price of oil went up and a campaign to economise was launched in France, initiated by the President himself, who even ordered that the Elysée be heated by wood.

At Rambouillet they lit fires in all the fireplaces but, whether through lack of use or the inexperience of the servants, the chimneys smoked badly. The whole château was filled with smoke and all the windows and doors had to be opened – and this was in December. So the experiment with the fireplaces had to be terminated, the radiators were turned on again, and suitable conditions for the talks were restored.

Giscard d'Estaing was defeated in the 1981 elections and his place was taken by François Mitterrand, leader of the French Socialist Party. Although the country was not shocked by the result, a definite polarisation of forces took place, to the disadvantage of the bourgeoisie. Socialists, communists and left radicals gained the upper hand and consequently communists were included in the government which was formed in June 1981.

Soon after this left-wing shift I had occasion to meet the French Foreign Minister Claude Cheysson in New York, during the UN General Assembly.

He declared, 'The new regime will lead the country along the path of socialist change.'

He was excited and emotional, but I and other members of the Soviet delegation thought it sounded too good to be true – as indeed it was. There were in fact no attempts to carry out, even experimentally, any serious socialist changes in France.

Distinct progress in Franco-Soviet relations, however, took place with the visit by Mitterrand to the USSR in June 1984, and again in 1985 and 1986. All these meetings, especially those with Gorbachev, enriched Franco-Soviet relations. To some extent, a spirit of true co-operation was born. The concrete results of the 1986 visit were reflected in speeches made by Gorbachev and Mitterrand and in documents published during and at the end of the visit.

As I was accompanying the President to the airport, he said, 'I rate this visit to Moscow of the highest importance, in terms both of bilateral relations and of broad international politics.'

The Soviet Union also saw the visit to be of great importance, as did other countries whose foreign policies were directed towards peace.

★

I have visited West Germany several times, and every time I have had depressing thoughts about the misery our people suffered at the hands of the Nazis. Of course, history has already identified predatory German imperialism as the evil which poisoned the German people's mind, and not even the most reactionary West German politicians today support the ideas which dominated the Third Reich. But those who are responsible for present West German policy should not forget that twenty million Soviet people and millions of others in the anti-Hitler coalition gave their lives so that the threat of war should never again arise in Germany.

The conditions for establishing normal relations between the Soviet Union and West Germany were not easy to create. The Soviet people remembered Hitler's aggression too well. Furthermore, the post-war West German leadership came from the same class that had nourished Hitler and his gang.

But as time passed the people learned what had been achieved at Potsdam. The question of establishing relations had to be tackled. Konrad Adenauer, head of the West German government, reached the same conclusion.

One could say that time itself compelled this reactionary, super-pedantic man, in life and in politics, to look at the East with different eyes – especially since a state with a new social order had arisen in the eastern part of the old Germany. Thus in 1955, at Moscow's Vnukovo airport, a tall man with stern features alighted from a plane. The task ahead of him was no easy one. After much weighty consideration, Adenauer had come to Moscow to establish diplomatic relations, and a major event in post-war European history took place.

I recall a typically conciliatory incident during Adenauer's visit to the Soviet capital. At that time large numbers of intelligence-gathering balloons were being launched from West Germany over Soviet territory. An exhibition devoted to this subject had been set up in the yard outside the house on Alexei Tolstoy Street where the talks were taking place, and Adenauer was shown it.

He shrugged his shoulders. 'It seems the Western powers are using West German territory for this purpose, and they haven't even consulted me.'

The talks were not easy, especially since Adenauer could not relinquish his dream of swallowing up East Germany, but common sense prevailed and diplomatic relations were established. If the West had been true to the Potsdam principles and not opted for a divided Germany, it is possible that events would have turned out differently; but one cannot put the clock back. Europe has two Germanys, and the facts themselves show the Soviet position.

On 10 March 1952 the Soviet government had submitted an outline for a peace treaty with Germany, in which the restoration of Germany as a united sovereign state was proposed with the guarantee of an equal place among the other European states. Germany would have the right to armed forces for national defence and the right to produce arms and technology for their use, but not for coalitions and alliances aimed against any state that had fought against Hitler. We proposed the rapid formation of an all-German government and free elections throughout the country.

The reaction of the Western powers was unenthusiastic. In Bonn, however, common sense deserted Adenauer and his circle altogether, the Soviet proposals became an object of propaganda, and the reunification of Germany was lost in the scrimmage.

No other European government in the postwar period made such a gross political miscalculation. Without doubt, Adenauer lost a historic opportunity. The Federal Republic, moreover, became a part of the anti-Soviet Western military bloc – at a time when the USSR and Germany were still technically in a state of war. This was ended only on 25 January 1955 by an order of the Supreme Soviet of the USSR.

Adenauer continued his policy of lost opportunities. In 1957 he rejected an East German proposal which put forward the idea of a German confederation. He was impervious to reason; once West Germany had been drawn into the Western military bloc, it was almost as if the Federal Republic had become more important to Adenauer than the idea of reunification.

I met Adenauer for the last time in 1959 in somewhat unusual circumstances. He was coming down the front steps of the White House as I and my colleagues, the Foreign Ministers of Britain and France, were going up them. We had come straight from our meeting in Geneva to attend Dulles's funeral, and now we were visiting Eisenhower.

Adenauer spotted me and stopped: 'I have lost a friend,' he said.

I did not disagree with him. He really had lost a friend. The whole world knew that Adenauer and Dulles were political soul-mates.

In fact, Adenauer probably did not abandon the idea of a united

Germany until the night of 13 August 1961, when measures were taken to strengthen the state borders and sovereignty of the German Democratic Republic.

The Western powers had shown no willingness to resolve the German problem or to regulate the position of West Berlin. Rejecting Soviet proposals, they had instead increased their military capability, and ignored important international agreements aimed at preventing German militarism. The governments of the Warsaw Pact countries appealed to the government and workers of East Germany to establish on its border with West Berlin reliable arrangements that would block the path for subversive activity against the states of the socialist community, and to organise reliable security and effective control around the entire territory of West Berlin, including its border with East Berlin. As a result, the East German Council of Ministers passed a resolution on measures for defending the state, especially its capital, Berlin. On the memorable night of 12–13 August 1961 the border between West and East Berlin was sealed.

This step was so effective that, within two years, Adenauer, the spiritual father of West Germany's militarist ambitions, went into retirement. Ludwig Erhard, his successor, tried to continue the same bankrupt policy of not recognising East Germany, but he was not long in office, and was succeeded by the Social Democrat, Willy Brandt.

In Moscow we already knew Brandt well. From my meetings with him, I can say he is one of the most outstanding statesmen in West Germany. He spent the war in exile in Sweden, preferring to leave his country rather than bow his head to the swastika, and he deserves credit for this.

By 1969, furthermore, Brandt had recognised that the firm stand of the Soviet Union and the other socialist states to gain recognition of European territorial realities had at last created conditions for the preparation of a treaty between the USSR and the Federal Republic. Both sides now wanted the treaty. So, headed by myself and Foreign Minister Walter Scheel, and armed with patience and well-honed arguments, the representatives began talks.

Our work went quite well. Although the West German emissaries fought hard for their positions, it was Brandt's views which dominated the talks. Despite many arguments, zigzags, dead ends and nervous outbursts, the participants did not lose sight of the main thread, and understanding was reached. Opponents of the treaty, who were more inclined to look backwards than forwards, put many obstacles in its path. In the end, thanks to a broad view and a desire to come to terms with reality, Brandt led the West German side with a firm hand to the successful completion and then ratification of the treaty. People say it cost him many a sleepless night.

It is both easy and hard to write about Brandt – easy because he explained his views fully when he was Chancellor, hard because he is a man of many parts. For some years before reaching the pinnacle of state power in Bonn, he had been the mayor of West Berlin. In that delicate and difficult post he had acquired considerable experience which came in useful later on. What was just as important, however, was that, being on the border between the socialist and the capitalist worlds, he was constantly in contact both with his East German counterparts and with the Soviet embassy. Soviet diplomats, including myself, noticed how often, during discussion of even quite routine matters, Mayor Brandt would find an opportunity to express his views on Soviet–West German relations; he would look beyond immediate issues and make subtle judgements about relations between East and West as a whole. He was already feeling out the ground on which relations between the USSR and West Germany could be established. Taking the idea of peaceful coexistence as the foundation of Soviet–German relations, he formulated an appropriately practical policy in this sphere.

Consistently in favour of a treaty with the Federal Republic, the USSR was, of course, largely responsible for its character. From the start, the Soviet Union saw that both sides must create conditions for peace. Accordingly there had to be plain acceptance of the post-war borders agreed by the three powers at Potsdam, including the Oder–Neisse line; the German Democratic Republic must be recognised as a sovereign state; and there must be agreement to develop mutually beneficial Soviet–West German economic relations and contacts in other fields. On all these points, and on others that emerged during discussion of the cardinal issues, opinion was exchanged at a level of detail such as neither I nor my colleagues had probably ever experienced at formal talks.

As we had expected, the border questions were those which proved most intractable. The question of recognising East Germany as an independent state at once turned into a question of the borders between the two German states. Our partners constantly attempted to avoid complete clarity on this issue, trying to leave the final definition of the border for the future. Additionally, the concept of a 'united Germany' or, more accurately, the absorption of East Germany into West Germany, remained a stumbling block to the very end.

Eventually, however, after long and difficult discussion, the West Germans could not hold out against the logic of historical justice. They withdrew their claims and restricted themselves to a letter addressed to the Supreme Soviet of the USSR, in which they expounded their views on the question. Consequently, the treaty is as precise as it could be on this main issue. Article 3 states: 'The Union of Soviet Socialist Republics and the Federal Republic of Germany are united in recognising that peace in Europe can only be preserved if no one encroaches on present-day borders; they declare that neither side has any territorial claims on anyone and that they will not advance such claims in the future; they regard all state borders in Europe as inviolable now and in the future, including the Oder–Neisse line, which is the western border of the Polish People's Republic and the border between the Federal Republic of Germany and the German Democratic Republic.'

Looking back on those days, I can say that the main work of drafting the treaty clauses was accomplished during my talks with Egon Bahr, state secretary in the Federal Chancellor's office. It was then that the idea of 'agreement on intentions' emerged. This would shape the measures taken to strengthen the territorial realities in Europe, and to bring about healthier political conditions.

It is clear to me now that, had there not been commitment and understanding on both sides, we would not have succeeded, and the outlook would have remained gloomy.

The signing took place on 12 August 1970 in the Kremlin. The Soviet side was represented by A.N. Kosygin and myself, the West German side by Willy Brandt and Walter Scheel. I must emphasise the important role played by Brandt, who conducted this, his most important negotiation as Chancellor, with courage and determination. The signing and ratification were greeted in Europe and the whole world with enthusiasm and relief.

The spirit of the treaty is the principle of the inviolability of European borders and it was this spirit that imbued the treaties that followed between Poland, East Germany, Czechoslovakia and West Germany, as well as the Four-Power Agreement on West Berlin – in connection with which, early in 1971, in the former Control Commission building at 196 Potsdamer Strasse, West Berlin, the Soviet ambassador to the German Democratic Republic and the US, British and French ambassadors to the Federal Republic of Germany met for talks. The subject of the talks at once raised an issue: the Western powers insisted that they were discussing 'Berlin as a whole', which did not correspond with the situation on the ground, while the USSR tried to gain acceptance for the phrase 'West Berlin'. We ended up with 'the Western sectors of Berlin'.

There was also much argument about the official name of the German Democratic Republic, without which there could be no final text. Whenever the initials of the GDR came up, they simply stuck in our Western partners' throats, and it was six months before they could bring themselves to utter those three simple letters. Eventually, however, on 3 September 1971, all parties put their signatures to the Four-Power Agreement, thus bringing to a successful conclusion a marathon of thirty-three sessions.

The signed agreement represented an important stage in the city's history and put an end to the twenty-year crisis surrounding West Berlin, fixing its status in terms of international law as an independent political entity. The document notes that Western sectors 'as before are not constituent parts of the Federal Republic and will henceforth not be governed by it'. Thus the Four-Power Agreement facilitated normalisation of this dangerous region, and was an important step towards securing peace in Europe.

Since the signing, the turnover of trade between the USSR and West Berlin has risen more than fifteen times, exceeding 400 million roubles in 1985. Some people in the West would like to terminate the agreement and make West Berlin a part of West Germany, but this would merely re-create the previous explosive situation. The only way of reducing tension and ensuring peace in the region is by strict observance of the agreement.

As the Soviet diplomat, V.S. Semyonov, who studied all the complicated moves of West German policy at the time, commented: 'Time will show whether those in West Germany, who set the country's political course, seriously understand that the border question is actually the question of war and peace. In other words, how much the Federal Republic liberates itself from the revanchist mentality that is still far from having disappeared in the ranks of the Bonn politicians.'

Shortly after the signing, I had a meeting with Foreign Minister Scheel, who in a free moment told me: 'You know, Mr Gromyko, we've had an addition to the family. We have a daughter and we're going to call her Andrea, in your honour. My wife and I agreed on this.'

I must confess I was somewhat embarrassed, so I decided to make a joke of it: 'That is a decision, you realise, that remains entirely the responsibility of yourself and your wife. In this you have one hundred per cent sovereignty. And I am very happy to hear the news.'

Hans-Dietrich Genscher was Minister of Internal Affairs in Willy Brandt's government when I first met him. He was later Foreign Minister under Helmut Schmidt and then under Helmut Kohl. We had many discussions on Soviet–West German relations and relations between the Warsaw Pact and NATO countries.

Genscher liked talks to go at an unhurried pace, as if we were rowing gently across a smooth lake, but one needed to have one's facts and figures at the ready, for he always came well prepared and able to present his country's position in the most favourable light. My impression, which reports from our people in Bonn confirmed, was that his policy was to keep things sweet with Washington while being careful not to upset relations with the Soviet Union.

On balance, despite the fact that Genscher was a difficult partner, our talks usually had a businesslike character and on the whole produced positive results. His later meetings with E.A. Shevard-nadze were also full of useful content and conducted on a high political level.

One of West Germany's major figures, and a man who left his mark on international affairs in the 1970s, is the Social Democrat, Helmut Schmidt. During the war he was an officer in the Wehr-macht, with a unit at Zavidovo in the south-eastern part of the region of Kalinin, so there can be no doubt he had seen the crimes committed by Hitler's men in the towns and villages of our country.

Significantly, when he talked to me once about his time in Zavidovo, he said, 'I belonged to that group of officers who felt that Hitler's adventure against the Soviet people was doomed,' and I am inclined to believe him. There were such people in the officer corps of the Nazi military. Even so, the majority of them carried out their orders punctiliously, regardless of the misery they were inflicting.

From my talks with Schmidt, when he was Defence Minister in the Brandt government and then Chancellor, I formed a definite opinion: although capable and strong-willed, he had not fully freed himself from the outlook of an officer in the German Wehrmacht. Certainly Schmidt had been in favour of concluding and implementing the West German 'Eastern treaties'. Furthermore, he declared his support for the existing strategic balance between NATO and the Warsaw Pact. Yet in every discussion I had with Chancellor Schmidt he was invariably concerned to justify the steps NATO took towards ever increasing its armaments. He somehow managed not to hear the statistics we introduced concerning the armed forces of the two blocs.

During one of my visits to Bonn I showed him a map which displayed the deployment in Europe of nuclear missiles of both groups of states. I awaited his comments.

He said, 'If it's possible, please leave me this map – I'd like to look at it more carefully.'

We gave him that opportunity. But all he then said was: 'I don't like those Soviet SS-20s.'

The logic was simple: he liked US missiles targeted on the USSR, but he didn't like Soviet missiles targeted on western Europe.

The government Schmidt headed until the autumn of 1982 was responsible for throwing the country open to new American Pershing-2 nuclear missiles, and it is on their conscience. Even Adenauer had not risked so much in 1957, when the Americans tried in vain to deploy the medium-range Thor and Jupiter missiles on West German territory. West Germany's safety has not been improved by the deployment of the US missiles, and many West German politicians know it.

Schmidt always put himself forward as a pragmatist, and liked to show himself capable of making quick decisions. It was an image he cultivated. Yet one need only compare what he wrote in his theoretical works with what he stood for as Chancellor, and one sees a curious difference. A good example is his position on the deployment of US medium-range missiles in West Germany. In his writings on strategic affairs he has said that a responsible politician will never allow rockets in West Germany, since they would act as a magnet to the other side's nuclear weapons; and that the place for such weapons is Alaska, Labrador, Greenland, etc., but not densely populated Europe. That was what he wrote; but in practice he did otherwise. After he retired he admitted the error of his ways – but by then it was too late.

In the same way, Schmidt made many an error in his economic judgements. It was Schmidt who advised the Americans to strengthen the dollar. In Washington they laughed at him and called him Schmidt-Napoleon. With the advent of Reagan, however, interest rates were raised and the USA received billions of dollars to finance its military programmes, at serious cost to West Germany as well as to the rest of western Europe.

Schmidt's colleagues in the Social Democratic Party said of him: 'At bottom, he has remained not so much a Social Democrat as a Prussian officer with conservative views.'

Justice demands that Schmidt nevertheless be credited with having done something to develop Soviet–West German economic relations. Even he was aware that life takes its revenge on those West German statesmen who will not recognise the basic truth that, despite all the differences of state and social structures and ideologies, both their country and the USSR have a broad common interest conditioned by such unchanging factors as geographical proximity, reciprocal economic potential, a need for cultural exchange and, especially important, the desire of both their peoples to live in peace.

Chancellor Helmut Kohl remains a controversial figure in West German politics. While one part of public opinion claims he is ineffective in both domestic and foreign affairs, another maintains he is just the man the country needs in a difficult time.

I can only comment on the foreign policy he and his government have pursued. Undoubtedly Kohl has perpetuated many of the follies of the past: there has been much in his policy that bears the stamp of Adenauer, to say nothing of Schmidt, especially on disarmament, including nuclear. To give credit where it is due, however, once Soviet–American relations began to ease, the West

German government took a more objective view of its ties with the USSR, of the international situation as a whole and of the role it could itself play in international affairs. Without doubt, the West German government made a major contribution to the resolution of questions relating to the Soviet–US treaty on the destruction of medium- and lesser-range missiles.

13

Again Europe

As a schoolboy I once came across a little book by De Amicis called *In Search of a Mother*, and since that day I have been fascinated by Italy. I had even made that little book into my own shorthand version of Italy.

As a student, and even later, I continued to be attracted by the stormy events of the Roman empire, its severe majesty, the colourful lives of its military leaders and statesmen. Like most Soviet people, however, my idea of modern Italy was much affected by the fact that fascism came to power there. I did not want to believe that the country of the great poets, artists and sculptors was being run by uncivilised monsters, that blackshirts were trampling Rome and strutting arrogantly in Venice and Florence.

But Italy survived, and for that we must thank, among many others, those veterans of the fight against fascism who took an active part in the Resistance. Every honest person will acknowledge that the Italian Resistance movement belonged to the communists, and the history of the Communist Party of Italy, including the period of the fascist dictatorship, is closely connected with the name of Palmiro Togliatti, who led it for many years. Not only those who knew him personally but even opponents of socialism will give him credit as a remarkable leader and indefatigable fighter.

I met Togliatti only twice. Our first meeting took place in Moscow at the end of the 1950s, when I was already Foreign Minister. I was told by the Central Committee that Togliatti wanted to see me and that they thought I should agree. Togliatti was staying at the Sovietskaya and I visited him there in his room.

After exchanging cordial greetings, he came straight to the point: 'I asked if I could see you as there are a number of international questions that are bothering me.'

At that time the cold war was in full swing, so I readily agreed to discuss the situation.

He began: 'I often wonder what the West really wants, especially Britain and the USA. We Italian communists tend not to believe their leaders when they say they want to improve East–West relations. Please tell me if we are right to be sceptical, or are we missing something?'

I replied: 'Your scepticism is fully justified, and two simple facts demonstrate it. First, the Americans have established military bases in various parts of the world, aimed at the USSR, and they are building more. Secondly, when the USSR declared at the Geneva four-power meeting of 1955 that, since the West regarded NATO as a defensive alliance, the USSR was ready to enter it itself, the US, British and French leaders couldn't even manage to give us an intelligible reply. I was in our delegation and I remember it very well. The most interesting thing was to observe Eisenhower and Dulles. Eisenhower was simply speechless.'

Togliatti smiled. 'I'd love to have seen that. Of course, NATO won't agree to belong to the same grouping as the Soviet Union – the aims of the USSR and her friends are diametrically opposed to those of NATO. And anyway the class barrier is insurmountable.'

He then asked: 'What is your view of the West German question? The Americans, the British and the French, too, all seem to want to push her into remilitarisation. We Italian communists continually point out what this policy means, but even Italy itself is gradually being drawn into NATO's military plans. The position is very difficult.'

I agreed. 'One of the most important issues in Europe is indeed the remilitarisation of West Germany, just as that of Japan is in the East. More and more attention may appear to be being paid to questions of disarmament, but you must have seen how the US and her allies in the Western bloc reject all Soviet proposals for arms reduction.'

Togliatti replied, 'Italian communists see it as one of our chief tasks to support the Soviet Union on disarmament, including the banning of nuclear weapons.'

He also made an interesting observation about the domestic situation in Italy and the mood of the bourgeoisie: 'They are increasingly in favour of collaboration with the USA, to the detriment of Italy's national interest.'

He seemed in excellent health and was agile in his responses to questions, as well as being extremely well informed on international affairs.

The second time I met him, early in 1964, he was ill and soon to die. It was sad to look at him, like a flickering candle. His mind was still as active as ever, but he was finding it hard to speak. He died in the Soviet Union, the land of the socialism he had fought for all his life.

After a sorrowful farewell with Togliatti in August 1964, the Italian communists chose Luigi Longo as their party leader. He too had been widely known since the early twenties, when he had gone to Moscow in 1922 as a delegate to the 4th Congress of the Communist International, where he heard Lenin speak.

I met Longo several times, but my happiest memories of him are of the mid-1950s in the Crimea, where he and his wife were holidaying at the same dacha as my wife and I, and we met and talked almost every day, on all manner of subjects. He was there on his doctors' advice for the sea-bathing and the dry, warm climate. Of course, Italy also has a good climate, but as he put it: 'I can only really relax in the Soviet Union, in the land of Lenin, where the air seems sweeter.'

Longo had great personal charm, in addition to which his life as a fighter against the exploitation of the working class had forged in him the deep convictions of a communist. He was a good talker and moved easily from one topic to another. I especially enjoyed his account of the 1922 Comintern Congress.

'It was 13 November,' he told me, 'when Lenin made his speech to the Congress. He called it "Five Years of the Russian Revolution and the Outlook for World Revolution" – it was a grandiose title, and in fact he only spoke about one small part of the subject, the New Economic Policy. But first of all he announced that Vladivostok had been taken, which meant that the Red Army had thrown the last of the Japanese forces into the sea and Soviet territory was completely free of all invaders. The news brought a thunder of applause that shook the roof.'

Longo remembered the occasion in detail and it was obviously not the first time he had told the story.

'Then Lenin outlined his plans for economic reconstruction. He told us that one could consider the rouble as significant only because it now exceeded a quadrillion in number. That got a laugh. But one could always cross out a few noughts, he said, hinting that the Soviet Union intended to take drastic steps to stabilise the currency and the economic chaos. That also made them laugh.'

I was fascinated. Any Leninist dearly loves to hear reminiscences of Lenin, especially if they are personal.

Longo went on: 'Obviously to pre-empt criticism from ill-wishers, Lenin admitted straight out that mistakes were being made. "We have just begun to learn," he said, "but we're determined to get things right. And anyway – what about those who criticise us: don't they ever make mistakes?" Lenin spoke with passion. But the chief thing for him was still the idea and its development. He wanted his listeners to understand exactly what he was proposing. It was this that won over his audience.'

Longo then told me about the Italian Resistance during the war, playing down his own prominent role. The main point he wanted to get over was that the communists were the soul of the Resistance: 'They knew many of them would die, yet they willingly made the sacrifice. There were Soviet men and women in the Italian Resistance too, people the Italians will never forget.'

He told me how the Italian Resistance had hunted down the wily Mussolini, and how they had sentenced and executed him. 'Of course, there were members of other parties fighting the fascists, particularly the socialists. This broadened the Resistance and gave it strength.

'In that way,' he concluded, 'the Italian people redeemed one of the blackest periods in their history.'

The Soviet Union re-established diplomatic relations with Italy in March 1944, and contacts and exchanges quickly ensued. Every time I landed in Rome and drove from the airport to the centre of the city, I had the fascinating thought that here I was, travelling the ancient Appian Way, over paving laid by Roman slaves. And there were so many ruins and monuments still to come!

It was a special feature of Italy's political life that after the war no single person enjoyed the sort of public recognition of a de Gaulle or an Adenauer. Instead, there was a circle of statesmen who rotated from one post to another at the top level of state power. It does not seem to matter, therefore, in what order one discusses them.

If I am asked which of the Italian political leaders I knew best, I answer without hesitation, Aldo Moro.

Although Moro was a representative of capitalism, he nevertheless believed that differences between states should be settled by peaceful means. Differences between social systems, however extreme, should not lead to the use of armed force.

When I first met Moro, he seemed somewhat slow-thinking, but the precision of his language and the concentrated nature of his arguments soon corrected that impression. We met frequently at the UN General Assembly, and also in Helsinki, during the last stage of the All-European meeting. While defending the position of the NATO countries, he never forgot that if East and West were to live in peace then they must maintain a dialogue and always consider each other's interests.

Before submitting the Soviet proposal to convene the All-European meeting to the governments concerned, the Soviet leadership decided to take a sounding. None of the NATO countries yet knew about the idea, and we chose to test it first in Italy. In April 1966 I went to Rome to get Prime Minister Moro's reaction.

He and Foreign Minister Amintore Fanfani, who was also present, thought it over lengthily, while I grew more and more impatient. Moro even asked for some clarification.

Then, at long last, he spoke: 'Certainly, the European states and the USA and Canada have reached the point where they should meet to discuss questions of European security. That's the only way to reach solutions acceptable to both Warsaw Pact and NATO countries.' After some more questions from Moro and explanations from me, he said: 'This idea of an All-European meeting will be welcomed by the Italian government.'

The Italians maintained this position while we had consultations with the other governments, and they were helpful throughout the talks in Helsinki. Moro headed the Italian delegation at the last stage and signed the Final Act on his country's behalf. Always calm and collected in his examination of a question, Moro never appeared nervous, and anyone who ever tried to disrupt his exposition of the Italian position was ruthlessly dealt with.

As we were leaving one of our meetings, I said to the Soviet ambassador to Italy, N.S. Ryzhkov: 'You know, Moro's got the same temperament as the young Roman, Scaevola, who held his hand in the flames to show his contempt for pain and death!'

He was a modest man too, never concerned about whether his statements or his photograph would appear in the press, and he had the rare gift of being able to talk about his fellow countrymen both with affection and objectively. On one occasion he suddenly asked me, 'In what way are Italians different from Russians?'

I replied, 'When I first became acquainted with your country through books and paintings, in those days I thought the Italians were always either singing and dancing or laughing and crying, when they were not going down canals in gondolas. I never thought about the fact that they also work.'

Moro showed no surprise. 'That's what people abroad usually think about the Italians. But what is the reality? The Italians are virtually the same as any other people. They work, and work makes people all over the world equal.' He smiled. 'One should not judge young Italians by their behaviour in gondolas.'

I remarked: 'Mr Fanfani has said to me many times that if I haven't been to his native Venice I haven't really seen Italy. But when I did go to that wonderful city there were no gondolas on the canals and it rained for two whole days. We told our Italian guides the CIA must have had a hand in it!'

This reminded Moro of a visit he himself had made to Venice. 'It was during the famous procession of the gondolas. A girl fell into the water from one of them and all the gondoliers raised the alarm. The girl was starting to drown, so several men dived in to help the signorina out. It was all very heroic.' He then observed: 'I think the whole thing may have been staged. It all looked real enough, but then we Italians sometimes find it difficult to distinguish fact from fantasy. In some ways, we are born actors. So, that's how we are different from the Russians.' He added: 'That, of course, does not apply to serious politics.'

This conversation came back to me when I read in 1978 that Moro's body had been found in the boot of a car in a street in the eternal city. His death in a terrorist killing added one more name to the long martyrology of Rome's 2500-year history.

Among Italian statesmen distinguished by the capacity to survive the ups and downs of domestic politics, the first prize undoubtedly goes to Amintore Fanfani of the Christian Democrats. He has been Prime Minister, President of the Senate and Foreign Minister and held a number of other portfolios. Always known as a dynamic power-house of a man, Fanfani holds firmly to the views of the leading bourgeois party. However, unlike some other Italian politicians, he is a master tactician, and has often demonstrated his talents in foreign policy.

A serious partner in talks, Fanfani obviously prepared himself thoroughly. Although never departing from the basic concepts of NATO, he avoided the clichés of other NATO representatives and conducted talks expertly, trying to understand the thinking behind the Soviet position. He would never demean himself, as other Western politicians might, by simply quoting lurid news-paper headlines, and he was always most courteous in his hospi-tality to his Soviet guests.

Frankness and a sincere wish to find ways of closing the gap between points of view are qualities which arouse one's respect for one's partners, even if they represent a different social ethos. I would include among such people Giulio Andreotti, a major figure in Italian politics. He came to the USSR in 1972 on an official visit as chairman of the Council of Ministers to sign the Soviet–Italian protocol on consultations, a document expressing the desire of both sides to work for a generally closer relationship. The signing was preceded by discussions on a wide range of subjects.

I had serious and businesslike talks with Andreotti then, in Rome, Madrid, Stockholm and again in Moscow. Whatever post he occupied, while defending his own country's point of view, Andreotti would always try to understand his partner's position and to seek points of contact.

Beginning in 1963, I had frequent meetings and talks – eight in all – with successive heads of the Roman Catholic Church and the Vatican State, the Popes: once with John XXIII (1963), five times with Paul VI (1965, 1966, 1970, 1974, 1975) and twice with John Paul II (1979, 1985). The meeting in 1965 took place in New York, the rest in the Vatican.

The initiative for these meetings came in every instance from the Vatican. Though not exactly given an official invitation, one was made to understand that the Pope wanted an exchange of opinion with the Soviet Foreign Minister. This in general fitted with our own wishes, since we knew the Vatican was in no way isolated from world politics.

Questions of war and peace were the main topic of my talks with Paul VI. On our last meeting in 1975, the Pope spoke highly of the USSR's foreign policy, our work in the interests of mutual understanding and agreement between people. Before this Vatican meeting, one of the priests asked us to consider the Holy Father's age and state of health, as every meeting was for him a difficult test, and this warning proved to be appropriate. During our conversation the Pope talked slowly and obviously with difficulty, as only sick people do.

I gave him to understand several times that I was ready to stop, but on each occasion the Pope, with dignity, shook his head and said: 'No, I think it is too soon to end. Let us continue.'

My meeting with Pope John Paul II (the Polish Cardinal Karol Wojtyla, as he had been) in January 1979 took place, after a short tour of the Vatican with our ambassador to Italy, N.S. Ryzhkov, in the state room where the Pope normally receives foreign visitors. It is a ceremonial hall so large that it dwarfs its occupants. Behind a table at the far end sits the Pope, with an interpreter to one side of him and a little further off a cardinal or two. When I was there, Bishop (later Cardinal) Casaroli, who ran the Vatican's foreign affairs, was present and very attentive.

John Paul greeted us and remarked, 'I want to underline the importance of contacts for helping to secure peace on earth.'

I agreed with him, of course, and then went on to describe some of the major Soviet initiatives designed to achieve that end.

'As far as I can judge,' I finished, 'the Catholic Church accords great importance to strengthening peace, to disarmament and to the liquidation of weapons of mass destruction. The Soviet leadership believes that this position has great value. As for ideological or religious differences, they must not be allowed to stand in the way of collaboration towards this noble goal.'

The Pope moved on to the issue of religious belief. 'It is possible that the obstacles to freedom of religion have not been removed everywhere.' He paused. 'According to some sources, something of this sort may be happening in the USSR.'

This kind of accusation was nothing new for us. I replied: 'Not all rumours deserve attention. The West spreads all kinds of misinformation about the state of the church in the Soviet Union, but the truth is that from the first day of its existence the Soviet state has guaranteed freedom of religious belief. After all, in the dark days of the war, the Russian Orthodox Church was on the side of the Soviet state and fought fascism in its own way. Would that have been possible if the church in our country had not been free? We have religious people, but that doesn't create problems either for them or for Soviet society.'

The Pope and Casaroli listened thoughtfully. Then the Pope said, 'That's more or less what we thought.'

No more was said on the subject.

In his way of speaking, John Paul II adopted a tone of voice and turn of phrase that might be called semi-ecclesiastical, as if to make what he said sound secular, and indeed the impression was created that our discussion was not going on in the Vatican, surrounded by the busts and portraits of the holy fathers, but rather in the ordinary little room at the United Nations.

This first meeting with John Paul II took place before the events of the early 1980s in Poland, in relation to which the Vatican took up a position that crossed the threshold dividing politics from religion. Unsurprisingly, this was an issue raised at our next meeting.

On 27 March 1985, during an official visit to Rome, and accompanied by Deputy Foreign Minister N.S. Ryzhkov and the Soviet ambassador to Italy N.M. Lunkov, when we arrived for our arranged visit in the Vatican we were met with an exceptional degree of courtesy. I noticed that we went along all the same endless corridors, except that where before we had hardly drawn attention to ourselves now we were closely observed. As we got closer to the audience room, the clerics of the Vatican hierarchy who stood along our way became ever more luxu-riously garbed and grander, until at the Pope's door there were two very senior bishops whom I recognised from my previous visits.

Entering the room, we found Pope John Paul II striding towards us energetically. We exchanged greetings like old friends. The Pope then made the following request: 'Please explain your country's views on the international situation and what ought to be done to prevent a nuclear catastrophe.'

Naturally I complied, briefly and frankly, ending with the following comment: 'It seems to us the Vatican is not using its influence fully in the struggle for peace. We know that statements have been made about mobilising Roman Catholic believers in the struggle, but little has been done in recent years to follow up these statements.' I then added: 'I understand that your believers expect only good to come from heaven. But there are men in certain countries who want to turn the heavens into a source of appalling misery and death. Everyone knows which country it is that wants to spread the arms race into outer space.'

I was closely observing the Pope and his two companions. None of them expressed any reservations about what I had said. On the contrary, the Pope told me: 'We share your concerns. The Vatican is collecting information on this issue and in due course will make a firm public judgement.'

He then asked me, 'Do not Catholics in the USSR suffer some limitations to their civil rights? Isn't that so?'

I replied, 'Religious leaders in the USSR, whatever their faith, should not engage in activities beyond their authority. In other words, their religious rights are in no way limited, but they should not meddle in state affairs.'

The Pope seemed to accept our explanation and we did not return to this topic.

As always in my meetings at the Vatican, I tried to fathom what actually motivated the Pope when he was talking about war and peace. Clearly the Vatican is aware of the catastrophic consequences that a nuclear war would bring, and yet it still does not want to do all it could to stop the arms race and to condemn the policy and philosophy of militarism. Indeed, the Vatican's practical activity is consistently slanted towards cultivating distrust for the socialist states, and even interfering to a degree in their internal affairs.

The Vatican has many ways of influencing its flock, and one could say that subtly, by back alleys and back doors, it encourages ideological unity with the exploiting class. All the excuses church leaders may make – for instance, that Catholics sympathise with the ruling classes only in matters of religious belief – do not hold water, for it is those same classes that are forging the weapons. Thus the Vatican frequently directs its believers into sympathy with precisely those forces which bear the most responsibility for increasing world tension.

If the Vatican was really willing to look this truth in the face, it would have to work for the unity of *all* people, whatever their differences of ideology or religious belief, in the interests of peace and the struggle against war and the nuclear threat.

All my life I have retained the memory of the news that came from Spain at the end of the 1930s, the years when Spanish fascism fought to crush the people's power into the ground. At first the news was encouraging, but then more and more depressing. Solidarity between Franco, Hitler and Mussolini did its bloody work. The anger of the Soviet people was roused, the Soviet Union gave substantial aid to the fight against Franco, and Soviet internationalists went to fight in Spain to defend the Republic, while later many Republican fighters found refuge in the Soviet Union.

During the Second World War, Spain under Franco and his clique was practically Hitler's ally: its so-called Blue Division joined the Nazi forces fighting against the USSR. With the defeat of Hitler's Reich, Spain was for a long time in a state of political convulsion until the death of the dictator in 1975, whereupon the country could breathe more freely. An attempted reactionary military coup in 1981 failed. The atmosphere had changed since Franco.

When re-establishing relations with Spain in 1977, we took account of the fact that there is always light and shade in the politics of a nation. If the Soviet Union and Spain were to build a bridge, it would have to be from both ends, and both sides knew that it would take time. Today at last we can say our relations are normal.

As I descended the steps from the aircraft on my first visit to Spain, I felt a certain thrill. I was, after all, stepping on to the soil of a country that had made many priceless contributions to world culture, a country where the heroes of Spanish literature had lived, a country through which Hannibal's army had passed on its terrible journey to Rome.

My official visit to Spain took place in 1979. I have very pleasant memories of my meeting with King Juan Carlos I. He gave me the impression that he fully understood his role in taking the country away from its Francoist past. Our talk was wholly friendly, and it concluded with the King saying: 'I want to thank the Soviet leadership for their invitation to visit the USSR. I have long dreamed of seeing your great country.'

After dinner with the King, I had businesslike talks with Prime Minister Adolfo Suárez and Foreign Minister Marcelino Oreja, both of whom emphasised Spain's need to develop trade relations and cultural ties with us.

I had the opportunity to talk again with the King, and with the senior members of his government, in September 1983, when I was in Madrid during the last phase of the meeting of participants in the European convention. As host nation, Spain did much to bring about positive results from this meeting.

In March 1985 I made a further visit to Spain, during which both sides expressed satisfaction with the widening of our collaboration in economic, scientific, technical and cultural spheres, and in May 1986 Prime Minister Felipe González made a state visit to the USSR. He had talks with General Secretary Gorbachev on deepening Soviet–Spanish co-operation in solving international problems, and with Prime Minister Ryzhkov, as a result of which a protocol was signed on the further development of economic and industrial collaboration.

In his meeting with me, as Chairman of the Presidium of the Supreme Soviet since March 1985, González tried to prove that the USSR and the USA bore equal responsibility for the present world situation. By quoting examples, we were able to show that this was not so.

One can say that the basic outcome of our many meetings with Spanish state officials since Franco is that Moscow and Madrid have learned to talk to each other, and that is quite an achievement. Indeed, on the question of nuclear weapons it has proved easier to find a common language with the Spanish than with many other West European governments.

The policies of all post-Franco Spanish governments have of course included solidarity with elements of NATO, but this is solidarity of a class character. In the last analysis, Spain is a capitalist country. Even so, where the danger of nuclear war is concerned, Spanish statesmen are agreed that to perish in the fires of such a war, even in the embrace of their class brethren abroad, is not acceptable.

For many years in Finland, Urho Kaleva Kekkonen was an inspiring figure, not only in Finnish political life but also in the international arena. As Foreign Minister, I met him many times for talks in either Moscow or Helsinki, and in purely personal circumstances during his hunting trips to Zavidovo near Moscow.

Kekkonen's name is well known in the USSR. The fact that he was Finnish President for more than twenty-five years and Prime Minister for five years before that already says much. The number of years, however, is less important than the great strides Soviet –Finnish relations made during his tenure.

In September 1944 Finland's part in Hitler's aggression against the USSR came to an end. Under J.K. Paasikivi the country's leaders drew lessons from the past and, realising that the only realistic course was peace with their great neighbour to the east, agreed to the Soviet proposal for a treaty on friendship, co-operation and mutual aid.

Among the Finns who came to Moscow for talks on this question was Kekkonen, who was to succeed Paasikivi as President and who, even during the war, had been in favour of restructuring Soviet–Finnish relations, shifting from hostility to neighbourliness. He actively facilitated the success of talks and the signing of the treaty in 1948. Kekkonen showed that good relations were in the interests of both countries, and he not only continued the work that had been begun but made his own contribution to many aspects of Soviet–Finnish friendship.

Not so long ago, an early-morning passer-by in the Lenin Hills in Moscow might have witnessed three joggers in tracksuits, a middle-aged man slightly in front of two strong, younger people. Nobody would have paid much attention, since Muscovites are quite used to joggers, morning, noon and night, but, having run for an hour, the trio would then turn into the gates of a particular building where the militiamen on duty gave a smart salute.

That was how President Kekkonen began his day when visiting the Soviet Union. He ran only until the snow came, after which he put on his cross-country skis. No doubt that was the secret of his long and active life.

Of peasant origin, Kekkonen went from journalist to lawyer to politician. A man of exceptional intelligence and rich experience, he had a great sense of humour, and was always simple and accessible in his behaviour. True to the identity and traditions of his own country, he was also interested in the Soviet Union and made trips to the Caucasus, Central Asia, Siberia and even Sakhalin. He gained respect both in Finland and beyond her borders, and it was his foreign policy that earned Finland the world's admiration.

I well remember meeting Kekkonen in Helsinki in 1975 during

the meeting on European security. By this time he had acquired the status of a wise elder statesman, a man amply qualified to act as host to the heads of the state and government of thirty-two European countries, the USA and Canada.

I also recall his last official visit to the USSR in November 1980. At a ceremony in the Sverdlov Hall of the Kremlin, he was awarded the international Lenin Prize for strengthening peace between peoples.

Accepting this high honour, Kekkonen said, 'The Finns remember with gratitude that the Soviet government under Lenin recognised Finland's independence and thus created the preconditions for mutual friendship and collaboration between our two countries.' From the rostrum he called on the Soviet people: 'Let us together guard this heritage well.'

The Soviet leadership has done much to ensure that relations between us remain neighbourly. As for Urho Kekkonen, until his death on 31 August 1986, he worked ceaselessly towards that end.

The first little piece of Sweden I saw was in New York harbour in 1948. It was the Swedish passenger ship *Gripsholm*. In a way, that ship may have saved the lives of myself and my family. We had intended returning home by the Soviet ship *Pobeda*, which was bound for Odessa, but that would have delayed our journey considerably and, since my mother was seriously ill in Moscow, my wife and I decided to take the quicker Swedish ship. Tragically a few weeks later the *Pobeda* caught fire in the Black Sea and many people died, including some of our family friends who had been on their way home from the USA.

The voyage on the Swedish ship gave us the chance to learn something about Sweden and the Swedes. In the restaurant, for instance, all the hors-d'oeuvres were both abundant and free, and one only paid for the hot dishes. The organisation of the food was top class, so clearly the Swedes, who know a thing or two about economics, have discovered there is a handsome profit to be made from operating this Swedish table, or smorgasbord. It is now widely used around the world, not just on ships. Washington restaurants often have a Swedish table and it is highly popular.

We disembarked in Göteborg and spent a day in Stockholm, then continued the journey home via Finland.

A more substantial acquaintance with Sweden came in 1964

during an official visit. Our hosts went out of their way to acquaint us with the Swedish capital, and everyone I met, from Prime Minister Tage Erlander to officials in the Foreign Ministry, said that the Swedes and their government welcomed the good relations that had formed between our two countries, especially in trade.

They emphasised Sweden's success in solving its social problems. The standard of living was higher than the average of other developed capitalist countries, and the Swedes claimed they would soon have the highest in the world. They were probably right. Sweden's neutrality over a long period does much to explain her present prosperity.

Since 1814 Sweden has been involved in no wars. Both its international and to a great extent its domestic policies have been characterised by relative stability. Neither Sweden nor its royal household has been subject to the violent fate of most of the rest of Europe, and this has created the soil for traditional Swedish neutrality.

My talk with King Gustavus VI, the grandfather of the present King Charles XVI Gustavus, left a special impression on me. I was met in the royal palace by a tall, middle-aged man, one of the few European monarchs to have stayed firmly on his throne. He was a cultivated man, his special interest being archaeology, in which he said he tried to keep up with all the latest findings.

'I am especially interested in archaeological literature, including Russian publications,' he said. 'Perhaps you would send me some of the latest works?'

In due course, I sent him some books from Moscow.

Scandinavian kings do not take part in the practical affairs of state but somehow stand above them. Only the Swedes really understand how this works and foreigners have a hard time trying to fathom it. One thing is clear, however: the monarch is expected to carry out many duties aimed at maintaining foreign contacts.

In 1978 Moscow received the young King Charles XVI Gustavus. His visit was to some extent a landmark in Soviet–Swedish affairs, as it showed that Sweden was genuinely interested in developing a businesslike relationship with her eastern neighbour.

When I spoke to the King again in January 1984, during my visit to Stockholm for the opening of the conference on strengthening confidence, security and disarmament in Europe, he was quite definite about this: 'I am in favour of businesslike relations between our countries and for their improvement.'

He did not avoid discussing political matters either. When our side raised them, he responded eagerly. It seemed to me that the limitations placed on the Swedish monarch were becoming less rigid – if not constitutionally, then at least *de facto*.

My talk with Prime Minister Olof Palme was equally substantive and along the same lines as with the King. Of course there are politicians in Sweden who apparently cannot bear it if nothing happens between us to cause a serious quarrel, so neither the Prime Minister nor I avoided certain more contentious issues. And indeed the diplomatic situation has remained difficult: it seems more time is needed before common sense prevails in Stockholm over relations with the USSR.

Of Olof Palme we sadly now have to speak in the past tense. He was killed on 1 March 1986 by a terrorist. There were reports that suggested he may have been the victim of a right-wing organisation that could not swallow the Prime Minister's liberal views, his predisposition to good relations with the Soviet Union and his role as initiator in creating the group of leaders of six countries – Argentina, Greece, India, Mexico, Tanzania and Sweden – which came out for peace, disarmament and international collaboration. Or, of course, he may simply have been the target of a lunatic. The Swedish courts are still searching for the truth.

After reading *Hamlet* as a youth, I formed certain distinct impressions about Denmark which I was able to compare with the reality (allowing for the difference in era, of course) when I made my first official visit to that country in 1964.

My wife and I visited the famous castle at Elsinore, so graphically a part of Shakespeare's drama. As one enters the castle and passes through its intricate labyrinth of passages and doorways, emplacements and dungeons, halls and bedchambers, one is mentally transported back to Hamlet's time. One feels that one has only to wait until dark and the ghost of Hamlet's father would appear.

The fortress is clad in bronze lattice-work that has long turned green and the blue window-panes give the place an eerie look. The battlements facing the straits bristle with cannon and, in the

Middle Ages, ships passing under them had to pay a tribute to the Danish crown.

The specialists say that Shakespeare never saw the place, but that a troupe of English actors performed there and that one of them, who later worked with Shakespeare, must have told him the story of the prince of Denmark. Since 1916 *Hamlet* has been staged at Elsinore every year. An English company performed the play there for the first time in 1937, with Laurence Olivier in the title role and Vivien Leigh as Ophelia, both of them later to become acquaintances of mine.

Our talks with Danish state officials were much the same as those we had had in Stockholm, though with one difference: Denmark is a partner in NATO and therefore the issue of defence was raised on every occasion.

In our talks, we often put the question bluntly to the Danes: 'What does membership of NATO do for Denmark?'

The answer was usually a simple one: 'Denmark belongs to the Western world and therefore it is natural for her to belong to the alliance of Western states.'

We would ask, 'What about NATO's military activities and the military obligations Denmark has taken upon herself by joining?'

The reply: 'NATO is a defensive organisation and all its activities are defensive.'

The Danes, like other members of NATO, generally refuse to examine the point of such questions. Representatives of the small NATO member states usually resort to clichés when discussing these issues. Yet Danish politicians, like the Danish public as a whole, are clearly aware that the USSR poses no threat to Denmark. The atmosphere would change dramatically for the better once the talk turned to trade and economic relations, which have traditionally been good and which benefit both countries.

I made two official visits to Denmark, my main talks being with the Foreign Ministers and Prime Ministers. I also met King Frederick IX, his daughter, Princess Margrethe, also being present. The King said Denmark wanted to expand its economic and trade ties with us. I noticed that Princess Margrethe was interested in political issues, and when she became Queen Margrethe II she visited the USSR with her husband in 1975. The good impressions she gained from her talks with L.I. Brezhnev and from seeing the Soviet Union helped Soviet–Danish relations.

My first impression of Norway was that the people lived much closer to nature than in other economically developed countries of the West. The towns and industrial centres blended so much with their surroundings that they gave the effect rather of being large, densely populated villages. Even the capital is closely ringed by fields and forest.

During the Second World War a close friendship developed between the Soviet people and the Norwegians in their common struggle against the Nazis. Having broken the fierce German resistance, the Red Army went on to liberate the people of Finmark above the Arctic Circle six months earlier than the rest of the country. More than 12,000 Soviet soldiers gave their lives in the liberation of Norway, and in a telegram to Kalinin, the Soviet head of state, King Haakon VII congratulated the Soviet armed forces 'whose valiant struggle is so vital for Norway'. In the common effort, the King said, 'I see a basis for permanent cordial relations between our peoples.'

Ten years later Prime Minister Einar Gerhardsen said: 'The Norwegian people will never forget the contribution made by the Soviet people in the Second World War, and particularly to the liberation of the Norwegian people.'

Words of gratitude to the Soviet forces are inscribed on monuments all over Norway. For their part, hundreds of Norwegians helped the Red Army and brought victory closer; eighty of them were awarded Soviet orders and medals.

Norway's proximity to the Soviet Union imposes many obligations – in particular, to live as good neighbours. Norwegian and Soviet state officials have met on numerous occasions and at various levels, including the highest. I had useful talks with former Prime Minister Gerhardsen, since we both knew that, although Norway was a member of NATO, it was impossible for our two countries not to be on good terms. Whatever positive actions have helped to lay down a firm foundation for good Soviet–Norwegian relations over the last decades, these have been the result of efforts by both sides, and it is in both countries' interests to protect that relationship.

★

The Soviet Union has always paid attention to its relationship with Belgium and Holland, and the differences in our social systems have not prevented much genuine cooperation. Although they are small in size and population, the importance of these countries in international politics should not be underrated. In both world wars conquering Germans marched through Belgium, and in the Second World War the Nazis occupied Holland. The Soviet Union has always seen Belgium and Holland as innocent victims of fascist aggression and that alone has created a basis for mutual friendship.

Whatever government has been in power, the Belgians have always declared themselves in favour of friendship with the USSR. This was said to me by such political figures as Paul-Henri Spaak, Pierre Harmel, Leo Tindemans and, during his official visit to Moscow in June 1975, King Baudouin. They all spoke gravely, aware that any war, especially a nuclear war, would spell the end of their country.

I recall a conversation I had at a meeting with the King in Brussels in October 1976. I had taken my wife at his request and we were received by the King and Queen.

The talk was in a friendly vein and the leitmotif of everything the King said was summed up in the single thought: 'We must guarantee peace. Belgium is a small country, but she is economically developed. She can trade many things with the USSR. As for culture and cultural ties, Belgium values the culture of the Soviet people and would like to expand cultural ties.'

The Queen supported this idea energetically.

In my talks with Belgian politicians I have stressed: 'Those who condone the arms race forget that the same rule applies in politics as in the sports stadium: wherever competitors try to overtake one another, if one gets ahead, the others will do everything not to remain behind.'

In Holland too the people are definitely drawn towards peace, but once again her obligations to NATO run counter to this real and natural desire. After all, the peoples of Russia and Holland have long been mutually attracted. For instance, at the end of the seventeenth century Tsar Peter the Great went especially to the shipyards of Zaandam where, as a carpenter, he learned shipbuilding from the famous Dutch masters. It is also noteworthy that the two countries have never been at war with each other.

The October revolution made a great impact on the hearts

and minds of the Dutch. We remember that the Dutch workers protested against Western intervention in Soviet Russia and disrupted the shipment of arms from Rotterdam, and they gave food aid during the famine in the Volga region. Sadly, however, relations have not always been smooth. Certain people at the top in Holland prevented diplomatic recognition of the Soviet Union right up until July 1942.

Then, in 1945, Queen Wilhelmina sent a telegram to the Chairman of the Supreme Soviet in which she said: 'In the hour of my people's complete liberation, I also want to express my deep admiration and my people's total gratitude for the important contribution made by the splendid victories of the wonderful Russian armies to the triumph of the just cause and liberation of the Netherlands.'

Nevertheless, a great deal of time and effort was needed to bring about any significant degree of Soviet–Dutch co-operation. The breakthrough came only in the 1960s, when international relations in general were shifting from the cold war to détente.

I remember with satisfaction the friendly meetings I had with Queen Juliana and the present Queen Beatrix. During my official visit in 1972, Queen Juliana and her husband, Prince Bernhard, invited my wife and myself to the royal palace; and I met Queen Beatrix, when she was still Crown Princess, in Moscow in 1973 with her husband Prince Claus.

At various times, I have also met Prime Minister Barend Biesheuvel, Foreign Ministers Wilhelmus Schmeltzer, Max van der Stul and Hans van den Bruk, and other leading Dutch figures. Despite understandable differences of approach to some international problems, they have all been united in recognising the need for peaceful coexistence.

Widening the political dialogue has been beneficial to all spheres of Soviet–Dutch relations. A sound basis for these relations was provided by such bilateral documents as the agreement on aviation and merchant shipping, on the development of economic, industrial and technical co-operation, and on cultural co-operation. Holland is one of the USSR's main export partners in western Europe.

Switzerland's 'eternal neutrality' is long established. It was proclaimed and guaranteed in a declaration signed in 1815 at the

Congress of Vienna, when issues connected with the defeat of Napoleonic France were under review. For more than a hundred years thereafter Switzerland was a refuge for political émigrés from Italy, France and elsewhere, and several generations of Russian revolutionaries also found a haven there. Lenin spent about seven years there altogether.

It is as if Switzerland were created to show the world that, amid her majestic mountains and spacious valleys, her snows and her flowers, those fighting against tyranny would find a refuge where they could breathe the air of freedom. Swiss state officials are well aware of these attractive aspects of their history and they are used to compliments about their country's past. But of this country's present it has to be said that Switzerland's post-war neutrality has been less than perfect.

Why does Switzerland constantly look over her shoulder at NATO? As a neutral country, Switzerland need not become involved with any grouping of states and should remain aloof from any conflict between NATO and the Warsaw Pact.

Switzerland would understandably like to remain the location for international gatherings and for several international bodies, including the European section of the United Nations. One can only hope that she will maintain her reputation for neutrality as successfully as her watches tick away the hours. Forty-five years ago, I became the owner of my first Swiss watch, and it still keeps perfect time.

Which other country in central Europe can one consider a pillar of neutrality? The answer must be Austria, which acquired neutral status by the Vienna State Treaty, signed on 15 May 1955 by the USSR, the USA, Great Britain, France and Austria. When Austria celebrated the thirtieth anniversary of that treaty in 1985, she made a clear demonstration of her neutrality.

Austria had emerged as a state in 1918 after the disintegration of Austria-Hungary, which had frequently raised the sword against other countries in Europe, but in March 1938 Austria became a victim of German fascism in the shameful Anschluss. When the victory over Hitler brought freedom to the Austrian people, the path to independent development lay open.

I have visited Austria many times and have met her statesmen, starting with Chancellor Julius Raab and Foreign Minister Leopold

Figl, and ending with the present generation. I knew President Kurt Waldheim when he was Secretary-General of the United Nations. All of these leaders accepted that Austria must hold steadfastly to its neutral policy.

Those across the Atlantic who do not like Austria's neutrality, and who criticise it as 'amoral', are deeply wrong. The Soviet Union's relations with Austria are a compelling example of balanced co-operation between states having different social systems. In fact, if there is amorality, it lies in any attempt to make Austria repudiate her neutrality.

Vienna, the capital of a neutral country, is a leading international centre, accommodating for example such an important body as the International Atomic Energy Agency. Vienna is also the site of major international conferences. For instance, it was here that on 18 June 1979 the treaty on strategic offensive arms limitations – SALT-2 – was signed by the USSR and USA.

One would like to think that for Austria the future holds no unpleasant surprises. Europe needs a neutral Austria, and so do the Austrian people.

14

Friends and neighbours

The notion of proximity between states has undergone substantial change in the present century. Some states have been turned into virtual neighbours by the scientific and technological revolution in air, sea and land transport and in communications. This is particularly true of the USSR and Canada, who look at each other, so to speak, across the North Pole. Both countries are aware that because of their geographical positions they have common interests in the Arctic region.

This idea was expressed most clearly by Canadian Prime Minister Pierre Trudeau, leader of the Liberal Party. In fact, no other Canadian politician ever expressed more plainly the need to find a common language in bilateral relations and trade links with the USSR. This does not mean that Soviet–Canadian relations always ran smoothly under Trudeau, but as a rule his government would find a way of easing any tensions.

Canada and the USSR are also drawn together by the fact that nowhere else in the capitalist world are there such large colonies of Russians and Ukrainians who have kept their language and culture.

There are about 30,000 Canadians of Russian origin, almost all of them descendants of the Dukhobors who emerged in Russia in the second half of the eighteenth century, rejecting the Orthodox rites, sacraments and priesthood, and refusing to serve in the army. Persecuted by the authorities, they emigrated to Canada at the end of the nineteenth century. They live there in colonies concentrated in the area around the towns of Trail and Vancouver in British Columbia, and much of their economy is based on the collective ownership of property.

Canadian Ukrainians number over half a million. The descendants of peasants who at the turn of the century were driven by sheer starvation to leave their white huts and stream across the ocean, they are scattered throughout Canada, but chiefly in Manitoba, where the prairie is very like the steppes of Kakhovka or Kherson. Outside the provincial legislature in Winnipeg, the capital of Manitoba, alongside statues of Louis Riel and Robert Burns, there are monuments to Taras Shevchenko and Ivan Franko, two great Ukrainians.

I met Pierre Trudeau, several times, and Brezhnev received him on his first visit to the USSR in 1971. Trudeau was a man of great ability and tact. He would not skirt around a problem but would express his opinion straight away, and although he always had a good supply of ammunition for use against his political opponents, he was careful never to insult anyone personally. It was a characteristic that everyone noted. People who know him well say he has no personal enemies. He even behaved gallantly when he divorced his wife.

Trudeau was always ready to speak critically of Canada's southern neighbour, where he was eyed with some caution. I found him well informed on international matters, and if at times his evaluations were muddled then it was probably NATO solidarity speaking, for when he received information from Washington it was often either uselessly subjective or plainly false. To his credit, on such occasions he always listened with an open mind to the Soviet explanation.

It is widely recognised that, as Prime Minister, Trudeau was a master of domestic affairs. It looked at times as if he was about to go under in the political ocean, but he showed remarkable vitality in his country's interest, driven perhaps by the knowledge that his main political enemies did not approve his line on gaining more independence for Canada within the NATO bloc. After the elections of September 1984, however, the opposition Progressive-Conservative Party came to power in Canada and Brian Mulroney became Prime Minister.

I would say this of Pierre Trudeau: of course he is a bourgeois politician and his ideological views derive from his class. Nevertheless, in international affairs he stood head and shoulders above statesmen of other NATO countries who are blinded by their hostility to socialism and either cannot or will not recognise the situation as it is. Countries which have different social systems must sort out their differences by peaceful means: there is no other rational way.

A glance at the globe will show the vastness of the Latin American continent. Its thirty-three countries each have their own history, traditions, culture and heroes of the past and present, all of them having shed their blood to attain their people's independence and the chance to develop. Some are still having to continue their struggle.

Distance has not stood in the way of the desire of the Soviet Union and the countries of Latin America to form friendly ties, and during the Second World War and in the years following it, one by one these countries established diplomatic relations with us.

The name of Salvador Allende lives in the memory of the Soviet people. As head of the Chilean government for a relatively short time, he wrote a bright page in the history of his country's struggle against foreign domination and the oppression of the American monopolies. Allende came on an official visit to the USSR in December 1972. Our talks were conducted in the friendliest atmosphere. He was not a communist, but his social and economic plans for his country represented a programme of progressive reform for liberating the economy from the thrall of US monopoly capital.

Ten months before the fascist coup that overthrew him, Allende made a speech at the UN General Assembly in which he expressed his fears for the fate of Chile. He said, 'We are victims of a new assault by imperialism, a cunning, insidious and dangerous imperialism whose aim is to prevent our sovereign state from realising its rights. We are opposed by forces that operate in the dark, without identifiable labels, but having powerful weapons and occupying influential positions in the most various fields . . . . Not only are we suffering from a financial blockade, but we are also the victims of barefaced aggression.'

The talks we had in the Kremlin with Allende and his entourage were cordial and frank and our discussions on international issues and bi-lateral relations were conducted in an atmosphere of complete mutual understanding. The Chilean President expressed his desire for certain economic aid which the Soviet Union agreed to give, not because we had resources to spare but because we

sincerely wished to help the Chilean people overcome their difficulties in combating the military, economic and political pressure
being put on them by the imperialists.

A modest man of noble disposition, Allende did not hide his
pleasure at being in Moscow among friends, and wherever he
appeared thousands of Muscovites would turn out to greet him.

His wife, Hortensia Bussi de Allende, is a remarkable person in
her own right. She remains a prominent figure in public life, and
her calls for peace, and for the liberation of the Chilean people,
still carry weight.

All the Soviet representatives had an opportunity to talk to
Allende and his ministers. Mine came during a reception in the
Kremlin. Naturally, our conversation revolved around an evalu-
ation of America's Latin American policy.

Allende said, 'I resolutely condemn the enmity and hostility
which Washington has felt towards Chile since the first day our
democratic regime came into being.'

He himself did not then know how far in skulduggery and
viciousness his enemies, inside and outside the country, were
preparing to go to overthrow him. Taking into account his utterances and the context in which he made them, it was plain to us
that Allende was the sort of statesman who was prepared to die
for his cause. This was the view of all those in the Soviet leadership
who had talks with him during his visit.

He was personally a very brave man, who set aside fear for his
own safety and dedicated himself to his beliefs. When Pinochet's
gangs surrounded the presidential palace, Allende, had he so
chosen, could have shown the white flag and saved his own life.
He did not do so. His comrades were being killed before his eyes
and the President himself took part in the battle, dying with an
automatic pistol in his hand. There can be no other example in
twentieth-century history of the president of a democratic country
taking up arms to fight and die for an ideal.

One can assert with assurance that the time will come when
sooner or later the cause for which Allende gave his life
will conquer and that the Chilean people will once again breathe
freely.

I well remember the fellow feelings our people had towards the
Serbs, even as long ago as the First World War. Everyone knew

that Russia had come to Serbia's defence when she was attacked by Germany and Austria-Hungary. This sympathy continued in the inter-war period and even survived the difficulties experienced in Soviet–Yugoslav relations after the Second World War.

As a member of the 1955 Soviet delegation to the talks in the capital of Yugoslavia that resulted in the Belgrade declaration, I was involved from the start in the process of normalising relations. This declaration fixed the main basis of relations between our two countries which were later reinforced in a joint announcement signed in Moscow in 1956. I had the opportunity to meet President Josip Broz Tito in both Moscow and Belgrade, and our talks were conducted in a friendly atmosphere.

Obviously the improvement in Soviet–Yugoslav relations arose because both sides realised that failure to mend the differences between us would only give satisfaction to our enemies. Subsequent events showed that the declaration signed in Belgrade by Khrushchev and Tito was a major event for both countries.

It was a sad occasion when I had to attend Tito's funeral. The Soviet people remember him as a brave anti-fascist fighter, the leader of the heroic partisan struggle against the Nazi occupiers.

Let me say something about the events that took place in Hungary in 1956. I was not yet Foreign Minister, but I was informed about the upheaval being experienced by a friendly country that had taken the path to socialism.

I must emphasise as strongly as I can that the help given to Hungary by the Soviet Union was absolutely justified. The forces that were bent on overthrowing the Hungarian leadership intended to liquidate the social order and restore the previous system that had been responsible for making Hungary a bridgehead for Hitler's aggression against the Soviet Union and many other countries.

The internal forces that were hostile to the new post-war Hungary derived help from outside the country. This much was plain from the moment they decided to resort to the use of force and to drown in blood everything that had been achieved in the country liberated by the Soviet army at a cost well known to both the Soviet and the Hungarian peoples. The foreign circles that condemned the Soviet action have presented the facts in a distorted light. They have generally pretended not to be aware that the

Soviet Union was acting in response to numerous and insistent requests from Hungary, from democratic bodies, including that part of the leadership that patriotically stood for the defence of Hungary's social order. As a result, Hungary has remained an independent state among the socialist countries, dedicated to the cause of peace and friendship between the peoples.

In evaluating the events of 1956, the Soviet Union and the people of Hungary have a clear conscience.

The Soviet Union and Czechoslovakia well remember the crisis that the country passed through in 1968. This was the new Czechoslovakia, where the people had triumphed and had set off on the path of socialist transformation and peace. Many sons of the Soviet people had laid down their lives in liberating Czechoslovakia from the Nazi aggressors.

By 1968 the country occupied a stable position among the fraternal states, and the people had demonstrated their ability to heal the wounds inflicted by the war and Nazi occupation and to make progress both in their economic development and in strengthening the social order under the leadership of the Communist Party.

Then suddenly the forces that were at one with the previous order, when power had been in the hands of politicians who had cared nothing for the people's welfare or the country's true national interests, decided to turn back the clock – and to do so with guns in their hands and without regard to casualties. In other words, they decided to stage a *coup d'état*, and for this purpose they used people who had managed to penetrate the state apparatus. Of course, outside help was also given to the enemies of the new Czechoslovakia, in much the same way as had happened in Hungary in 1956.

News swept Prague and the rest of the country that actions were taking place in the Czech capital that were aimed at seizing state institutions by force, in other words, a seizure of power. The first targets were the party committees. At fixed times, mostly at night, house numbers, and in some cases also street names, were changed. This was evidence that the enemies of the new Czechoslovakia were getting ready in good time and with care.

But they miscalculated. Requests to the Soviet Union for help were transmitted to the capitals of the other socialist countries in order to block the path of the counter-revolution. The fraternal countries gave immediate and effective support.

Once events had been channelled in the desired direction and the collapse of the counter-revolution was an established fact, it was necessary to strengthen the country's internal forces. The people expected nothing less.

I recall the arrival in Moscow of the official Czechoslovak delegation, led by Dubček, then First Secretary of the Czechoslovak Party Central Committee. A banquet was arranged in their honour in the Kremlin. Dubček's speech on behalf of the delegation made an odd impression. He condemned the counter-revolution, but he said nothing sensible about how to deal with the situation. It was a speech full of innuendo, and it lacked realism. Dubček, of course, did not remain in his job, since he lacked the necessary authority in the country.

Czechoslovakia and her people found the assurance that their country would continue along the sure path of socialist construction and firm friendship with the Soviet Union and the other socialist countries.

If you ask Soviet citizens what they know about Turkey, ninety-nine out of a hundred will tell you: 'It is a neighbouring country with which tsarist Russia was at war on and off for at least two hundred years.'

The history of Christianity and Islam shows that both religions often served the god of war. The Christian fathers would bless their flocks with the sign of the cross as they marched off to kill other Christians, and similarly the Muslim mullahs would call on Allah to help them in their wars with other Muslims. From 1979 to 1988 a war was fought by Iranian Muslims against Iraqi Muslims, senselessly wiping out the flower of both nations.

However, when the warring sides profess different religions, the ferocity increases. The literature and paintings depicting the wars between Christian Russia and Muslim Turkey are replete with bloodthirsty scenes, and it took hundreds of years before the implacable processes of history forced the Ottoman conquerors to a standstill. The situation on the Russo-Turkish border was stabilised, and the peoples of the Balkans, with Russian help, achieved their independence.

Of course, present-day Turkey is not responsible for the aggressive wars inflicted in the past on Russia or elsewhere. The October revolution was the turning-point in our relations and it came at a moment in Turkish history when a number of far-sighted men had emerged, among them Kemal Atatürk.

The letters exchanged by Lenin and Atatürk will long serve as a source of enlightenment for those who work towards good relations between countries. Lenin saw in Atatürk a figure standing above the narrow interests of the Turkish bourgeoisie and land-owning upper classes. Atatürk for his part wanted his people to see their future not in the gloom of the Middle Ages, ringed with unfriendly neighbouring countries, but in forward progress, slow but steady.

Prominent among Atatürk's successors was Ismet Inönü. He enjoyed wide respect in the country, was President from 1938 to 1950 and Prime Minister from 1961 to 1965. Admittedly Inönü served in the interests of the bourgeoisie and landowners, and did not exactly hurry his country along the path of social reform, but nevertheless the traditions of the People's Republican Party, that is Atatürk's party, survived and urged the country forward. The party has suffered defeats in recent years, however. Inönü's retirement from political life made the goals set by Atatürk harder to achieve, and Turkey's entry into NATO made this achievement even more difficult.

I made an official visit to Turkey in 1965. By this time Inönü was not in any official post, but he asked to see me nevertheless, and I agreed. The mere fact that he had been a comrade of Atatürk's aroused respect. Certainly not everything his government had done corresponded with Atatürk's aims in Soviet–Turkish relations, but we let this pass.

Inönü, now in opposition, was able to express himself freely on the subject and I was amazed by his clarity of mind, even though he was in his ninth decade. In the course of our talk, he returned frequently to the main fact he wanted to emphasise: 'Far from everything that is happening in Turkey has my approval. Even less does it correspond to the precepts of my late mentor. But I hold to the belief that Turkey must and can build relations with her mighty northern neighbour on the basis which Lenin and Atatürk understood so well.'

★

When international problems are discussed with the Turks, the question of Cyprus inevitably arises. We tell the Turkish leaders frankly that the Soviet Union supports the Cypriot people's right to build their own destiny, while taking into account the legitimate interests of both Cypriot communities, Greek and Turkish.

Since the war the Cypriot situation has heated up more than once, and crises have occurred both within Cyprus itself and between Cyprus and her neighbours. On every occasion, the justice of the Soviet position has been confirmed, since it is based on the need to guarantee peace in the region.

I have flown over Cyprus many times when visiting, say, Egypt or Syria. As I look down on the island, which in good weather you see in its entirety as clearly as the palm of your hand, the idea comes into my mind: down there are British bases – that means NATO bases. Then another thought: this small, elegant piece of earth, green the year round, was once a centre of modern civilisation, a place of delicate and priceless treasures. Surely the Greek and Turkish communities would have found a common language long ago, if the leading countries in NATO had respected Cyprus's independence?

The Soviet Union understands the problems faced by the Cypriot leadership. Heading this leadership from 1959 to 1977 was the brave fighter against British domination, Archbishop Makarios, who with faith and justice served his people. To hear Makarios putting his case, one would have had to be made of stone to remain unmoved by his situation, and the same is true today. Yet Washington, London and other NATO capitals are relentless: neither the UN Charter nor international law can shake this determination.

I shall illustrate this by describing an episode that took place in May 1974. It was mutually agreed that one of my trips to Cairo should coincide with a visit to the Middle East by Henry Kissinger, who was then Secretary of State in the Nixon administration. We met in Nicosia, the capital of Cyprus, and discussed a number of issues, including that of Cyprus.

Having heard Kissinger's explanation of the US position, I asked him point blank, 'Does the US government support the independence and territorial integrity of Cyprus, or not?'

He was evasive, but his answer boiled down to the admission that Washington would basically be happy to see the division of the island into two parts, Greek and Turkish – that is, the creation of two separate states. He also made a number of sarcastic remarks about Makarios. Although he refrained from a direct attack, his veiled and sugar-coated gibes made it plain that he personally, and the US administration, regarded Makarios as an anomaly, a church man who would be better sticking to church affairs.

Anyone overhearing my conversation with Kissinger about Cyprus would have been amazed. Here was I, the representative of a socialist state, with its dominant atheistic ideology, supporting an archbishop as head of the Cyprus government, while the representative of a capitalist state, with its professedly Christian attitudes, was making that archbishop an object of scorn.

Once again Washington was showing its indifference to the principle of non-interference in the affairs of other states, which meant nothing when set against the economic and strategic interests of the USA and NATO.

Both Kissinger and I had separate talks with Makarios. Mine were extremely friendly, as once again the Soviet position on Cyprus was shown to be consistent and humane.

Many years have passed since these meetings took place, yet still the problem remains unresolved, and indeed in the summer of 1974 was greatly worsened when, in connection with an anti-government *putsch* organised by the military junta in Athens, Turkey landed troops on the island on the pretext of protecting the Turkish Cypriot population. Since then Cyprus has been divided (*pace* Kissinger) into two completely separate parts.

All this has taken place despite resolutions passed by the UN General Assembly and Security Council. Nevertheless the Soviet Union persists in protesting against attempts to settle the Cyprus issue in terms of NATO and against the will of the Cypriots themselves. Our position is that the island should be freed of the foreign military presence. The Soviet proposal for holding a representative international conference on Cyprus under the auspices of the UN is the only way to reach a just solution of the problem.

Before discussing Iran's recent history, I should like to mention events which took place thousands of miles away and somewhat earlier than my first meeting with the Shah.

The setting was New York. The United Nations had just begun to function, but the UN building did not yet exist in its present

form; its offices were accommodated in various temporary locations scattered around the city. The Security Council was in the
Bronx, and I was the Soviet representative.

At that time there were still some Soviet troops in northern
Iran: they had been sent in during the war for security reasons,
since the Nazis also had their eyes on Iran, and at the end of the
war the USSR felt it could not withdraw these troops before
a number of questions had been settled – principally, the continued existence of British bases in Iraq and India, and the large
number of US bases around the perimeter of our frontier, to say
nothing of British naval forces in the Persian Gulf. Therefore,
the USSR declared it would keep its troops in Iran for the time
being.

A murky wave of anti-Soviet feeling at once rose up and a
question was tabled at the Security Council – which was what
Washington and London wanted. I received the following instructions from Moscow: 'If this question is tabled, say that our troops
are being kept in Iran because of unforeseeable circumstances.'

When the initiators of the discussion heard our explanation,
they asked: 'Would you mind telling us, please, just what these
unforeseeable circumstances are?'

I replied, 'Unforeseeable circumstances are unforeseeable precisely because you can't foresee them.'

This brought loud applause from the auditorium, which I had
not expected. The Western powers nevertheless set their voting
machine in motion and substantive discussion of the issue began.
I got up and left the session, the first time in the history of the
United Nations that a representative of a powerful country walked
out as a sign of protest.

Several times in the following years Moscow was visited by
a small, dark, well-educated man, the Shah, Mohammed Reza
Pahlevi, who for several decades determined the domestic and
foreign policies of Iran. He had ascended the throne in September
1941 after the abdication of his father, Reza Shah Pahlevi. The
former commander of a tsarist Russian Cossack regiment in Persia,
Reza Shah had been elected to the throne after an internal revolt
in 1925, as a result of which a bourgeois–landowning dictatorship
had been established.

What can one say of the Shah, leaving aside his ignominious
end? He and his entourage realised that Iran's northern neighbour
was a state with which they needed to have good relations.

Accordingly the Shah made diplomatic visits to Moscow. One might have said of these that they represented cautious neighbourliness plus a large dose of suspicion.

The talks during the Shah's visits to Moscow in 1974 were particularly difficult. It had become clear by this time that the Shah was starting to acquire heavy weapons, such as tanks and planes, in impressive quantities from other countries, primarily the USA. We decided, therefore, to raise this matter with the Shah during the official talks in the Kremlin.

Brezhnev expressed our basic disquiet in the form of a question: 'Why does Iran need so many weapons? She has nobody to fight with. Her neighbour, the Soviet Union, wants to maintain neighbourly relations. The Soviet–Iranian treaty of 1921 moreover obligates both sides to live in peace and neighbourliness.'

The gist of what the Shah had to say in reply was: the Iranian government and the Shah personally have good intentions towards our northern neighbour; Iran has nothing against the Soviet Union.

Undeniably, however, the Shah and his political advisers were less than respectful towards the 1921 treaty which Lenin had initiated and which had laid the foundation for good relations. As a matter of fact, it was under article 6 of this treaty that Soviet troops had been stationed in Iran during the Second World War. This clause stated that, in the event of aggressive attempts by third countries against Iran or, using Iran as a bridgehead, against the Soviet Union, both sides agreed that if the Iranian government itself were unable to avert such a danger then 'the Soviet government would have the right to introduce its own troops into Persian territory in order to take the necessary military measures in the interests of self-defence.'

I remember the Shah boarding the plane at the end of his 1974 visit. He turned to me and said, 'And when will you be able to come to us on an official visit, Mr Gromyko?' He added reproachfully, 'We have after all asked you repeatedly.'

I replied, 'I'm afraid I can't answer that just at the moment. We'll have to think about a date.'

It was a suitable reply in the circumstances, especially in the light of subsequent events.

Neither I nor the Soviet Union need have any regrets that the bearer of the Shah's crown had to make a rapid dash for the border and ended his days as an exile. We welcomed the Iranian revolution and have never hidden the fact that we want to have only friendly relations with the new Iranian government.

Shortly after the October 1917 revolution, the Soviet Republic and its neighbour, Afghanistan, established diplomatic relations. Soviet political and material support was one of the chief factors in Afghanistan's victory in its almost one-hundred-year struggle for independence from its British colonisers. It is therefore not surprising that Soviet–Afghan relations have long been of a friendly nature.

When I began to wonder what I would say in my memoirs about Afghanistan, I found myself in a quandary. This was not for any lack of factual material relating to my meetings with Afghan state officials over a forty-year period, nor for any lack of problems connected with Afghanistan that might have arisen over the last few years. The difficulties were of a different order. Out of all this mass of material I had to select enough that was not already well known about the major changes that have taken place in that country.

So, here I am in Kabul some time before the Afghan revolution. I am in the royal palace in the luxurious study of the King, Zahir Shah, who is sitting behind his desk. This man is interesting and cultivated, and knows very well how best to begin a conversation with a foreign official.

After mutual greetings, the basic point is emphasised, namely that Soviet–Afghan relations must proceed on the basis of strict non-interference in each other's internal affairs.

The King spoke principally of Soviet foreign policy which he recognised was aimed at maintaining peace. I must underline the fact that the King did not even mention the internal situation in his country. This was not surprising, since neither he nor his government paid any attention to practical domestic matters such as the economy, industry or agriculture. In effect, they simply ignored the social problems that affected millions of their people; but in any case tribal organisation and lack of resources probably prevented them from taking any effective measures in the economic life of the state.

Numerous meetings with Afghan representatives in Moscow later produced much the same impression, even though the Soviet Union was by then already giving substantial aid to the country.

Throughout all our talks at all levels, one fundamental principle predominated, namely that the Soviet leadership's position fully conformed to the UN Charter and Afghanistan's desire to remain independent. Therefore, when Western politicians today, many years after the Afghan revolution, assert that the Soviet Union wants to grab Afghanistan for itself, they are deceiving both their own people and the Afghans. It is a deception that is obviously required if they are to continue their crude interference in Afghanistan's internal affairs.

It would be hard to count the number of meetings held by Western and Pakistani officials, each one designed to frustrate a solution of the Afghan problem on the basis of the national conciliation proposed by the Afghan government. At these meetings the Western representatives invariably adopted an unfriendly, not to say openly hostile, attitude to the Afghan government.

Their arguments were primitive. They stated that their anti-government support could be stopped only after the complete withdrawal of Soviet troops from Afghanistan, even though everyone knows that these troops were introduced solely as neighbourly assistance between one country and another.

It is good that two such countries as the Soviet Union and India should be geographically close to each other. Both are genuinely peace-loving, and this fact alone exerts an enormous influence on the international scene.

As a direct result of both sides' efforts, the Soviet Union and India have developed mutually rewarding relations. This desire for neighbourly exchange and co-operation has its roots in ancient times. The Russians have since time immemorial been drawn to a knowledge of India and its people; the medieval chronicles of Rus mention India; and for their part the Indians have always been interested in the social and cultural life of Russia. Thus the leaders of the Indian national liberation movement, Tilak and Gandhi, took a close interest in the evolution of Russian thought.

The correspondence between Leo Tolstoy and Mahatma Gandhi is full of mutual respect. In this connection, I recall an incident from my first visit to India in 1955. When I was taken to my hotel I asked my hosts: 'I wonder if you could bring me a few local books that I could read or at least glance through in my free moments?'

They brought me some books and among them I found Gandhi's autobiography. In the little time I had, I leafed through the pages and came across an arresting detail. The author described how he had once been sitting in a train, reading the works of Tolstoy. Suddenly the idea dawned on him: why not follow Tolstoy's call to the Russian people not to resist evil with force? Tolstoy thus gave Gandhi the impulse to form his own philosophy of non-violent resistance, and Gandhi speaks of it frankly in his book.

The October revolution was a mighty stimulus for the national liberation movements of the colonial and dependent countries, including India, whose democratic forces were heartened by our success.

Showing unswerving solidarity with the Indian people's struggle for freedom, the Soviet Union welcomed Indian independence in 1947 and in the same year established diplomatic relations.

Already in the period when it was being created, India's foreign policy had been powerfully influenced by such pillars of the independence movement as Mahatma Gandhi and Jawaharlal Nehru. Although I never met Gandhi, at the Security Council in 1948, on Moscow's instructions, I was privileged to express our condolences after his assassination. I met Nehru, however, on countless occasions – in Delhi, in Moscow and in New York at the UN. He was in my opinion an outstanding statesman. A man of powerful intellect, he was at once a distinguished politician, historian and philosopher. One was struck above all by his erudition, but he also revealed an inexhaustible hatred for colonialism, and this to a great extent underpinned his whole assessment of the international situation.

Speaking at meetings, it was not through the volume and timbre of his voice or gesticulation that he conquered his audience, but rather by the logic and depth of his thinking. I was at a meeting attended by hundreds of thousands of Indians in Delhi. Nehru's speech was a fierce condemnation of imperialism and a call for friendship with the Soviet Union, and his words were carefully considered, formed and projected in elegant and precise phrases. He emphasised that India's future lay along the path of peace and peaceful co-operation with other countries, and his vast audience roared in response.

Conversation with Nehru always took place in a relaxed manner, but one quickly realised that this was not someone satisfied with paltry ideas, that everything he said was thought out, as if it were the concentrated experience of his life. Nehru never used prepared notes – at least I never saw him do so. He improvised, freely choosing phrases and words to express his thoughts, but it was improvisation which only a politician of his calibre could have produced.

Nehru had learned to think through his problems when he had been held for many years in solitary confinement by the British. Indeed, since he had spent more than ten years in prison, it was maybe there that he had acquired the unusual habit of suddenly going quiet during a conversation and sitting motionless with his eyes half shut, as if gazing into himself. From his experience under British domination Nehru learned inner peace and the ascetic way of life. He became India's leader following independence, and he was even more respected and loved by the people after the tragic death of his mentor, Gandhi.

I was also struck by the fact that in conversation he did not avoid the sort of specific questions that senior politicians often prefer not to discuss; he was, on the contrary, interested in detail. For instance, he wanted to know the structure of the UN, how decisions were taken, what were its numerous agencies and the differences in their functions. At the same time he did not express any doubt that the UN and its operation were well designed. He knew the part the USSR played in its machinery and he appreciated it.

With the appearance of the atom bomb, Nehru was aware of its dire implications for the world. His thinking was similar to that of the Soviet Union, which soon after the war proposed the banning of this weapon for ever.

I remember Nehru's words, during a conversation in November 1955 in Delhi with the Soviet delegation, headed by Bulganin and Khrushchev, in which I also took part.

Khrushchev was talking about the results of the meeting that had just taken place in Geneva between the leaders of the USSR, the USA, Britain and France. He said, 'The cold war is now a thing of the past.'

Nehru was thoughtful. 'I would warn you against excessive optimism.' With a restrained smile on his face, he added sadly: 'We will hear of the cold war again.'

Nehru's voice in defence of the freedom and independence of peoples rang out authoritatively and weightily at the UN General Assembly in 1960, when the Soviet proposal on the liquidation of colonialism was debated. In the end, the Assembly adopted the declaration on granting independence to the colonial countries and peoples. This historic decision had been initiated by our country.

Nehru has gone down in history as one of the founders of the policy of non-alignment, the fundamental principles of which are a commitment to the cause of peace, to the equality of states in both political and economic relations, and to the repudiation of all forms of colonialism and racism.

Krishna Menon, a comrade of Gandhi and Nehru, was given a series of important government posts when India gained independence. From 1947 to 1952 he was Indian High Commissioner in London, from 1956 Minister without portfolio, and then from 1957 to 1962 Minister of Defence.

He frequently headed the Indian delegation to the UN General Assembly, representing India and defending her interests effectively. I first got to know him during the UN debate on the Kashmir question. As the Kashmir question wasn't resolved for many months, we met dozens of times.

It quickly became clear to me and my Soviet colleagues that Menon believed deeply in the justice of India's case. It was also plain that he was personally friendly towards the Soviet Union. He would say to me heatedly: 'You cannot imagine the hatred the Indian people felt and still feel towards the colonialists, the British.'

His eyes would shine and he would go on to assert: 'Colonialism and imperialism are twins. It's no accident that the biggest imperialists are also the colonialists.'

He vehemently rejected the idea that the USA should not be thought of as a colonial power: 'Look at Puerto Rico or the Philippines, which have not yet thrown off the colonial yoke of America.' He added, 'The methods used by American capital to exploit the backward countries may be oblique, but they're just as harsh.'

The governments and diplomats of the West were well aware of Menon's views and they took their revenge whenever they could. The press was especially zealous in this regard, inventing all kinds of preposterous stories about him.

Menon found it hard to do his work in this atmosphere, but he stuck it out. His speeches at the UN tended to be long and they took a lot out of him. After one such speech, he collapsed from exhaustion and had to be carried out on a stretcher.

On European affairs, Menon expressed his government's opposition to the rearmament of West Germany, a sober and bold position which did credit to independent India. Everything Menon said at international meetings represented a significant contribution to the policy which India still follows as one of the most influential states in the non-alignment movement. Even though I remember John Foster Dulles saying, 'Non-alignment is amoral,' this policy has gained wide respect, and is embraced by a hundred countries today.

There were many stories about Menon. I heard for instance that in order to toughen himself he slept without a mattress, blankets or a pillow. Over a cup of tea, I once asked him if this was true.

'Of course it is,' he laughed. 'Millions of us in India sleep like that.' He went on, still smiling: 'I find it especially hard when I'm on a trip and I have to stay in American hotels. I arrive and say, "Take everything off the bed." They never know what I mean, so I have to turn the room upside-down myself, which only puzzles the staff even more.'

I have many happy memories of my chats with Menon, who argued well and liked a joke. He has not held office for some years, but has been active as president of the All-India Peace Council.

To the Soviet people, Indira Gandhi was the very embodiment of India – wise with the experience of millennia yet thrusting into the future, matriarchal yet eternally young, constant in seeking good and opposing evil and oppression.

Mrs Gandhi enjoyed widespread popularity and sympathy in the Soviet Union, as witness the large number of Soviet babies who were given the unusual name Indira. Certainly, on the frequent occasions that I met her, Indira Gandhi left a deep impression on me. Thin, light of step, with an open, soft, gentle smile, large, lively eyes and greying hair, she exhibited enormous integrity, a clear mind and great firmness of character. On an individual basis she knew how to charm and make one feel well disposed towards her, and at large meetings she also knew how to reach the heart of her audience.

The daughter of India's first Prime Minister, Nehru, Indira was to a great extent influenced by her father. Although not himself a Marxist-Leninist, Nehru readily admitted that the study of Marx and Lenin had helped him to see the modern world in a new light. Linking the realisation of his high philanthropic ideals with the struggle for the social and political freedom of the individual and the people, and with the development of India's national liberation movement, he sought to pass this view of the world on to his daughter. In consequence, she too linked her ideas with those of the Russian revolution. Born only a few days after that great event, on 19 November 1917, she liked to think of herself as the same age as the revolution.

Like her father, she did not show emotion. Possibly her restraint was due also to the modesty which is innate in Indian women. Without the risk of exaggeration, one can say that in the ten years or so of her rule, Indira will always occupy a place of honour in India's history. She did everything possible to make her country strong and able to stand on its own feet, while preserving its rich cultural heritage and at the same time trying to end its poverty, its backwardness and its outdated institutions and traditions. Thanks to her policies, India achieved self-sufficiency in food, and industrial production increased dramatically; yet, significantly, India today is one of the few developing countries where the share of foreign capital in the financing of national construction is minimal.

In the development of Soviet–Indian relations, Indira was a consistent supporter of friendship and co-operation. As early as the Second World War, she was an active member of the Friends of the Soviet Union. After her first trip to the USSR in 1953, she became a frequent visitor and her name is closely linked with the signing of the 1971 treaty of peace and co-operation between our two countries. Co-operation with the Soviet Union meant more to Indira Gandhi than simply an aspect of international relations; she repeatedly stressed that the Soviet Union had always been on India's side in her difficult moments.

After her assassination in 1984, she was succeeded by her son, Rajiv, who in his very first statements declared: 'The Republic of India will remain faithful to the independence and peace-loving course along which Jawaharlal Nehru and Indira Gandhi led her.' He emphasised: 'India treasures the friendly relations she has with the Soviet Union, which are widely supported by the country's political forces and by the entire people. With this in mind, great attention will be paid to the further strengthening of relations with the USSR.'

An event of great international importance was Rajiv Gandhi's official visit to the USSR in May 1985. This meeting resulted in the signing of an agreement of general economic, industrial, scientific and technical co-operation until the year 2000 and an agreement on Soviet–Indian co-operation in the building of several large specific new projects in India.

The further talks General Secretary Gorbachev had with Rajiv Gandhi during his visit to India in November 1986 resulted in the Delhi declaration, which called for 'a nuclear-free and non-violent world', a new political term which has since entered the daily vocabulary of international discourse. Clearly contacts between the leaders of the USSR and India are a working mechanism for strengthening friendship and trust.

The partition of the sub-continent into India and Pakistan which took place after independence left both countries with a difficult legacy.

In the autumn of 1965, when the situation sharply worsened as a result of Indian–Pakistani military actions, the Soviet government declared itself ready to seek an early end to the conflict. Our proposal having received a positive response, in Tashkent on 4 –10 January 1966 the Indian delegation, led by Lal Bahadur Shastri, met the Pakistani delegation, led by Ayub Khan, in the presence of A.N. Kosygin and the Foreign Ministers of all three states. Despite the fundamental differences between the two sides, the armour of suspicion, mistrust and national hatred was nevertheless broken down.

Unfortunately, the last stage of the talks was overshadowed by the tragic death of Prime Minister Shastri. It happened late in the evening, following the farewell reception at which Shastri had made a short speech. At about one in the morning I was informed that something was wrong and I went at once to his residence. He was lying in bed and seated beside him was a very depressed-looking Kosygin, who had arrived two minutes ahead of me. Apart from Indian officials, there was a Soviet doctor in attendance who was giving the patient artificial respiration as I arrived. Kosygin and I watched his efforts with great concern; Shastri was showing no sign of life. The doctor and his team did all they could, but to no avail.

The Tashkent meeting nevertheless resulted in the signing of a declaration according to which the two countries would undertake all measures to create neighbourly relations.

However, their relations remained bad. One inflammatory factor was the insidious web into which Pakistan fell almost at the outset of her existence as an independent state. The West, above all the USA, in order to keep Pakistan within the orbit of their policies, applied a number of political, economic and military pressures. The Soviet Union nevertheless always tried to maintain good relations with Pakistan and, prior to the problems in Afghanistan, even tried to help Pakistan overcome her economic backwardness.

It was 15 November 1982 in the St Catherine's Hall of the Great Kremlin Palace. On one side of the table sat Yu.V. Andropov and myself, as Foreign Minister, on the other side sat General Zia ul-Haq, who had headed the Pakistani military government after the army takeover of 1977 and had since become President. With him was his Foreign Minister, Yaqub Khan.

The Soviet side gave the general our assessment of all the actions that had been carried out from Pakistani territory by armed groups operating in Afghanistan. We told him, 'Any attempt to pretend that Pakistan has nothing to do with what is happening around Afghanistan is pointless. Pakistan is a partner in the war against Afghanistan. You must understand that the Soviet Union will stand by Afghanistan, with which she has long and close ties, formalised in a treaty of friendship and co-operation after the April revolution. The Soviet Union is giving and will continue to give help of one kind or another to the Afghan people. Pakistan is completely wrong to carry out a hostile policy towards Afghanistan, and is thereby dangerously undermining Soviet–Pakistani relations.'

Zia ul-Haq assured us: 'Pakistan genuinely wishes to have friendly relations with Afghanistan and the Soviet Union, and seeks a peaceful political solution of the Afghan problem.'

Yet his words were just words. His emphatic politeness and his gentleness of manner and expression might, in other circumstances, have been convincing, but everything he said was in sharp contrast to Pakistan's real policy, and the Pakistani government acted in precisely the opposite manner.

I often think of Zia's predecessors who conducted a more rational policy towards their neighbours and the USSR. Today we have a long distance to cover before we can achieve good relations with Pakistan again, and our frequent contacts with the Pakistani leadership have shown us that the main obstacle is the unrealistic position adopted by ruling circles in Pakistan. It is truly amazing that they allow themselves to be used by others, as tools in a conflict that can only damage their own national interests.

No sensible person will disagree that the relations which have existed between the Soviet Union and China over the last thirty years are an anomaly. The development of good Sino-Soviet relations, based on mutual respect for the interests of each side, and of course without detriment to other countries, would serve to improve the political atmosphere of the whole world.

I do not propose to comment on the domestic policies of Mao Zedong. His activities had a great impact on China's internal situation and have been amply evaluated by the Communist Party of the Soviet Union and fraternal parties as well. Less has been written, however, about Mao's influence on international affairs; yet for several decades China's foreign policy was directed entirely by his ideas and his philosophical outlook. For this reason, I believe that some of the things he said, either in my presence or in direct conversation with me, may be of interest.

I first met Mao in December 1949 during his visit to the USSR (from December 1949 to February 1950). China was celebrating its workers' victory. Led by the Communist Party, the people had seized power from the bourgeoisie and landowners. Chiang Kai-shek's armies had been routed, and the country rejoiced at the opportunity to create an independent state which would move along the path of socialist transformation in its economic and social life.

Stalin and the other Soviet leaders welcomed Mao in Moscow in the most friendly way. In addition to offering formal expressions of mutual sympathy, both host and guest wanted to strengthen their friendship by means of a political treaty.

On 14 February 1950 the prepared thirty-year treaty was ceremonially signed, and relations between the two states became at least nominally those of two allies. The treaty thus represented a major step towards guaranteeing security not only for the Soviet

Union and China but also for the Far East, Asia and the world as a whole – although unfortunately, by the time the thirty years had expired, China had adopted a new position in relation to the USSR and declined to renew the treaty.

The dinner held in the Metropole Hotel to celebrate the occasion, hosted by Stalin and the Soviet leadership, was a very cordial affair. Even so, I was not the only one to notice that conversation between the two leaders, who sat side by side at dinner, was sporadic, to say the least. They would exchange a few phrases, through an interpreter of course, and then a seemingly endless pause would ensue. I was sitting opposite and did my best to help them out, but without much success. My chief impression was that they did not have enough in common of a personal nature to make the necessary minimum of contact.

No doubt, if a psychologist had been present, he could have given a more precise account of the situation. On the other hand, when one is speaking of Stalin and Mao, it would take more than the standard psychological formulations to tell even half the story.

As we were leaving the room, my wife, who had been sitting next to them, whispered to me, 'Stalin and Mao didn't seem to say much to each other.'

I replied, 'I was thinking just the same thing.'

Next day, other comrades said that in their opinion there had not been much cordiality between the Big Two the night before. The atmosphere over the next few days remained much the same.

I next met Mao in 1957, and by then relations between our two nations had already begun to deteriorate.

Soon after the formation of the Chinese People's Republic, the Chinese had proposed talks with the USSR on the creation of two joint-stock companies, one Sovkitneft (Soviet–Chinese Oil) and the other Sovkitmetal (Soviet–Chinese Metal), to be built in the north-western part of China, in the province of Xinjiang. It only remained to put it all on paper.

The two sides accordingly agreed that specially appointed delegations should conduct the talks. I was deputed to head the Soviet delegation, while the Chinese side was headed by the Xinjiang official, Saifuddin. After a few sessions in Moscow, however, it became clear the Chinese had changed their minds, and, when I reported this to the Politburo, Stalin vented his feelings on the matter in the strongest terms. A breach ensued, which did little for relations between the USSR and China in general, and left a bad taste in the mouth of the Soviet leadership.

When Mao came to Moscow for the second time, in November 1957, I was informed that he would like to meet me to discuss questions of international policy. Our meeting took place in the Kremlin.

Mao was conciliatory, assuring me: 'China will never cause relations with the Soviet Union to worsen and we will march shoulder to shoulder with you in the struggle for peace.'

He was chiefly interested in the following questions: 'Is it reasonable to define US policy, or more precisely that of the Eisenhower administration, as aggressive?' and 'Is the USA so economically strong that it would be hard to win a war against her?'

The conversation ranged far on both these questions, and my replies contained these familiar ideas: 'The creation of the NATO military bloc and the countless bases scattered around the world suggest that the US is anything but peace-loving. This is also shown in Washington's rejection of all the Soviet proposals on disarmament and the banning of nuclear weapons.

'As for America's economic potential,' I went on, 'one must remember that much of her industrial plant was renewed during the war, and that she transferred many laboratories from West Germany. This of course increased her productive and economic capacity. But that does not at all mean that the USA is impregnable or that one cannot compete with her. Americans like to talk about their economic potential, but they quieten down when they are visited by that old but fierce guest, economic crisis. Socialism has only to open up, and so it will when the time comes.'

Mao said much the same thing, but in his own way. He was particularly fond of the expression 'American imperialism is a paper tiger'. He also talked energetically about the inevitability of economic crises. Clearly he was familiar with those passages in Marx's *Kapital* which discuss economic crises, and he wanted me to know how well he knew them.

After the conversation, as usual, I asked myself: What were the salient features of what Mao said and what was he trying to tell us?

I came to the conclusion that in effect he wanted to weigh up aloud China's possibilities as a great power, especially in the economic sphere. He also wanted to know how far it was possible to prevent US imperialism from imposing its will on others, above all on China.

Then in August 1958 my government decided I should go to the Chinese capital, as Foreign Minister, to talk to Mao about a number of issues, especially those connected with the tense situation that had arisen between China and the USA over the offshore islands. The Chinese leadership eagerly agreed to my visit, which I undertook incognito, that is to say without informing the mass media.

A crisis had developed in the Far East in August–September 1958, with the USA issuing direct threats against China. On 4 September Dulles openly stated that, in order to ensure US 'security' and protect Chiang Kai-shek's (and hence US) positions on Taiwan and the offshore islands, the President 'was fully resolved' to take 'timely and effective measures'. This was simply armed blackmail, intended to frighten the Chinese people.

In a message to Eisenhower of 7 September, Khrushchev gave a clear warning of the consequences of Washington's actions. These actions qualified as interference in China's internal affairs and were therefore unjustifiable in international law. At the same time, the Soviet Union expressed its willingness to co-operate in a peaceful settlement of the Taiwan problem and in the restoration of China's legitimate rights in the United Nations.

My conversation with Mao concentrated chiefly on this issue and on co-ordinating Soviet and Chinese action on the political level. The general drift of Mao's attitude was that there should be no giving way to the Americans and that we should act on the principle of meeting force with force.

He said: 'I suppose the Americans might go so far as to unleash a war against China. China must reckon with this possibility, and we do. But we have no intention of capitulating! If the USA attacks China with nuclear weapons, the Chinese armies must retreat from the border regions into the depths of the country. They must draw the enemy in deep so as to grip US forces in a pincer inside China.'

Developing these thoughts and underlining the importance of co-ordination between the Soviet Union and China as allies, he then went on to give the Soviet leadership advice on what it should do in turn: 'In the event of war, the Soviet Union should not take any military measures against the Americans in the first stage. Instead, you should let them penetrate deep inside the territory of the Chinese giant. Only when the Americans are right in the central provinces should you give them everything you've got.'

I was flabbergasted. Before this meeting, I had heard many of Mao's statements about war and peace and American imperialism, but this was the first time that I heard at first hand utterances that showed a willingness to accept the possibility of an American nuclear attack on China, and then to discuss means by which to fight against it.

In the proper form, I was obliged to tell him: 'Such a proposal would not meet with a positive response from us. I can say that definitely.'

With that our discussion of strategic issues came to an end. But it shows how wide the gap was between his views and policies and those of the socialist states in the Warsaw Pact and the majority of the fraternal parties.

A Soviet delegation, consisting of Khrushchev, Central Committee secretary M.A. Suslov, trade-union secretary T.N. Nikolaev, and myself as Foreign Minister, visited Peking in October 1959 for talks with Mao and other members of the Chinese leadership. Once again, deep differences emerged between us.

The Soviet side emphasised yet again that it did not want a worsening of relations and would do everything possible to preserve what we had so far achieved. It was clear, however, that the other side had adopted a line calculated to disrupt those relations.

Of Mao himself, I might add that, if one disregarded his theoretical aims, philosophical concepts and peculiar views on politics, he was on the whole a nice man, and courteous too. He liked a good joke and could tell his own. He had studied ancient Chinese philosophy and was fond of talking about it.

Mao liked people he could have a good argument with, but when a difficult political question arose his expression glazed over and he became a different person, utterly remote. In Peking I once saw with my own eyes how he sat throughout dinner without uttering more than a dozen formal words to his chief guest, Khrushchev. Neither my own efforts nor those of Chinese Minister Chen Yi could do anything to ease the situation.

I also had the opportunity to meet and to watch at close quarters such Chinese party and state officials as Liu Shaoqi and Zhou Enlai, both of whom occupied important posts for many years and were considered Mao's chief support.

Zhou Enlai was Prime Minister without interruption from the

moment the Chinese People's Republic came into being in 1949 until his death in January 1976. He came with Mao to Moscow, took part in the Sino-Soviet talks of January–February 1950 and signed the treaty on behalf of his government. He and I met on frequent occasions, especially in Geneva in 1954 during the conference on Indo-China, then during the Sino-Soviet talks in Peking in 1959 on the occasion of the tenth anniversary of the Chinese People's Republic, and in Moscow in 1964, when Zhou attended the forty-seventh anniversary of the October revolution.

The Soviet position on China supports the creation of friendly relations, which would be in the interest of the USSR, of China, of socialism and of peace everywhere in the world. I discussed this on two occasions with Chinese Foreign Minister Wu Xueqian, when we were both attending the General Assembly in New York in September 1984.

For the Soviet side, I said: 'We believe we must keep the future of Sino-Soviet relations constantly in view. Obviously the international situation at present is difficult. The forces of imperialism are striving for military superiority, from which position they plan to impose their will on other countries. They have declared a holy war against socialism and they lay special stress on playing the socialist countries off against each other. In the face of this, it is all the more important to strengthen socialist unity, and it would be easier to improve the political climate and consolidate the foundations of peace if there were a greater degree of mutual understanding between the USSR and China.'

Wu Xueqian interpreted the causes of world tension in a different way. 'They are the product of Soviet and American efforts to achieve military superiority over one another,' he claimed.

While asserting that the normalisation of relations was one of the basic political aims of the current Chinese leadership, Wu in effect repeated the views expressed by the Chinese side in previous years, namely, that such normalisation was dependent on the USSR's agreeing to the proposals China put forward concerning, in particular, the interests of Vietnam, Kampuchea, Afghanistan and Mongolia.

On these and other issues, I gave Wu Xueqian appropriately firm answers, but added: 'We think it important to maintain lines of communication between us.'

He agreed.

There has recently been some improvement in Sino-Soviet

relations. Speaking in Vladivostok on 28 July 1986, General Secretary Gorbachev remarked on the noticeable increase in economic
ties. Both sides are discussing the joint exploitation of the rich
natural resources of the Amur river basin and the building of the
Xinjiang–Uigur–Kazakhstan railway. Talks on the border issues
are being conducted in a businesslike and pleasant atmosphere,
and the Chinese have also proposed co-operation in space.

I am convinced that whatever happens between the Soviet
Union and China has historic importance. Countries of this scale,
with their vast natural resources, their rich cultures and their
tradition of good relations in the recent past, are compelled to
recognise the serious need for neighbourliness and friendship.

15

The East and Africa

At a conference in San Francisco on 4–8 September 1951, Washington presented a plan for a treaty with Japan that clearly favoured the USA. The Soviet delegation, which I was heading, wanted to negotiate a treaty that instead served the broader interests of peace, but the Truman administration would not change its position. The Soviet Union therefore refused to sign the treaty with Japan.

'This treaty,' I said, 'contradicts agreed Allied resolutions. It does not guarantee the security of the countries that have suffered from Japanese aggression, it ignores their legitimate demands, and it creates conditions for the rebirth of Japanese militarism which would have very serious worldwide consequences.'

An active part in preparing the treaty had been taken by Dean Acheson and John Foster Dulles, who was then Secretary of State. By exerting considerable energy, they finally got this treaty past the conference, against the objections of the USSR. But even they could not ignore the Soviet demand that Japan be denied all rights and claims to the southern part of Sakhalin and the Kurile Islands, since agreement on this had been reached by the USA and USSR during President Roosevelt's tenure. Nevertheless, despite the obligations undertaken by America and Britain at Yalta, as well as historical justice, the San Francisco treaty avoids any acknowledgement that these islands belong to the Soviet Union as its aboriginal territory. It merely requires that Japan should cede them to the USSR. This fact elegantly characterises the hostility of President Truman and his entourage towards the Soviet Union.

Soon after the official signing ceremony, moreover, the USA and Japan concluded a security treaty which permitted the USA to maintain a military presence in Japan for many years, turning that country into a US strategic bridgehead in the Far East.

It is no secret that Soviet relations with Japan in the post-war period have developed unevenly. In fact, over the years they have passed through phases of relative cordiality, followed by long intervals of stagnation, if not outright antipathy. This has been far from our fault. The unevenness in our relations derives from the zigzag nature of Japanese politics. Tokyo's policy in the past has alternated between reason and hypocrisy, with a growing tendency towards the latter.

In the 1950s Japanese public opinion was disturbed by this, and a movement for the improvement of relations with the USSR became active in the period 1954–6, when the Prime Minister, Itiro Hatoyama, set himself the task of restoring normal diplomatic relations with us. As a result of talks lasting nearly two years, on 19 October 1956 in Moscow both sides signed a draft treaty designed to end the state of war and restore diplomatic and consular relations. Virtually every condition one would expect to find in a peace treaty is there, yet to this day the treaty has not been ratified in Tokyo, owing to the unrealistic approach of the Japanese, who will still not accept the conditions that prevailed at the end of the war.

Nevertheless, the signing of the treaty bore witness to the fact that Hatoyama was a far-sighted statesman, for in this treaty he made a serious effort to conduct an independent foreign policy. In time, however, this independence plainly declined and became subordinated to America's global interests. Tokyo began looking for any excuse to slow down, if not reverse, any progress made in relations with the Soviet Union. Our negotiations were frequently interrupted by sudden outbursts of anti-Sovietism in Japan, and many questions of bilateral co-operation were hindered by entirely artificial obstacles invented by the Japanese officials.

I myself have visited Japan three times, in 1966, 1972 and 1976, three times have admired the great natural beauty of Fujiyama, and three times have gazed down enthralled by the sight of Tokyo from the air. Tokyo's streets are narrow, and by day they are all but obliterated by advertisement hoardings; but by night the city is a vast, brightly coloured, shimmering jewel.

Of the Japanese statesmen I have met, I must now single out Eisaku Sato, Prime Minister from November 1964 to July 1972.

An episode that occurred during my 1972 visit is worth recalling. My wife and I had returned from a trip to various cities and

I went to see Sato, as arranged, in the company of our ambassador to Japan, O.A. Troyanovsky. When we entered the Prime Minister's study we saw at once that he looked very worried. Showing the greatest courtesy and concern, he said:

'Before we discuss the questions that interest us both, I want to apologise, Mr Minister, for the bomb that exploded on the road in front of your car as you were returning from the station. Luckily neither you nor anyone in your party was hurt, but I am very upset and want to apologise for what happened.'

I replied, 'In fact, my wife and I did hear an unusual noise as we were passing a crowd that seemed excited about something. Some policemen were dealing with a man in civilian clothes.'

In the car my wife and I had said nothing and the Japanese Deputy Foreign Minister who was with us, and his driver, had tried to look as if nothing had happened.

The Prime Minister was still apologising when I said, 'Mr Sato, there is nothing to worry about, everything is all right.'

He was relieved to hear this and our meeting got on to a more normal track.

When I arrived back in Moscow, Brezhnev said: 'The foreign news agencies have been putting out alarming reports about something happening to a Soviet minister's car. Then it was all explained.'

Japanese prime ministers came and went in quick succession after the war, usually every two or three years. Thus Sato was something of a champion for having stayed in office for so long, and this explains his political influence.

I found that, uniquely among Japanese Prime Ministers, Sato understood very well the importance of maintaining good relations with the USSR, and it was during his tenure that we signed a number of agreements which to some extent strengthened the official basis of our ties – for instance, the Consular Convention and the agreement on direct flights. Naturally, Sato raised the issue of the northern territories so unsatisfactorily dealt with in San Francisco, but he knew that it was one thing to have a big appetite and quite another to satisfy it.

However, Sato knew how to listen. His way of conducting a discussion inspired respect. On one occasion, in 1972, he told me: 'Japan has broken with militarism. Look at our constitution and the laws we have passed in accordance with it – the situation is not what it was.'

History has taught us to be cautious when Japanese statesmen express their good intentions. In 1904 the Japanese broke an agreement and attacked Port Arthur – which led to the outbreak of the Russo-Japanese war. Then there were the events of 1937 at Lake Khasan and 1939 at the Khalkhin Gol river, when Japanese militarists suddenly undertook to test the defences of the Soviet frontier. There was also the unexpected attack on the US naval base at Pearl Harbor. Finally, we have also been put on our guard by the American military bases the Japanese have over the last few decades permitted on their territory.

After her defeat in the Second World War, Japan spent almost nothing on armaments: virtually everything she produced was for peaceful purposes, and in large measure thanks to this she made a great economic and technological leap forward.

The lesson for Japan, therefore, is that if she wants to continue to develop successfully she must not take the path of militarisation, whether alone or in the company of other states. In our opinion, Japan's historic task is not to permit the noose placed around her neck by the military treaties with the USA to strangle her as an independent country, and on behalf of the Soviet leadership, as Foreign Minister, I have repeated these views in talks with Japanese officials on all levels. Soviet representatives of the relevant agencies have also underlined the importance of widening economic co-op-eration between the two countries – especially in fishing. We have indicated that such co-operation would do much to warm up our relations in general.

This approach coincides with that of Japanese business circles, where interest in developing relations with us has never waned. However, while Japan has been rapidly developing economically and in science and technology, the fall-out from poor political relations still fetters our economic and trade relations. By adapting herself in general to NATO strategy, Japan has been dragged steadily towards the old quagmire of expansionism.

In view of the fact that she is not prepared to sign a peace treaty with the USSR without unacceptable conditions, we have suggested that, without prejudice to future agreements, we could discuss a treaty on good-neighbourliness and co-operation in order to give stability to our relations; but the Japanese at that time did not show enthusiasm for this proposal either. Equally, our proposal guaranteeing the non-use of nuclear weapons against Japan, while Japan in return would maintain her own non-nuclear status, is still on the table.

It was in April 1976, that I first met Yasuhiro Nakasone on the occasion of my official visit. He was later to become Prime Minister (1982) but at that time held no government post, being the general secretary, or second-in-command, of the Liberal-Democratic Party. We met on his initiative. He stood out among Japanese statesmen perhaps because he was more fervent than most in his apparent devotion to the idea of genuine friendship with the Soviet Union. Furthermore, at the time of my visit the international situation had improved considerably, and there were sound reasons for hoping for an advance in Soviet–Japanese relations.

I therefore declared to Nakasone: 'One glance at the map is enough to show that Japan and the Soviet Union must live in peace. This is what the USSR wants. It is not a question of current fashion; it is fundamental to our approach.'

Nakasone gave an unequivocal reply: 'We are for the development of Soviet–Japanese relations, and I would especially like to emphasise their importance for peace in the Far East.' He added, 'I share the view of those Japanese statesmen who believe that attempts to play on the differences between the USSR and China are pointless and in the end could harm Japan's own interests.'

It seemed then that Nakasone was a politician who thought realistically and who understood the importance of maintaining good relations with the USSR. In the Liberal-Democratic Party, however, as far as I understood, he had gained the reputation of a conservative and had vigorously advocated increasing Japan's military potential. He was credited with having said: 'Japan must be turned into an unsinkable aircraft-carrier.' Still, if a man is honest and cares about the good of his people, he will admit his mistakes and try to help his country along the path to peace. I always like to think that reason and realism will in the end revive in the minds of Japanese politicians.

Nakasone became Prime Minister in 1982. Unfortunately, his speeches were inconsistent: on the one hand he spoke of the need for co-operation, while on the other hand he yet again raised Japan's groundless territorial claims against us.

On 14 March 1985 General Secretary Gorbachev received Nakasone in the Kremlin and had a brief exchange of opinions on key questions. I took part in the conversation. Gorbachev reaffirmed the Soviet Union's willingness to develop mutually beneficial contacts with Japan, and in reply Nakasone repeated all his old territorial arguments, although slightly more tactfully than when he was at home.

Nakasone's personal style is unusual. At the beginning of a meeting he adopts a physical posture which remains fixed throughout, while his face is utterly inscrutable. His self-possession and his control over his reactions are phenomenal. I point this out not because I disapprove. Everyone is free to adopt whatever style puts him most at ease, as long as he does not exceed the bounds of decorum. I mention it only because it is not the sort of behaviour I meet every day.

In a frank and substantive talk I had with Japanese Foreign Minister Abe at the UN General Assembly of September 1984, I told him that in my opinion Tokyo's foreign policy was leading to a loss of personal identity in international affairs, and this undermined her authority. Some of those in power in Tokyo apparently yearned for tanks, warships and piles of weapons. They were longing for a return to the past, even though it had brought the Japanese people so much misery, and it was a situation that could not but cast a shadow over Soviet–Japanese relations.

I then assured Abe: 'If Tokyo chooses neighbourliness, then our country will be Japan's partner in the struggle for a reduction of world tension. Admittedly, the Japanese leadership makes statements about improving relations with the USSR – but can Tokyo's behaviour honestly be described as moving in that direction? One would need a very powerful magnifying glass to see any sign of it.'

Yet another new impulse was given to our relations by the proposals made by Gorbachev in Vladivostok on 28 July 1986, in which he spoke of broadening economic co-operation in the coastal regions, creating joint enterprises in areas close to both countries, co-operating in long-term research into the ocean's resources, and combining programmes on the peaceful study and use of space. In this way, 'economic diplomacy', which comes naturally to the Japanese, can also serve Soviet–Japanese co-operation. The Vladivostok speech reaffirmed the Soviet Union's position on all basic policy issues in the Pacific region. It represented a broad platform for co-operation in the interests of universal peace and security, while studiously avoiding addressing the narrow interest of any one country.

Soviet–Japanese relations, I am convinced, have potentially a great future. The Soviet Union manifestly wants to develop relations with the land of the rising sun, but regrettably over the last few decades little more has been accomplished than a few economic deals. In the field of politics the thinking of Japanese statesmen is still affected by the cold war, and this is a great pity. Being out of tune with present reality, it seriously hampers the establishment of new relations on the basis of political thinking suited to the end of the twentieth century. Moscow's position is absolutely clear: today the situation is qualitatively different, offering the possibility of major breakthroughs, and it is time to look each other straight in the eye and get down to creating a basis of co-operation worthy of two such great states.

As people of the twentieth century, we can scarcely begin to imagine the fantastic possibilities opening up before us. To a certain extent we have been wearing blindfolds made of old political stereotypes, and have been either unable or unwilling to remove them. The Japanese say, 'Time flies like an arrow', and they are right. But wisdom gives man wings and helps him to overtake time.

The restructuring of the Soviet economy is under way and sooner or later we will be able to create a broadly developed economic region in what is for us the Far East and for the Japanese the near north-west. Science, technology and the resources of both countries can provide an economic base for Soviet–Japanese relations of a new type. And, if people have brilliant and inspiring thoughts about the future, they can do much in the present.

In great measure, it was the victory over Germany and Japan that for the first time gave the Soviet Union an opportunity to establish ties with the countries of south-east Asia and Oceania.

One of these is Indonesia. When the flag of Indonesian independence was unfurled there was not a single Soviet representative in independent Indonesia, and not one Indonesian official had visited the USSR. Even so, there was a growing desire for friendship with the Soviet Union among the Indonesian people, who knew almost instinctively that our socialist state had by its very existence assisted in breaking the entire system of colonial oppression.

When a newly emerged state embarks on its development, a striking figure often emerges to leave his mark on its history. Such personalities may perhaps constitute a heavy burden and a brake on a society's progress, but there are many other examples of individuals who have nobly identified their own fate with that of their people.

One such man was Sukarno, whom the Indonesians dubbed 'the father of the republic'. Under colonialism, Sukarno had recognised the interests of the people, but he did not have a socialist outlook and did not set out to transform Indonesia along socialist lines. With the banner of independence in hand, he defended the interests of the national bourgeoisie by setting out to overcome the economic backwardness of the country.

My meetings with him as head of state left me with lively and colourful impressions. As Foreign Minister, I accompanied a Soviet delegation headed by Khrushchev, and for twelve days in 1960 I was able to observe the President. He hardly left the Soviet delegation for an hour, and we were amazed by his energy. He was able to hold talks, to entertain his guests magnificently and at the same time personally keep all the machinery of government running.

He was masterly at asking for favours, especially economic ones. Every request would be accompanied by a lengthy explanation, giving the economic, political, historical and psychological background. It seemed at times that the President was about to burst into tears.

It was impossible to reproach him for this. Indonesia was only just getting on its feet. They were short of practically everything, industry was just beginning, their agriculture was still primitive, while trade and the entire financial system were in the hands of foreigners. For some years, therefore, the Soviet Union gave Indonesia substantial aid with which to develop its industry and agriculture.

Indonesia also lacked experience in public administration and the conduct of foreign affairs, which no doubt partly explains the innocent fondness Sukarno and his government had for public ceremony. Once the country had its own flag and national anthem, they had to be used to the full, so, whatever the venue and however insignificant the occasion, the national anthem would be played, sometimes twice over. Possibly the population liked these events; certainly they must eventually have got used to them.

As head of state and the leading political figure, in talks Sukarno showed that he knew what he wanted and what his country needed. Educated and sociable, he struck me as a man of great ability. Since he was utterly absorbed in Indonesia's politics, the ideology or outlook of others did not interest him. He liked to think in clear categories – colonialism and independence, rich and poor, socialism and capitalism, war and peace – and he could do so with masterly skill and conviction.

Sukarno was a good orator and knew just what his public wanted to hear. He loved putting on entertainment for his guests, especially dancing, which he organised at every spare moment during talks. He was an excellent dancer himself, his Indonesian wife Hartini was just as good, and they say he taught his second wife, a Japanese, to dance too.

Sukarno's political crash came in 1967, a tragic time in Indonesia's history, when many innocent heads rolled.

International events move on, however. Soviet–Indonesian relations have now passed their thirty-year milestone and, although they have not always been smooth, a wealth of experience in co-operation has already been accumulated, experience that we must continue to develop.

In talks I had with Indonesian Foreign Minister Mochtar Kusumaatmadja, during his official visit to the USSR in April 1984, both sides noted with satisfaction that our positions on a number of key international issues were very close. This prompts an optimistic outlook. So different from each other, the USSR, as the greatest land mass in the world, and Indonesia, a vast collection of islands, have a duty not merely to get along with each other, but to make friends.

After the Second World War, the Philippines also set out on the path of independence. Much has been said and written in the USA about the need to respect Philippine independence, but in fact, since Spanish colonialism was replaced by the American variety, the USA has for many years regarded the Philippines as little more than a distant 'backyard'.

For some time, American monopolies fiercely exploited the Philippine people, but they were unable to maintain their position when the British empire fell apart at the seams and the same fate overtook the French, Belgian and Dutch colonies. In 1946, therefore, the country was declared independent. Yet even now the independence process cannot be considered complete, since there are still US bases located there, with all that this implies.

Soviet–Philippine diplomatic relations were established in 1976 and have developed normally ever since, especially in the fields of trade and culture.

President Marcos and his government represented the interests of the private landowners and comprador bourgeoisie, the middle men who sold to foreign buyers. Under his rule, his country became increasingly dependent on the USA, which for historical reasons had put down deep roots in the political and economic life of the country. Even so, President Marcos came on an official visit to the USSR in June 1986, and as always our talks were friendly, with both sides emphasising the need to deepen our relations.

Marcos's hold on power was assured, yet everything pointed to the fact that the Philippines were ripe for major changes. More and more people were openly protesting against his autocratic rule. Plainly his days as president were numbered. Nevertheless, out of respect for the country he represented, we observed protocol.

Since the changes which took place in the Philippine leadership in 1986, the USSR has been ready, as before, to develop good relations, and we hope that the new government, under President Corazón Aquino, will preserve and build upon everything of value that we achieved in our past relations with the Philippines.

Africa! However exotic the word may sound, the bitter reality is rather one of economic crises, a kaleidoscope of army coups, and constant famine which annually carries off millions, especially children.

I had the opportunity to see life in North Africa – in Egypt, Algeria, Tunisia and Morocco – with my own eyes, not only during the hard times of the Second World War, but also when Africans were fighting for their independence. What struck me most was the poverty, the miserable housing and quite often a sense of total apathy.

Africa has seen dramatic changes. Looking at the history of the continent from the vantage-point of the late twentieth century, a number of conclusions for all of us can be drawn.

Africa had its own civilisation long before colonialism arrived. It was here indeed that, according to science, man took his first steps. The ancient African states, however, were unable to withstand the pressure of the Europeans, who came with the Bible in one hand and gun in the other. In sub-Saharan Africa, the European takeover was made easier by illiteracy and the fact that African society was fragmented and weak, based as it was on tribal organisation and religious cults. As a result, the 'civilising' armies cut through to the heart of the continent like a knife through butter.

Fatally weakened by the slave trade, the continent's economic development was further held back under colonialism. Many people lost faith in their own skills, agricultural methods stagnated, and, by the end of the nineteenth century, the colonialists were in possession of almost all Africa's territory, plus an endless supply of cheap labour.

The crushing defeat of fascism in 1945, however, meant that the days of colonialism were numbered, and by the 1980s the overwhelming majority of African countries had gained independence. However, this new freedom is nevertheless restricted by economic dependence on European centres of economic power. Often the prices of African exports are depressed and the costs of imported manufactured goods are inflated; the old pattern of economic oppression is repeated.

On the other hand, over the last twenty-five years African politicians have gained in strength, studied their own achievements and failures, and have almost decisively shed their former sense of inferiority. All that is now required is for the healthy elements in Africa to be set in motion, reinforcing the local culture and in the process developing their economy, science and technology.

The question is, can the Africans do this on their own? I think not. When the growth rate of the population exceeds the rate of food production, the economic possibilities for progress are cruelly restricted. Therefore it is up to the international community to give proper aid, and it is time that the countries that once held colonies in Africa honoured this debt to her. And it is what the Africans expect. It is no more than justice demands.

At the end of the war, the only independent countries in Africa were Ethiopia, Egypt, Liberia and the Union of South Africa. Now there are more than fifty independent African member states of the United Nations and, as each one has emerged, the Soviet Union has consistently maintained a policy of establishing relations and developing co-operation to our mutual benefit.

By contrast, the former colonial powers adopted a policy – carried out on numerous occasions – of 'leaving in order to remain'. The tragic events that took place in 1960 in Zaïre, formerly the Belgian Congo, are memorable in this respect. When Congo's independence was declared, on 30 July of that year, the colonialists quickly discovered to their surprise that the new government of Patrice Lumumba intended to have genuine independence. They therefore resolved to detach Katanga, Congo's most valuable province, with its copper, diamond, uranium and gold mines. Events unfolded dramatically. An army revolt was organised so that the colonialists, on their favourite pretext of 'protecting human life and property', could send in heavy units of Belgian troops whose task was to secure the establishment of a puppet government in Katanga.

The Lumumba government was not to the taste of the United States either, but Washington resolved to act on a grander scale, and to bring the whole country, rather than simply Katanga, under its domination. It chose as its instruments direct terrorism and subversive activity, together with manipulation of UN forces. Today, anyone can read published official American sources which show, right to the day and the hour, how Washington planned to get rid of Lumumba, how President Eisenhower sanctioned the crime, the exact names of the CIA agents and their accomplices who were commissioned to carry it out, and the means they used to exterminate the head of the legitimate Congolese government. The plot which the USA hatched against an outstanding son of Africa, and which left the area in a state of unrest for many years to come, is a glaring example of how much Washington's claims to the 'moral leadership of the world' really mean.

When the USSR and Mexico established diplomatic relations in 1926, our first ambassador was Alexandra Kollontai, with whom I became friendly many years later, and who set our relations on an upward trend that has continued ever since.

An important threshold in our relations was crossed when in 1938 the government of President Lázaro Cárdenas nationalised the country's oil industry, thus putting an end to the domination of the American oil monopolies. The Mexicans knew that the USSR sympathised with this move, even though it was an internal matter.

Relations were broken off temporarily in 1940, when a reactionary government was returned, but they were restored again in

1942, when Mexico declared war on Nazi Germany. While I was working in Washington I frequently met the Mexican representatives, including Luis Quintanilla, who before going as ambassador to Moscow was Mexico's envoy in the American capital. The Mexican diplomats I knew were on the whole people with sound political views, and they were always on guard in relation to US policy. Apparently the long period of American exploitation of Mexico's natural resources had left a deep scar on the national consciousness.

I remember the Mexican ambassador once touched on the question of Trotsky, who was then in exile in Mexico.

He said: 'This emigrant represents no interest whatever to Mexicans. You could be driving along the street and passing near the house where Trotsky lives, and someone might tell you, quite casually: "By the way, some emigrant or other from Russia is living there." People regard him as a not very interesting museum piece.'

I replied, 'I can quite understand it.'

None of this is meant to suggest that historians should not study Trotsky's role in the Russian revolution, or in the early years of Soviet power, or his collaboration (and even his struggle) with Lenin, and still more with Stalin. Trotsky, however, fashioned his own fate, not always in his own best interest, and it was crowned by his being expelled from the land of the Soviets.

16

The crossroads of the Middle East

The actions the Soviet Union has taken to secure a settlement of the Middle East problem are well known. To this end we have submitted countless proposals, had endless meetings at all levels with foreign representatives, and defended the legitimate demands of the Arab people.

Israel's attack in 1967 on Egypt, Syria and Jordan gave new force to the question whether an aggressor should be permitted to use the territory he has occupied as a political bargaining counter, and thus be rewarded for his expanionist foreign policy. Should he be curbed or indulged? That is the choice which states have been made to face by the logic of events. The Soviet position was that everything must be done to bring about the immediate withdrawal of his troops. The support we have given the Arab countries has done much to curb the Israelis, and yet the position in the Middle East remains critical, thanks to the endless intrigues of Israel, her accomplices and protectors.

Soviet diplomacy and the efforts of other countries scored a success with the convening of the Middle East peace conference in Geneva in 1973.

Explaining the Soviet position, I said: 'We demand the removal of Israeli troops from all occupied Arab territories and recognition of the legitimate rights of the Palestinians to create their own state. Our position provides for effective guarantees of the right of all the nations of the Middle East, including Israel, to exist independently in peaceful conditions.'

In following this line, the USSR, like many other countries, condemned and still condemns Israel for her aggressive actions.

Egypt's exit from the Arab bloc delivered a serious blow to the interests of the entire Arab world. What had seemed the least likely had happened. Egypt agreed to a deal with the Israeli aggressor and Washington and Tel Aviv rubbed their hands with satisfaction.

This took place after the departure from the international scene of Gamal Abdel Nasser, and my memories of the world's statesmen would be the poorer if I did not mention Nasser, especially as it was precisely during his rule that the greatest improvement occurred in Soviet–Egyptian relations. A fitting symbol of that period is the light that is supplied to Egypt by the energy from the Aswan Dam, which was built with the Soviet Union's active participation. It is the best evidence that friendship with the USSR brings concrete benefits. The advance in our relations owed much to Nasser's realisation that at that time Egypt could not expect help from the West, either to develop her economy, or to strengthen her defence potential, or to liberate the Arab lands seized by Israel. Many times I heard Nasser say that the Arabs must never capitulate to Israel: 'All the Arab territories under Israeli occupation must be freed.'

From our first meeting to our last, Nasser was friendly towards the USSR. He valued the help we gave for the Aswan Dam which he regarded as a noble gesture on our part. He believed in the USSR. Under Nasser, Egypt also had friendly ties with the other socialist states. He was one of the founders of the non-alignment movement and did much to enlarge the scope of its activities.

As for the West, to say nothing of Israel, Nasser's position was uncompromising. He would dismiss any suggestion of making concessions. More than once he said to me: 'One must not believe the politicians of the major Western countries. They will undoubtedly deceive the Arabs if they can.'

It would, however, be wrong to suppose that Nasser at once embarked on changing Egypt's elitist social structure. The revolution of 1952 that overthrew the monarchy was carried out by the army under the leadership of a group of officers, and had no theoretical foundation for the future development of the country. Nasser said this himself. Its main aim was to secure Egypt's independence.

The question nevertheless arose of improving the lot of the labouring people, especially that of the *fellahin*, who constituted 75 per cent of the population, and the agrarian reform of 1952 was intended to do just this. Egypt was the first country in the Middle

East and Africa to introduce such a reform, and no one, including Nasser, expected it to destroy the basis of the old social order totally. However, its positive effect on the lives of the subsistence peasants was beyond dispute.

Slowly but surely Nasser came to realise that the successful economic development of the country was impossible without a solution to its social and economic problems. He began to show greater interest in the social sciences, including Marxism-Leninism, and he studied the Soviet experience. In this context, his efforts to develop the economy according to some sort of planned programme, his recognition of the existence of class struggle in Egyptian society and his wish to create a party as a political support for the regime – all appear natural, even inevitable. Nasser was thinking of the future of Egypt and her people. He bent all his efforts towards making that future a better, brighter one.

In our meetings with him, Nasser was always attentive. I liked the way he conducted a conversation. He did not like long perorations, and he thought discussion of an agenda a waste of time. Usually he would settle back in his chair, name the question he wished to discuss and then briefly state his position. He did not mind whether he spoke first or second.

He was not inclined to look back at history. Naturally he expressed pride in his country's antiquities, but more as a patriotic duty in conversation with foreigners. When someone admired the Pyramids, Nasser liked to joke, and once said to me: 'What on earth did those eccentric pharaohs build them for? They're just as useless to the working people today as they were then.'

He may not always have known what was best for the future, but he always insisted: 'Everything must be subordinated to the needs of the people.'

I never once heard him raise his voice, even when he was talking about Israel and imperialism. He seemed to lack any emotion, though of course this was because he had remarkable self-control. Often I saw and heard him speak at meetings, usually from a prepared text. His voice was rather quiet, but sounded convincing. Although he paid little heed to the orator's art, his words would always get an enthusiastic response.

Nasser and his family lived in modest circumstances. Their house in Cairo, which I visited several times, was much like any other and contained no sign of luxury at all. He had no time for royal mansions, and the people evidently appreciated this. Nor did he show off either his position or his power as President, although in fact he exercised enormous authority.

Even for Nasser's sturdy constitution, however, the burden of responsibility proved too much, and his health began to decline. After taking a cure in the Caucasus he improved somewhat, but he would not have been Nasser if, on returning to Cairo, he had not ignored his doctors' advice, including that of the Soviet physicians, and thrown himself back into the political maelstrom.

He once said to me, when I was visiting Cairo, 'After returning from the Caucasus, I was seventy-five per cent fit, and twenty-five per cent ill. But it's my own fault. The twenty-five per cent is my own doing.'

A few months later, in September 1970, this remarkable man died.

At the risk of exaggerating the role of any one individual in the history of the Middle East, I'm sure I can say that, had he lived a few years longer, the situation in the region might today be very different. After all, by the time of his death Nasser had already acted as a powerful catalyst in the Arabs' self-awareness and understanding of their legitimate rights; and this in itself was of historic importance.

Egypt's history is full of sudden turns. Thus Nasser was succeeded by Anwar Sadat. Where Nasser was a fighter for Egypt's security and for the Arabs' legitimate interests, Sadat demonstrated a truly astounding ability to ignore both factors.

Confusingly, when Nasser was leader, Sadat was regarded as his loyal supporter. Those who knew Sadat well, however, were always cautious of him and quite rightly suspected that Nasser did not entirely trust him. Certainly the Soviet leadership had received background information on Sadat of a distinctly negative kind, and it must be supposed that this was also known to Nasser. At any rate, it is widely accepted that Nasser did not let him in on his most important plans, even when Sadat was Vice-President.

Sadat's political history reveals much. In his time, he had engaged in terroristic activity, belonged to the Muslim Brotherhood, sympathised with Hitler and his racist philosophy, admired extreme right-wing social democrats and showed himself to be a rabid opponent of communist ideology. It was ironic that he died at the hands of the very Muslim Brotherhood of which he had once been so ardent a supporter.

I remember a trip to Alexandria in May 1964, when a Soviet delegation, headed by Khrushchev, was visiting Egypt. Nasser and Khrushchev were travelling in the chief car in the motorcade, and Sadat and I were in the car following. As the whole journey took about three hours, we had plenty of time to talk.

And Sadat turned out to be very talkative. I got the feeling he had set himself the task of repeating one idea in as many variations as possible, namely: 'Egypt and the USSR are natural allies.'

'Egypt and her leaders are devoted to friendship with the Soviet Union,' he said, 'and we admire your success in the building of socialism.'

I waited for him to start shouting: 'Long live socialism in Egypt!'

He did not do that, but instead went on: 'The Egyptian leadership is bringing about the situation in which, as in the USSR, the people run the country, and not some narrow grouping of society.'

For my part, I observed: 'The people of every country must of course be allowed to choose the social system they want to live under. Naturally, we Soviets are pleased when we see socialism succeed, for we are convinced that the future lies along the path of socialist transformation.'

Sadat replied, 'We are not at all afraid of this idea. We ourselves are engaged in what might, in a socialist country, be called embryonic social transformation.' He explained: 'I have in mind the emergence of farms in which the land and means of production are in effect the property of the state, and not in private ownership.'

As a matter of fact, we were shown one such farm in northern Egypt, where Soviet equipment was being used, but from what we saw and heard it was difficult to discover what it and other farms like it represented in terms of their social influence. They were probably little more than some sort of experiment in its early stages.

Sadat and I were still absorbed in our discussion of Soviet–Egyptian friendship when I looked out of the car window just as we were approaching Alexandria. There, before my eyes, was the Mediterranean coast.

I said to Sadat, 'Look, there's the sea!'

He calmly replied, 'We still have twenty kilometres to go before we reach the coast.'

'But there it is, right in front of us,' I insisted.

He explained: 'It is not the coast. It's a genuine mirage, which one sees quite often at this altitude.'

It was the first and only time in my life I saw such a phenomenon.

Some time later, while I was on leave in Moscow, the news came that Nasser had died. Millions of Egyptians poured into Cairo to accompany him on his final journey. Police tried to hold the crowds back from the gun-carriage which bore the coffin, but thousands tore tiny shreds from the white cloth covering the coffin.

Sadat became President of Egypt. Initially, from sheer inertia, Soviet–Egyptian relations were not reversed, but as the months passed there were increasing signs that Sadat was abandoning Nasser's line. In our negotiations over military and economic aid, for example, he began systematically to increase his demands. Moreover, he took little notice when, with the facts and figures in our hands, the Soviet side repeatedly proved to him that the aid we supplied had not merely put Egypt on a par with Israel but had in a number of categories given Cairo superiority.

Everyone who took part in talks with Sadat at that time observed that he looked for any excuse to make difficulties, and Soviet attempts to inject some realism into the discussion met with little success. It became plainer day by day that Sadat's line was to bring about changes in Soviet–Egyptian relations, and when information reached us that Washington was offering him all kinds of blandishments and promises we realised that some sort of arrangement between Egypt and the USA was in the offing. Later came Sadat's trip to Jerusalem in October 1977 and the anti-Arab deal that was struck with President Carter at Camp David in 1979.

Sadat knew what he was doing: his actions were an expression of his conviction. It is a particularly bitter irony that both Sadat and Israel's Prime Minister Begin should have been awarded the Nobel Prize as 'fighters for peace'! Begin, who continued his policy of aggression against peaceful Arab populations, as in the Lebanon; and Sadat, who had betrayed the interests of the Palestinians and all Arabs, went on to put Egyptian territory at the disposal of the USA.

Sadat's political bankruptcy was total. He has been called the 'Egyptian darkness', after the biggest dust clouds in human history, which settled on Egypt 3500 years ago when the volcanic island of Santorini erupted.

As a person, however, Sadat was unfailingly courteous. When entertaining representatives of a major power, he would ask his guests: 'Do you prefer coffee or tea?' And he would ask each of us several times, telling his servants: 'Bring fruit juices as well.'

That was Sadat at home – all consideration and solicitude. He would take you round his house, pointing out his favourite photographs, so you would see all the famous people he had met. In conversation he always had a smile on his face. I sometimes wondered if he did not have excess flesh just for the purpose. He usually spoke in a soft, ingratiating voice which seemed made only for nice words. Depending on the situation, however, he could also use it to harshest effect.

I had the opportunity to observe Sadat, both at the conference table and at large meetings. He was a middling orator. I never heard him speak without detailed notes at a large gathering, but at the conference table he could improvise for hours. When he became nervous and was expressing disquiet over something or other, he would blatantly contradict himself. He had an extraordinary ability to distort the facts.

All his life he had suffered from megalomania, but this acquired pathological proportions when he became President. Many people were puzzled when he built one of his numerous residences close to the Pyramids at Giza. It was Sadat himself who cleared up the mystery: he had a photograph taken of himself at his residence, against the background of the Pyramids. The photograph was widely distributed, and when he entertained foreign guests there he would always sit so that they could not look at the Pyramids without seeing him in the foreground. He often said: 'See how the people demonstrate in my support in their thousands.'

When I visited him in March 1974, he invited me to this residence for talks on the Middle East. I spent several hours with him. It was already clear that his allegiances were drifting towards the West.

When Sadat was buried, the cortège consisted of a few of his closest colleagues, three former US Presidents, Israeli Prime Minister Begin and a number of foreign delegations. Not one prominent Arab state was represented, and the streets of Cairo were empty. That surely was the Arabs' judgement on him.

★

Unlike Egypt, the other most influential Arab country in the Middle East, Syria, has long held to the view that Israel must release the occupied Arab territories, including the Golan Heights, which she seized by force in 1967, and must respect the national rights of the Palestinian people and their claim to have their own state.

Having taken a principled stand from the outset on Israeli aggression, Syria's President Hafez Assad condemned the Camp David agreement. A powerful and far-sighted leader, respected in the Arab world and beyond, President Assad has always understood the importance of Soviet–Arab friendship. I have met him in Moscow and during my trips to Damascus, and I found that his attitudes were always serious and well informed. Smartly dressed, a hint of a smile sometimes appearing on his face, he might look slightly ineffectual, but in fact he was highly self-controlled with a spring-like inner tension. He would follow his partner's train of thought attentively, never missing a thing. He never wasted time uttering curses against his enemy, and what he said was always to the point. We were in total agreement, furthermore, that the Israeli 'solution' to the Palestinian problem – giving the Palestinians limited 'administrative autonomy' on the West Bank and the Gaza Strip – would simply deny a nation of four million the right to form their own independent state.

The Palestine Liberation Organisation is not recognised either by the USA or Israel. Washington, moreover, undertook the obligation not to engage in any talks or to make any contact with the PLO, even though this body has received wide international recognition and is represented in the UN and its agencies.

The job of chairman of the PLO, held by Yasir Arafat, is a difficult one. He must hold together the host of different groups within his organisation, and sort out the political disagreements which emerge at times in sharp form.

Arafat is a colourful figure, both as a politician and as a man. He can be instantly recognised by the Palestinian national head-dress that he wears. I have met him on many occasions and I cannot think of him without it. Of outstanding character, the Palestinian leader is convinced of the rightness of his cause. He would smile and explain his views, but he would not change them. Generally, he does not raise his voice, but when he speaks about his people his eyes shine with emotion. He usually opens with, 'We Palestinians are a people who have been deprived of our national hearth. We have nowhere to lay our heads.'

US and Israeli obstruction of the Palestinian people's right to form their own state is in contravention of the United Nations resolution of 1947, which envisaged the creation of both an Arab and a Jewish state in Palestine. This resolution has never been withdrawn and the Soviet Union is still in favour of its implementation; but so far only the Jewish state has been created.

I well remember the time when the Jewish population of Palestine was seeking to create its own state. In those days, in conversation with Soviet representatives, Jewish politicians missed no opportunity to express their gratitude to the USSR, to the Red Army and the Soviet leadership, for what they did to save the Jews from Hitler's gas chambers. Later, many Israeli statesmen told me of their gratitude to the Soviet Union for supporting the creation of the Jewish state.

Since its creation, however, Israel has followed expansionist policies. I have met many Israeli leaders and to each one I have pointed out that the state of Israel cannot secure its own happiness while building up an atmosphere of hatred and hostility in the Middle East. Any sensible person can see that from year to year the Arab states are getting stronger, and that their voice carries correspondingly greater weight in the international arena. Does Israel really intend to remain permanently at war with these countries?

In September 1984, while attending the UN General Assembly in New York, I received Israeli Foreign Minister Yitzhak Shamir, at his request.

I said to him: 'In supporting the creation of Israel right from the start, the Soviet Union was adhering to the principle that the Jewish people had the right to form their own state, just as the Palestinian Arabs had the right to form theirs. The Jewish people's right was reinforced by what they had suffered in the Second World War at the bestial hands of the Nazis. And even now, when Israel is not friendly towards the USSR, we do not support those who call for the liquidation of Israel as an independent state.'

Shamir listened attentively and, it seemed, with understanding.

I underlined the basic point: 'While we maintain this position, we severely condemn Tel Aviv's policy of seizing lands to which it has no right. Ask yourself whether Israel has gained or lost from this policy. We of course believe that Israel has lost.'

It is impossible to believe that the Arab world and international public opinion will ever accept Israel's expansionist policy. To rely on the bomb and the rifle is hopeless. Perhaps not tomorrow or the day after tomorrow, but sooner or later justice will triumph and Israel will hand back the Arab lands to the Arabs and learn to live within her internationally recognised borders.

There is probably no other region in the world with such a complex mix of countries, having profoundly different levels of political and economic development, as the Middle East. Monarchies rub shoulders with socialist states, and all within a highly compressed territorial area.

The Soviet Union is not prejudiced towards or against any one Arab country. We are in favour of normal, good relations with all of them, regardless of their social structures. The Soviet Union does not seek any privileges or profit for itself in the Middle East: our role is as a neighbour. We are in close geographical proximity to the region, however, and we cannot therefore be an uninvolved bystander. We believe that the best way towards a Middle East settlement is through an international conference which should result in the signing of a treaty or treaties, embracing the following organically linked components:

Withdrawal of Israeli forces from all Arab territories occupied in 1967;
Realisation of the legitimate national rights of the Arab population of Palestine, including their right to an independent state;
Establishment of a peace which guarantees the security and independent development of all states presently involved in the conflict.

17

From Nixon to Reagan

As the experience of the Second World War graphically demonstrated, when the Soviet Union and the USA adopt a course of mutual understanding and co-operation both they and international security benefit.

The improvement in Soviet–US relations in the early 1970s came about primarily through an active Soviet foreign policy, but also through the steady growth of Soviet influence in international affairs, as Soviet military strength achieved parity with that of the USA. In consequence American foreign policy began to adopt a more realistic posture: the understanding gained ground in Washington that permanent tension in Soviet–US relations was not in their own interests, and that the only reliable basis for relations with the USSR was peaceful co-existence and a mutual recognition of the security interests of both states.

The Republican administration of Richard Nixon perhaps came closest to a true understanding of the need for peaceful relations. Richard Nixon was possibly the most controversial figure ever to hold the office of President of the United States. Returned to office a second time in a landslide electoral victory in 1972, in August 1974, two years before the constitutional end of his tenure, Nixon was forced to resign when it looked as if he was in danger of impeachment over what became known as the Watergate affair. This political scandal blew up over a series of illegal activities committed during the election campaign, including an attempt to install electronic listening devices in the Democratic Party headquarters in the Watergate Hotel in Washington, corruption, threats, false evidence – all implicating leading figures in the

Republican Party and senior officials of Nixon's own White House staff.

Watergate will give historians work for a long time to come, but it actually boils down to nothing more than a symptom of social decline. Was Nixon any worse than the others? Not at all. Maybe they used more subtle methods.

However, here it is pertinent to ask: is there any more criminal aim than preparing nuclear war? Every thinking person can only answer no. Yet think of the cascades of deceptive statements that pour from the highest platforms, the torrents of unprincipled propaganda intended to prevent the banning of nuclear tests and the destruction of all forms of nuclear weapons. In comparison, the Watergate affair was a minor episode, and an internal one at that; but it has almost totally obscured the positive aspects of the Nixon administration's activities in the sphere of relations with the Soviet Union.

During Khrushchev's visit to the USA in September 1959 I had to accompany him on his trip around the country, flying from east to west and back, following our own special route and stopping over in various cities. We flew over the southern parts of the country and returned mostly by the northern route.

It was obviously an exhausting journey, and one of our comrades was curled up in the train from Los Angeles to San Francisco. The sun was shining above our heads through a glass roof. The train suddenly emerged on to a stretch of the track that ran alongside the ocean. Someone shouted out: 'Look at that beautiful ocean!'

We were moving above a steep ravine and could see a sandy beach and white surf below.

Our drowsy comrade half woke, raised his head and asked: 'What, the Atlantic?'

'No, the Pacific,' he was told.

'Mmm,' he mumbled, disappointed, and went back to sleep. 'Wake me up when we get to the Atlantic,' he seemed to be telling us.

I saw the Pacific coast again when I accompanied Brezhnev on his visit to the USA in June 1973. On that occasion, we stayed as guests in President Nixon's private home. Perched above the ocean, it was regarded as his summer residence.

'I only bought it a little while ago,' he told us with some pride, as he showed us over the large wooden structure and the lawns and trees surrounding it. 'I'm very fond of it.'

After the official talks in Washington, and the scarcely less formal meeting at Camp David, the house near Los Angeles was noticeably different, much more domesticated. One felt one could forget about official constraints. The house, which was moderate in both size and its interior decor, itself contributed to this feeling.

However, Nixon had arranged an evening gala reception to which the flower of Californian 'high society' had been invited. Of course there were many big businessmen there, as well as quite a few cultural personalities and actors, especially since Hollywood was nearby. Not that any reception in America can ever be held without some film actors being present: they add prestige to the host's reputation. There were also some local political bigwigs, and the guest list was crowned by the presence of California Governor Ronald Reagan himself.

The queue to greet the guests of honour was quite long. Brezhnev shook the hand of everyone who approached. As Foreign Minister I was standing next to him. To my left was the Soviet ambassador to the USA, A.F. Dobrynin, and we too greeted the guests.

Reagan shook hands and stayed long enough to utter the customary words of welcome, then added briefly, but making plain his warm feelings towards us: 'Representatives of our two countries should meet each other.'

It was the first time I had spoken to Reagan.

The other guests who were following him waited their turn with patience and respect. Some time later at the reception, one of the Americans happened to make a remark to the effect that Reagan had his own ideas about Washington and that he wouldn't mind making it his own residence. But we didn't pay particular attention to this remark, because Reagan's future plans were still unknown, especially as regards his standing as the candidate for the Republican Party which Nixon represented.

The rest of the reception followed the normal course. Nixon's hospitality was very much in evidence. Both host and chief guest made a pretty good job competing with each other in lavishing their smiles.

The first meeting between Nixon and Brezhnev had already taken place that day, and they had agreed to continue next morning at a specific time. Naturally, our ambassador and I, having taken part in the first meeting, were expected to be present at the second.

Next morning Dobrynin informed me that Nixon was already pacing around the house and was obviously waiting for his partner to appear. However, there was still no sign of life in the rooms where Brezhnev was staying, and so Nixon had to carry on strolling around his own house. Secretary of State Rogers and the President's adviser Kissinger had already been wandering up and down outside for some time. Dobrynin and I joined Nixon.

Brezhnev emerged from the house late. For obvious reasons the discussion began with a certain stiffness, especially as our host did not see fit to say that he had been ready too early, and his guest did not express regret that he had broken their agreement about when to begin.

They greeted one another, and to break the ice Nixon joked: 'I used the time to walk around my garden again and get a different view of the house.'

From a sharp incline we could see the Pacific Ocean in the distance.

Discussing it among ourselves, we came to the conclusion that when he bought the property Nixon had been more interested in the wonderful view of the ocean than the house itself, which was not especially luxurious. It was even rather modest.

I remember Nixon's words to Brezhnev at the end of his first visit to Moscow, in May 1972: 'According to American data, the USA and the USSR have built up enough weapons to destroy each other many times over.'

To which Brezhnev replied: 'We have come to the same conclusion.'

It was just this sort of openly expressed mutual understanding that informed the work preparing the provisional agreement on measures to limit strategic offensive weapons, or SALT-1, which was completed while Nixon was in Moscow, when the treaty was signed also. True, it concerned only ground-based intercontinental and submarine-based ballistic missiles. Strategic bombers were left aside for later talks. SALT-1 nevertheless was enormously important in limiting the nuclear arms race. News of the agreement quickly spread and all around the world people breathed more freely.

Undoubtedly a large part was played by US public opinion which was strongly in favour of arms limitation, but it should not be assumed that the Nixon administration was defying the American military-industrial complex. It was simply acting against the most extremist politicians and military and giving preference to the more moderate groups in big business. Although the US side has not yet ratified this treaty, by mutual agreement it has been in force for a number of years, and the fact that SALT-1 had at least been signed made it possible to proceed to prepare and sign SALT-2.

Another important achievement of Nixon's visit in 1972 was the Soviet–American treaty on anti-ballistic missile systems (ABMs). Both sides agreed not to develop naval, air, space or mobile land-based systems, or to give such systems to other states or to deploy them in foreign territory. In May 1972 both sides also declared their conviction that 'in the nuclear age there could be no other basis for maintaining relations than peaceful coexistence'. These words should be cast in bronze, for they remind us that, in place of great power ambitions, reason should prevail in the minds of the world's decision-makers.

It was also agreed that differences of ideology were no obstacle to normal relations on the basis of sovereignty, equality, non-interference in each other's internal affairs and mutual benefit. Interestingly, the USA and USSR had originally established diplomatic relations in 1933 on much the same basis.

A further important event in Soviet–American relations took place in 1973, when agreement was reached on preventing nuclear war by avoiding situations which could raise tension to a dangerous level. It would be hard to exaggerate the importance of an agreement according to which the world's two most powerful states undertook to regulate their relations in such a way as to reduce and ultimately eliminate the risk of nuclear conflict. If in fact this risk in recent years was not reduced but rather increased, then the responsibility must fall on the American side, which set out to intensify the nuclear arms race and to achieve US and NATO superiority over the USSR and the Warsaw Pact.

During Brezhnev's visit to the USA in June 1973 and Nixon's two visits to the USSR (the second one taking place in June–July 1974), the sides signed a number of agreements on co-operation in various fields, ranging from trade and culture, to research into the peaceful use of space, protection of the environment and development of the artificial heart.

During that period the USSR and the USA signed more agreements than throughout the entire period of their previous diplomatic relations. These agreements created a broad structure for bilateral relations and a mechanism for political talks and consultation, as well as raising the possibility of slowing down the arms race.

When weighing up the successes and failures of the Nixon administration, historians – Americans included – realise that by the end of his tenure Nixon had come to accept the pointlessness of America's adventure against the Vietnamese people, and that he showed enough common sense to take steps to end it. In January 1973 the USA signed the agreement to end the war and withdraw US troops from Vietnam, which was carried out by Nixon's successor, Gerald Ford.

On the other hand, the Nixon administration also did much to stifle legitimate regimes in a number of countries. A glaring example was Chile, where conspiracy, terror and bribery were used to bring down Allende's popular government. Acting in collaboration with the Nixon administration was the powerful Anaconda corporation, which had long had a stranglehold on the Chilean economy, especially the important copper industry. The responsibility for this lies directly with Nixon.

What of Nixon as a partner in talks? He would keep the threads of the main issues in his hands, but he was not always able to grasp the detail, which he left to others. On the whole, he conducted talks with Soviet representatives, myself included, in an even tone. He could control his nerves, but it was obvious that he was a stubborn man and that it would be no easy task to reach an understanding with him.

My impression was that he genuinely wanted to reach an understanding with the Soviet Union; indeed, our meetings usually led to some progress. I cannot remember an occasion when he launched into a digression on the differing social structures of our states. He always presented himself as a pragmatist uninterested in the theoretical aspects of an issue, a man who preferred to keep discussions on a purely practical level.

★

It sometimes happens that a man will occupy a high state position, and yet will be written of and spoken of only in passing. Gerald Ford, President for barely two years, belongs in this category.

It is perhaps easier for a foreigner than for an American to characterise Ford objectively as a politician. In general terms, his administration continued the line set out by Nixon which was designated as the shift from the era of confrontation to the era of negotiations. However, certain events connected with his presidency, which left their mark on international policy, should be emphasised.

I remember when President Ford and Secretary of State Kissinger arrived in Vladivostok in November 1974 for talks with Brezhnev. The President's plane landed not far from the city and Ford came boldly down the steps. We saw a quite tall man of athletic build. He turned out to be an affable type, with a pleasant, easygoing simplicity; certainly he did not look like an intellectual.

The road from the airport produced a marked impression on our guests. For its entire length, they travelled through vast fields alternating with forest, and the autumn colours were enchanting.

The talks were directed towards a new agreement on limiting stategic offensive weapons. They lasted for three days, during which I felt that both sides were seeking to clear the way for an agreement.

I will single out one issue which later became public property and at the same time – after Ford had left office – a stumbling block. Ford and Kissinger persistently wanted the USSR to relinquish a significant number of so-called heavy, land-based ICBMs (intercontinental ballistic missiles). This would have seriously damaged our national interest and would have been against the principle of parity and equal security. The Soviet side could therefore not concede this, and we explained why.

Brezhnev said: 'We must adopt a realistic approach. Neither side should attempt to gain strategic superiority. The Soviet Union is not happy that the USA has nuclear weapons in forward positions in Europe and in other regions close to our country. Yet the American leaders will not even discuss this. In such circumstances, the American request concerning Soviet ICBMs cannot be discussed either.'

Ford finally withdrew the question from the agenda – no doubt after careful analysis by the experts and approval from the military – thus opening the way to agreement on SALT-2 and contributing to a climate of moderation in Soviet–US relations in which each side took account of the other's interests.

Similarly, the Ford administration witnessed America's participation in the Helsinki Final Act, when Ford added his name to those of the leaders of the thirty-five member states in the European conference, proving that there was still the possibility in US politics for dialogue in the search for peaceful solutions to difficult problems.

Finally, it was under Ford's administration that the Vietnam war came to an end. He said himself, 'Vietnam was a trauma for our country for fifteen years or more. The war in Vietnam is over. It was a sad and tragic event in many respects . . . I think the lessons of the past in Vietnam will be learnt by Presidents, by Congress and by the American people.'

These were sober judgements, and one hopes that Washington has not forgotten them.

However, there were also negative trends in US foreign policy under Gerald Ford. In particular, in December 1974 Congress voted to accord trade and credit facilities, at most-favoured-nation level, to the Soviet Union, but made these dependent on the settlement of issues which had nothing to do with trade or international economic ties. The USSR declared that it would not enter into trade relations on a discriminatory basis.

It was also symptomatic that in March 1976 President Ford, in tune with extreme right-wing forces, ordered that his staff stop using the word 'détente' and instead start talking about 'peace through strength'. If there had not been serious issues at stake behind this, one might have thought the man in the White House was simply indulging in a little semantic exercise.

A special place in the formation of US foreign policy under Nixon and Ford belongs to Henry Kissinger, the Secretary of State whom I met more often than any other holder of that post after the war.

I have known generations of American state officials, each man with his own personality and way of thinking, and each with a supply of negotiating ammunition already well tested in his political career. Kissinger, however, had spent the war in US intelligence somewhere in Europe, and had not climbed the ladder of state service. Even so, he seemed perfectly at home in his jobs, first as Nixon's assistant and then as Secretary of State.

It took quite a few meetings at various levels to prepare SALT-1, and Kissinger and I drank many a cup of tea together at them. Our meetings in Moscow, Washington, Vienna, New York and Geneva were businesslike and dealt with the nuts and bolts of the issues. The summit meetings took place in order to draw all the ends together, to set the seal on the understandings we had reached and to maintain impetus for the future.

Whenever we two ministers took our seats at the table, each could be sure that his opposite number, first of all, wanted an agreement – otherwise he wouldn't be there – and, secondly, was properly prepared for the discussion. This ruled out any notion of outsmarting each other or of pulling the wool over anyone's eyes, and indeed the prestige of any man who attempted such tactics would have been damaged. It is surprising, therefore, to read in Kissinger's memoirs suggestions that in certain cases, referring even to summit talks, he was supposedly able to 'outsmart the Russians'. He does not, of course, produce any facts to support his claim, since there aren't any. In practice, the Secretary of State behaved with dignity at the talks, and did not resort to any of the methods he hints at in his memoirs.

Kissinger is without doubt a capable, even a highly capable, man, who has acquired considerable experience in foreign affairs. Within the limits allowed him, he was able to put forward genuinely constructive proposals, and I always found it extremely interesting to conduct talks with him. He never stated the obvious or took refuge in the platitudes of less experienced diplomats. The arguments he brought into play always contained elements so powerful that it was not enough merely to say they were unconvincing – one had to show *why* they were unconvincing.

Kissinger was also given to widening the terms of his analysis, especially when the subject was world tension, the mistrust between states and between the USA and USSR. He liked to introduce theoretical reasons for Washington's policy on a given question. When we debated arms reduction and disarmament, he would return repeatedly to his belief that all the problems which divided East and West, including the USSR and USA, were interconnected: 'These problems cannot be solved separately, in isolation. They are all connected. Therefore they have to be solved interrelatedly.'

His judgements, however, were often dubious, offending both logic and history. For instance, he frequently cited Metternich

With Sir Alec Douglas-
Home and William
Rogers, US Secretary of
State, at the UN in 1970

An audience with Pope
Paul VI in the Vatican,
1970

With Alexei Kosygin and
U Thant in the Kremlin,
1971

RIGHT Sharing a joke with
Richard M. Nixon, 1971

LEFT Moscow, July 1974: Leonid Brezhnev and Nixon sign an agreement of scientific co-operation
BELOW With Nixon and Henry Kissinger during the same visit

BELOW September 1974, the UN, New York. *From left to right:* Huang Hua, China's UN representative; Jean Sauvaghargues, French Foreign Minister; Kissinger; UN Secretary-General Kurt Waldheim; myself and James Callaghan, then British Foreign Minister. Walheim was hosting a dinner for the five countries who are permanent representatives of the Security Council

With Czech Communist Party leader Gustav Husák, Prague 1975, after receiving the Order of the White Lion

With Brezhnev and K.U. Chernenko during a European meeting on security, Helsinki 1975

With President Josip Broz Tito of Yugoslavia in 197

With Cyrus Vance,
Geneva 1978

ABOVE With Indira
Gandhi, New Delhi 1980

RIGHT With Fidel Castro,
Havana 1980

Talks with Jimmy Carter in Moscow, 1977. On my left are Brezhnev and Marshal Ustinov, on my right is Chernenko. On Carter's left is Zbigniew Brzezinski

With Hafez Assad in Damascus, 1980

With Chernenko and Asad in the Kremlin, October 1984

With Yitzhak Shamir of Israel. We had an interpreter with us, although Shamir spoke Russian

Meeting with Chancellor
Helmut Schmidt in West
Germany in November
1979

With Wojciech Jaruzelski
of Poland, Moscow 1984

With Chancellor Helmut Kohl and Hans-Dietrich Genscher in West Germany in 1983

With Pope John Paul II in the Vatican in 1985 with Cardinal Casaroli

With Mikhail Gorbachev
and Javier Pérez de
Cuéllar

With Francois Mitterand
in the Kremlin in 1985

With Ronald Reagan in
1984

With George Schultz,
Geneva 1984

With George Bush in 1984

From left to right, front row: Dmitri Ustinov, Nikolai Tikhonov, Yuri Andropov and myself, at a meeting of party and government leaders of the Warsaw Pact countries held in Moscow, June 1983

Gorbachev signs an extension of the Warsaw Pact, 1985

With Gorbachev, November 1987, on Lenin's Mausoleum for the anniversary of the 1917 Revolution

With Lydia and Ronald and Nancy Reagan in Moscow, May 1988

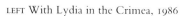

LEFT With Lydia in the Crimea, 1986

BELOW With my granddaughter Anna. She is reading Drabkina's memoirs of Lenin

FAR BELOW A family group, Summer 1988. *From left to right:* Anatoly's wife Valentina, Anatoly, my granddaughters, Emilia and Anna, myself, Lydia and Emilia

Top, left to right: Grandson
Alexei, Anatoly's wife
Valentina, Emilia's
husband Alexander,
grandsons Andrei and
Igor. *Middle:* Anatoly,
Lydia, myself and Emilia.
Bottom: Great–grandson
Oleg, granddaughters
Lydia and Anna

as his idol in nineteenth-century European political history. He believed that Metternich, the Foreign Minister of the Austro-Hungarian empire and later its Chancellor, had been right when he claimed that the problems dividing the European states should not be treated in isolation from each other, but that their solution should somehow be embodied in a single process. Kissinger had nothing convincing to offer, however, when it was pointed out to him that Metternich and his successors were in large measure responsible for the eventual collapse of the Austro-Hungarian empire; and that even before its collapse it had been endlessly engaged in largely unsuccessful wars. Fortunately for the world, Kissinger did not practise what he preached with total consistency. Thus most of the successes he eventually achieved in combination with the Soviet side – particularly in the field of nuclear arms limitations – occurred because Washington did *not* make agreement in one area conditional upon agreement in another.

Even so, for almost the entire period of his tenure as Secretary of State, Kissinger practised the technique of applying pressure on the Soviet Union wherever possible, whether in Asia, Africa, the Middle East or anywhere else, as a way of forcing us to make concessions. Clearly this was a straight transfer to international affairs of the sort of wheeling and dealing that goes on throughout American domestic politics, and for as long as Washington employed this approach nothing useful could be achieved in talks with us. It was only when realism triumphed and the USA learned to take account of the interests of both sides that things improved.

The former Secretary of State has one particular quality of which he says nothing in his memoirs – his extraordinary ability to switch positions. For example, in our talks on strategic arms, he had accepted the principle that they were based on Soviet–US parity. He liked to repeat: 'The principle of parity is of fundamental impcrtance.' Now, however, when he is out of office, the same Kissinger who contributed so much to our agreements regards this principle as a virtual anathema. Moreover, he tries to assert that the agreements made by the two powers no longer fully meet the needs of this principle. He brings no evidence for this; it is pure opportunism.

To ignore principles, as Kissinger had frequently done, is a game that takes its toll. Having immersed himself in the world of his memoirs after leaving office, Kissinger tried to join public life again by offering his services to the Reagan administration. This was the administration which denigrated everything of value that had previously been achieved in Soviet–US relations, yet Kissinger approached it without batting an eyelid, in the hope that the new President would want him in his cabinet. However, his attempt was unsuccessful; apparently he was not quite what Ronald Reagan was looking for.

Seneca, the Roman philosopher and Nero's tutor, once uttered this wise saying: 'When a man does not know which harbour to head for, no wind is fair.'

With the advent of Jimmy Carter to the presidency in 1977, the myth of the 'Soviet threat' was again dragged out and US foreign policy once more became contradictory and inconsistent. During his term of office, Carter himself slid steadily towards confrontation.

Indeed, our very first contact with the Carter administration made it plain that the USA intended to withdraw from the Soviet–US accords reached at the Vladivostok summit, and to try instead for a treaty that would give the USA significant superiority in strategic nuclear arms. It was with this mission that Secretary of State Cyrus Vance came to Moscow in March 1977.

Vance met Brezhnev and had a general discussion on nuclear weapons. I too had a number of meetings with him to discuss the issue in greater detail. I explained to him: 'The chief demand being made by the USA, namely that we destroy half our land-based ICBMs, is absurd. We are wholly opposed to tampering with the Vladivostok accords. They took so much effort from both our sides to achieve, and we must use them as a basis for a second treaty on limiting strategic offensive weapons.' I reaffirmed our position at a Moscow press conference for Soviet and foreign journalists on 31 March 1977, and international public opinion on the whole supported it.

SALT-2 was the main subject of my first meeting with President Carter, in Washington in September 1977. I arrived at the White House together with Soviet Deputy Foreign Minister G.M. Korniyenko and our ambassador, A.F. Dobrynin. We were shown through to the cabinet room, where Cyrus Vance was waiting with the President's ubiquitous foreign policy adviser, Zbigniew Brzezinski, and the US ambassador to Moscow, Malcolm Toon. We all waited for President Carter to appear.

He came in unannounced through one of the many doors, and approached us with the famous half-smile on his face. He greeted us warmly, clearly wanting to show that he intended serious business.

We sat down at an oval table, the Soviet team on one side, the Americans on the other. Any other President – and I can speak from personal experience of many – would have held a meeting of this sort in his private study, where everyone would have sat in easy chairs and been extremely uncomfortable whenever they tried to speak even to their most immediate neighbours. Carter, in contrast, evidently preferred a degree of formality that positioned his advisers close at hand, where they could pass him any information he might need. This made sense, as Carter was not overburdened with foreign policy expertise and anyway he had not been in the White House very long.

It was up to me to open the discussion. I raised some key issues, notably a number of unresolved questions concerning the SALT-2 treaty, and set out our position for settling them.

Carter replied, 'We are ready to speed up completion of the work that has already been done over the last few years on this treaty.'

However, as soon as the discussion got down to brass tacks, it became clear that mutual understanding was not going to be so easy to achieve. Particular difficulties arose when we reached the point of actually defining what constituted a nuclear ballistic missile. There was also hesitation when it came to naming the locations of such weapons, even though they had long been known to both sides.

Being a diligent man, Carter did his best, but when he tried to pronounce the names of towns and regions in the Soviet Union all that came out was a sequence of incomprehensible noises. More worryingly, we quickly discovered that he had difficulty in grasping even the most elementary basic features of the Soviet–US relationship. Clearly, therefore, the President's advisers had urged him to devote his main attention to the Soviet ICBMs which he must persuade us to agree to reduce in number, and indeed he had managed to retain what they explained to him – in words of one syllable, as it were. Thus, at a certain moment, he produced a souvenir set of plastic missiles consisting of a row each of American and Soviet missiles, and set them down on the table. Pointing to two Soviet missiles which were clearly much bigger than the US ones, he said: 'These are the ones we are most afraid of.' He seemed satisfied, and evidently thought his demonstration a proper substitute for real debate.

Carter's chief aim, like that of his predecessors, was to reduce the Soviet nuclear arsenal while keeping America's main offensive potential intact. It was only with difficulty, persuaded by our arguments and the pressure of world public opinion, that he shifted his position and we were able to make progress.

Everyone knows, from books or films, the effects of an atomic explosion, but Carter – uniquely among American Presidents – had personal experience. As a young submarine officer he worked at General Electric on the production of plutonium reactors for America's second nuclear submarine, *Sea Wolf*. He had been sent with a group of officers to deal with the breakdown of one of the reactors and, remaining in the danger zone for more than a minute, had been exposed to a full year's radiation limit. This had been no ordinary act of courage.

One might imagine that Carter, having felt the breath of nuclear death, would have a special attitude to everything connected with nuclear war, but it seems he had learned no particular lessons from the experience.

The discussions lasted a little over three hours, during which time we managed to make some progress towards an understanding. Difficulties still remained, however, and to settle them we had to go back to issues we thought had already been dealt with. In reality it would take another eighteen months of detailed work, and several further meetings with Carter and Vance, before the SALT-2 treaty was ready, and even then, before the signing in Vienna, Carter had reservations about actually putting the treaty into force.

'Both sides still have to ratify the treaty, of course,' he said.

The Soviet side declared: 'This treaty is so important for peace and security that it must be ratified by the legislatures of both the USSR and the USA without delay.'

As we were to discover in due course, Carter's warning about ratification had been entirely appropriate.

It was 18 June 1979. The Redoubt Hall of the Hofburg Palace, where the ceremony took place, was brilliantly decked out for the occasion.

The moment approached. The lawyers had checked every comma and full stop for the umpteenth time, in case one of them had jumped out of place and changed the treaty's whole meaning. After all, the whole world was waiting.

Each leader picked up a pen, adjusted his position and wrote his signature.

They had not yet got up when I quietly asked Defence Minister Dmitri Ustinov, who was standing next to me: 'What do you think, will they kiss?'

'No,' came the reply. 'There's nothing to kiss for.'

We were both pleasantly surprised therefore when President Carter took the initiative, sealing the treaty with a formal embrace and a kiss, to the loud applause of everyone present.

Both delegations later attended the opera, where, in boxes bedecked with the Soviet, US and Austrian flags, we watched Mozart's *Abduction from the Seraglio*.

The treaty went considerably further than SALT-1, embracing the entire range of strategic weapons and establishing a bridge to the next stage of talks which would deal with further limitation and reduction of nuclear weapons.

During the Vienna meeting the leaders exchanged views on a number of international issues and expressed their readiness for further talks. This was put to me by Cyrus Vance, who did not conceal his great satisfaction with the treaty, and the same thing was said to Ustinov by Defense Secretary Harold Brown and the chairman of the joint chiefs of staff, David Jones. Such emotional declarations by the US side, however, were no basis for reliable predictions about the future.

Later actions of the Carter administration, both towards the USSR and in international affairs generally, were to strengthen the opponents of the treaty – so much so that the administration was clearly looking for any means to prevent its implementation. In these circumstances, Carter's feeble calls for Congress to ratify the treaty were an opportunistic ploy, designed simply to make it look as if he was carrying out the obligations he had undertaken earlier. In January 1980 he declared the issue postponed to an unspecified date.

In its efforts to shift the strategic balance in favour of the USA and NATO, Washington now sharply increased its military expenditure. The NATO allies were urged to do the same, in addition to which new US missiles were deployed in western Europe. Simultaneously, and without any excuse, Washington broke off earlier talks on a number of important arms limitation issues.

The Carter administration set out to undermine the process of

détente in Europe. This intention had been foreshadowed at the
Belgrade meeting of October 1977 to March 1978, where the USA
adopted an obstructionist position. The USA also took steps to
wind up trade and cultural links with the USSR. They broke their
obligations by cancelling existing contracts, banning the sale of
grain to the USSR and the export of certain goods which were
declared 'strategic'.

One absurdity followed another. Washington declared that
henceforth it would base its Soviet policy on the principle of
'linkage' – that is, the level of co-operation would be dependent
on the Soviet Union's fulfilment of conditions, improperly set by
the USA and relating to the USSR's own domestic concerns or
those involving a third country. It was in this context that a
propaganda campaign was launched in the USA alleging that
human rights were being violated in the USSR and the other
socialist countries.

Talk on this topic, accompanied by inventions about 'the Soviet
threat' and 'Soviet expansionism', became the Carter administration's favourite negotiating tool, as Washington engaged
more and more actively in ideological subversion against the
USSR. The aim was to confuse public opinion and to camouflage
Washington's real strategy, which was to intensify the arms
race.

Carter took a personal hand in the campaign of provocation.
Sounding like a zealous TV commercial, he seemed to think it
was his duty to raise the matter of human rights every time he
met a Soviet representative. I endured it myself.

We were in the White House and had just been talking about
the need for a second treaty on limiting strategic nuclear weapons,
when Carter suddenly said: 'I would like to raise a question in a
different area, the area of human rights.' This boiled down to the
demand that the USSR release some dissident.

I replied: 'I can only express my amazement that this question
should have been raised in this discussion on the President's
initiative. As for the particular dissident, I have never even heard
his name before.'

It later transpired that the person in question was a dropout,
someone who had moreover been convicted and sent to gaol for
breaking the law.

The American side of the table began whispering among themselves, and then Carter reiterated his question, asserting that the

release of this criminal would be in the interests of 'observing human rights'.

This episode made a gloomy impression on us. The issue Carter had whipped up was plainly not a serious one. In fact, it represented a frivolous abuse of his powers as President, since it was a purely internal Soviet matter.

I asked the President straight out: 'Isn't it time to drop such ploys as utterly unproductive?'

On that note, the discussion came to a close.

In Soviet–American talks during the 1960s and 1970s, both sides raised the issue of human rights, since it is obviously an important one. If we ask ourselves what is the chief human right, the plain answer is, the right to life. This can hardly be refuted: only if you are alive can you enjoy all the other rights – the right to work, to housing, education, medical service, emigration and so on. On this basis, I have always thought it my duty to do everything possible to advance the process of disarmament and to create conditions in which nuclear weapons and the use of force in international relations should be a thing of the past.

Several Western countries have interpreted human rights in a far narrower way, often making up simplistic clichés that try to reduce the problem of human rights to the issue of emigration from the USSR. And that is not all: the right to emigrate of this or that individual, usually of Jewish origin, is declared to be the touchstone of 'Soviet sincerity'. The effort to put pressure on us does not stop there either, for the right to emigrate is made a condition for resolving other important questions.

In fact, many initiatives that would have smoothed Soviet–US relations were deliberately slowed down by endless new conditions connected with the question of emigration. A pathetic example of this was the Jackson–Vanik amendment passed by Congress in 1974. In effect it froze Soviet–US trade by linking it to Soviet policy on Jewish emigration. Was this sensible? Could it possibly secure the rights of individuals to life and their other vital rights? Of course not.

Our position, when individual cases of emigration were raised in talks, was that we would examine them in the context of Soviet law and try to help when possible in cases of reuniting families. As a matter of fact, the success of our efforts was demonstrated by the fact that in some years the Soviet Jewish emigration reached tens of thousands. The Americans not only did not express their satisfaction at this, but rather tried instead to whip up anti-Soviet hysteria by seizing on some 'hard cases'.

Since we genuinely wanted to improve our relations with Washington, we made occasional concessions on individual cases of emigration. In reply, we were confronted by more and more demands, not all of which, unfortunately, could be met for reasons of national security. It is also possible that at times there were unjustified decisions and unnecessary delays. But, after all, there were enormous numbers of cases to be looked at and red tape does no doubt take precedence over common sense at times. These problems can only be solved by due process and not through interference by other countries.

In the present further democratisation of Soviet society, under *perestroika* and with *glasnost*, there is a good chance that conditions will be created in which controversy over the right to emigrate will no longer be available to add grist to our opponents' mill.

Another ploy in Washington's line was the arbitrary declaration of this or that region of the world as 'a sphere of vital US interest', where the Carter administration could intervene with its specially created 'rapid response forces'. In the latter part of the twentieth century we were witnessing the most basic principles of international law being trampled upon. The godfather of this dangerous idea was Carter and it was just applied during his term of office.

From my own experience, I would say Carter had a certain amount of goodwill, but this quality only showed itself when questions of war and peace were not being discussed. He could raise his glass in ten toasts and do it intelligently too. But when the big problems appeared on the agenda he was visibly uncomfortable.

In the course of a discussion, Carter would sometimes create a diversion, perhaps in the interests of giving his partner and himself a breather. Thus, before one of our meetings in the White House, he brought in an elderly lady.

'Let me introduce you,' he said to me. 'This is my mother. She often visits with us in the White House.'

The President's mother turned out to be a pleasantly sociable lady. She greeted me warmly with the words: 'All decent Americans, Mr Gromyko, would like to have friendly relations with you Russians.'

We supported this motion enthusiastically and I added: 'It would be a good thing if some of the Americans who share your views could be involved in these talks.'

Carter and his mother laughed good-naturedly.

For most of Carter's term the Secretary of State was Cyrus Vance, an interesting and significant figure in the field of American foreign policy. He had been Carter's foreign policy adviser during the 1976 campaign and, before that, they had both taken part in the Trilateral Commission, which David Rockefeller had created in 1973 and which included businessmen, politicians and political scientists from the USA, western Europe and Japan. Its purpose had been to study the political and economic problems of interaction between the leading capitalist powers. It was not surprising, therefore, that Carter should entrust to him one of the top posts in his administration.

His workload was enormous and of course included negotiating the future of nuclear weapons. As he was swept from side to side in the whirlpool of his government's policy, he tried to remain the optimist he was by nature. In our meetings, I would be highly aware not only of what he was saying on the administration's behalf but also of the way he was saying it. His views were sometimes original. Of course he defended the official position, but he did it with an unusual degree of flexibility.

He clearly understood the issues more subtly than most, and his differences with Carter over foreign policy eventually made his position as Secretary of State untenable. The immediate cause of his departure was his open disapproval of the disastrous action taken to release the American hostages in Iran, which was undertaken in April 1980 with the President's approval.

As often happens to politicians, an event that appears outwardly unfavourable turns to their ultimate advantage, and so it was with Vance. His resignation was seen at home and abroad as proof that he was a man of firm principles. Now out of office, Vance is an authoritative representative of the American movement for arms limitation and for improving the political climate in the world. Having been an experienced and capable lawyer, a prominent politician and public figure before holding office, Vance has gone back into private practice as a partner with the respectable law firm of Simpson, Thacher and Barlett. But he also takes part in the work of the international commission for disarmament and security which was headed in 1986 by the late Swedish Prime Minister Olof Palme.

I always enjoyed talking with Vance. He came, of course, from another social world, but that did not prevent him from wanting to overcome the differences between the USA and USSR by peaceful means. Several times he said to me: 'The American people reject war, the risk of war appals them. I believe in the objective possibility of reaching mutual understanding between the two great powers.'

Always correct in his behaviour, even at the worst moments in Soviet–US relations, and never one to resort to harsh words – unlike some public utterances of the Reagan administration – Vance reminds me very much of Anthony Eden. If he lacks something, it may be Eden's inventiveness in matters of tactics. Optimistic, lively, energetic and capable, he might easily be labelled a 'pro-communist' or a 'communist sympathiser', but that would be nonsense. He is simply one of those rare people in American public life who do not look at the world through the narrow window of profit or money-grubbing.

One other US Secretary of State I ought to mention briefly is Edmund Muskie, who was appointed in place of Vance. I met him only once, in Vienna in May 1980, during the twenty-fifth anniversary celebrations of the Austrian state treaty. As was to be expected, Muskie expressed the Carter administration's basic attitudes. Its hostility towards the USSR was openly paraded. Everything Muskie said confirmed that the Carter administration was drifting in the direction of raising world tension, sharpening Soviet–US relations and widening the gulf between us on nuclear issues.

In fact Muskie's line in Vienna, like Carter's in Washington, was obviously designed to appeal to the electors in Carter's competition with Reagan for the presidency. But in doing this, ironically, Carter was only making things easier for Reagan. Reagan's line as the Republican candidate was simply to take a position to the right of Carter on every aspect of foreign policy; the further Carter moved to the right, the further Reagan moved also, to the delight of his backers on the extreme right.

Muskie's statements and general demeanour were coolly rational, if only in comparison with what was to come under

Reagan. He was known in Washington for his calm approach to international affairs, but his moderation was overwhelmed by Washington politics when he became Secretary of State, especially regarding the question of Soviet–US relations and nuclear weapons.

If I were asked whether I would like Muskie as a partner in discussions on international problems, I would say: 'Yes, but only Muskie without the burden of the policy he was forced to carry in Vienna.'

On the coming to power of the Reagan administration, tension in Soviet–US relations increased, with a resultant cooling in the international climate. The new US government did everything it could to undo the work of its predecessors, striking blows at one agreement after another, either emasculating them or, as in the case of SALT-2, declaring them defunct.

Then came a certain night in August 1983.

Events sometimes occur in international life which by their scale seem at first not to be important, but which quickly take on a very serious political significance. One such event was the incident which took place in the Far East on the night of 31 August 1983, when a South Korean airliner that had blatantly violated the Soviet state border was shot down.

News of the event flashed round the world with varied reactions. This was only a few days before the final stage of the Foreign Ministers' meeting on European security which was taking place in Madrid, and the response from Washington was a wave of insinuations against the USSR, brazenly exploiting the incident for propaganda purposes.

US agencies vied with each other in putting out false and often contradictory versions of what had happened. The fact that it was the US administration that assumed the role of chief slanderer was itself extremely indicative, and to anyone with a grain of intelligence it soon became clear that Washington was in fact defending a plane of its own, that the airliner had simply been carrying a South Korean label.

In Madrid, meanwhile, there was a distinct atmosphere of uncertainty. Everyone was wondering what would happen. As always, there were the pessimists who thought the meeting would break up, and there were the optimists who thought that Washington would not go so far, bearing in mind the consequences for the USA. The other Soviet delegates and I were inundated with questions about what to expect. We, of course, were no prophets, but we made it plain that only those who did not want the meeting to take place would break it up. The meeting opened on 8 September 1983. Each minister began by putting his government's own position. Most of the NATO members supported Washington's version of the plane incident. Some, however, said it was tragic, but made it plain they did not take on trust the explanation served up by the Pentagon and the US special services.

Secretary of State George Shultz made a speech that was generally hostile to the USSR.

I had to reply with a rebuff: 'The violation of Soviet airspace was carried out for purposes of military intelligence. I declare in the name of the Soviet leadership that the Soviet Union had the right to protect its frontiers. That is its sovereign right. Other states have the same right.'

The tension reached a peak after the US and Soviet speeches. Everyone was waiting to see what would happen – would the meeting sink or swim?

It had already been agreed that Shultz and I would meet privately in Madrid to exchange views on Soviet–US relations and such key international issues as the limitation of strategic and European nuclear arms. We held this meeting on the day after our speeches, in an old mansion that had no doubt once belonged to a grandee and was now the US ambassador's residence in Madrid. It took no great perception to see that Shultz looked depressed. We had what is called a frank discussion.

He started off straight away about human rights in the Soviet Union.

I tactfully pointed out: 'It doesn't make sense to discuss this subject, as it only concerns our internal affairs.'

Shultz then repeated almost word for word what he had just said, adding, 'The President instructed me to say this.'

Again I told him: 'We have no intention of discussing our internal affairs with anyone. As for the orders you have been given as Secretary of State, I am not bound, as the representative of another government, by the instructions of the American President. Wouldn't it be better therefore for us to leave this little room and go into the larger room next door where we can discuss genuinely international problems in the presence of our advisers?'

Shultz had no choice but to agree to move into the other room and engage in discussion with a broader participation. The Soviet side included Deputy Foreign Minister V.G. Komplektov and the interpreter V.M. Sukhodrev, while the American delegation included the President's special adviser on Soviet affairs Jack Matlock, Assistant Secretary of State Richard Burt and the US ambassador to Moscow Arthur Hartman.

As I expected, Shultz had barely sat down when he began with the aeroplane incident. Ignoring a point of order from me, he began setting out his government's views on the issue, again referring to his President's instructions. Shultz was simply imposing his own order on the talks, and I had to.stop him.

'Your attempt to act out a plan worked out previously in Washington,' I said, 'cannot be allowed to succeed. We have to debate fundamental issues of Soviet–US relations, the question of nuclear weapons in Europe and a world situation which is becoming more and more tense.' I added: 'If the Secretary of State will not enter into debate on important issues, then there will be nothing for us to discuss and we shall consider the conversation closed.'

I cannot recall another occasion when a US Secretary of State tried so persistently to shift the discussion and impose his own agenda. Shultz's next statement was equally hard to fathom: 'The Reagan administration is devoted to constructive dialogue with the Soviet Union.'

In reality, the USA was obviously not at all interested in seeking solutions, and I said as much to Shultz. I then set out our position on the key issues of nuclear disarmament, remarking: 'To claim that the aeroplane incident is problem number one is exaggerated. Problem number one for the whole world is to avert nuclear war.'

In the name of the Soviet leadership, I declared: 'The world situation is now slipping towards a very dangerous precipice. It is plain that the great responsibility for not allowing a nuclear catastrophe to occur must be borne by the USSR and the USA together. In our opinion, the USA should re-evaluate its policies, and the President and his administration should look at international affairs in a new way. How many constructive proposals for restricting the arms race, let alone reducing nuclear weapons, has the USSR advanced, only to have them turned down by the USA? Many.

'The Soviet leadership,' I continued, 'assumes that both the

USSR and the USA are committed actively to averting the threat of a nuclear catastrophe. There is a joint official document to this effect that commits both our governments to this task.'

Shultz sat in silence.

I went on: 'The Soviet Union persists in striving for just this. It may seem paradoxical, but this present meeting shows that even in difficult circumstances dialogue is still possible. A bad dialogue is better than war.'

This was a slight paraphrase of the well-known Russian saying: 'A poor peace is better than a good quarrel.'

I told Shultz: 'We cling to the hope that the American administration has not given up the idea of negotiation. Therefore, we call on the President and yourself, as Secretary of State, to seek understanding with a sense of responsibility, and to use every opportunity to narrow our differences on questions of the nuclear arms race and disarmament.'

I then asked: 'If the USA carries out its intention of deploying new nuclear missiles in western Europe, what will follow? Inevitably, the Soviet Union will not slumber. We will try to restore parity and we will succeed. Peace will be even more fragile, since the new balance of power will rest at an even higher level. That is where US policy is leading us.'

Shultz just sat and listened.

I continued: 'You and I have the responsibility of setting out our countries' positions to each other, and of informing our governments about the proposals each side has put.' And at this point I repeated the proposal made by Andropov on nuclear weapons in Europe.

What did the Secretary of State give in reply?

Shultz parroted the formula, 'No one is more dedicated to the ideas of peace than President Reagan', and then returned to the aeroplane incident. He had apparently paid no attention to a single word I had said.

Resignedly I set out the Soviet point of view: 'We accuse the American side of carrying out a serious and premeditated action against the Soviet Union. The American statement cannot shake our conviction. How could the plane accidentally divert from the established corridor of five hundred kilometres, not towards international waters but towards the Soviet border, over vitally important military territory in the Soviet Far East, and penetrate and fly in Soviet airspace for more than two hours?'

I asked: 'Why did this plane, flying as it was in Soviet airspace, not obey warning signals and the order to land which were given in strict accordance with international and Soviet law?'

Shultz made no replies to any of my questions.

I concluded: 'That is why we accuse the US administration of organising a criminal act against the USSR, only one of many such attacks on us. At the same time, we object most strongly to words which have become the administration's common currency in its abuse of the USSR and our social system.'

That was virtually the end of my talk with Shultz. It was probably the sharpest exchange I ever had with an American Secretary of State, and I have had talks with fourteen of them.

I met Shultz for several talks, both before and after Madrid, each time with a different agenda and occasionally with a different tone.

Our first talk, during a UN General Assembly meeting in New York, was quite extended. I had intended our talk to be constructive, but that could only happen if the other side did not shy away from examining our differences on key issues. Shultz, it turned out, was willing only to state the differences but not to seek a way of overcoming them. This became clear at once.

He began with the assertion: 'The Soviet Union's actions in the international arena, and what it does to guarantee its own security, represent a threat to the United States.'

Rather than provide evidence of this threat, Shultz then offered a number of mythical instances when we had allegedly pushed a number of countries into hostile attitudes towards the USA, and ended by repeating his statement that the USSR's nuclear weapons represented a threat to the USA and western Europe.

Our talk continued. From time to time Shultz would rummage for data in the folder he had either on his lap or on the table in front of him. I would then imagine that we were going to get down to specifics, but it never happened. When our side brought out the facts and figures, Shultz would simply look uncomfortable. He did not even try to dispute them. For example, we were able to show conclusively that the medium-range missiles Washington and its allies were so worried about did not give the USSR superiority over NATO in that class of weapons, but merely parity.

We came away from this talk with the definite opinion that

Washington was vainly hoping to gain US superiority by putting military pressure on the USSR.

In my next meeting with Shultz, which took place in Stockholm on 18 January 1984, nothing new was added. Again the sharp differences in our positions were plainly felt.

The Soviet side had come to the Stockholm meeting with the firm intention of making it a success. We made two proposals. The first was that all member nuclear states should follow the Soviet Union's example and renounce the first use of nuclear weapons. The second was for a treaty on banning altogether the use of force in relations between states. We also announced that we were ready to work out more detailed and wider measures for building trust in the military sphere among the present participants.

It soon became clear that Shultz had come to Stockholm with the same baggage he'd brought with him to our talks in New York and Madrid.

The American and foreign media have sometimes compared Shultz with his predecessors, suggesting that he was better than Haig because he was more pragmatic in foreign policy matters. It has even been said that he was the most flexible Secretary of State of recent years.

It is difficult to talk of flexibility in connection with great powers and the differences between them on key issues of war and peace. As the representative of the leading capitalist power and the spokesman for a particular social order, Shultz was inevitably programmed by a special code. I had many interesting conversations on international matters with this outstanding American statesman, and I believe he really did understand that the idea of liquidating socialism is nonsensical. If so, this alone put him head and shoulders above some other statesmen whose verbal piggy-banks are stuffed with all manner of simplistic anti-communist phrases.

However, I think it would not be appropriate for me to compare Shultz with his predecessors. No doubt his international business background helped him in political debate, but it is not for me to determine whether as a statesman he was one who led rather than one who was led. It is too risky to guess. I am always sceptical of hasty descriptions of this statesman or that. Usually it is only people who are trying to be sensational who indulge in them.

★

The character of US policy, causing as it did tension between the USA and the Soviet Union, long ago gave rise to growing alarm among many sensible American politicians, social figures and certain big businessmen. Among those who have pointed out the dangers inherent in the arms race and who have called on Washington to move from confrontation to détente one should mention Cyrus Vance, Edward Kennedy, Paul Warnke and many others. Also worthy of note is the former diplomat and distinguished historian, George Kennan.

Kennan has a high reputation in the USA. For some thirty years his name has frequently appeared in the press, in journals and in books. First noticed on the diplomatic scene as early as 1925, Kennan was one of the authors of the Truman Doctrine and the Marshall Plan, and he was among those theorists who espoused the notion of acting from a position of strength in relation to the USSR.

I first met Kennan in the autumn of 1939 in the US embassy in Moscow, where he served as temporary chargé d'affaires. We talked in general terms about US policy, the situation in Europe and the Far East.

He repeatedly asserted: 'The aims of US foreign policy in the post-war settlement, both in Europe and on a wider scale, are peace-loving.' He also spoke of the need to develop US–Soviet relations.

Kennan appeared to hold interesting views on the international events of the time, and I believed that the post he was then occupying was merely a stepping-stone in his diplomatic career. I think this would have turned out to be the case, had he had more prior experience – but Washington was to decide otherwise.

In March 1952 Kennan was made ambassador to the USSR. This post turned out to be a test which Kennan could not handle, not because he lacked training, but because he failed to be aware – as any ambassador should – of the borderline between the permissible and the impermissible, especially when making remarks about the country to which he was accredited. This borderline may change, depending on circumstances, on the nature of the relations between the two countries and on international conditions.

What happened was that, en route from Moscow to London, at Tempelhof airport in West Berlin on 19 September 1952, Ambassador Kennan made hostile remarks about the Soviet Union which were at once reported in the world's press. Taking all the circumstances into account, the Soviet government not only made representations to the US government but also declared Kennan *persona non grata* and demanded his removal from the post of ambassador.

Kennan's brief stay in Moscow was hardly enough to enrich his knowledge of the country by much, while the notoriety the incident attracted in the West did little to enhance his position. For quite a long time thereafter, when Kennan's name was mentioned in diplomatic circles, people would say: 'Oh, yes, the ambassador who was declared *persona non grata* by the Soviet Union.'

To this day, he has not lived down this 'fame'. Yet, to give him credit, Kennan eventually found the strength in himself to overcome the personal injury and hurt pride. On a number of issues of Soviet–US relations he has taken an incomparably more objective position than the Reagan administration, or indeed some of its predecessors. He has frequently and on various platforms taken the administration to task for undermining relations with the USSR, for whipping up anti-Soviet hysteria, for the arms race and for raising international tension. He has often called on the administration to think again before it is too late and to take the path of moderation and understanding.

These views do not mean that Kennan is close to the USSR in his ideology; on the contrary, he is a representative and spokesman of his class, the bourgeoisie, 100 per cent. However, he has understood the simple truth that differences between socialism and capitalism must be resolved within the framework of peaceful competition, that disputes between them must be settled at the conference table and not by armed conflict. Growing numbers of people in American society and business are adopting these views.

Washington's repeated attempts to stir up an economic cold war have failed internationally, and have yielded few dividends in American domestic politics either. They simply intensify the disorder in the economy, reducing demand in some areas and causing unemployment. It was the right-wing politicians themselves who lifted the grain embargo against the USSR when they saw it was harming the interests of American farmers, and the embargo on the sale of equipment for the oil and gas industry produced equally negative results.

The Reagan administration nevertheless attempted to discrimi-
nate against the USSR in trade and economic relations. This
aroused the disquiet of a substantial section of American business
which wants a political climate that will encourage co-operation.

Armand Hammer is the head of a major American enterprise,
the Occidental Oil corporation. A dynamo of a man, he is in
permanent motion, always making plans and talking in terms of
hundreds of millions of dollars. His strong point is his political
realism, tinged with a good dose of social idealism. 'A businessman,' he says, 'shouldn't look at what's going on through rose-
coloured spectacles, nor through dark glasses either.'

Hammer's family emigrated from Russia to the USA before the
revolution. He is deeply rooted in American business, but he has
a lot of the dash and merchant bravado that was characteristic of
the magnates of the Volga region in the old days. Uninterested in
the small time, they would only get excited when the figures were
astronomical. For Hammer, it doesn't matter if the business is in
mineral fertilisers or works of art, as long as the scale is large
enough, there is a profit and a tingling of the nerves. Without
these priorities, in his world, he would be trampled underfoot.

He told me once, 'Business for me is a kind of sport, with the
big difference that for some reason fate has decreed that I have the
chance of increasing my capital.' By a little less, perhaps, or a little
more, but always a profit. He also said, 'One thing is clear – I've
had fewer failures than successes.'

This is due to his experience, native wit, even a sort of talent –
and a lot of luck: to say that fortune has smiled on him would be
an understatement.

In the difficult period following the civil war, Hammer was in
Russia and was received by Lenin. He was granted a concession
to help in the campaign against illiteracy. Millions of children –
myself among them – wrote out their first alphabet with a pencil
stamped with the name 'Hammer'. For Hammer it was a business,
and a profitable one at that. Soviet industry soon managed to end
the pencil famine and Hammer's monopoly declined, but his
interest in doing business with the Soviet Union remained alive.

Although he was not prominent during the Roosevelt era, his
ideas were embodied in the President's general political line.
Whatever the state of Soviet–American relations, Hammer has
been in favour of trading with the USSR. He is without doubt his
own man in the world of American big business, but I have

noticed that the big corporations eye him with a degree of caution. They don't like his friendly attitude towards the Soviet Union. Hammer knows this, but is not deterred.

On 28 September 1984, after a four-year break in top-level Soviet–US political contacts, I met President Reagan for the first time. Until then, he had given the impression that Soviet–US relations or contacts with the Soviet leadership were of no great interest to him.

As one could have anticipated, when the campaign for the 1984 presidential election came round, his advisers suddenly realised that the dearth of political contact between the two powers might have a negative impact on Mr Reagan's prospects. Accordingly, when I flew out in the second half of September 1984 as head of delegation to the UN General Assembly, an invitation to meet President Reagan was in my pocket.

Accompanied by Deputy Foreign Minister Korniyenko and Soviet ambassador Dobrynin, I had a two-hour talk with the President in the Oval Office of the White House, continuing over lunch in the company of Vice-President George Bush, Secretary of State George Shultz, Defense Secretary Caspar Weinberger, Secretary of the Treasury Donald Regan, and presidential advisers James Baker, Edwin Meese, Robert McFarlane, Michael Deaver and other senior White House and State Department officials.

The conversation was edgy, and of course there was the inevitable confrontation. The President's remarks boiled down to this: 'Virtually all the Soviet Union's plans are designed to destroy the capitalist order in the West. Therefore the USA must arm, so that we're never faced with the choice between surrender or death.'

I objected strongly to this. 'The essence of our political philosophy is this: in the course of historical development, one social order is inevitably replaced by another. Certainly we take the view that the capitalist order will be replaced by the socialist order – we believe this in the way people believe the sun will rise tomorrow morning – but this process will occur quite naturally, as a result of historical development. We do not believe in political or military intimidation, and nobody should accuse us of trying to change America's social structure by force, nor that of any other country. We have no such plans and never have had.'

The President then put forward the familiar theory that the

Soviet Union's military effort represented a danger for the West.

I asked him: 'After the war, when the guns had fallen silent, who was it who set up military bases all round the world? It was the United States. Our efforts to get them dismantled and to start disarmament were unsuccessful. The USA blocked our every initiative.

'The USA and its Western allies,' I went on, 'have undertaken a relentless arms build-up. The road they have taken is lined with posters saying: "Give us more guns!" Behind all this lies the clear calculation that the USSR will exhaust its material resources before the USA and therefore will finally be forced to surrender.'

'This, Mr President,' I said, 'will never happen. Of course, the arms race forces us to expend massive material and intellectual resources. But we will hold on. We held on during a war of unprecedented ferocity. Our people showed their iron will and their ability to make do with what they had. We were victorious, despite colossal losses. That is why your hope of gaining military superiority over the USSR is unrealistic. Such plans should be dropped.'

I concluded: 'Our two countries now possess vast reserves of arms. We are both sitting on top of a mountain of nuclear weapons and we keep on inventing new ones. The mountain is growing. One wonders, what happens next? How much more can it grow?'

Having listened to all this, Reagan still defended his administration's arms policy. He even reached into the drawer of a side-table next to his armchair, and took out some diagrams which purported to show that Soviet arms were growing at a faster rate than US arms. Certainly he included high-flown words about contact, meetings, dialogue, but there was no content in them, nor even a hint that he might change his country's political course in a more positive direction.

Even so, it seemed to me that, all things considered, the US President must have realised that attempts to put pressure on the Soviet Union would get him nowhere.

At a later stage of the discussion, I said to Shultz: 'There are inconsistencies between US declarations of loyalty to the historic agreements made by the anti-Hitler coalition and current American international policy.'

Shultz was much concerned to show that there had been no change in the US position: 'The USA is loyal to its treaty obligations, including the question of European frontiers.'

To which I replied: 'We are pleased to hear that, but where is the practical proof of it? The Soviet Union is zealous in observing past agreements and will continue to be. We're waiting for the Americans to match their words with deeds.'

Like the rest of his team, Reagan was very courteous during the talks. I detected no frostiness, despite the inner tension that they all must have felt. After all, for the last four years the President had been making consistently unfriendly remarks about the USSR. His handshake was firm. During the photo session, he eyed his guests with frank curiosity, and kept fidgeting in his chair.

I was amazed by the number of English long-case clocks there were in the White House. It must be the President's hobby to collect them. A small chamber orchestra played classical music in the room next to where we were given lunch. Nancy Reagan was there to welcome us, but she did not join us for the meal.

The President introduced her to me and I had the impression of an energetic and self-assured woman. We had a brief conversation, the contents of which she quickly relayed to the ubiquitous American newsmen. It appeared in the press in the following form:

'Gromyko arrived with my husband. After we were introduced, he proposed a toast to me. He had cranberry juice, I had soda water. We're both great drinkers! He then turned to me and said: "Is your husband for peace or war?" "He's for peace," I replied. This seemed to surprise him, as he asked: "Are you sure about that?" I replied: "Yes." He then said: "Then why doesn't he accept our proposals?" "What proposals would they be?" I asked. At this point people came over and interrupted us. Then, just before lunch, he came back to me and said: "You should whisper peace in the President's ear at night." "Oh, sure," I said. "But I'll whisper it in yours, too." Gromyko smiled in reply.'

Her account was pretty close to what was said.

The main part in these talks was played by Shultz, who gave most of the official responses both in the Oval Office and at lunch. Weinberger was not present in the Oval Office and was sitting rather to one side at the lunch. Although he tried to involve himself in the conversation with the guests, he fell silent the moment Reagan spoke. Bush sat rather stolidly and did not care to air his views.

A few days later, when we had just completed talks between our delegations, President Reagan suddenly asked me: 'Mr Gromyko, why don't you and I have a little talk on our own, just for a while?'

'Certainly,' I agreed.

We had what might be called a standing conversation.

The President began: 'I want to say in all frankness that I'm doing all I can to find ways to improve relations between the USA and the USSR. I think about it a lot, but nothing happens. I'm trying to understand the reason for this.' He paused, and then went on: 'I think it's the habit of mistrust that has built up between our two nations.'

'Obviously mistrust has indeed built up,' I replied. 'But the real trouble is that Americans ascribe to the Soviet Union all sorts of aggressive plans which we have never had. You even spoke of such plans in the talks that have just ended. Lenin never said capitalism would have to be buried by force. Someone invented the quote, then passed it off on to you, and you repeat it, despite the fact that we have frequently repudiated it.'

Reagan listened in silence. I don't think he had ever tried looking up the source of Lenin's alleged utterance, but he would not have found it if he tried, since it does not exist. Looking at him, I couldn't tell from his face whether he believed me, but I never heard anything further on the matter from the White House.

As for his remarks about seeking ways of improving relations, I said to the President: 'As always, the Soviet Union sincerely wants to co-operate in reducing tension. I am empowered to say that that is the view of the entire Soviet leadership. As for our long-term policies, and relations with the capitalist countries, including the USA, we hold to the principle of peaceful coexistence. We have never planned and we do not now plan to use force against capitalist countries in order to eliminate their social systems. We do believe, however, that in the normal course of social development socialism will win because it is the superior system.'

I expressed the hope that the President would think over what I'd said.

Yet, in our talks after this, neither the President nor any of his representatives ever expressed support for the idea of peaceful coexistence between states having different social systems. When he met General-Secretary Gorbachev in Geneva in 1985 and again in Reykjavík in 1986, both meetings of major significance in our relations, the President still made no statements indicating US commitment to that principle.

Throughout the history of Soviet–US relations, we have dealt with many different administrations. When the American leadership is being realistic, our relations are good and this is reflected beneficially in the world situation. When there is no realism, relations worsen, with a corresponding effect worldwide.

For there to be genuine improvement, there has to be the political will. The USSR has that will. If the Americans can show the same will, many problems which divide us can be settled.

A new course has begun, in my opinion, with the signing of the agreement on eliminating medium- and shorter-range missiles which took place on 8 December 1987. Let us hope this new course is allowed to continue.

18

Diplomats and others

In the whole of my life as a diplomat, only once, in 1952, have I had to put on a tailcoat, or more accurately a morning-coat. Carrying the top hat – which I could not bring myself to put on – I ensconced myself in a spacious horse-drawn carriage, while two gold-braided, top-hatted footmen took up their positions on the footboards. The well-trained horses then drew us slowly through the streets of London, past gawping crowds of Londoners and tourists.

They found it an arresting scene, and so did I – a citizen of the Soviet Union, where we hadn't had kings and noblemen for quite a while, decked out in aristocratic fancy dress, and riding to meet the Queen of England! In accordance with protocol, I was going to Buckingham Palace to present my credentials as Ambassador Extraordinary and Plenipotentiary of the Soviet Union.

I was thinking at that moment of Maxim Litvinov, the first Soviet ambassador to London after the revolution. He had presented himself as accredited to the British working class rather than to the Court of St James, but Lenin had been sharply critical and had ticked him off about it.

These diplomatic anachronisms still survive. In 1986, in order to present his credentials to the Spanish King, the Soviet ambassador to Spain, S.K. Romanovsky, rode through the streets of Madrid in an antique carriage, drawn by several pairs, and escorted by a troop of Mauritanian cavalry in picturesque medieval dress.

We have to coexist with countries which have different social orders from our own. As long as their rules of diplomatic protocol do not offend the dignity of our country or our diplomats personally, why should we not accept them? Moreover, in accepting them we are showing our respect to the country concerned. That is why a Soviet diplomat sometimes wears a morning-coat and carries a top hat, even though everyone knows he would manage perfectly well without them.

Among some of the best-known figures of the Soviet diplomatic service, Georgy Vasilyevich Chicherin was a leading light. Born into an aristocratic family in St Petersburg, he served in the tsarist foreign ministry, joined the revolutionary movement in 1904, went abroad and spent the First World War in London. In the summer of 1917 he was arrested for anti-war agitation and incarcerated in Brixton Prison, by which time he had broken with the Mensheviks and become a Bolshevik. The new Soviet government secured his release in January 1918.

Lenin greatly admired Chicherin's erudition and perceptiveness, and it is therefore not surprising that in March 1918, at an internationally difficult political moment, he appointed him Commissar of Foreign Affairs. Chicherin became a diplomat literally of the Lenin school, working with Lenin and taking orders from him personally.

Lenin himself had been supposed to head the Soviet delegation to the Genoa international conference of 1922, but he was unable to attend and sent Chicherin in his place. A man of outstanding intellect and considerable experience in dealing with foreigners, at the conference Chicherin ably defended the interests of the young Soviet state.

On Lenin's instructions Chicherin advanced the thesis of peaceful coexistence and economic co-operation between states with different social orders. Furthermore, at the time of the Genoa conference, at nearby Rapallo, on behalf of Soviet Russia Chicherin concluded a treaty with capitalist Germany by which they established diplomatic relations and settled their outstanding differences. Lenin regarded this as the 'only correct approach' to relations between states, and went on to link peaceful coexistence with the need for universal disarmament, the first such proposal in human history.

Chicherin was also responsible for concluding treaties with Turkey, Iran and Afghanistan. He remained Foreign Commissar until 1930 and died in 1936.

His successor, Maxim Maximovich Litvinov, whose real name

was Max Vallakh, held the post until he was replaced by V.M. Molotov in May 1939, and was sent as ambassador to the USA in December 1941.

During Molotov's visit to Washington in June 1942, I was struck by a conversation between him and Litvinov while the three of us were driving to the Appalachian mountains. We were talking about the French and the British, and Molotov sharply criticised their pre-war policy, which was aimed at pushing Hitler into war against the USSR. In other words, he voiced the official party line. Litvinov disagreed. This had been the prime reason for his removal from the post of Foreign Commissar in 1939, yet here he was, still stubbornly defending Britain and France's refusal to join the Soviet Union and give Hitler a firm rebuff before he could make his fateful attack upon the USSR. Despite having been relieved of his post for such views, Litvinov continued to defend them in front of Molotov, and consequently in front of Stalin.

It was strange listening to someone who appeared not to have noticed Munich and its consequences – Munich, which our party and people had roundly condemned and which remained a symbol of treachery in international affairs.

I was in no doubt that Molotov would report the argument to Stalin when he got back to Moscow, and that as a result Litvinov's prospects as ambassador to the USA were dim. And so they turned out to be. I replaced him as ambassador less than a year later.

Among other distinguished members of the first Soviet government was Alexandra Mikhailovna Kollontai. Born into an intelligentsia family of Baltic origin, she had been swept into the revolutionary movement. She fluctuated somewhat in her political affiliations, moving from Menshevism to Bolshevism in the middle of the war, but she was spotted by Lenin and in 1919 was put in charge of the section for work among women. From 1923 to 1952, however, she was to be a diplomat, first as ambassador to Norway – the first woman ambassador in the world – then briefly as envoy to Mexico, and then as ambassador to Sweden.

She was remarkably successful, considering that not all countries could get accustomed to the idea of having a great socialist nation's embassy in their capital city. But monarchies and bourgeois republics got used to this in the end, and the fact that the Soviet Union was represented by a woman, and a woman moreover who had known Lenin, eased Kollontai's task. A witty woman with a sharp tongue, she could handle herself expertly in debate, and in several languages.

I met her in Moscow in 1949–50. She was ill by then, paralysed and in a wheelchair. My family and I were staying in the same rest home as she, and we got on very well. For me, as a relatively young man of forty, she was the living history of the revolution, a party fighter who had talked and corresponded with Lenin, and for that alone she deserved respect.

I did what I could to make things easier for her. Although she was by then only a pale shadow of her former ebullient self, I particularly remember one of our conversations. I had asked her about Mexico but she did not have much to say about her work there: she was more talkative about her time in Sweden, where she had spent the last fifteen years.

'Just think, Andrei Andreevich,' she said, 'I was once declared *persona non grata* in Sweden and thrown out by the police and local security. It happened before the revolution, when our party was still underground and Russian social democrats were feared like the plague in some capitals. But the years went by and suddenly the Soviet government was asking for approval as ambassador for the same Kollontai who had once been chucked out of Stockholm. Either the Swedes didn't remember my name, or they thought it was someone else, or they knew perfectly well but didn't want to spoil their relations with the Soviet Union over me, I just don't know. It was probably the last reason, but anyway they gave their approval and I got in, and there I was being received by the King, the Prime Minister and the Foreign Minister. Anyway, I had frequent cause to remind the Swedes not to be provoked by the Nazis into breaking their neutrality, which in fact they did several times. I never stopped thinking of our people, there across the Baltic, dying . . .'

At that moment she broke down and wept. Sitting in her wheelchair, she looked such a frail old lady. I tried to console her and I was sorry I had asked her questions that had clearly aroused painful memories.

Unquestionably, V.M. Molotov occupies a special place in the history of Soviet diplomacy. While continuing to hold a series of senior party jobs, he took over as Foreign Commissar from Litvinov in 1939, was succeeded as Foreign Minister – the title of the post of commissar having been changed to minister in 1946 – by A. Ya. Vyshinsky in 1949, and then held the post again from 1953 to 1956. He was in effect second in command throughout the Stalin period.

Of course, the main guidelines of foreign policy were determined by the Politburo, but even there Stalin's opinion was decisive, and he left Molotov responsible for dealing with a number of issues involving other countries. In the USA, Britain and other Western countries Molotov was regarded as a 'hardliner' in foreign policy, but in fact he was no harder than the party and its Central Committee.

Although it is true that Stalin's attitude to him was uneven, as Stalin's right-hand man at the wartime and post-war Allied conferences Molotov exercised a considerable degree of influence on Stalin.

Molotov's high position can best be explained by the fact that he was an old revolutionary, an able man with an enormous capacity for work and for organisation. On occasion, admittedly, his passion for organising things took curious forms, verging on the obsessive. For instance, once, when he had been working on a document for some hours, he suddenly announced: 'I'm going next door to rest for thirteen minutes.' He went out and thirteen minutes later, on the dot, he returned looking fresh and resumed his work.

At times he would appear to lose his temper and let fly at his assistants, but everyone knew that in fact the scene was contrived and that he'd have well-thought-out reasons for it. A real failing, however, was his excessive conventionality in the preparation of a document. For example, if there was an opportunity to formulate an idea in a fresh way, and if it looked in the least unusual to Molotov, let alone unprecedented, he absolutely refused to allow it. I experienced this more than once myself. It had nothing to do with his severe sense of prose style or literary form: it was simply Molotov being unreasonable.

He died – a member of the Communist Party – on 8 November 1986 at the age of ninety-six.

Western statesmen and journalists sometimes ask Soviet representatives to explain how it was that communists like Molotov, Malenkov, Kaganovich or Bulganin, who once held great power, could be expelled from the party.

I don't think the question is difficult to answer. The party has given its own account of these people's activities. Both the party and the people have been told the reasons for taking such action. As a member of the Central Committee myself, I both heard the speeches of Stalin's former comrades-in-arms and voted for the severe decisions taken in regard to their anti-party activities. I shall illustrate this with one example.

When it became clear that the supply of grain required new measures to improve the situation, the overwhelming majority of the Central Committee came to the conclusion that some improvement could be achieved by bringing into agricultural production the virgin lands of the east, primarily in Kazakhstan. Molotov came out against this idea most vehemently. His argument was simple to the point of being primitive.

'Why plough virgin land,' he said, 'when we can raise the productivity of the fields in the European region of the country?'

As we know, the problem has not been solved even to this day, though much is being done. As it was, even in bad years, grain from the virgin lands made substantial contributions to the country's granaries. Molotov nevertheless stuck to his position.

It should also be noted that under Stalin the people in the leadership on whom he relied were in many cases also guilty of the harsh oppression of innocent people, communist and non-party alike. Sometimes their own families became victims, but that does not excuse them for having been involved in the deaths of countless innocent Soviet people.

Did any of these characters ever express sincere repentance for the past? Not a bit of it. They all welcomed the verdict of the court on Beria and applauded Khrushchev's speech at the 20th Party Congress of 1956. But was that enough? Of course not.

Therefore the removal of Stalin's former accomplices from top posts was justified, as was their expulsion from the ranks of Lenin's party. True, Molotov, whose wife had been exiled and who was therefore himself to some extent an object of repression, was, at his own request to the Politburo, reinstated later as a member of the party, but that magnanimous gesture changes little in the assessment of his guilt in the period of Stalinism and the positions he took on economic policy.

Throughout my working life in Moscow, two enigmas remained unsolved for me, as for millions of other people: L.P. Beria and

A. Ya. Vyshinsky. Beria was Minister of the Interior and head of the NKVD, and Vyshinsky was Chief Procurator.

About Beria I knew mostly what I had read in the press. I heard about the enormous influence he exerted on Stalin, and I saw him when he attended Politburo meetings or bigger occasions, but there were episodes which gave me the impression that he was not all that the papers made him out to be.

It was a short time after Stalin's death, during the so-called 'interregnum' of March to September 1953, when the Politburo (or Presidium as it was called between 1952 and 1966) consisted of only ten people, and a new General Secretary (at that time called First Secretary) had not yet been found. Sessions were being chaired by Malenkov and were no longer held in Stalin's study. At one meeting when the Politburo was discussing the question of East Germany, the discussion was getting quite lively. Malenkov was in the chair with Molotov and Beria alongside him. On either side of the table were Kaganovich, Mikoyan and Bulganin. Vyshinsky and I, as Deputy Foreign Ministers, had been summoned that day, since the GDR was on the agenda.

Malenkov opened the discussion, pointing out the importance of the GDR, since it was in the forefront of our negotiations with the Western powers. Everyone agreed that the time was ripe for a serious debate. The GDR itself was of course not represented in the room, but most of those present said their piece, and in quite precise terms. It soon became plain that, although not everyone held the same point of view, the differences were not over matters of principle.

Until suddenly Beria spoke up: 'The GDR? What does it amount to, this GDR? It's not even a real state. It's only kept in being by Soviet troops, even if we do call it the "German Democratic Republic".'

We were all shocked by such political crudeness, and that he could say this about a socialist country in a dismissive tone and with a sneer on his face.

The first reproof came from Molotov. Speaking firmly, he said: 'The Democratic Republic is in the same position as the Federal Republic. I strongly object to such an attitude to a friendly country. It has the right to exist as an independent state.'

Then Malenkov spoke. Although his tone was milder than Molotov's, there was no mistaking the fact that he did not share Beria's point of view. Bulganin, Kaganovich and Mikoyan all agreed with Molotov and Malenkov and expressed warm support for the GDR. The discussion then came to a close. Beria was confounded.

Two days later Vyshinsky expressed his satisfaction with the outcome of the meeting. He said to me: 'You can see what it means to be a member of the Politburo! Their minds don't work like other people's.' And, smiling, he raised both hands above his ears with the palms turned out, as if to say, those people have got much bigger brains than ordinary mortals.

Beria's dismissive judgement of the GDR was enough to get him kicked out of the leadership. His position reflected a hostile and insulting attitude to the first workers' state on German soil. This sort of thing happened with him more than once, and Beria was finally exposed in full later that year, when he was arrested, tried and shot.

The other enigma was Stalin's chief prosecutor, Vyshinsky himself. He had been appointed First Deputy Foreign Minister – or Commissar, as the post was called until 1943 – in 1940. I met him for the first time only after the war, though I saw him frequently later on. What struck me especially was his excellent education and his ability to express his thoughts in a literate manner, without ever having to search for a word. It must be said, though, that he often abused this talent and lost a great deal by it. As Foreign Minister, Molotov treated him on the whole politely, though he did not share his point of view on a number of diplomatic issues, as I observed many times.

Staff at the Foreign Ministry did not discuss the purge trials of the 1930s; as diplomats, we avoided the subject. However, many of us often saw Vyshinsky sitting plunged in thought. What he was thinking about I did not know. Only later did I realise that Stalin knew his chief prosecutor's biography down to the last detail, and he had plenty to think about.

When I piece together what I know about Vyshinsky during the Stalin period and the trials of the so-called 'enemies of the people', I come to the conclusion that Vyshinsky could not have been a true communist, but that he was a leftover from an alien political world. He had once been an active Menshevik and in the summer of 1917 had been involved in the Provisional Government's search for Lenin, who was hiding in Finland. It was not so much that he had been a Menshevik as that he was a careerist without honour or conscience.

Speaking for myself, I found him a sinister figure. Stalin obviously needed him for his own power-seeking purposes: he used Vyshinsky to create the semblance of legal process in order to cover up the criminality of his mass repressions. Vyshinsky's job was to drown the truth in a sea of lies and half-truths, using foul and violent methods against his victims in the dock, and mocking those lawyers who attacked the legal principle he worked by, namely that an accused person's confession was in all cases sufficient grounds for conviction. This principle, widely applied at that time, encouraged illegal methods of investigation, coercion and even refined techniques of physical and psychological torture.

For Vyshinsky, confession was 'the queen of justice', as he was fond of saying, and it did not matter how it was obtained. A simple argument followed from this: if there was a confession, the judges could hand down a sentence and the accused was doomed from the start. Vyshinsky of course knew what depths of criminality lay beneath such court procedure, but with dumb loyalty he continued to serve the chief architect of the repressions and the entire machinery of terror.

I am one of the few people left who had the opportunity to observe Vyshinsky at close quarters. He was harsh and, it seemed, made to be the sort of lawyer who can cause people pain, especially if it gained him a pat on the back from his superior. In 1940, after he had completed his dirty business as Chief Procurator, Stalin transferred him to foreign affairs and in 1949 he became Foreign Minister. The repressions still continued, but he was now in a different job.

Some time later, I was present during a telephone conversation he had with Beria. As soon as he heard Beria's voice Vyshinsky leapt respectfully out of his chair. The conversation itself also presented an unusual picture: Vyshinsky cringed like a servant before his master. It was clear now just how obsequiously he had carried out any 'legal' sentence Beria chose to demand during Vyshinsky's time as Chief Procurator of the USSR.

On another occasion, when I went into his office one evening for our usual discussion of current events in foreign affairs, I found him sitting at his desk in a state of near oblivion. His face was flabby, and he looked tired and tense. When he saw me, he stared at me frenziedly, as if he was expecting some appalling news. I actually wondered if something terrible had happened to him. He half rose, obviously still expecting me to tell him something.

'What's the matter?' I asked him.

He replied, 'I tell you, I'm only theoretically alive. I just get through the day. Well, at least that's something, thank God.'

For the first time I realised that the powerful machine he was part of threatened him too. Tactfully, I made no comment about exactly what might be tormenting him – I knew nothing, anyway – and he quietly pulled himself together. We started to talk about ministry business.

In itself this scene may seem insignificant, but it does suggest that people who used the terror for personal advancement were themselves being held hostage by Stalin, from his seat at the top of the pyramid of power and lawlessness.

Unsurprisingly, Vyshinsky was totally thoughtless of others. I remember an episode in this connection. I had arrived home after work at four o'clock in the morning. Senior officials in those days thought it was clever to sit at their desks until late into the small hours. Stalin did his work at night, and all the other leaders simply followed suit. But Stalin did not begin his working day at nine in the morning, like everyone else. He slept all day and worked at night, starting at one or two o'clock in the morning.

As soon as I got in, I fell asleep. Suddenly the phone rang. I struggled awake and lifted the receiver.

'This is Vyshinsky speaking.'

He launched into an issue we had just been talking about. I reminded him: 'But we went over that together not two hours ago.'

In fact I knew very well that he had gone home for a three-hour nap the previous evening and then returned to work. But he didn't apologise: instead he flew into a rage at my discreet rebuke.

Another sign of his ugly nature was that when he summoned an assistant he would generally open on a high-pitched note of accusation, if not downright abuse. He spoke like this even to ambassadors and envoys. He took the view that you had to start by throwing a scare into the man and then continue the discussion in an atmosphere of fear. I knew that he did this to emulate Beria.

On one occasion, when he had just reprimanded one of our own ambassadors in the most abusive fashion, I lost patience and said, outwardly cool, but furious inside: 'Clearly, you lost your temper. My friendly advice would be for you to talk to diplomats in a calmer way. After all, they *are* working for the legitimate interests of the Soviet state.'

Instead of accepting my counsel, Vyshinsky made it plain that he had no intention of changing his ways. 'I believe in keeping people on edge,' he exploded.

After that, he harboured ill feelings towards me which would emerge at the most unexpected moments. One such episode that I was told about later is worth recounting.

During a discussion on current policies at a meeting of the Politburo, Vyshinsky suddenly announced: 'My assistants are nearly all too young. They haven't had the necessary experience. Take Gromyko, for instance. I'm not criticising his work, but he certainly never took part in the fierce struggle against Trotskyism.'

He was referring to the mid-1920s, and one of the Politburo members asked: 'How was he supposed to do that at the age of, what, sixteen?'

Everyone waited to see who was going to speak next. It was Molotov: 'Yes, he could hardly have been more than seventeen at the time.'

Vyshinsky said nothing. Molotov was of course right, and everyone smiled, including Stalin.

Vyshinsky had never studied diplomacy: Molotov always got the upper hand in discussions and arguments, and in time their relations became severely strained. Vyshinsky's temper and lack of experience were especially marked when we were in New York for a session of the UN General Assembly. The senior members of the Soviet, Ukrainian and Belorussian delegations were meeting at our UN delegation's country house at Glencoe, some thirty miles from New York, to discuss an accusation by some Western powers that the Soviet Union would not accept NATO's proposals on arms controls because it did not want disarmament.

Molotov, who was head of delegation, expressed his view: 'We must give a reasoned reply, which should show that our disagreement with the West is not over whether or not to allow controls. We do insist, however, that any controls be applied equally to both the USSR and the NATO countries. We have to make that clear.'

Those present at the meeting – Manuilsky, Kiselev, Zorin, Novikov, Sobolev and Galunsky – all agreed with Molotov that the Soviet position had to be explained with patience and firmness. Everyone, that is, except Vyshinsky, who thought we should issue a brief statement pointing out simply that the West was engaging in slander. None of us could agree with him; when he realised he was isolated, he suddenly jumped up from his chair and strode out of the room, slamming the door behind him. Like most of the others in the room, I was dumbfounded. Molotov, however, did not so much as raise his head, but continued the discussion as if nothing had happened. Thirty minutes later, Vyshinsky reappeared, silently resumed his seat and sat through-out the rest of the meeting like a statue. Molotov, still giving the impression of not even having noticed him, calmly went on chairing the discussion, which was mostly being conducted by Manuilsky and myself.

Vyshinsky was involved in another incident in the early 1950s, on the occasion of Zhou Enlai's official visit to the USSR. He hosted an official dinner organised in the Chinese leader's honour in a house belonging to the Foreign Ministry. At the table, friendly conversations were struck up covering a wide range of topics and everything seemed orderly and relaxed.

After dinner, Vyshinsky and I and two other Soviet officials took Zhou Enlai, the Chinese ambassador and a couple of their diplomats into the drawing-room. When we had found our seats, I noticed that Vyshinsky, who usually had plenty to say, simply wasn't speaking. Ten minutes passed. Suddenly he got up and, without a word to anyone, headed for the main staircase and the exit. Everyone was taken aback, especially Zhou Enlai. Even I was caught unawares, but as I was next in seniority it was up to me to lead the conversation.

I apologised to Zhou Enlai: 'Apparently Vyshinsky isn't feeling well.'

'Yes, it looks like it,' he replied.

Conversation continued, the guests evidently unconcerned by what had transpired, and all in all it hadn't amounted to much.

However, about half an hour after I had got home, Stalin telephoned me. 'What happened tonight to Vyshinsky?'

I described exactly what had happened.

Stalin asked, 'Had he been drinking? Was he drunk?'

I replied, 'From what I could see, sitting as I was right opposite him, he drank only one glass of white wine, and I don't think anyone could have got drunk from that amount.'

'So why he did run out and cut short the meeting with Zhou Enlai?'

'I don't think he was drunk. He was steady on his feet.'

'But the doctors say he's an alcoholic,' Stalin remarked.

'Then maybe he'd had a drink before dinner.'

There was a pause while Stalin was thinking. 'Oh well,' he said, 'all right,' and put down the receiver.

Why had I protected Vyshinsky? No doubt because I couldn't be sure whether or not he had had a lot to drink – I simply hadn't noticed. It was hardly for me to check up on how much a minister was drinking. I had seen bottles and glasses on the table, but clear vodka in a clear glass is easily missed. I therefore acted on the principle of the presumption of innocence, the opposite of Vyshinsky's approach as prosecutor in the purge trials. As for Stalin's phone call, I never mentioned it to Vyshinsky.

Changes were made in the Foreign Ministry after Stalin's death. Molotov became Foreign Minister again, and Vyshinsky was demoted to First Deputy Minister – with something more remote in mind for the future.

One day Molotov came back from the Politburo in a highly excited state and summoned all his assistants: Vyshinsky and myself, as his First Deputies, and two others. This always happened when the minister had been charged with reporting a particularly important decision of the party's top body; he would normally inform his senior staff before telling the press.

What we were told on this occasion, however, was utterly unexpected. Molotov announced: 'Beria has just been arrested!'

I looked at Vyshinsky, who was sitting next to me. He seemed to have collapsed, with his arms on the green-baize table and his head resting on them awkwardly. He was plainly in a state of shock.

Molotov briefly described Beria's arrest: 'He was taken straight from the Politburo meeting into the next room under guard. The rest of us remained at the table and did our best to carry on with the session.'

Vyshinsky listened to this without getting up from his chair. It took him a while to get over the news. Finally he straightened up, but he uttered not a word for the rest of the meeting. Vyshinsky died two years after Stalin.

Readers may be wondering whether a cloud ever hung over my own head during those years, when, seeking to advance their own careers, liars and provocateurs were making obscene slanders in a flood of letters and reports. Was there never a single such filthy note ever sent about me? Well, yes there was.

As soon as I was appointed ambassador to London in 1952, I started to read as much as I could about Britain, studying many documents, official and unofficial, in the Foreign Ministry archives. I also read recent despatches from the London embassy, among them a letter from the chargé d'affaires, giving an account of the economic situation in Britain. It was brief and dealt mainly with basic issues, but, as was customary, it provided a list of the sources used, including books and periodicals published in the British Isles.

I made a list of some of the titles that I intended to obtain on arrival in my new post and gave it to the diplomatic couriers who were travelling with us to London. In due course, some of the titles arrived at the embassy, and turned out to be very useful, containing as they did material on both Britain and the USA. I was gathering data at the time for a book I intended writing on the export of American capital. It was published later in Moscow and submitted to the academic council when I defended my doctoral dissertation in economics at Moscow University.

After I had been at my new job for only a matter of a few months, I was summoned to Moscow to go over a number of issues and when we had completed our business, Vyshinsky said, 'By the way, a report on you has come in from your embassy about some secret materials that you had sent by the diplomatic bag to London, addressed to you personally.'

I was amazed. He went on, 'You realise, of course, where the report has ended up. You'd better write a letter to Stalin, explaining.'

I told Vyshinsky precisely what the report referred to and I had the distinct impression that he regarded its author as a loathsome creature. He nevertheless said, 'Still, you must write that explanation.'

'I will,' I said curtly. I did so soon after.

Up to this day, I still do not know whether my letter was ever dealt with, and, if it was, what reaction it provoked. As a matter of fact, I never gave it another thought. The main point I want to underline here is that the whole business did not cause me the least concern. Looking back now, however, and knowing what I do about Stalin's repressive activities, I should have realised then that such a report, however ludicrous, could lead to dire consequences for myself. But I felt completely safe.

The question is, why? First of all, because I believed that Stalin himself, or the people who worked close to him, would have realised at once that the affair had been blown up by the ignorant, unprincipled person who had initiated the slander. Secondly, I was still feeling the effect of what I had learned from Charles Bohlen, US ambassador to Moscow: namely, that Stalin had told Roosevelt at Tehran that he was highly satisfied with my work as ambassador in Washington.

We know now that Stalin was capable of making reassuring promises to people and even of expressing his respect, and then treating them in the harshest way. But in those days, most of us were not aware that he had these diabolical qualities.

A diplomat abroad sometimes faces unexpected situations requiring an instant response. This happened to me when the Soviet Union launched the first spacecraft. I was at a diplomatic reception in New York when a bunch of newspaper correspondents suddenly burst in noisily. They were all demanding to know where the Soviet representative was: 'Where's Gromyko?'

I was quickly surrounded by a dense crowd of journalists, all either photographing me with their flash cameras or bombarding me with the same question: 'Mr Gromyko, what can you tell us about the sputnik?'

In fact, I knew nothing, since I'd been at the reception when the radio announced the news, but of course I couldn't let on. Instead I tried to glean what information I could from the questions that were being shouted at me. As I stood there, turning this way and that in front of the crowd of photographers, I learned that Moscow had just announced the launch of the first ever artificial space satellite. Keeping as cool as possible, I told the newsmen: 'I regard this as a great achievement by Soviet science and technology, and by the Soviet people as a whole.'

'How long has the USSR been working on this?'

'When did you hear about the launch?'

'How long will it stay up?'

The questions came thick and fast, most of them requiring an immediate reply. I gave them the impression that I knew more than I was telling them. Then one of them asked: 'And when will the Soviets launch a man into space?'

I answered this by saying: 'When that happens it will be announced straight away.'

I had no idea that it would happen in only four years' time, or that Yuri Gagarin would be that man.

It was in New York that I got to know Yuri Gagarin. He was at the peak of his fame, everyone knew about him and countries from all over the world were inviting him to visit them. By that time, space flights had been accomplished also by Titov, Bykovsky and Tereshkova. Yuri Gagarin and Valentina Tereshkova, accompanied by General N.P. Kamanin, arrived in New York from Mexico in October 1963 and stayed a mere two days. Their names were on all the front pages. The United Nations Secretary-General U Thant had invited them to visit the UN headquarters.

At a crowded and very lively reception held for them by the Soviet UN delegation, I discreetly asked the cosmonauts: 'What about the two of you making a speech at the UN General Assembly during the debate on banning the launch of objects carrying nuclear weapons in space?'

'Well, I don't know, Andrei Andreevich,' Gagarin muttered diffidently. 'It *is* the General Assembly, after all.'

'There's nothing to be afraid of,' I said. 'Your speeches can be short. You can both sort out your ideas tonight. I'll help you.'

I could see they were both somewhat alarmed at my suggestion. Next day a small lunch was given for them by the Soviet UN delegation. The dozen or so of us round the table were lavishing congratulations on both guests of honour, who thanked us modestly.

Then, when someone made a particularly ecstatic speech, Gagarin said: 'It was not me, but our country that has been honoured by my flight.'

'There's a diplomat for you,' General Kamanin remarked.

Someone once joked that Gagarin had not been alone in space because he always had his smile with him, and it was no exaggeration. Whoever picked him to be the first man in space made a brilliant choice: Gagarin wasn't just a strong, brave, decisive, heroic figure; he was also the perfect diplomat. I was able to confirm what I had read in the press about his being an interesting conversationalist. He was ready to talk on many topics, but when the subject of space travel came up everyone else fell silent and listened to the man who had looked at Earth through the window of a sputnik.

That day, the cosmonauts' arrival at the UN headquarters building was greeted by a blaze of lights from the cameras of

press reporters, TV crews and tourists. Accompanied by the UN
Assistant Secretary-General, V.P. Suslov, we took them to the
Soviet delegation's seats in the General Assembly.

When the chairman, Venezuela's ambassador to the UN, Carlos
Sosa Rodríguez, opened the session, he announced: 'We have here
today the two Soviet cosmonauts, Colonel Yuri Gagarin and
Valentina Tereshkova.'

The public galleries were full of journalists and spectators who
all started applauding.

'I invite the Soviet cosmonauts to sit in the Assembly chairman's
and Secretary-General's seats,' Sosa Rodríguez said.

The whole audience rose and cheered as Gagarin and Tereshkova
took their places alongside the top officials. 'Speech! Speech!' they
called out. 'Let them speak!'

Valentina Tereshkova spoke first. She gave a short speech,
describing how her country was sending people into space in
order to carry out peaceful research for the good of mankind.
Gagarin's speech was equally short and was followed by a long
ovation.

Then, surrounded by reporters and cameramen, the cosmonauts
were shown over the building, stopping to give their autographs
and shake hands every step of the way. They were similarly
mobbed as they made a hurried visit to the Security Council. It
was then time for the press conference.

I don't remember another occasion when there were so many
TV, radio and newspapermen present: the room was packed.
Among the questions and answers were the following.

'Do you think American–Soviet co-operation in space is a
possibility?'

'Yes, it is possible,' Gagarin replied, 'and it can take place
through the exchange of scientific information, by creating an
international system of communication and tracking, by giving
help to cosmonauts when they land in other countries, by joint
study of meteorology and in many other ways.'

'Does the appearance of Soviet navy ships in parts of the Pacific
mean another spacecraft is about to be launched?'

'Better rely on Tass to tell you if a spacecraft has been launched,
not navy ships.'

'What do you think of the resolution that is now under debate
in the UN on banning the launch of nuclear weapons in space?'

'I would be happy to see it passed, and I know I speak for all

Soviet cosmonauts. It is very important for us. A ban on nuclear testing in space and on the launch of objects carrying nuclear weapons would eliminate the risk of radiation and the threat to space travel. Nuclear weapons in space would hang like a sword of Damocles which could fall at any time. We welcome the proposal that has been tabled by the Soviet Union.'

At that very moment, the General Assembly was voting to ban the launching of objects carrying nuclear weapons in space. As Gagarin told well-wishers when he heard the news: 'We accept this gift from the UN with pleasure.'

During the memorable official visit of Khrushchev to the USA in September 1959, I spent virtually every day in the company of the writer Mikhail Sholokhov, who was a member of our delegation. The author of *And Quiet Flows the Don* had been recognised as a major writer while he was still relatively young, and by now he was world famous.

'Are you getting ideas for your writing here in America, Mikhail Alexandrovich?' I asked him one day.

'I don't think so,' he said. 'It isn't relevant to my work and won't add anything. My world is the Don, my home country, my village and towns. That's where I was born and grew up and I'm tied to it for the rest of my life. This is an interesting trip, but I don't propose to write about it.'

He had set himself the aim of getting to know American culture, but very little of it had been included in the programme.

One day he said to me: 'The Americans have achieved a lot in the sphere of technology, and anyone involved in it or owning a piece of it can become a millionaire. They seem to grow like mushrooms after warm rain. But what I've seen of their culture so far seems like so much light entertainment. Where's the true humanistic culture that can meet the people's needs? It can't be the Can-Can we saw when we were in Hollywood, surely? They should have been ashamed . . .'

Indeed, during our visit to the Twentieth Century Fox studios in Hollywood, a group of half-naked females had been made to cavort in front of us, and both they and we had felt distinctly awkward.

While we were there, Sholokhov had an acerbic conversation with the actor Charlton Heston. Obviously wishing to please the

Soviet writer, the actor said: 'You know, I've read extracts of some of your books.'

To which Sholokhov replied with a wry grin: 'I'm most grateful to you. When your films are shown in my country, I'll be sure to go and see some extracts.'

Sholokhov, having spent one of the last days of the trip watching television, came to the conclusion: 'If you sat in front of their TV long enough, you'd become an idiot.' Of the trip in general, he said: 'I don't know about high politics, which is your business, but, as far as culture is concerned, we have little to learn from the Americans.'

To which I replied: 'It's pretty much the same with high politics.'

Our dacha outside Moscow was next door to the Alexandrovs'. He was the film director, Grigory Alexandrov, and she was Lyubov Orlova, the song-and-dance star of films that still draw big audiences, are shown on television and are regarded by present-day film-makers as having laid the foundation for the Soviet film musical.

Alexandrov once told me about the filming of *The Battleship Potemkin*. 'I was co-director,' he said. 'When we got to the final scene, where the sailors have to throw their officers overboard, it was autumn, the water was cold, and the actors who were playing the officers refused to go into the water. So I put on an officer's uniform myself and got them to film me being thrown over the side. Then we did the same thing from another part of the ship, and so on, until every one of the officers who was supposed to be thrown over, according to the script, had been, and every one of them was me.'

He also told me about the filming of the first Soviet musical, *The Happy Children*, and about the censorship difficulties they'd had. 'It was 1934 and a number of people, including even some famous writers and poets, had attacked the film.'

'How did you manage to get it released, then? Who helped you?' I wanted to know.

'At first, Maxim Gorky,' he replied. 'We took the film to him in the country where he was resting. He got all the people of the village together and we ran the film. Everyone enjoyed it enormously, and Gorky suggested we show it to Stalin. He even arranged it himself.'

'What happened then?'

'Stalin invited the Politburo to view it with him. They all turned up at the State Film Industry Board on Gnezdnikov Street. This was before the Central Committee had its own viewing-room. The chairman of the board was Boris Shumyatsky, and before the screening he said to me: "I'm only going to show them two parts. You sit next door in the cutting-room. If anyone wants to see any more, tell them you're still working on it and you don't want to show it before it's finished. Got it?" It was his way of raising the film's value. We ran the two parts, but then Stalin said, "Show the rest of it." Shumyatsky objected: "The director still wants to do some editing." Stalin insisted, so Shumyatsky came to me and said: "You're wanted in court, better go in there." I went into the viewing-room and announced, "I think the film needs more work done on it", but they weren't in a mood to discuss the point. "Show it!" I was told. I gave the cans to the operator and, when the film was over, Stalin said: "It's a very jolly film. I felt I'd had a month's holiday. It would be useful to show it to all the workers and collective farmers." Then he added: "And take it away from the director. He might spoil it."'

I have never been a sports addict, but neither have I been indifferent to it. As children, we used to play the ancient Russian game of lapta, which is somewhat reminiscent of American baseball: you hit the ball with a bat and run to a boundary fifty metres away, and if you can hit the ball far enough, you try to get there and back, making a 'home' run. The team that can get all its members to the boundary and back without a loss is the winner and has the right to start the new game.

Lapta was played in different ways in my childhood. I can still see the twisting body of a boy throwing me a tricky ball. For such traditional games to flourish once more, every village would need at least one enthusiast, if not several, and it is not very likely that enough could be found to breathe new life into the old game; at any rate there are none in sight at the moment.

American baseball is a much more complicated game. It is an entire industry, attracting tens of thousands of spectators. In itself, it is a beautiful game, in that nobody gets hurt. Like soccer, it is also a democratic game, since the gear is not too expensive.

Boxing, in my opinion, is at the opposite end of the scale from baseball. What memories I have of it! I once went with Bernard Baruch to watch the legendary Joe Louis fight Billy Conn. Louis was black and Conn was white. I think the difference in skin colour raised the passions of the enormous crowd at New York's Madison Square Garden, where we watched the match.

Right from the start, I didn't like what I saw, either in the hall or in the ring. Everyone was smoking and there was a lot of shouting and screaming. When Louis landed a punch on Conn's body, with the loud thwack of leather, some of the women would jump up and down with delight. Others, when the figures were really swapping punches, would cover their faces, though there weren't too many in this squeamish category.

I glanced at Baruch and saw that his face was calm and that he showed no particular emotion. Then I thought to myself that, as he was hard of hearing, the noise wouldn't count for much, anyway. Guessing my thoughts, he gave me a sly look and pointed to his hearing-aid.

He asked me: 'Well, how do you like all this?'

Not wishing to offend my host, I said: 'It's all very interesting and very noisy.'

'Strength, skill and willpower,' he said, 'that's what it's all about.' Then he asked me suddenly, 'Who's going to win?'

'Joe Louis, I think.'

For some reason, Baruch made no response, but sat in silence, his eyes glued to the sweaty bodies of the contestants. As with all professional fights, there were three or four times as many rounds as in amateur boxing, and during the breaks Baruch and I watched the spectators. Girls and energetic young men were selling cool drinks, beer and brightly coloured packets of peanuts.

While the fight was going on, it occurred to me that boxing was the very antithesis of diplomacy. In diplomacy, there is a healthy tendency to compromise, whereas in sport, and especially in boxing, there is absolutely no such inclination. To land a stronger punch than one's opponent, to knock him off balance, or fell him with a knockout blow, in other words to achieve a one-sided victory – that's what counts in boxing.

Some American statesmen, entering the post-war scene with the atom bomb in their hands, behaved like boxers, as they sought to gain overwhelming supremacy, trying to give the 'one-two' to their former ally, the Soviet Union, in the international arena. There was no sign of their wanting to reach a compromise either, only to score victory. Plainly, they wanted to retain the monopoly of nuclear weapons.

I don't know if such thoughts occurred to Baruch as he watched the fight in which passions were reaching their limit and more and more Joe Louis was getting Billy Conn into the corner. The 'Brown Bomber' won the fight and most of the spectators supported the decision, though a small number weren't too pleased. They booed and tore up their programmes and threw the pieces on the floor. Baruch gave me an enquiring look.

'Very interesting,' I said. 'Force overcomes force, it's quite obvious.'

Many years have passed since those days, but I often think of that fierce duel of two young Americans in the ring and of Baruch's amusing boxer stance the last time we met. It was even somewhat symbolic: the USSR and the USA were in permanent cold war. In the international arena we were fending off Washington's attempts to isolate Moscow by force.

There is another American sport that is also very interesting and similarly very tough, and that is football, though in fact the players use their hands to break through with the leather ball into the opposing team's territory. Feet are only used to score off a penalty. The game is dominated by dirty tactics, occasionally making cripples of the modern gladiators, however well built they may be. It contrasts sharply with such elegant sports as track athletics, basket-ball, volley-ball and, of course, soccer.

During a World Cup not so long ago, the name of Diego Maradona was frequently heard on the air. I don't claim to know very much about soccer – I've watched it occasionally on television – but what I saw when Argentina played England in Mexico simply captivated me. Maradona was the inimitable personification of skill. Watching him get past the barriers of strapping defenders and then scoring was to see a real artist at work. By the laws of gravity there were times when it seemed he must fall, yet he didn't. The powerful legs of the swarthy, tough young athlete kept him up, as he flowed like mercury towards the enemy goal. At times, his inspired face would appear on the screen and it looked almost as if he was in some kind of ecstasy, though never losing his composure – a rare combination!

The press reported that it appeared Maradona had beaten England by a hand-ball, and he was widely criticised for not admitting that he had committed a foul. But I think it is unreasonable to expect a player to judge himself, when the game has been played at such a high pitch of emotion, when he is playing at the very limit of his psychological and physical strength and can easily forget himself. If there was a foul, it was England that suffered, but that was the referee's fault and not Maradona's. Although I could sympathise with the England players, I could not condemn Maradona.

On the same level as Maradona I would place our goalkeeper, Lev Yashin, whose skill and personal bravery I have always admired and whose name was held in high regard abroad in his time.

Born professionals are as rare as large diamonds, but whereas diamonds last for ever, people don't: their skill sparkles for maybe ten or fifteen years. The true athlete gives the game all his strength, strength which would otherwise last him for a minimum of twenty, if not thirty years. It is not surprising that one rarely finds a top athlete who has lived to a great age, so we should not envy them.

As for myself, I made some efforts to play football when I was a student. Another game I tried was volley-ball, and at the amateur, student level I didn't do badly; but I never took it up seriously.

As a spectator I prefer to watch games between different countries. Games between Soviet sides have never interested me. I have never cared which side won or lost, since whatever the result, a Soviet team would win. An international match is something different, and I have always enjoyed everything taking place on the pitch, on the ground or in the hall, when my own country's team was playing. I have never once had my mood or my sleep disturbed by our team losing, however, and sleep has never been my strong point.

On occasion I have been drawn by famous foreign teams, though I have to say that, when my wife and I have been to football matches where no Soviet players are involved, I have tended to watch the spectators, rather than the field. It was especially enjoyable to watch the English spectators during a match.

When I was ambassador in London, we used to make up a small party on our free days and go for a drive out of town: 'studying England' was how we jokingly described our little outings.

We really enjoyed those trips. Barely any distance outside London you would come across a well-kept football pitch, usually in use. Another half-dozen miles and there would be another pitch fully laid out. If we drove out forty or fifty miles, as we did occasionally, we would see at least a dozen such well-kept pitches, and often we would park the car and join the spectators on the most crowded benches to watch the game.

It was a really interesting experience. We frequently came to the conclusion that football and the famous English reserve were incompatible concepts. During the match it seemed as if someone else had taken the Englishman's place, as he kept up a constant, loud commentary, leapt for joy or slapped his neighbour on the knee. Such scenes would be repeated on the stands of any English stadium.

Football matches were not my only taste of English sporting events. I must recount one interesting incident, when my wife and I were invited to attend the Brighton races with the Queen Mother. We accepted with pleasure, even though we did not then – nor do we now – know much about racing.

We duly arrived in Brighton. The meeting began in a lively way and for the first time in our lives we felt something of the excitement of this sport. People and horses seemed to work in harmony with each other, as if they were communicating in a language which only they understood. We were told, 'Now you're going to see the Queen's horse show its paces.'

And they were off. It started wonderfully. The Queen Mother and everyone near her, including her Soviet guests, were getting ready to applaud the Queen's horse and shake Her Majesty by the hand. Then suddenly, at the last fence, her horse fell. The jockey got up slowly. The spectators let out a great sigh, something between an 'Ah!' and an 'Oh!' I did my best to avoid looking at the Queen Mother at that moment. I was upset, too. We heard someone say, 'The Queen Mother has shed some tears,' and we all felt sympathy for her. That was the only time in my life I have been to the races.

Long ago, in my youth, there was a great artist I wanted to meet, someone everyone knew – or, at any rate, everyone who was interested in art. His name was Pablo Picasso.

The most famous artist of his time and an anti-fascist, Picasso decided to remain in Paris when it was occupied by Nazi German troops. This in itself was a brave act of patriotism.

My duties took me to France several times, but a delegation's time is usually entirely occupied, and introducing changes is seldom convenient, since it means either cancelling an official engagement or shortening it. Sometimes accidental meetings do take place, nevertheless; and sometimes, when one side is not expecting the meeting while the other side wants it very much, such meetings are only 'half-accidental'. It was in this way that I 'bumped into' Picasso, for I afterwards discovered that the French protocol department at his request had secretly arranged my meeting with the artistic colossus so that it would look like an accident.

During one of Brezhnev's visits a tour of the Louvre was organised. The Soviet guests, including myself, arrived at the appointed hour and were graciously met by the museum administrators in the biggest gallery on the second floor.

Suddenly a short man bustled his way through the circle of people, thrust his hand first at Brezhnev and then at me and the other comrades, and announced: 'Hello. I'm Pablo Picasso.'

Brezhnev exchanged a few words of greeting with the artist and then Picasso stepped back to let the visitors see the pictures. The party moved on, anxious to reach the part of the gallery where Leonardo's *Mona Lisa* was exhibited.

At that moment Picasso came quickly over to me. 'Monsieur Gromyko, I've seen you before.'

I stopped. I couldn't be sure if he was just being polite or if he really had seen me, but for myself I knew perfectly well I had never met him before. I would not have forgotten that.

Picasso asked, 'I wonder if you would stay for a moment and talk to me?'

'With pleasure,' I replied.

He began: 'You know, I have very little contact with people in the Soviet Union. Members of the intelligentsia drop in on me, but I have no idea what the people in general think about me as an artist.' He continued: 'I do realise that I've never exhibited my pictures in the Soviet Union as I would like to, and that maybe that's my own fault. I wouldn't want a lot of my pictures to disappear for a long time. I like to be able to keep my eye on them. But I do often wonder how to get more exposure in the USSR.'

He was making it clear that he was not satisfied with the exhibition of his work that had been staged in Moscow and

Leningrad in 1956. He was also referring to the Soviet public's unsympathetic attitude to his painting. He was after all the founder of cubism; some of his work had been close to surrealism, and nature was frequently deformed apparently arbitrarily in his painting. He himself had said that his art was not simple and there was no single approach to it.

Picasso was accompanied by three friends, also painters, but neither he nor they went round the museum with the Soviet delegation. I had held back to talk to him, and his three friends remained with us. We were standing by *The Coronation of Josephine* by David, a vast canvas of which an artist's copy hangs at Versailles.

I remarked, 'I like the David paintings here in the Louvre.'

Picasso said, 'David is undeniably one of France's greatest painters.' He paused. 'But times are different now. Painting and art don't stand still.'

I thought he was finding it hard to stand still himself. Despite his age – he was born in 1881 – he was remarkably agile.

He asked me, 'Have you ever been in the Louvre before?'

'I must have been here five or six times,' I replied. It then occurred to me I ought to say I knew his work too. 'But I've also been to the Museum of Modern Art and I've seen your pictures there. I especially liked the portrait of your father. It's in the realistic manner and would appeal to any lover of painting.'

'Yes, I painted that portrait with love. It's in what is now called the neo-classical manner. But a lot of things have changed since then, including myself as an artist.'

Towards the end of the conversation we returned to our earlier topic.

'I know,' he said, 'that I am generally respected in the Soviet Union. Most likely it's my name, rather than my pictures. I do hope the situation will change with time.'

I decided not to go deeper into this subject. It was inappropriate and would have sounded false to try to assure him that his art was widely admired in the Soviet Union.

Regrettably, his work is indeed little appreciated in the USSR, although the artist himself is widely known for having joined the Communist Party during the war, for his famous *Peace Dove*, the emblem of the peace movement, and as a winner of the Lenin Prize for strengthening peace between peoples.

I said goodbye to him, as the other delegates had already reached the exit. After shaking hands, he said: 'Picasso can only be Picasso. He can be nobody else.'

Time passed, and one day, during an official visit to Moscow, the French Minister for External Relations, Roland Dumas, brought me a souvenir from Paris.

'I know you love art,' he said, 'so I've brought you this Picasso. I didn't have the chance before.'

Picasso had died in 1973 and this was a good ten years later. Dumas had brought me the *Peace Dove*, of which Picasso had made repeated copies, and it now hangs in my home, an original of the famous picture, with the number 32 in one corner.

Pasternak's work, too, has appealed to me since my youth. His own verse and prose, and his translations from English, German and French, show him to have been unusually gifted.

I first met him in 1952 at the house of our friend Boris Livanov, the actor. There was a lively company of friends, including the writer Konstantin Fedin, the film director Alexander Dovzhenko and a number of other cultural figures. Everyone was chatting and telling amusing stories, but they would always fall silent when anyone rose to propose a toast. And now it was Pasternak's turn . . .

No one would disagree that he was a striking personality and that he left a deep mark on Soviet literature. I would go further and say that, even if all he had left us were his translations of Shakespeare and Goethe, he would have performed enormous service; but he also translated Shelley, Schiller, Verlaine and many others, and as a poet and novelist he has immortalised his own name.

When he rose to speak that evening, he did not mention his own achievements, even though by that time he had done much for Soviet literature and for his country.

He said, 'I want to underline the great successes of our literature as the literature of socialist realism.'

He named a number of Soviet writers and poets whom he considered to be the pride of Soviet literature, and the burden of his speech was: 'Every writer, whether he has a great talent or not, must have his own personality. No attempt to impose external standards can be justified. They only shackle an artist's inspiration and his ability to depict life and man's inner world.'

Pasternak then proposed a toast to Soviet writers and literature.

Pasternak's novel *Doctor Zhivago* was criticised in the Soviet Union after being published abroad. The circumstances were admittedly unusual, but the criticism itself appeared to be principally in the nature of an official outcry against the author, without any serious argument being advanced against the book itself. The persecution of Pasternak began as a result of Khrushchev's utterly uncalled-for interference in matters of art and literature – a negative feature in the life of that politician. However, writers themselves were committing blunders at the time, as many of them later admitted. Some openly attacked Pasternak, while others remained silent. The whole business was a blatant injustice and the poet was not protected from it as he should have been.

I remember Boris Livanov coming to see me at our dacha at Vnukovo. In a melancholy mood, he told us how hard Pasternak was taking all the harsh criticism. 'Why are they doing it? Pasternak is a *Soviet* poet, after all!'

I did not know what to say. I couldn't see any common sense in what was going on myself. Owing to my diplomatic work I had not yet managed to read *Doctor Zhivago*, and when I did so later I found nothing wrong with it. Injustice always wounds, sometimes seriously, and it wounded Boris Pasternak, an outstanding poet of the twentieth century. Pasternak was deservedly awarded the Nobel Prize, but under the pressure of circumstances declined to receive it.

I want to say what I think of *Doctor Zhivago*. It is true that, in his way of thinking and his outlook, the book's main character is not a hero who merits admiration; but is he so different from the hero of Sholokhov's *And Quiet Flows the Don*, Grigory Melekhov, who also vacillates and for a long time cannot understand how the Don Cossacks will come to terms with the new order created by the revolution? Admittedly Sholokhov tries to liberate Grigory from the social encrustations of the past, but he does not manage to do so completely. Thanks largely to the part played by his beautiful, tender and intuitive heroine, Aksinia, we may believe by the end of the book that the hero has gained in insight but – perhaps significantly – Sholokhov leaves him at that point.

Doctor Zhivago's fate is different. A complex figure, he has no reliable, wise hand to guide him into the new world or to help him accept the new spiritual life as special and precious. Pasternak's

Doctor Zhivago moves from the beginning of the century into the 1930s, a world he does not understand.

I do not think *Doctor Zhivago* is Pasternak's best work. I think the novel has structural flaws, but I would not undertake to judge its literary merits and shortcomings. In any event, there was not the least excuse for cutting off this great artist from the collective of Soviet writers and ostracising him.

We visited Pasternak at his dacha in Peredelkino. The company was much the same as we had met at Livanov's and included his friend Fedin. Pasternak and his wife were charming hosts and did everything to make one feel at home. Our visit was made all the more memorable by his writing a short verse to my wife, which touched us both.

Pasternak asked me a lot of questions about my impressions of the USA, as former ambassador. He accompanied my remarks with a witty commentary. He and Fedin knew American literature well; both agreed that even talented writers had to please a reading public whose idea of creative literature was highly distorted, and that, while the American reader's mind needed to be stimulated only in moderation, his nervous system required maximum excitement.

It is important to see Pasternak in the context of the events and changes that were taking place in our country and in the world at large. For some reason he had gained the reputation during his lifetime of having become remote from society and its problems, so that his poetry was mannered and incomprehensible to the average reader. Yet it was Mayakovsky who had described Pasternak's verse as one of the models 'of the new poetry, in perfect tune with the times'.

How could he have been thought remote from society's problems, when in the twenties he had written his two revolutionary poems, *Nineteen Hundred and Five* and *Lieutenant Schmidt*, and when he could write in 1934: 'I have become a particle of my time and my state, and its interests are my interests'?

My meetings with Pasternak confirmed me in the belief that he was a patriot, that his country's literature and her people were precious to him, as were her fields and forests, rivers and mountains, and of course his native Moscow.

19

The party carries Lenin's torch

I thought I had said everything I wanted to, had reminisced about all the people and places, without overcrowding my book. Then, suddenly, I heard the sad news of the death of Yuri Vladimirovich Andropov, with whom I had worked closely over a long period. I can still see his half-smile and hear his soft, calm, even voice. He remained the same when he was in hospital, bedridden, except for a few occasions when he tried to get up and have a cup of tea. Even there he was looking into the future and making plans, and colleagues and I, when we visited him, would try not to dampen his enthusiasm.

He closely watched our reaction to his condition. Any expression of sympathy or even wishes for a rapid recovery would be received in silence. He perked up, however, when we talked about our work, as it raised his hopes that he might return to it with us.

Instead, on the evening of 9 February 1984, the phone rang at the dacha and K.U. Chernenko gave me the sad news.

The next day, when the Politburo met, I was touched by Gorbachev's proposal that I should give a funeral speech, in addition to the one Chernenko would give as General Secretary. And so, speaking from Lenin's Mausoleum, I voiced our farewell and then we buried our comrade's remains at the Kremlin wall.

One day in March 1985, Chernenko, whom I had known for twenty years, phoned me: 'Andrei Andreevich,' he said. 'I'm not well. I'm wondering whether I oughtn't to retire? I want your advice.' There was a pause while I considered my reply.

'Wouldn't that be rather premature? As I understand it, the doctors are not so pessimistic.'

'You mean, I shouldn't make up my mind in a hurry?'

'Exactly. Don't rush into it. There's no need.'

He seemed pleased with this. 'Well, I won't, then.' With that the conversation ended. But his long illness brought him down and three days later he died; soon we were all again at the Kremlin wall, bidding farewell to him.

In three years the country had lost three leaders and we in the leadership had gone through a period of considerable nervous strain. None the less, the party and the people showed their capacity for closing ranks and everyone got on with the job.

Of course, the next task was to choose a new General Secretary. It was up to the Politburo to take the first step in this process, and it wholeheartedly proposed Gorbachev as the candidate it wished the Central Committee to approve. At an emergency Plenum of the Central Committee in March 1985, I put the proposal on behalf of the Politburo and the Plenum voted unanimously for Gorbachev. Already before his selection, Mikhail Sergeevich Gorbachev enjoyed high authority in the party. He was well known to the country at large and for nearly seven years had worked in Moscow in top party posts.

Back in November 1978, three days before the regular Central Committee Plenum, Brezhnev had called me.

'There's something I need your opinion about,' he said. 'What do you think of the idea of bringing Comrade Gorbachev into the Secretariat of the Central Committee? He's first secretary of the Stavropol regional party committee at the moment. What's your view?'

I replied: 'I have never actually worked with Gorbachev, so I can't speak from personal experience. But I have talked with members of the Politburo and Central Committee secretaries, and I've heard many good things about the Stavropol secretary. He sounds like a communist – straightforward, honest and very well trained.' I added: 'If you've heard the same sort of thing about him, then I suggest you propose his candidacy at the next Plenum. I'm sure it will be accepted.'

Brezhnev said: 'I haven't had any direct experience of working with Gorbachev either, but I've heard a lot of good things about him too, so I think I'll put him forward.' And so he did.

The subsequent period revealed Gorbachev's wealth of talent as an outstanding and perspicacious statesman, a subtle and farsighted politician, and a man with a sharp and powerful mind. This is precisely how he is seen by both the party and the people.

For nearly ten years I watched him work, and not from the sidelines. We worked closely together in the Politburo and many times had intensive discussions on the most varied aspects of domestic and foreign policy. I have to say that he possesses that rare gift of being able to convince people. If he is sure his position is correct, he knows how to set out a host of arguments, deploying them one after the other in order of importance.

Perhaps ten years is not such a long period, but in that time the General Secretary has acquired a wealth of the most varied experience, which has made him skilful not only at identifying the problems but at exposing the facets which make it plain that a decision needs to be taken and determining the solution he sees as most appropriate. It will often happen that, during discussion of a particular issue, a solution or decision will emerge, but then suddenly Gorbachev will point out a side of the question that cannot be ignored, often indeed an aspect that presents the best solution. The General Secretary is always ready to listen to the views of any participant in the debate. He has a phenomenal memory and he uses it to advantage.

The changes in the leadership had their effect on my own life, as is well known. At the Supreme Soviet of 2 July 1985 I was elected Chairman of the Presidium, that is, President of the USSR.

The 27th Party Congress of February 1986 created a new leadership under Gorbachev. The country and the whole world know this leadership to be capable of the great tasks facing the party and the people. Cool-headedness and perseverance, calm, accurate calculation, careful planning of every step and of its consequences, and reliance on the entire spectrum of political, scientific and technical information available to the leadership – all these are combined with purposefulness and the will to carry out far-reaching plans for our future development.

Meeting Politburo comrades and party secretaries almost every day, I have been able to watch them in varied circumstances. At the 27th Congress – a meeting of the like-minded – I saw them as fighters against routine and stagnation, as the designers of *perestroika* and the acceleration of our constructive activities. I saw them during the alarming period following the disaster at the Chernobyl nuclear power station, as they worked to eliminate its consequences. And I saw them at the 19th All-Union Party Conference of June 1988.

If I were asked what I wish our country and its people for the foreseeable future, I would say this. The leadership under Gorbachev should continue to head the country. This leadership is capable of solving the historically important questions of both economic construction and the country's social development. It is also dealing with complex foreign policy tasks and is defending the cause of peace with initiative and conviction.

An important turning-point in our party's history came with the Central Committee Plenum of April 1985. One of its theses – Lenin's April Theses of 1917 inevitably come to mind – called for the acceleration of our social development in order to raise productivity and restructure the economy, and thus ameliorate our social problems. This thesis, which Gorbachev presented to the Plenum in precise form, was elaborated in his political report to the 27th Party Congress and was profoundly Marxist in its conception.

One of Marx's greatest contributions was his formulation of the theory of surplus value, which exposed the exploitative nature of the capitalist form of production. He proved that, under capitalism, a surplus value is created, while labour power can be bought and sold at a fixed price. Marx showed that in this lies the way in which human labour differs from other commodities in the normal sense of the word. Under capitalism, it is the capitalist who can use this surplus value at his own discretion, turning it into personal profit if he so chooses.

Under socialism, however, the surplus product goes to the whole of society which owns and disposes of the material resources. It is society that determines this in accordance with the proper proportions and priorities. By its nature, socialist society creates the possibility of limitless expansion but, in order for that possibility to become a reality, everyone's total effort at the workplace is needed, as well as the focusing of their way of thinking.

While attending the 27th Party Congress in 1986 I suddenly found myself thinking of what Lenin had said of the Second Congress of 1903, when the party was just beginning: 'What a wonderful thing our Congress is!' Now, the party has become a mighty force of nearly twenty million, and the Congress noted that what is required is a decisive restructuring (*perestroika*) of all party organisations, of the soviets, of the country's entire economy and of the people's thinking, and all on the basis of freely accessible information, or *glasnost*, and democratisation.

The Plenum of January 1987 put the task of *perestroika* before the party with still greater force, mercilessly exposing our failure up to now to put our maximum effort into developing the country while remaining alert to the structure of society. It also drew attention to the need for further revolutionary restructuring in the management of the economy in order to accelerate the nation's social and economic development. The Plenum reviewed the question of 'restructuring the party's personnel (cadre) policy', noting the serious inadequacies which had led to the failure of our development plans in the 1970s and early 1980s. The Central Committee called on the party to maintain Leninist unity in its ranks, while pursuing the task of refining Soviet democracy and strengthening the fraternal bonds of all the peoples of the Union. The Plenum's decisions were underpinned by the assurance, which the General Secretary emphasised in his report, that they would be carried out.

Our strategy is based on fusing the achievements of the scientific and technological revolution with the planned socialist economy, thus bringing the full potential of socialism into play. Our general line on foreign policy can be expressed briefly: it is to work for peace on earth. Our main foreign policy strategy remains as always to find means to prevent a nuclear catastrophe.

Gorbachev's statement of 15 January 1986, ratified by the Party Congress and calling for the complete elimination of all nuclear and other weapons of mass destruction by the end of the century, was of world importance, while the measures proposed at the Congress for a programme aimed at disarmament and the creation of a universal system of international security represent a significant intermediate stage.

The Soviet proposals at the 1986 Reykjavík Soviet–US summit moved nuclear and space issues to the very edge of a breakthrough. Both sides came very close to an agreement of historic importance, but unfortunately the US administration made its final settlement impossible.

On 28 February 1987 the Soviet Union proposed to remove medium-range missiles from the question of nuclear disarmament and to seek a separate agreement on them. This was seen throughout the world as a major step towards realising the Soviet plan ratified by the Party Congress in early 1986. The signing at the 1987 Washington summit of a treaty on eliminating medium and shorter-range missiles was a major victory for the new thinking and was widely interpreted as the start of disarmament.

The USSR pays great attention to strengthening its ties with the Warsaw Pact countries. The principle of socialist international solidarity has been translated into practice as never before.

I am convinced that when we reach the year 2000, which has been set as the completion date for these far-reaching plans, the Soviet people will be able to look back at the previous fifteen years and see that the party has indeed successfully mobilised the country's vast reserves, and that the leadership has indeed acted correctly in carrying out the Leninist line.

As a communist to the marrow of my bones, I respect the profound learning of Marx, Engels and Lenin, and the great spirit of our people as they build the communist society. When I cast my gaze over our great country, I feel I want to share my sense of confidence in tomorrow. What gives me that confidence? First, the fact that we have a wonderful people who are capable of solving the most difficult problems. Secondly, we have a wise and perceptive party, closely bound to the people. Thirdly, we have a leadership worthy of the great tasks it has set before society at this crucial stage in its development and in the international situation.

The German philosopher Herder remarked that the two greatest tyrants in life are accident and time. After my seventy-ninth birthday, I became more acutely aware of the burden of age and decided it was time to retire. I wrote accordingly to the party Central Committee and to General Secretary Gorbachev.

The Politburo discussed my request and accepted my resignation, and this was ratified by the Central Committee Plenum on 30 September 1988. General Secretary Gorbachev made the following kind remarks about me:

'The Politburo has discussed Andrei Andreevich's request and agreed to grant it. We all know him as a great political and state figure. For more than thirty years he has been a member of the Central Committee. He devoted almost fifty years of his life to diplomatic service: as ambassador to the USA and Britain, as Soviet representative in the Security Council of the United

Nations, as Deputy Foreign Minister and then as Foreign Minister. The documents establishing the United Nations bear his signature on behalf of the Soviet state.

'In 1973 Andrei Andreevich was elected a member of the Politburo and in 1985 Chairman of the Supreme Soviet of the USSR.

'As you can see, comrades, he has had a long working life, over a varied and at times difficult period. His work has received recognition both at home and abroad.

'His has been a rich political career. One could say that both Andrei Andreevich and we who have known him well for a long time have much to remember.

'Today Andrei Andreevich is leaving to take his well-earned rest, and on behalf of his colleagues in the Politburo – and I hope the participants in the Plenum as well – I want to thank him for the enormous work and loyal service he has given to the party and the state, and to wish him good health.

'However, I am sure that Andrei Andreevich will continue to take an active part in the social and political life of the country and to give us the benefit of his experience.

'Once more, allow me to wish Andrei Andreevich Gromyko all the best.'

On 1 October 1988 in the Great Kremlin Hall I made a speech before the deputies of the Supreme Soviet in which I requested their permission to lay down my responsibilities as chairman in view of my retirement. Perhaps it is fitting to include this speech in my memoirs.

'First, I wish to thank General Secretary Gorbachev for everything he said about me yesterday at the Plenum, for his comments on my work as Foreign Minister and Chairman of the Supreme Soviet.

'The Party Plenum has granted my request to retire.

'I think my work is well known. For almost the whole of my working life, beginning with my diplomatic service, my work has been on public view, and it lasted for just short of half a century.

'I am deeply grateful to you, comrade deputies, for the work we have done together in these first years of *perestroika*.

'Our entire people and the party are engaged in realising grandiose plans, and the people's representatives, the deputies of the soviets, are also facing new tasks. To perfect the political system and to achieve the creation of a socialist state based on the rule of law will demand enormous efforts. But the Party of Communists and its Central Committee are full of determination to accomplish their bold and well-grounded programme of development for the country.

'*Glasnost*, which has enriched Soviet democracy, is a mighty source from which the people can draw strength for their new achievements, both in the domestic life of the country and in carrying out the Leninist policy of peace in international affairs.

'I believe in the powerful force of our ideas and principles. With this faith, our people have come through the hard but heroic time since the great October revolution. We are all aware of the sacrifices that have been made at various stages in the history of the Soviet state.

'But our land of socialism – and, I repeat, land of socialism – has not merely survived. It has acquired the strength to go forward with a sure stride.

'We have seen disruptions in our history. They are well known. We have condemned them decisively, and justly so. But the star of socialism has never stopped shining since October 1917. It was ignited so as never to grow dim in the Land of the Soviets.

'The people today expect the soviets of all levels to make their contribution to *perestroika*, a contribution worthy of the majestic plans drawn up by the party.

'Past experience shows that, to accomplish the great affairs facing the country, our Leninist party needs a clear head and broad shoulders, but it also needs unity in its ranks.

'This has been shown by our entire history since the revolution. Unity in the party's ranks and the party's unity with the people are as essential for solving the serious tasks facing us as is the air we breathe.

'We have that unity, and it is also there in the Central Committee and Politburo.

'The party and the country, together with the fraternal parties and socialist countries, will continue the untiring struggle for peace among nations. That is the chief cause; it is the meaning of our lives and of our children's and grandchildren's lives.

'Thank you, comrade deputies, for the trust you placed in me. I have valued it dearly, and will continue to do so.

'I especially value the wish expressed at the Plenum that I should continue to take part in social and political life and to give the leadership the benefit of my experience.'

Lenin's spark lit the flame of the October revolution and, bearing a torch from the same fire, the Communist Party of the Soviet Union, of which I have been a member for more than half a century, is going forward along the Leninist path.

20

More about Stalin

I have already expressed my views about Stalin's international activity, chiefly in the context of the Allied conferences and meetings during and after the war. I selected that sphere to write about because I had the opportunity to observe it personally, having myself participated in the three-power meetings and similar events. I also met with Stalin alone and discussed various important questions with him.

But the Stalin phenomenon is an extraordinarily broad concept. In whatever colours one may choose to depict him, especially as a politician and human being, the task is enormously difficult. And it will take more than one generation of historians, politicians and writers to do it,

Nevertheless, it is for the people who were his contemporaries to say their piece about him, even if they were not among his comrades-in-arms in the leadership. They bear a moral obligation before the people, and not merely before their compatriots. And this applies in particular to those who had the opportunity to meet and observe him at close hand. It was this notion that prompted me to take up my pencil again and to write down my thoughts about Stalin in the context of the country's domestic life.

I do not claim to attempt a complete analysis of the circumstances over the entire thirty years of Stalin's rule, if only because I hadn't even seen him in the first ten years, except for his photograph in the newspapers. But fate decreed that I was to have my first meeting with him in 1939, as I have described elsewhere in this book. That meeting inaugurated my lifetime of state service.

Whatever one says of Stalin, anyone who knew and observed him is bound to compare his knowledge and impressions of him in the past with what is now generally known, and I am of course no exception.

If one were to ask, say, a hundred thousand people of roughly the same age and education who had had similar opportunities to observe Stalin, or who had merely heard about him, to express their opinion of him, their views would not be the same. Yet the law of the greatest number also applies to political portraiture, as it flows from the pen.

One can say with a high degree of certainty that the overwhelming majority of those questioned would say that, at a certain time, the people believed in Stalin. In their eyes, he was working to make their country strong and capable of defending their security. They would also say that their view of him when he was alive was different from what it became later, after he had died and his crimes were revealed.

As for the war period, most people would probably agree that Stalin led the country against the fascist aggressors with energy. After all, his was the last word even on military matters and questions of national defence.

After the 20th Party Congress in 1956, and especially now, during the period of *perestroika*, there has been a veritable flood of information on Stalin's crimes, about which the mass of the Soviet people knew nothing during his lifetime.

It should also be remembered that for nearly thirty years Stalin ran a repressive apparatus which, as is now clear, had a dual task: to destroy a host of innocent persons as 'enemies of the people', and by means of a sophisticated system of illegality to hide all trace of its crimes. People perished at the hands of executioners who were then themselves destroyed. This chilling picture is now being revealed in its entirety, as is the fact that Stalin himself stood at the top of the structure.

Some of Stalin's features have emerged in sharper relief with the passing of time. After all, the official documents and the various kinds of other sources, as well as the memoirs of eye witnesses, now make it possible to construct a far fuller account of the Stalin period. We are surrounded by veritable mountains of information.

The Stalin phenomenon demands that the people as a whole, and historians in particular, add their own contribution to a new assessment of the nation's past, now that we are passing through the period of revolutionary restructuring. This assessment must be objective, impartial and, given the crimes involved, merciless.

It is not always easy to handle the facts and figures produced since Stalin's death. The discovery of countless traces of the repressions, including the massacre of party and state functionaries, testifies to the fact that Stalin operated a complex system designed for that purpose.

How can one explain the fact that most of the population did not connect Stalin directly with the lawless treatment of those accused of crimes against the party and state?

Life itself gives us the most convincing reply to this question. People simply did not know about the crimes being perpetrated by the central authority. Nor did they have the possibility of finding out. They were not permitted to make contact with the accused, even if they were relatives and loved ones. Stalin invented and launched his phoney, strident slogan of 'enemy of the people' and it was parroted by his minions in the NKVD, from the top to the bottom. Judges and investigators, newspapers and magazines repeated it, and it was echoed from the platform of every kind of auditorium, including party meetings.

The treatment of those who were arrested, including those who went through the so-called judicial process, was a mockery of what in any civilised society are the accepted legal norms. And any attempt to reprove a member of the repressive apparatus was itself harshly punished.

Only the most vicious, utterly arbitrary form of investigation and of so-called due process can explain why the great mass of the population was ignorant of the crimes being carried out on Stalin's orders. Most of the decisions he made either on his own or with a small number of his accomplices. Arrests were often not discussed even by the Politburo.

Stalin did not like to make long speeches at Politburo meetings, especially about the repressions. He always tried to expound his views tersely. It would on occasion appear that he was about to explain in greater detail an idea he had just voiced, but the time would pass and he would sit in silence and see what the others had to say. He might also express himself two or three times on an issue, if not even more often. But he always put his points concisely, especially when difficult questions of policy and the arrests were being discussed.

In an effort to emulate Stalin, the others would also try to be brief. I observed this myself during discussions on foreign policy.

It's true that some Politburo members did not follow this pattern. K.E. Voroshilov, for instance, sometimes spoke with great energy, not that he was present at many meetings, for reasons that remained obscure to me. But everyone had become accustomed to his way of speaking. Even now, I cannot imagine him speaking quietly. L.M. Kaganovich had a booming voice which he evidently found it hard to moderate.

N.A. Voznesensky stood out in this regard. He spoke well, like an educated man. This was already after the war. I did not see him at many meetings. I never understood why he got excited during his speeches. His area of specialisation was economic problems, including aspects of theory. He often had to speak to large audiences and no doubt that was where he had acquired his speaking manner.

I remember on one occasion when Voznesensky was making one of his lively speeches, Stalin, who as usual was pacing up and down alongside the table, suddenly stopped, went up close to Voznesensky and stared straight at him. It was almost a theatrical gesture, though I don't think Voznesensky felt very comfortable under that piercing gaze. Without uttering a word, Stalin continued pacing the room.

Ther was nothing in what Voznesensky was saying that could have aroused Stalin's displeasure. He was speaking in the same vein as the other members of the Politburo, though I can't remember what we were discussing. Stalin's piercing look can hardly have been accidental.

The idea has occasionally been expressed in print that, if one were to examine Stalin's speeches carefully, one would find a clue to his harshness, to his true character. Things he said are supposed to contain hints that he was preparing to accuse innocent individuals of hostile acts against the people. I don't think Stalin was such a simpleton. It was not easy to read his thoughts. He organised his speeches so that the listener's attention was concentrated on incontrovertible, or seemingly incontrovertible, propositions.

Some authors, especially abroad, even assert that it was impossible not to notice in Stalin's eyes his harshness towards his intended victims, though I do not think they have the evidence to prove it.

Nobody I knew who saw Stalin at close quarters ever suggested that his eyes held a harsh expression. Certainly, I never saw such a thing myself. A look is a look. At times, if anything, he had rather a mild look. In any case, none of the people in his entourage, including those whose own families were later arrested, ever claimed to have seen something harsh in Stalin's behaviour at an earlier period.

Thinking about him and what he did, especially during the period of mass arrests, it seems to me that nature had endowed him with the ability to hide the harsh side of his character, and very effectively so. He also seems to have had the capacity to appear at times even gentle and sensitive to others. The conversations he had with some foreign personalities, especially writers, confirm this.

In my opinion, nobody can say whether or not Stalin ever considered the possibility that one day his policies and his activities would be condemned by the country he ruled. And if he did ask himself the question, he took the answer with him to the grave. It is quite likely that his mind was so imprisoned in his own convictions that such a question would never have occurred to him. Was he a victim of his own self-confidence? Without any doubt whatsoever. That was an indelible feature of his character.

Obviously, a creative writer has greater licence to analyse the way he surmises that Stalin's mind worked. That is his right as an artist. It is quite another matter to describe one's own direct impressions and to try to cast light on and understand the man's personality as one has actually observed it. In such circumstances, one is obliged to keep one's gaze fixed on the subject and not allow oneself to fall under the thrall of invention.

The question nevertheless remains: was it possible after the revolution of 1917 to avoid the development of a socialist state in which one man was enabled to concentrate unlimited power in his hands, when all major questions of governing that state were decided by him, even though nobody – nobody, ever – had actually given him that power?

It is a difficult question. It is not surprising that a number of historians have come to the conclusion that Stalin could not have shaped events in the country in such a way as to make himself the virtual dictator entirely by his own efforts. They argue logically that it was the circumstances that permitted him to achieve his goals.

But then two different questions arise here. First, was there an objective *need* for the country and its political system to develop along the lines chosen by Stalin?

Secondly, did the *possibility* exist, despite the character of the socialist revolution, of turning the country significantly from the path set out by Lenin, and of directing it along a path dominated by the cult of a single individual?

The answers to these two questions have to be different.

There were *no* objective conditions that would have *dictated*, I repeat *dictated*, the emergence of Stalinism. Power was in the hands of the workers and peasants, and that was the main thing. The chief means of production and the land were public property. Leadership was in the hands of the Party of Communists, Lenin's party.

As for the second question, it is more complicated. What was merely a possibility unfortunately became a reality. The situation that emerged after Lenin's death enabled Stalin to set the internal development of the country on a path that was profoundly alien to Lenin's ideas and Lenin's precepts, in terms of both economic and social policy.

The whole Stalin period was characterised by a persistent tendency towards arbitrary, anti-democratic methods in the exercise of power. Stalin's personal cult radiated down to his subordinates and from them down further and further. This helped him, for it fixed the image of the supreme *vozhd*, the Leader, in the minds of the people. He regarded these sources of support as both useful and necessary. Can one describe it as degeneration? In a certain sense, yes. In the sense that it represented degeneration of the supreme power, degeneration of Stalin the usurper. Not, however, degeneration of the socialist character of the state or of the revolution.

The question properly arises: where was the party in all this, and its committees, including its Central Committee? We have to look at the history of the party and the country to find an answer to this question.

Stalin was so convinced of his own infallibility and the strength of his own authority that for thirteen years after 1939 he did not regard it as necessary to call a Party Congress. The first one was convened only in 1952. And those thirteen years included the most fateful and decisive time for the country, when it was fighting Hitler's aggression. Even if one accepts the proposition that war-time was not the most appropriate time for a Party Congress, the seven years after the war were a time when countless problems of an economic and social kind needed to be dealt with in the party's highest forum. But Stalin thought that he was the only person competent to deal with such issues. He behaved like an arrogant dictator, intoxicated by his limitless power.

Perhaps one of the reasons he did not convene a Congress was that he was afraid he might be asked: why had he destroyed the flower of the Soviet armed forces high command in 1937, when even a blind man could see that a war was coming? Stalin went to the grave without ever giving an answer to this awkward question.

Of course, a large part in all this was played by his entourage, especially that part of it that was composed of obedient yes-men. No doubt it would not have been easy to persuade their paranoid leader, even over the question of the Congress, but none of them ever made the effort.

Before the war, and indeed even during the period following Lenin's death, the Central Committee was engaged in a constant debate over cardinal questions of the country's future development. Stalin won the debate, and one consequence was a multitude of victims. With diabolical cunning, he managed to present his case as though it were the Leninist line. This was of course a lie, but the majority of the party and the population were unable to expose the fact that he was creating his own cult, although there were individual efforts to do so. As a result of the repressions, those who might have defended the true Leninist line simply melted away. The facts are known. The country and the people suffered terrible consequences.

An effective weapon in Stalin's hands during that time was the repressive apparatus he had created, the prostituted legal system. An atmosphere of struggle against 'enemies of the people' was generated, even though none existed. Nor were there enough sufficiently devoted people to fight against this lie and to defend the truth. Stalin meanwhile exhibited monstrous inventiveness. He was well endowed in this respect. He used his system of repression to prevent communists in all branches of the party from getting the country back onto the Leninist path. The political signposts were buried in concentration camps and in the graves of the victims.

It emerged later that even the 1937 case against the Soviet military leadership had been falsified from start to finish. From the point of view of common sense and strict political and human logic, the accusation that Marshal M.N. Tukhachevsky and the others were implicated in a plot against Stalin was plainly absurd.

If anything confirms the idea that a political pathology was at work, then it was Stalin's way of thinking in the 'case' of the military, which turned out to be a great tragedy for the country, particularly in the course of the Second World War. One would think that the 'Leader' should have realised that, if the top leadership of the armed forces were conspiring against him, then nobody would be in a position to hinder their plans. It was naive to imagine that the army leaders couldn't have found their Brutus or Cassius. But the fact is, they weren't looking for them, as they too believed in Stalin, because they believed in the party.

But Stalin was not strong on logic, and this case shows it. His massacre of the army leaders remains one of his worst crimes against the country and the Soviet people.

The term 'Stalin's entourage' has come into common usage lately. He did have an entourage, but it was not monolithic, and one should therefore speak about it in rather relative terms. Stalin used his NKVD operatives to get the information he needed on his own entourage, who knew what he was up to and drew the appropriate conclusions.

Stalin did not encourage Politburo members to associate with each other outside of their official business. Only in the first years after Lenin's death did such socialising occur. Stalin calculated that it was better to have them know each other less well than to give them the opportunity to mix freely. He was constantly on the watch for the threat of a conspiracy: who could say when and how a plot was being hatched? It was consequently unusual for, say, two members of the Politburo to relax together, with or without their families.

For the same reason, two or more members of the Politburo never rode in the same car. They knew they would be noticed. Who knows, the 'all-seeing eye' might jump to the wrong conclusion! They all knew how one careless step or unguarded conversation might end.

This does not mean that every one of Stalin's bodyguards and the members of the Politburo was ready to tell the 'boss' everything he heard. Not at all. But even if one tenth of them did so, it would be taken note of 'up there'. That was how V.M. Molotov explained it all when he spoke about it after Stalin died, and he was perhaps the closest to Stalin.

To the end of his life, Stalin never lost his ingrained, pathological suspiciousness. And this was widely known. It could reduce the others in the leadership to trembling jelly. And what was worse, Stalin's paranoia grew more acute with time, and more and more people fell victim to it. The criminal conveyor-belt for slaughtering the 'enemies of the people' kept on running right up to the war and again after it. And even during the war itself it continued operating.

It is hardly surprising, therefore, that numerous secret burial grounds of Stalin's victims are now being unearthed, despite having been covered over for decades.

Could the people who were discussing the situation in the country, while sitting at the same table with Stalin, have known that innocent people were being slaughtered?

Everyone is free to answer the question according to his own convictions. My opinion is that *everyone at the highest level of authority did know* about the criminal orgy of blood-letting that was going on and knew that utterly innocent people were dying on the 'Leader's' instructions.

As for the scale of the repressions, the system of concealment that had been devised makes it difficult to give even an approximation of the total number of victims. That was part of Stalin's policy, and his entourage knew it.

These people somehow managed to hide all this away in a locked drawer, thus helping Stalin to avoid making the appalling facts public. It was as if the situation had brought their conscience and their loyalty to the 'Leader' into a head-on clash.

I heard something interesting just after Stalin's death. Stalin was not yet buried. Gales of loud laughter could be heard coming from inside Khrushchev's office. Who was in there? The Politburo members who the very next day, with heads bent low and melancholy faces, would be burying Stalin. Molotov would even wipe away a tear. Further comment on how they greeted Stalin's death seems unnecessary, though maybe this cannot be said of all of them.

They all knew what had been going on for many years. Some of them had themselves even signed the death warrants of innocent people.

Without doubt, what happened under Stalin will be studied and analysed more fully. It is important to understand how these people, who were at one time respected and who exercised considerable authority, managed to turn themselves into uncomplaining executors of the will of one man who had vowed to rule the state by illegal means.

How had the usurper managed to bewitch those in the leadership and virtually paralyse their will?

Stalin inculcated in the minds of his entourage the idea that a great country needed a strong authority. He sought out historical parallels and was not ashamed to demonstrate them.

My attention was once drawn to Stalin's comments on Ivan the Terrible. It was after the war. Late one evening I was summoned to a meeting of the Politburo. A number of issues submitted by the Ministry of Foreign Affairs were to be debated.

I arrived at the Kremlin. A.N. Poskrebyshev, Stalin's personal secretary, said to me: 'The members of the Politburo are watching a film, so the session will begin later.' And he suggested I go through into the viewing-room where the film was being shown. 'You'll be able to see how things are done,' he added.

I was led into a small, cosy cinema, where I found Stalin and a number of other members of the Politburo.

They were showing the first part of Eisenstein's *Ivan the Terrible*. I have to admit I didn't watch the screen very attentively, as my mind was on the forthcoming meeting.

A little over an hour later the viewing came to an end, but before leaving the cinema, Stalin, in the presence of everyone there, said: 'It's a good film. It should get wide distribution. How he manages to convey Ivan's strong character! Just the way the historian Karamzin wrote about him. You can see how the tsar loved discipline and order. The film-maker obviously wanted to emphasise that side of the autocrat's character.'

The other Politburo members agreed with Stalin, but they did not express any ideas of their own. They contented themselves with silent approval of what he had said.

Stalin's comments became known outside the Kremlin, especially among the intelligentsia, and this aroused great interest in the film. Eisenstein himself was not at the viewing.

Stalin's remarks are interesting because they show that he was impressed, not only in life but also in art, by people whose personalities were not unlike his own. It was as if he were seeking justification for himself in history, looking for his doubles.

I find it difficult to evaluate the meagre, if positive, reactions of the other members of the Politburo to Stalin's comments.

Stalin will remain an object of study for a long time to come.

Khrushchev said a lot more about him after the 20th Party Congress. Often he referred in conversation to Stalin's dislike of frank discussion of a number of issues among the leadership. Khrushchev underlined the fact that both he and his family had adapted well to the norms of behaviour imposed by Stalin, even though they despised them.

In reading these reflections of mine, the reader may well wonder what was going on. Why couldn't the nation fathom the reasons for all the lawlessness? Who was guilty? After all, it's not as if it lasted only two or three years – it went on for almost thirty years.

Apart from what we now know about Stalinism, there is another question. Were not the reasons for the situation purely historical, but outside the framework of what happened in October 1917? I think history may provide an answer.

For centuries, the nation had lived under the domination of the monarchy. A long line of great (and not so great) princes and tsars, emperors and empresses had followed one another. The nation, which consisted mostly of peasants, went on and on bearing the burden of the monarchy on its shoulders.

If one approaches the history of the Russian state as a series of major stages, it becomes plain that the Russian people lived for most of it under monarchs. Thanks also to the general lack of culture and literacy, the monarch was the highest law.

It is not surprising, therefore, that every attempt at a revolt was suppressed. Under the monarchs, those elements flourished which the monarchy itself gave rise to and which in turn it relied upon. From one century to the next, the working people waited for their hour to come.

The people's deep-seated faith in the 'Little Father' – the tsar – could not, however, kill individual and at times striking outbursts of peasant discontent, and this went on for generation after generation. Such an historical legacy was bound to make itself felt, even after the banner of the October revolution was raised above Petersburg. The arbitrary rule that Stalin wielded for thirty years must have been based to some extent on the traditional submissiveness that millions of people had shown for one person, and one person for whose well-being they prayed to God.

Even the last years, and especially the last months, of the Romanov dynasty showed that the burden of tradition hung heavy in the people's minds and helped keep the tsar in power. The minuscule concessions the tsar made before the war to the demands of the pseudo-parliament, or State Duma, which was dominated by middle-class and landowner elements, were reduced to nothing while they were still only at the planning stage, and it was only the workers' delegates who consistently opposed the treacherous position taken by the majority in the Duma under Nicholas II.

And it was the party under Lenin's leadership which accomplished the great feat of October 1917, unparalleled in world history as an event of social significance. The working class demonstrated its allegiance to Lenin's policies and ideas, and the overwhelming mass of the peasantry accepted this policy and these ideas as their own, including creating an alliance with the working class.

All this is incontestable.

But what is also incontestable is that, within the very nucleus of the party, a permanent struggle for power was going on. This struggle reached severe proportions and became pregnant with danger after the death of Lenin in 1924.

As we know, almost always at the very centre of this struggle stood the fateful figure of Stalin. Those who associated themselves with him and his plans slid with him down the slippery slope, whether they realised it or not. With their own hands, sometimes unwillingly, they cleared the path for Stalin and one-man rule, until finally one single individual had acquired the power to decide the affairs of state as he alone thought fit. This included politics, economics and the lives of every citizen, one way or another. In a word, it amounted to the usurpation of supreme power.

Of course, questions arose as to how this or that individual or group should conduct itself, but Stalin acquired such status that the fate of individuals and groups was decided simply by his instructions. Those who timidly thought their actions should be guided by notions of justice simply packed their ideas away, generally in order to survive. Stalin was already operating on the principle that the highest law was his own will. Not many tsars had been able to say that.

In view of all this, I wonder if we are right to dismiss the heritage of history when we try to explain why, after the victory of the revolution, during the building of socialism and even after the worst war ever, the country and the party proved incapable of avoiding the tragedy of Stalinism?

On the other hand, it would be profoundly wrong to take the fatalistic view that Stalinism was inevitable. Age-old traditions were only one component in the rise of the cult which remorselessly slithered like a snake up the tree of power.

No less important was Stalin's highly developed ability to keep himself in the public eye. I myself saw on many occasions how, say, entering a ceremonial meeting or mounting Lenin's Mausoleum with a group of other government leaders, Stalin would behave as if there were nobody else around. He seemed not to notice anyone else. As a rule, he made no effort to chat or make a joke with anyone.

His walk was deliberate and assured, and when he paced, he did so firmly. People who had frequent access to him told me that he rehearsed for this purpose in private, so as not to spoil the effect. For the same reason, he preferred to appear in leather boots, as he felt they made his movements look more authoritative. In his last years he exchanged his boots for shoes only when he wore the uniform of Generalissimo.

He was enormously concerned not to show any sign of unevenness in his walk. Documentary films show how, unlike the others with him on Lenin's Mausoleum, he would always be on the move, making himself more visible to the crowds. People would say: 'Look, Stalin never stops moving about: that means he isn't tired, it means he's feeling well.'

His qualities as an orator were distinctly limited. Molotov once told me, after Stalin's death, that in his youth Stalin had once made an effort to improve his abilities in this regard. But evidently without success. He couldn't conquer his nature. Probably this was one reason he was not keen to speak at large meetings, a fact that was well known.

There is something else about Stalin I should like to mention. Without doubt, he had a powerful mind, and he had the ability to expound his ideas in a precise, if dull, way. He lacked the spark that any orator needs if he wants to gain his audience's sympathy.

Stalin was well aware of this deficiency and did his best to make sure that what he said in his speeches did not depart from his written text. He did not want people to say that, though his writing was not bad, his speaking did not amount to much. But that is precisely what they thought. His speeches somehow induced in the reader or the listener the desire to add something more human or vital in order to give his style a livelier and more natural feel.

I do not agree with those who say that Stalin was uncultivated.

That is far from the truth, and the fact that he was well read is widely known. His knowledge was soundly based, as I myself had frequent occasion to observe. I doubt if there will be any new discoveries on this score.

It is true that, though he was an educated man in the broadest sense of the word, he was no scholar. His intellect was not that of a scholar, but rather that of a practical man, an organiser and, above all, a very capable and subtle manipulator. None of this prevented him from trying to appear in the role of linguistician, say, or of theorist in the field of political economy and philosophy, though nothing came of it. I am convinced that it would be a waste of time to try to find evidence of Stalin's contribution to the science of Marxism-Leninism.

It is impossible to get away from the personality aspect of the Stalin phenomenon. Most people who saw him, saw his portraits, heard him speak, or simply read his speeches had already formed a view of him. In other words, millions of people had his image fixed in their minds before they gave any thought to what he had to say about the internal state of the country or the international situation. One might adjust a feature or two of the image in due course, but the basic elements had been firmly set in place beforehand. Before any alteration to the image could be made, however, whether in the mind of a worker, peasant, scholar or student, knowledge and experience were needed, as well as the ability to take many circumstances into account.

Could people in the 1930s and '40s forget the photographs and paintings they had seen of Stalin looking at someone with a calm, understanding expression on his face, or shaking hands with a model worker, with schoolchildren, or with who knows who else, often with a smile?

Of course, it would be true to say that the people who lived, worked, studied, and died for their country, fighting against real enemies – the fascist aggressors – that these people, who were moved by Stalin's portraits, did not know the truth about him. That is so. That was the reality, and that reality was triumphant. Stalin was not the man most of the people took him for, and that goes especially for the party. Only his death could dispel the myth of the 'great genius'.

The Stalin cult was dealt a decisive blow by the 20th Party Congress of 1956, and it should not be underestimated. The party, its Central Committee and Khrushchev personally performed a great service. It is sometimes said in the press that Khrushchev was himself to some extent an accomplice of Stalin, and he is reproached for somehow managing to deflect criticism from himself. It is said that he did not see to it that Stalin's vassals, who were responsible for the deaths of millions, were dealt with at once.

One can understand why people should think this way, but who can seriously suggest that such sudden measures might not have provoked some new tragedy for the country? Even one chance in a hundred that this could happen was too much. It was an unacceptable risk and it was right to act with caution and assurance.

It is true that Khrushchev said nothing about himself, but this is not a weighty argument. His role under Stalinism does not compare with the impact that his exposure of the Stalin cult had. The 20th Party Congress inspired the party with confidence in the future of the country.

Yet no matter how many facets of the Stalin phenomenon we uncover, not one of them, nor all of them taken together, can provide a convincing answer to the question: why was it that the cohort of Lenin's comrades-in-arms, supposedly all hardened fighters for the workers' cause, were so bewitched and paralysed by Stalin's personality that they proved incapable of recognising in good time the danger he posed to the success of Lenin's ideas and to the country?

Certainly at times quite a number of Central Committee members did not share Stalin's views, or took a reserved attitude. But after Lenin's death the majority generally supported Stalin. And the process was reinforced with time. The majority became larger and the minority smaller.

Dozens of years ago, communists, and not only communists, were asking the question which people are asking again today: how was it that the old revolutionaries who had gone through the school of Lenin did not see the direction in which the party and the country were moving under Stalin? More than that, how was it that some of them became accomplices in the political repressions, signing illegal sentences and official lists condemning innocent people to death?

Throughout the country there was an epidemic of spying on people. And shady individuals were systematically planted in the staffs of our overseas embassies, doing nothing but harm to the state.

Let me give a typical example. It took place after the war. A message was suddenly received from the Central Committee to the effect that I had been appointed to a commission whose task it was to look into the work of our embassy in Tehran. One of the embassy staff was arousing deep suspicion. We were told that it looked as though he was 'connected with British intelligence'. But no clues had been found.

There were three of us on the commission, which met twice. We thoroughly checked all the materials on the 'case' which might have thrown some light on the matter. But we found nothing reprehensible. The spy psychosis turned out to be without foundation.

It would appear that the matter could have been closed then and there. But since a high 'person' had cast his glance over the file, the commission had to continue its work of investigation. In the end we decided to reduce the embassy personnel by a third and to recall the suspicious individual, even though we knew there were no grounds for doing so.

This shows that diplomats were also not above suspicion. Informers were as a rule nothing more than slanderers, but their reports could often have serious consequences. For some reason, they seemed to direct most of their false denunciations against the most active members of the diplomatic service.

And what was the point of Stalin's criminal decision to apply physical torture during investigation? If someone was merely suspected of having committed an impermissible act, he was already condemned to arrest, concentration camp and probably execution. All this is now being exposed as it never was before.

There is a great mystery: why did such figures as Molotov, Kaganovich, Voroshilov, G.M. Malenkov, and later A.A. Zhdanov and many others, not raise their voices against the lawlessness being perpetrated in the country? They were perfectly well aware of the rot that was taking over the country, even if they did not know every last detail.

Let us grant that some of them were simply too frightened, once the political Rubicon had been crossed and the cult of the Leader had become an established fact. But, first of all, what sort of revolutionaries were they, to sacrifice their revolutionary principles? Secondly, there was a time when they could have replaced Stalin with someone else, thus fulfilling Lenin's wish that he be removed from the post of General Secretary. Yes, they could have done that, but they did not, and instead they obediently followed Stalin. This side of the problem is quite a puzzle.

However one looks at it, one cannot avoid the logical conclusion that responsibility for Stalinism and the mass destruction of the Soviet people lies also on the shoulders of the people Stalin relied upon. After all, there was a time when the Rubicon had not been crossed!

A precise, historically based assessment of Stalin's role in the history of the party and the country was given by General Secretary Gorbachev on the occasion of the seventieth anniversary of the October revolution. He gave a profoundly balanced view. He pointed out Stalin's services during the war, in defeating Hitler and in securing for the Soviet Union a firm place in the post-war world, and he indicated what Stalin had done to implement plans for the country's internal development, especially its industrialisation. All this was said plainly to the party, the people and the world as a whole.

But he also spoke with striking truth about the painful consequences of the Stalin cult, which had caused the deaths of millions of Soviet people and the trampling of Lenin's sacred principles of socialism.

How, for instance, can one read with equanimity Molotov's correspondence with the well-known physicist I.P. Pavlov? In his typically frank manner, Pavlov writes about the intolerable situation that had been created in Leningrad, and he criticises Molotov's negative replies to his letters. Pavlov openly makes accusations about the illegal arrests of utterly untainted individuals, and Molotov replies with nothing more than formal answers, admitting that some mistakes could have been made, but giving not one instance in which such a mistake had been corrected.

I remember the oppressive circumstances in Moscow during the period from 1934 to 1939. People would walk along the street with tense expressions on their faces. Workers and staff in institutes and enterprises were afraid to talk to each other, unless they were close friends. It was well known that every night the NKVD were 'taking' people, as we said then. They were taking them in towns and in the countryside, on the street and in their homes. Those who were 'taken' simply disappeared and, as a rule, nothing would be heard of them again. Grownups tried to hide the truth from their children, but that couldn't go on for long. The children found out sooner or later, and it made them serious beyond their years. Many people perished morally as well as physically.

In the Institute of Economics of the USSR Academy of Sciences, where I was then working, as in other scientific institutes, the atmosphere was equally strained. The scientific secretary of our institute was arrested and I was appointed in his place. I have to admit I did not feel good about it. It scared me to think that the man who had been in the job until then had just been arrested for no reason. My predecessor had a spotless reputation. He was of course a victim of slander.

On one occasion at that period, I remember attending a meeting of the Social Sciences Division of the Academy. The main address was given by Academician Grekov. All the speeches were impeccably anti-fascist in content and tone, debunking the Nazis' anti-scientific inventions about the Slav race. Clearly, the Germans were preparing themselves ideologically for aggression against the Soviet Union. One of the speakers was G.E. Zinoviev, who was then still at large. I remember his speech. It was very forceful and he delivered it impromptu; from the political point of view there was not the slightest dubiousness about it. He did a good job in debunking the misanthropic racism being peddled by the Nazi theorists. His speech was well received by the audience. I applauded too. Soon thereafter, however, Zinoviev found himself in the prisoner's dock, with well-known consequences.

Many times I have tried to retrieve from my memory the complex of thoughts and feelings that haunted me in those days. And I am still trying. Like most people at the time, I too thought that Stalin and the leadership must know what had to be done. Who should know better? They also knew that the Soviet people were for socialism, for the revolution and what Lenin and the communists had devoted their lives to fighting for.

But what was one supposed to make of the fact that people were being arrested and disappearing? The courts were a parody, as one heard from time to time. But most of those arrested simply disappeared in silence. Also in silence and generally unnoticed by outsiders, relatives bemoaned the loss of their nearest and dearest. Some hope was kept alive that perhaps they would return. People thought and often said that Stalin would not allow injustice to occur. But nobody was coming back and the number of those who disappeared kept on growing.

The thoughts in people's minds at that time were mixed. One

was that the population were devoted to the country and to Stalin and were ready to defend Soviet power against any enemy with their lives. Another thought was, who are these enemies about whom everyone keeps talking and writing, what sort of people are they? Who are these 'enemies of the people'? Where are they and where did they come from? Night and day, people asked themselves these nagging questions.

One's mind and feelings were, as it were, split in two. After all, people have to live, they have to work. And so they lived and worked with these thoughts going round and round in their heads. Nobody ever saw any enemies, even though the press wrote about them and there were special meetings about them and they were talked about on the street. The nation worked, the nation loved the country, it loved the party, and it loved the Soviet regime.

At that time, you could take any street at random in Moscow or Leningrad, and without fail you would find a house where the children of arrested people had been left as orphans, often without any means of support. And all the time, the man with the pipe in his mouth was pacing, in his deliberate, self-confident way, back and forth in his Kremlin office.

Looking back now, it all seems like a fantasy. But sadly it was reality, and the country had to live through it.

I would not hesitate to say that Stalin's punitive apparatus degenerated through its own momentum. It ground its victims into a pulp systematically, methodically, at times consuming many of those who had themselves operated the machine. In other words, it devoured itself as it went along.

Only its creator was beyond its reach. Even the heads of the NKVD, G.G. Yagoda and following him N.I. Yezhov, fell into the meat-grinder. L.P. Beria managed to escape, only to be dealt with by the dispensation of justice after Stalin's death.

I have a memory etched in my mind concerning Beria and his relations with Stalin. It is well known that Stalin had in his armoury a number of personality skills which he used to impress, among others, Churchill and Roosevelt. Primary among these was his resort to direct, frank speech.

During a dinner at Yalta given by the Soviet delegation in honour of the Americans and British, Roosevelt turned to Stalin and asked: 'Who is that gentleman sitting across from us?' To be more precise, he indicated the gentleman sitting opposite Ambassador Gromyko. This occurred at the very beginning of the meal. Evidently, Beria had not introduced himself to the President before we had sat down, and Stalin hadn't introduced him either.

Stalin replied: 'Ah, that's our Himmler! That's Beria.' Roosevelt was obviously uncomfortable with the comparison, especially as Beria had heard everything. It was quite plain that Stalin's remark had thrown Roosevelt into a state of confusion, and he had no idea how to react. He settled for something resembling a smile. As for Beria, he was plainly more than embarrassed – he must have been nonplussed.

That evening, and at other official occasions in general, Beria was not very talkative. His behaviour was constrained. Nor did he take part in any of the official meetings throughout the conference.

The foreigners who made their appearance among us seemed not to notice Beria. Apart from some remarks he made during dinner to other members of the Soviet delegation, I did not hear him express himself on anything. He seemed like someone made for secret work. Mounting intrigues and slander against honest people, and having all kinds of forgeries made – that was the element in which he felt most at home. Party veterans regarded him as an upstart.

He had reached his high office only because Stalin's 'glory' was reflected on him when he was still working in Georgia, whence they both hailed. Everyone knew that he enjoyed a high degree of trust in the 'Leader's' eyes. But I am inclined to agree with those historians who are now saying that, had Stalin lived a little longer, Beria would in all probability have ended up in the colossal meat-grinder he had helped to build with his own hands.

After Stalin's death, the following fact soon became known. Stalin was in his last throes, and when he regained consciousness for a few seconds, Beria immediately threw himself on his knees by the bed and started kissing Stalin's hands. But as soon as the dying man's eyes closed again and his hands fell lifelessly onto the bed, Beria at once recoiled. Why did he put on such a Shakespearean act? I was told this story personally by Molotov and Khrushchev, who had seen it all.

From the late 1920s, the country watched what was being done in the countryside with a growing sense of alarm. People could see that labouring folk were being arrested and sent into exile. And this was taking place in the villages which had not had time to get accustomed to collective agriculture and which still had little idea of what a kolkhoz was. What took place was a fundamental change in the peasants' very way of life, in the age-old structure of their community life.

As a student, I made many trips to various villages at the time of collectivisation, and I came to see that many peasants were not hostile to the idea of collectivisation as such. They simply could not understand why their land was being taken away from them and turned into public property in such haste. And why was it necessary to take their last cow, to say nothing of their horses, and then force them to join the collective?

On one of my official trips into the depths of the countryside, in an area administered today by Minsk, I witnessed the following scene. On the edge of a small hamlet, a peasant of about thirty-five to forty was sitting and staring at the land. He did not notice me and my comrade, another student. His eyes were full of tears. At a small distance from him sat another, older man, together with a boy of five or six, no doubt his grandson. We found it very hard to strike up a conversation with the older man. He told us that none of them had anything to eat. In the whole family there was nothing they could eat. He said they were probably going to be moved to some place to the east of Minsk. We did what we could to help the starving trio. In the village, we were told that the family was likely to be deported, even though they had done nothing of a criminal nature. It was just that they weren't willing to join a collective straightaway. In due course, they were classified as 'enemies of the people'.

I witnessed many such scenes in other districts. On another occasion, I had to go to Vitebsk on a research expedition as part of my graduate studies course. I spent the night in a hotel and next morning went out and encountered a column of men moving along the street. There were at least two hundred of them. They were walking in ragged ranks under NKVD guards placed at precise distances from each other. I asked a local inhabitant where the men were being taken and was told they were on their way to the railway station and from there would be transported to the east, to concentration camps, because they had refused to join collective farms.

As far as I can recall, they were all men. I noticed that some of them were even smiling as they talked to each other, but this only intensified the sense of despair that one felt at the sight of this heart-rending scene of inhuman treatment. More than fifty years have passed since those days, and yet I still retain a vivid image of the scene.

Another incident relating to the year 1934 comes to mind. I was sent on a mission from Moscow to the Kharkov area in the Ukraine. The instructions, given to me by one of the sections of the Central Committee, were to see how things were going in the recently created collectives in the area. One kolkhoz in particular was singled out, the 'V.I. Lenin Commune' in the district of Starobelsk. I found the manager, who got me a night's lodging and told me about the farm.

Of course, what he had to say about the economic state of his farm was uninspiring, to say the least. But that was no more than I expected. The kolkhozes everywhere were pretty much in the same condition. What really amazed me was a specific incident this farm manager and other kolkhozniks told me about.

In 1932, when the policy of mass collectivisation was under way, a peasant, whose hut I was shown, had been arrested for refusing to join the collective. His wife and two small children were left without any means of support. After a short time the villagers noticed that there was no sign of the woman or her children. They seemed to be absent. The villagers started asking what had happened, and it turned out that the woman, who was stil alive, had lost her reason and killed her two children. The people told me about it with tears in their eyes.

One can imagine the horrible scene the inhabitants of the 'commune' had found. Even now, I can't erase the picture of it from my mind. It's as if I had heard the story and seen the boarded-up peasant hut only yesterday. That hut should have been shown to Stalin, with the whole story as a commentary. I reported it all to the responsible staff in the Central Committee.

Another experience comes to mind. In August 1948 I was transferred to Moscow as Deputy Foreign Minister. We left New York in a hurry, as my mother was then seriously ill. I spoke to the physicians and was advised to take a break myself, if only for a few days. So my wife and I decided to go to a rest-home in Sochi. We took the train, stopping in Tula late at night.

Unexpectedly, the local party secretary and his deputy entered our compartment. They told me Molotov had telephoned to say that Stalin had ordered me to return to Moscow for a day's consultation on a particular issue. By the next morning we were back in the capital. It turned out that an instruction on an important matter had to be sent to the Soviet representative on the UN Security Council. Stalin thought I should first approve it. There was nothing extraordinary in this. My wife, however, was terrified. After all, that was a time when people were being arrested constantly, and this was not the first wave of arrests either. I myself was not concerned, but I could well understand my wife's anxiety. And, anyway, I was only relatively unconcerned.

It is well known that Stalin knew nothing about peasant life and labour. Nor did he want to know. His understanding of the rural economy was purely that of a bureaucrat. He received his information from reports, reports which were laced with a hefty dose of lies dictated by considerations of careerism. Effects were turned into causes, which is the norm for any anti-democratic regime.

The same thing can be said of Stalin's knowledge of the real life of the urban workers. Not once did I hear him comment on something he had actually witnessed in that environment. As for the itinerant, semi-peasant workers, he couldn't abide them, and this was well known, as he made no secret of it.

In both city and village throughout the period of Stalinism the atmosphere was poisoned with tension. But on the whole, the population lived with the thought that the Soviet Union was a great country, that it had carrried out a great revolution, and that Lenin in his genius had guided it politically for six years. Surely that was a guarantee that his pupils would lead the country along the same Leninist path? And was not the party, which he had created, in itself a guarantee that the future development of the socialist state would follow the Leninist course? That was how people – in towns and villages – reasoned in those days.

Today we can say that the harsh experience of the past has taught the party and the people to look hard at their future in order to make sure that our progress along the Leninist path is secure. A reliable guarantee that this is so was given by the 27th Party Congress, the 19th Party Conference and the implementation of *perestroika*, the great restructuring of our society and its democratisation, of which *glasnost* is an essential part.

The Soviet press of late has asked the question, which is essentially philosophical in its implications: where did Stalinism come from, and why?

The fact that people are asking this question is not surprising. Scholars will return to it again and again in their attempts to shed light on some of the obscure aspects of the Stalinist phenomenon. On the one hand, it looks like a simple proposition: a revolutionary, a contemporary and comrade-in-arms of Lenin, Stalin managed to seize the power that made him a dictator. He then proceeded to abuse that power severely and with impunity. But many aspects of the political life of the country and the party, especially following Lenin's death, remain unexplained.

And matters are made more difficult because scarcely any contemporaries, let alone participants or members of the ruling nucleus, are still around. It is plain enough that the aura of infallibility around Stalin was not created by him alone. His comrades-in-arms must share the blame. But why did these former Leninists adopt a course which made of Stalin the bearer of absolute power? After all, the country did not ask for it, nor did the country need it.

It is true that there were serious disagreements within the leadership over the future of the state. And it is true that Trotsky, who linked the country's future with a kind of command, or barracks, type of regime which he himself could not explain, had no support in the country. In these circumstances, one would expect to find within the ruling nucleus a strategy for both political and economic policy which derived from the major decisions of the party and the fundamental precepts and advice of Lenin.

Why, after Lenin died, was the ruling nucleus incapable of following his admonition to remove Stalin as General Secretary? The full text of Lenin's 'Testament' was not published until 1956, thirty-two years later, although contrary to Stalin's wishes its general message was well known. Had Lenin's comrades-in-arms shown the requisite responsibility and taken a principled stand, they could have settled one historic task after another. Had they behaved with dignity and relied directly on his ideas, even before his death, they could have done much.

What happened? Because the Central Committee supported Stalin, the people and the party absorbed the idea, which the propaganda media reinforced, that Stalin was the first person in the state. Once Lenin had died, Stalin made sure that everything was done to praise and glorify his own name. Only he could be called Lenin's successor.

And yet, looking back, one cannot help marvelling at the speed with which the idea of the Stalin cult took hold of the popular mind. It is one of the most mysterious aspects of the question, and one that puzzles researchers even today.

Did Stalin manage to hoodwink everyone? One could say that this is precisely what he did. But only because the others wanted it. Their own political ambitions played an important part.

Among the reasons which explain why Stalin with such determination settled the score with those leaders who had views of their own was his ingrained feeling of inferiority as a political leader. And Lenin's advice to the party about removing him as General Secretary had wounded him deeply. The entire Central Committee knew what Lenin had written. And indeed several dozen Central Committee members voted against Stalin at the 13th Party Congress in 1924, and this too was a painful blow to him.

Everything that happened subsequently was basically subordinated to the task of settling the score, not only with his open enemies but also with those who at any time in the past had not supported him. Typical in this respect were his relations with L.B. Kamenev and with Zinoviev. When he needed their help to overthrow Trotsky, he reached out to them. Once Trotsky was out of the way, he would destroy them both. He followed essentially the same logical pattern with N.I. Bukharin.

Stalin was a virtuoso at hiding his thoughts, especially about other powerful figures in the party. He had an astonishing talent for finding allies at precisely the right moment. He had his own understanding of what loyalty to principles, duty and honour meant. Everything was permissible in dealing with his opponents, even with those who the day before might have been his allies. The worst of medieval Europe's scheming monarchs would not have been up to the job for Stalin's purposes.

Stalin had no use for the panorama of leaders who were at one time or another either his allies or his opponents and who all had personalities of their own. What he wanted was his own gallery of monochromatic, even cemetery-dull, minions, who would belong to him and him alone, to Stalin, the man with the iron fist and the iron will.

In his skirmishes with his opponents, Stalin always tried to put things in such a way that he appeared to be defending Lenin's position. He was able to do this even during the debates over industrialisation in the late 1920s. It cost him little effort to show that the command methods that Trotsky had wanted to foist on the party for managing industry and its development had nothing in common with Lenin's ideas. As things turned out, Trotsky's political opportunism did not represent the future of socialist industry. The party gained the upper hand and the country achieved one of its greatest victories, as the war was to prove.

As for his agrarian policy, Stalin's approach was utterly un-principled. The idea that mass collectivisation should be ac-complished within a short space of time was both reckless and ignorant. Bland slogans and quotations from Stalin's speeches took the place of scientific analysis and debate. Pathological obstinacy completed the picture. All this caused not merely economic losses but a real tragedy for the millions of people who were left to go hungry. The blow was aimed not only against the rich peasants, the kulaks, but against the peasants as a whole. By the time Stalin published his 1933 article, 'Dizzy with Success', which called for a slow-down in the pace of collectivisation, the damage had been done. The famine had become a reality. It had carried off millions, especially in the countryside.

We students watched with aching hearts as thousands of horses and carts carrying men, women and children rumbled through the environs of Minsk, Borisov and Vitebsk on their way to the north and further and further away from the Ukraine. When we asked the peasants where they were going, they would usually reply, 'The north, just to survive.' They sold their few remaining possessions along the way for a crust of bread. Belorussia was not much better off. But the main brunt of forced collectivisation and Stalin's utter lack of concern was most severely felt in the Ukraine. Many of these farmers died along the way. And yet they had a better chance of surviving on their carts than by remaining in their homeland, the celebrated southern bread-basket of the Soviet Union.

It was only thanks to the peasants' tenacity, learned over many centuries, that the countryside, although seriously wounded, was saved at all. The villages entered the war with tattered resources, in the material and human sense. Only the limitless patriotism of the people kept up the spirit of the collectivised rural population and that of the peasants wearing their soldiers' greatcoats.

From the very first day of the new Soviet state's existence Lenin considered the party's main task to be that of carrying out the chief aims of the revolution. This was as true during the Civil War of 1918–21 as it was thereafter, when the new regime ap-proached the problem of organising the country's economy. In-stead of concentrating their efforts and attention on making the New Economic Policy function effectively, however, the party leadership was locked in a permanent conflict, in the course of which Stalin emerged as the dominant force.

Historians correctly point to what happened in France at the end of the eighteenth century as an analogy. Instead of dedicating themselves to the defence of the great French revolution in a spirit of unity, the leaders fought among themselves. As a result, even Danton's head was not spared, though that only hastened the moment for Robespierre's own head to roll at the feet of the counter-revolution.

While the others were arguing about principles and theory, Stalin set about organising the exercise of his already unlimited power. His measures were becoming more assured.

One frequently reads in the press that Stalinism had all the features of a myth. Human history has provided examples of myth-making, and not only in the realm of religion. Many historical figures had legends and tales created around their names, which in time acquired the status of myth, or something like it.

Under the influence of lying propaganda, the people endowed Stalin with an abundance of positive qualities which he did not have. From top to bottom, whether in the party or the population as a whole, the situation in the country was painted in bright colours, economic statistics were falsified, and the 'Leader' was perpetually glorified. This could not but have a lasting impact on the minds of the people. The Stalin myth paralysed any sober attempt to make a rational assessment of the situation. If criticism centered on agrarian policy, the label of 'kulak ideologist' was applied. In philosophy, one would be accused of 'Menshevik idealism'. If things weren't going too well in industry, 'wreckers' and 'enemies of the people' were sure to be found. History provides no other example of a myth being so well concealed under a cloak of lies, defects in the administration of the state, and so many crimes, as was the case when Stalin was in power.

The creation and character of the myth as a whole were the direct result of the Stalin cult in politics. A model of it was reconstructed in the people's minds. Consequently, the creation of the myth was directly linked with the life of society and its problems.

It ought not to be difficult to describe a cross-section of the actions perpetrated by Stalin, but one has to ask why they happened and why the party and the people let them happen? Why was he not stopped?

In this connection, the special nature of the relationship between Stalin and his entourage is of relevance, as emerged clearly after the repression of his former supporters during the wave of arrests in the late 1930s.

Past experience taught Stalin both the strategy and tactics for further consolidating his power. During the subsequent period, on the one hand, he pursued a clear line to secure support for his policies among his entourage, while on the other hand, he formed his relations with the Politburo and its candidate members and secretaries, and with the Central Committee, so as to keep them at a certain distance. Naturally, Stalin's reserve was not intended to push any of the members of the ruling centre into such liaisons among themselves as might pose a danger to the apex of the pyramid.

These tactics worked in Stalin's favour. The liquidation of Zinoviev, Kamenev, Bukharin, S. V. Kossior, and the others who were sentenced to death made the 'Leader's' position secure, despite his cruel arrest of the wives of some Politburo members, although that took place at a time when Stalin thought all danger to his dictatorship had passed. It is not surprising, therefore, that in time Stalin acquired his own peculiar ideas as to what was expedient and what was inexpedient when forming his relations with his entourage.

People today are no doubt curious about the relations Stalin had with his closest comrades. It is not a simple question. I would like to express my own opinion, however meagrely and without claiming that it represents things exactly as they were. All I can disclose is what I witnessed myself. For obvious enough reasons, I cannot comment on the generation of revolutionaries who were most active during Lenin's time and who were subsequently liquidated in the purges.

That area had to do neither with foreign nor with domestic policy. It concerned what today we would call cadres, or personnel issues, however they may have been linked with domestic and foreign policy matters. It was through those cadre questions that the various figures in the leadership expressed their views and made their marks.

From my first conversation with Stalin it was clear to me that he regarded Molotov as a major figure. He took notice of Molotov, and often it was Molotov's word – more precisely his advice – that would determine a decision, if one was needed, or a course of action. This first impression was confirmed again and again.

That does not mean, however, that Stalin and Molotov were close friends. After all, there was a time when Molotov (like A.I. Mikoyan) was not included in the inner circle of the Presidium (the name given to the Politburo between 1952 and 1966), something nobody could explain.

Stalin, moreover, sometimes showed personal animosity towards Molotov. For instance, I was a witness when Stalin expressed his annoyance at Molotov's being a few minutes late for a Politburo meeting. 'Well, when is the blockhead going to come?' he inquired. He himself had stuck that nickname on Molotov. Everyone knew Stalin was referring to the unusual shape of Molotov's head, and Molotov, who was familiar with Stalin's wounding remarks, pretended to take it as a joke.

I remember vividly one incident that had a distinctly political tinge. I had been summoned alone to have the conversation with Stalin at Yalta referred to elsewhere in this book, on the day he received Roosevelt's letter stating the US position on Sakhalin and the Kurile Islands. He had not asked Molotov to attend.

I had to begin by giving Stalin a verbal translation of the letter. He listened intently as I spoke. I expected that he would at once summon Molotov, whose residence was close by, but he did not, even though he asked me a number of questions about Sakhalin and the Kuriles. And Molotov did not appear at Stalin's residence until just before our departure for the meeting at the Livadiya Palace. I am still unable to explain why this was so.

Molotov only learned about the contents of the letter when he was sent the Russian translation later on. I might add that Stalin and Molotov hardly exchanged a word in the car as we drove to Livadiya.

It is worth mentioning also that Molotov's Jewish wife, Polina Zhemchuzhina, was arrested in 1952 and was not brought back to Moscow until Stalin died the following year. Her exile to Central Asia was of course an act of unjustified hostility towards Molotov as well, especially as there were no grounds for it. Presumably Stalin wanted to keep her as a hostage for Molotov's good behaviour. How Stalin arrived at these calculations is something only he could have explained.

Three days after Stalin's funeral, I was in conversation with Molotov in his office. He was in an exultant and far from funereal mood. 'Personal joy has entered my home,' he said. 'My wife has just come back from exile.' The pronouncement came as a complete surprise to me, as did his good humour.

That was how Stalin treated the one political figure widely identified as his most sturdy supporter.

Voroshilov was regarded as being close to Stalin, but their intimacy was of a different kind. Voroshilov carried out all of Stalin's instructions on military affairs. Stalin appreciated that, but he did not think of Voroshilov as particularly intelligent, though he did avoid criticising Voroshilov in the company of others. On balance, Voroshilov survived on the glory he had acquired during the Civil War, and he had no inkling of what the Red Army required on the eve of the 1940s. Towards the end of Stalin's life, Voroshilov's star was definitely on the wane, especially as he had not acquitted himself well in the Second World War.

Stalin rated Malenkov very highly. All personnel matters, other than those Stalin dealt with himself, passed through Malenkov's hands. His experience and grasp, and his ability to divine the 'Leader's' taste, were especially appreciated. Because Malenkov belonged to a later generation of the entourage, nobody thought of him as close to Stalin, and Stalin himself did not regard Malenkov as a close associate.

Kaganovich, who was not close to Stalin, nevertheless represented a constant voice in his master's support. From my own observations, it was not, however, an especially prudent voice. Often, before Stalin had even finished what he was saying, Kaganovich would pipe up with an approving remark. He is responsible for shamelessly having written 'Hooray!' in the margin of the NVKD lists of names of those sentenced to death as 'enemies of the people'.

Nobody would have included the name of N.A. Bulganin among the political figures of any importance in Stalin's last years, even though he had given blind approval to the NKVD in his time. Endowed with the mind of a crude soldier, he had the serious drawback that he was quite ignorant of military affairs. Nor did the insignia of Field Marshal that he wore compensate for this deficiency.

As a rule, the list of Stalin's entourage is closed by Mikoyan. He was a clever man, but there were more than enough cunning foxes of his ilk. For that reason, Stalin was always careful with him. One cunning fox is never fond of another.

I ought to conclude my remarks on Stalin's entourage with M.I.

Kalinin. I observed him several times at meetings of the Politburo. He was not very active. Apparently his ill health was already having an effect. The 'All-Union Elder', as he was called, suffered a serious blow when his wife was arrested in 1937 and deported to imprisonment in the Far East, where she spent seven years. Her punishment was meant as a sign to Kalinin.

One can only marvel at the fact that after being subjected to such humiliation by Stalin, Kalinin could carry on performing his high functions, serving as head of state from 1938 to 1946. He had no backbone.

It is fair to say that Stalin had no real friends. Even Beria was nothing more than his faithful cur. Stalin had only political adherents.

When and where did Stalin acquire this armoury, this harsh, anti-human philosophy that so manifestly destroyed in him the innate, natural instincts of a normal human being? The appalling thing is that the people who supported him behaved in exactly the same way. The NKVD lists of the condemned bear their savage marginal notes next to the words 'to be shot' – an obvious indication of their servility and mindless obedience to the 'Leader', without any doubt. One wonders how these people could look each other in the eye as they signed death sentences on people they knew to be innocent. If they did not know, it was only because they did not want to know. And yet they must have looked at each other! Not even the executioners of the slaves in ancient Rome behaved like this. The worst features of Nietzsche's philosophy of the superman seem humane in comparison with the philosophy of Stalinism.

Everything that happened in the Soviet Union during the period of the Stalin cult leads one to the conclusion that Stalin had his own particular, twisted notion of socialism in the USSR and of the tasks facing the country, a notion that was alien to Marxism-Leninism. He apparently believed that the country had to pass through a vale of harsh internal cataclysms involving the mass destruction of human beings. Along with this gloomy 'philosophy' went the proposition, also formulated by him, that as the building of Soviet socialism progressed, the class struggle would become sharper. It is this that makes us tremble today at the thought of what took place at that time.

The country has nevertheless overcome Stalinism. Only the heroic people and the party which is dedicated to the ideas of

Marx, Engels and Lenin, only the people, strong in heart and spirit, could force the fascist aggressor to his knees and then, having gone through another hard time of development, come out with a grandiose programme for the reconstruction of Soviet society today.

Instead of an epilogue

An epilogue in Greek tragedy takes place when the actors address their farewells to the audience. It has the sense of a denouement or ending. I don't feel like putting a full stop to my book, any more than I do to my life, and therefore I do not want to call my concluding words an epilogue. I would like to continue writing the book of my life in the literal and metaphorical sense.

I confess I enjoy writing and I am always excited when I know there's some free time ahead for it. Then I take up my pencil – I've always had the habit for some reason of writing with a blue pencil – face the blank page and let my memory flow. Or crawl at snail's pace. Sometimes it seems the snail has come to a complete halt and then there's no harder work than writing.

After reading my book, my reader may still be wondering how it was that someone born in a tiny village near Gomel could have become what I have become.

Yes, it was a tiny village, and, yes, there was usually not enough to go round by the second half of the winter. There were maybe two or three households which had enough to see them through, and the position was no better in the neighbouring villages. The men would therefore leave for the winter to do seasonal labour elsewhere, but they would need to come home to their families and plough their little patch of land when the sun returned in the spring, so they could not go very far.

I remember that once, in the summer of 1917, I happened to see our former landowner after his two or three thousand acres had been divided up among our peasants. His name was Ivanovsky and I watched him walking round the village with his wife and daughter, he in polished shoes, the women in pretty dresses. It was a beautiful, warm day. A bunch of us barefoot urchins followed them around, while the grown-ups looked at them shyly from the corner of their eyes. Then the family got into a light carriage and drove away, never to be seen in Old Gromyki again. Either they got stuck somewhere in the country, or they left for abroad, like many thousands of their ilk. But I wondered: Where have the gentlefolk gone?

I used to daydream all the time as a child. Imagine the picture – a boy of nine or ten sitting at the window. His parents are still out in the fields and have left him at home to look after the little ones and get the supper ready. But when he's done that he goes and sits at the window and thinks: I'll be grown up one day. What does it mean, to be grown up? It means you have to study and earn a living to keep your family and yourself. Round and round in my head went the thought: study to work. It seemed like the way out of the maze of my daydreaming.

After the revolution, when we started getting propaganda leaflets in the village, we youngsters used to love reading about the lives of the revolutionaries and we were filled with admiration for the workers in the towns. It was after all basically the urban workers who had made the revolution, and if they had not acted as they had none of us would have been able to do anything about the bewhiskered constables and district police officers who rode watchfully around the villages with the bells tinkling on their horses' harness.

The years passed. The children became adolescents, the adolescents became young men and women. The more inquisitive of them began to turn their dreams into reality. Most of us reasoned that if the workers could struggle against the exploiters then why shouldn't the peasants join them and become workers too? Surely they would welcome us? Some of us youngsters actually went off to the town.

I had a close friend called Vasya. After a long debate Vasya and I agreed to persuade our parents to let us get work in a factory. We were sure we'd find jobs if we simply walked east. Just then, though, we heard a rumour that they were looking for factory workers in the nearby town of either Klintsy or Novozybkovo. Nobody had any idea where the factory was, but we weren't choosy – any factory would do. We imagined that there'd be vast numbers of people and that a factory siren would summon us to work. It was especially the idea of the siren that fired our imaginations. Anyway, no sooner said than done: we packed some hard tack, a few apples and a hunk of cheese. We were confident that at our age we'd survive, but we didn't want to get weak from hunger. I was barely twelve and Vasya was thirteen. We set off for town.

Six miles along the way we sat down to rest and then walked the last six miles, scanning the horizon for the factory which never seemed to appear. We reached Novozybkovo and there we found what we had been looking for, the embodiment of our dreams. Small though it was in reality, to us it seemed gigantic, and, what was more, it had a chimney stack, which meant there'd be a siren. Our hearts beat faster.

It was summer, so we could sleep out in the open, under some market awnings, without freezing or catching cold. In the morning the siren hooted and we approached the factory entrance and spotted the gatekeeper, who also spotted us.

'Who are you two looking for – your mothers or your fathers?'

'Neither, we've come for a job.'

'A job? You're not old enough. And anyway we've taken on all the workers we need. There are no more vacancies.'

He spoke to us in a patient, fatherly way, but of course we were utterly downcast. What could we tell our parents? We decided it had to be the truth, so we set off back on the return journey. We had come to the factory with such high hopes and now we were leaving it with our hopes shattered. But youth is youth. On the way home, we found a secluded spot in the shade and sat down to discuss our options. We thought maybe we'd try a brick factory; there were plenty of them in the district, and at concerts all over the country the singer Valentina Krychinina was performing a song called 'Little Bricks'. I remember the words to this day:

> At first it was hard,
> But a year in the yard
> And I was in love
> With my little brick plant.

As luck would have it, there was no brick factory on our route, so back we went to the village. Our parents treated us with understanding, and for our part we went on doing what we could to help around the house.

Then we heard a rumour that clever boys and girls could join the Young Communist League, or Komsomol, which would open up all sorts of educational possibilities. No one knew how to get into the league, but then some Komsomol representatives arrived from town and explained how anyone wishing to join could be registered. They were empowered to set up cells where possible in every village. The new life was coming into its own.

Naturally we joined and at once set about organising Komsomol cells in Old Gromyki and New Gromyki. We felt we could set them up anywhere in the world, if asked.

We had to read a great deal. People brought in all the books and magazines they could find in their lofts or cellars, and reading-huts were started up in the villages. The Komsomols organised regular meetings at which they themselves gave speeches and proceeded to convince each other of the need for the victory of Marxism and the world revolution.

We also formed groups of two or three people to go from one village to another to help set up other cells, to organise political circles and reading-huts and to hold meetings at the same time.

It was the time when young men would do anything to get hold of a *budyonovka*, the tall pointed Red Cavalry helmet made famous by Budyonny. Even the girls preferred boys who had one, and this of course flattered the vanity of the boys, who in any case thought a revolution without a *budyonovka* was not a revolution.

But, try as I may, I still have not answered the questions: How could a village boy, like you, get the opportunity to be swept out into the political arena? Why didn't you become a farm labourer, the kind of man who, like your brothers and so many of your family, would most likely end up dead on the field of battle in the Great Patriotic War?

It is hard to answer these questions. Of course, there is always luck, and I'm the first to admit I had my fair share of it. It was luck that I entered a research institute where I began to study economic problems, and then it was luck that I was summoned to the Central Committee in 1939 to discuss my working abroad.

But was it only luck? Would they have asked me if I hadn't been prepared for it? That call had been preceded by many years of work and study. Also, I had the habit of thinking carefully before deciding anything, and usually in circumstances where I had only my own counsel to rely on.

They say everything begins in childhood, so perhaps we have to go back to mine for an explanation. I was still facing the

question: what now? There was not much in the mind of a boy
of thirteen to draw on for an answer. Vasya and I were still
puzzling over our futures. We could always stay in the village and
do peasant work. After all, peasant labour and seasonal work in
the towns was what most of the grown-ups did, year in, year out.

Then, one fine day, probably on the advice of one of his
relatives, Vasya left the village and entered the land-improvement
technical school in Novozybkovo. Naturally, I was filled with
envy and wanted to follow him, but it turned out they weren't
taking any more pupils. When Vasya came home for the summer
holidays, we decided we would become proletarians for a while,
and the best way to do this, we thought, was to go to the
nearest 'big' town. Obviously the technical school had been a
disappointment to my friend, otherwise he wouldn't have been
so keen to find something else to do.

So, with our parents' permission, we set off for Gomel, naturally on foot, some twenty miles away. We got there and wondered which institution to approach, and what to ask. The best
we could come up with was the labour exchange. There was still
unemployment and if you registered as unemployed you might
be given some sort of work, usually of a temporary nature. And
that is what we were offered.

A large railway administration building was under construction
in the town. Building work in those days involved hardly any
mechanisation, and our job consisted in carrying planks to the
upper floors from morning till night. We were more interested in
the meal they gave us. In the middle of the day they doled out
food in a special canteen. You could have one dish only, but it
was just the sort of meal for a real working man, for a real
proletarian! We worked there for three months.

Our lodgings were no more than a place to lay our heads, but
we found the time to have a look at the town, to see how people
there lived and how different it was from life in the village. We
read the notices outside institutions and schools, factories and
offices, and we soon realised we weren't going to be hired at any
of them. You had to have some training or skill, and we had none.
So, after a few months, we went home, with not much to speak
of in the way of savings in our pockets.

Our families tried to cheer us up, but we knew we were a
burden to them and that we had to find a way out of the situation.
We were helped by the fact that both our families encouraged us

in our desire to study, and, in the end, Vasya went back to Novozybkovo, got his diploma and became a land-improvement specialist, which he remained for many years. At that point our lives diverged, though I often think of my old friend.

I went to school in the village of Rechki, the local centre not far from our own village. The school was supposed to be upgraded to a trade school, specialising in some as yet unspecified technical branch. Soon, however, the school, together with the pupils and teachers, was transferred to Gomel, where it was set up in a former nunnery on the outskirts of the town. It was there that at last I felt there was a genuine possibility of further education, and I was overjoyed. After secondary school, I thought, I'd go on to a speciality. But what? Technical, maybe.

I think that was the decisive phase of my life. None of us pupils knew where we would end up – we could be scattered to any part of the country – but we felt the flames of the October revolution in our everyday lives. Our dreams were wrapped up in the name of Lenin. His pamphlets were being printed in huge numbers. The libraries and reading-huts, the schools and institutes, all were filled with communist literature, and it made a powerful impact on us all.

When I am asked, as I often am, what advice to give a young person just starting out in life, I always say: learn to study. At a time of universal literacy, furthermore, when we are inundated with information, we must be able to select what is right for ourselves, if we are to try to make a life that is of service to the community.

And so it's time to stop. I have done what I set out to do. As I was writing, it seemed to me the events and people I communed with were arguing with each other as to which of them was the more important. It is an eternal argument. People live in time and great historical events take place in time, and you cannot separate one from the other. That was the principle I worked on.

International affairs naturally predominate in my memoirs, because I spent so much of my life involved in them. It may be thought that I did not pay proper due to certain events and individuals, or that I dwelt too much on others. Well, I doubt if it is possible to satisfy everyone. The connecting thread that I tried not to lose was my wish to give an objective account of the events in which I participated and a fair picture of the people I knew who were involved in those events.

In other words, Marxism-Leninism has always been and remains my guide to practical action, including the writing of my memoirs.

Moscow, 1979–89

Appendix

Recalling the past

On 17 January 1989, Dr Henry A. Kissinger paid a call upon Mr Gromyko in the Kremlin. Their conversation was the last Mr Gromyko was to have with a Western statesman before his death.

Kissinger: I'm very glad to meet you again, Mr Gromyko. It's quite a while since we last met, the winter of 1987, I think. I'm reminded of your love of the double negative. I imagine that now you're retired you don't use it any more.

Gromyko: Well, it's not for me to judge. Yes, it's true it's some time since we met – so many summers and so many winters, as we say. By the way, I am familiar with your memoirs and I must say I think the book is full of interest.

Kissinger: There's just one passage in my book that I now regret, and that is where I describe some of your leaders.

Gromyko: I don't know which passage you have in mind, but all in all there is a lot that is positive in the book. I might even say it contains a number of observations that are different from your earlier views. But that said, I must add that one thing is clear: it is a book by a man of experience.

I may mention that I am often asked what I think of Henry Kissinger, not only by Soviet people, but by foreigners too, especially journalists. I tell them: 'You know, Mr Kissinger is an extremely talented man.' I would like to take the opportunity of this meeting to repeat this opinion. As you know, I am not given to scattering kind words around, like so many peas. I don't like that sort of thing at all, but that is my opinion of you.

Kissinger: Over the ten years that I've known you, it's true that you haven't scattered kind words around. Now here I am in Moscow and I remember our relations with warmth. I recall how stubbornly you defended your country's interests, which didn't always coincide with our point of view, but you always had our great respect. I have told many people that I have the deepest regard for Mr Gromyko. I was once asked on US television – and this was at a time when our relations were at a difficult stage – what I thought about Gromyko. I replied: 'God may punish me for saying so, but I like Mr Gromyko.' Some time later I happened to be dining with the son of King Faisal and when I told him that I had established the best possible relations with his father, he replied: 'There, you see, God has already punished you.' What are you doing with yourself now?

Gromyko: I'm reading and writing a lot. I go for walks in the evening. I walk three, five, even six miles a day. I must say I always feel better after a walk. My wife jokes: 'Everyone else gets tired from walking, but you're just the opposite – you relax.'

Kissinger: If you come to the US, you must visit me. I have a house outside the city and I also love to go for walks.

Gromyko: To be serious, I don't know if you find this is true of your own way of life now, but I devote a lot of time to literary and semi-literary activity. Recently I also gave an interview to a British television company. And I write a bit, mostly on past foreign policy. There's a good market for it, as they say in the Western business world. I'm finding outlets for my energy. I talk with my comrades from time to time. So, that's how I keep myself busy now. It suits me. After all, I was the one who raised the question of my retirement, you know. I had spent about fifty years in state service.

I am glad that relations between our countries have taken a turn for genuine improvement. It would be nice to think things will continue in the same direction.

Kissinger: I think the new American administration will do its best to see to it. I wonder, is your book going to be published in English?

Gromyko: Yes, it will. I have to say that a big part in improving relations between our countries has been played by our present leadership and M.S. Gorbachev. His own role has been enormous in this. You know that perfectly well. This has been shown in particular in the excellent speech he made recently at the UN General Assembly. What did you think of it? What do you think of the outlook, let us say, the most immediate outlook?

Kissinger: I know Bush well. We've worked together. I also know Scowcroft and Eagleburger and other colleagues. What Bush wants is to conduct affairs so as to come to a basic mutual political understanding with the Soviet Union, and not only in the field of arms control, but also in improving the political situation in many regions of the world. In my opinion, that's what he's going to try to do. As for the outlook, I take an optimistic view.

Gromyko: I'm glad to hear all that.

Kissinger: I spoke with Mr Gorbachev this morning. There's going to be an appropriate press release. I think the Soviet leader shares my positive assessment.

Gromyko: Yes, the Soviet government and Gorbachev – and I know this and can say it with assurance – want to follow the course that has been currently laid down. I think you in the USA will not be mistaken if you also take the view that for our part we intend to hold to the principles we have laid down. But it's also desirable that there should be no unpleasant surprises. Don't you agree? After all, success must be assured not only in disarmament and arms control, but also in the sphere of political and economic relations in general. That's what we're in favour of.

Kissinger: As far as I know, from what some prominent figures have said, the USA will not cause any unpleasant surprises. We also hope they will be avoided by other sides. If any should in fact arise, then any hidden dangers must be contained.

Gromyko: Sound thinking. You know, there's no more pressing and important problem at present than the total elimination of nuclear weapons from the face of the Earth. Otherwise, mankind could be overcome by a catastrophe. There is of course the danger that people have become so used to the expression 'catastrophe' that they no longer react to it as acutely as they should. It's been talked about so often.

They have been told about the catastrophe that threatens them but it hasn't happened up to now. A catastrophe is a catastrophe precisely because it's not something that happens very often. But it has to be averted and the threat of it completely eliminated. If mankind does not bury nuclear weapons, nuclear weapons will bury mankind and that will be the end of us all. Once, just once, I had the occasion to meet Albert Einstein in America. He said to me we had to do everything possible to eliminate nuclear weapons. Otherewise they would destroy everyone in this 'round ship' that we call Earth. They were wise words from a wise man. He was true to that idea to the end of his life.

Kissinger: I would like to be sure that if we are both going to destroy our nuclear weapons, someone else won't conceal theirs and then start blackmailing us.

Gromyko: That would be impermissible.

Kissinger: War must never be allowed to break out. Looking at the situation in the world, it seems to me that neither the USA nor the USSR can gain anything from each other by war. We would only weaken each other to the advantage of others, if we were to be drawn into a conflict.

In the eight years of working with you, Mr Gromyko, you rarely used the expression 'absolutely true'. You sometimes said 'that is not correct'. And you were famous for your double negatives. I warmly recall those double negatives of yours.

Mr Gromyko, I would like to ask you a question of an historical nature about an event which took place a long time ago, if you will allow me, since you are one of the few people still living from those times and can give a complete answer to my question. Some friends and I were once discussing the Berlin blockade of 1948. We wondered why Stalin was prepared to risk war for the sake of an insignificant advantage. I myself have wondered what he was trying to achieve. And if we had gone to war on that occasion, then what would his aim have been? I don't ask this in a spirit of criticism, but rather in the context of analysis of something that troubled people's minds.

Gromyko: I'd like to answer your question backwards. I believe that Stalin – of course nobody actually asked him directly –

embarked on that affair in the certain knowledge that the conflict would not lead to nuclear war. That's the first thing. He reckoned that the American administration was not run by frivolous people who would start a nuclear war over such a situation. That's the explanation of the first point.

Kissinger: But surely even a war with conventional weapons would have been dangerous for the Soviet Union?

Gromyko: As for other, so-called conventional weapons, the Soviet side – and Stalin personally – reckoned on having to respond to any action by the USA. That's the second point. Unilateral concessions by the Soviet Union were not on the agenda. And finally the third point. At the first sign that the USA was prepared to disengage peacefully – and bear in mind that Soviet and American tanks were a matter of a few metres from each other – as soon as there were such signs, we acted in the same spirit. It was Stalin's view, too, that we should disengage.* I have to tell you now that Stalin showed great foresight in this connection and he was sure that things would go as they did. And that was the decision that was eventually taken, the only correct decision. We disengaged. Figuratively speaking, it was as if a mighty voice had resounded from below the earth, expressing both countries serious interests and saying to both of us: 'What are you thinking of? Stop and take stock of the situation!' It was that voice which prompted both sides to see the need to disengage peacefully. If I were a creative writer, that's precisely how I would describe it. Of course, this wasn't an issue over which to risk the danger of plunging both our countries into the fires of war.

Kissinger: I'm looking forward with great interst to reading your book in English. I want to say that I look back with pleasure on the time when I had dealings with you as Foreign Minister and Head of State. You were a stubborn and persistent negotiator. But still we managed to conclude a number of agreements which turned out to be extremely firm.

Gromyko: Do you remember the time in Vladivostok with President Ford when we got stuck on two issues? One concerned the forward American bases, a question which we tabled, while

---

* On this point, see Dr Kissinger's comment in the Foreword.

you stumbled over the Soviet heavy missiles, the SS-18s. We had to unravel both these issues simultaneously before we could make any further progress. Brezhnev and I moved to the side of the room where the talks were actually taking place and sat down in a corner by the phone. Brezhnev telephoned two or three members of the Soviet leadership in Moscow to let them know how we proposed to resolve these two questions in Vladivostok. We told Ford and yourself about this. And at that point we found agreement. They were the two main issues that had needed to be resolved. And then we got the green light to come to an understanding, even though it would be another five years before a treaty was actually signed.

Kissinger: I well remember the time, here in Moscow in 1972, when you and I were negotiating over a period of several days and nights. Then one morning a shift began to take shape and by that evening we were ready to sign. We sent identical instructions to our delegations in Helsinki on the anti-ballistic missiles treaty and SALT-1.

Gromyko: Yes, I remember how we reached agreement, but the instructions we sent to our delegations weren't precisely identical, though they did follow a common line.

Kissinger: We had reached the last day of the negotiations and it was already eleven in the morning, and the agreement had to be signed by nine that evening. But there were still a number of outstanding technical issues to be settled.

Gromyko: I was asked precisely about this when I was interviewed on British television. I said we had agreed on the general tenor of our instructions, though they weren't absolutely identical. I think on that occasion you and I made a contribution towards securing major progress in the talks.

Kissinger: I agree with that. Unfortunately, my time is up, but I want to repeat how pleased I am to have seen you again. Please give your wife kind regards from Mrs Kissinger. Do you have any plans to visit the USA, or are you restricting your activities to Soviet territory?

Gromyko: I have no reason to make a trip at the moment, but as for the future, I won't rule it out. One should always keep one's options open. If you ever get lost in New York or Washington, you can always ask me and I'll help you find the street you're looking for.

Kissinger: You really know our country well. Still, if you do decide to visit the USA, I hope you'll call on me. I have a house in the suburbs outside New York where I take a daily walk. We could go for a walk together. Or we could have dinner in my apartment in the city.

Gromyko: I also walk from three to six miles a day. But what are you doing with yourself nowadays?

Kissinger: Mostly private business, though not very actively, to tell the truth. Making money is actually boring, even if it is necessary.

Gromyko: I remember meeting Bernard Baruch on one occasion. He was no longer occupying any official position. He asked me if I'd read his book *How I Became a Millionaire*. I told him I had read it with great interest, but I hadn't followed his advice. Please give Mrs Kissinger kind regards from myself and my wife.

Moscow, The Kremlin, 17 January 1989

Editor's Note

Readers of this book who are familiar with the Russian edition (*Pamyatnoe*, 2 volumes, Politizdat, Moscow, 1988) will be aware that much of the original material has not been included, while a considerable amount of new writing has. This came about as the result of an agreement between the publisher and the author, according to which the editor/translator had discretion as to what to retain, and the author undertook to write new pieces on a number of topics selected by the editor. The author and editor met in Moscow to review the finished manuscript and to iron out remaining questions, as far as possible. For the editor, this has been a unique experience and he hopes that for the author it represented, albeit in microcosmic form, an example of the sort of East-West co-operation to which his lifetime of diplomacy was dedicated. Shortly after completing Chapter 20 of this volume, the author died on July 2, 1989.

Index